The Canadian Write

Seventeenth Revised Edition

THE CANADIAN WRITER'S MARKET

Seventeenth Revised Edition

Sandra B. Tooze

McCLELLAND & STEWART

Library and Archives Canada has catalogued this publication as follows:

The Canadian writer's market.

[1st ed.]-
ISSN 1193-3305
ISBN: 0-7710-8528-4 (17th edition)

1. Authorship—Handbooks, manuals, etc. 2. Publishers and publishing – Canada—Directories. 3. Canadian periodicals—Directories. 4. Advertising agencies – Canada – Directories. 5. Journalism – Study and teaching – Canada – Directories.

PN161.C3   070.5'2'02571   C92-032255-7

We acknowledge the financial support of the Government of Canada through the Book Publishing Industry Development Program and that of the Government of Ontario through the Ontario Media Development Corporation's Ontario Book Initiative. We further acknowledge the support of the Canada Council for the Arts and the Ontario Arts Council for our publishing program.

Typeset in Plantin by M&S, Toronto
Printed and bound in Canada

This book is printed on acid-free paper that is 100% recycled, ancient-forest friendly (100% post-consumer recycled).

McClelland & Stewart Ltd.
75 Sherbourne Street
Toronto, Ontario
M5A 2P9
www.mcclelland.com

2 3 4 5   11 10 09 08

Contents

INTRODUCTION

You may write for your own enjoyment or for the challenge of it, but it's not until your work is published – made public – that you can truly call yourself a writer. Presumably, too, you write in the hope of making some money. If, however, you have to begin by writing for publishers who can't afford to pay you, you will still gain valuable experience, compile a clipping file, and increase your confidence for more lucrative assignments to come.

The Canadian Writer's Market is designed to serve both the aspiring and the experienced freelance writer who wants to get his or her work published but needs some guidelines and/or accurate up-to-date listings of potential markets. Use this reference tool as a guide to prepare your manuscript, acquire a literary agent, approach an editor, evaluate a contract, choose a writing class, find style guides and how-to writing books, join a writers' organization, obtain funding, or enter a writers' competition. Refer to it also to determine which publishers to pursue and what they pay for freelance work.

This new, seventeenth edition of *The Canadian Writer's Market* includes the most current information available on market opportunities in Canadian publishing. It is an industry in flux and expansion, where data change with regularity, making it imperative that this reference book maintain the standard of accuracy freelance writers have come to depend upon. Back in the 1970s, when *The Canadian Writer's Market* was first published, the country sported a mere 100 consumer magazines, about 150 trade journals, two dozen or so farm publications, and 147 book publishers. Today there are almost 1,800 Canadian magazines listed in *CARD* (Canadian Advertising Rates and Data) alone, and over 800 English and French book publishers. *The Canadian Writer's Market* has always kept pace.

This edition lists only English-language publishers and publications, although some publishers are bilingual. Readers looking to sell their work in the French-language market in Canada should examine *CARD* for French-language magazines and *Quill & Quire*'s biannual guide, the *Canadian Publishers Directory*, for a full listing of French-language book publishers.

As in previous issues, *The Canadian Writer's Market* puts magazines into three groups: Consumer Magazines; Literary & Scholarly Publications; and Trade, Business, Farm, & Professional Publications. To facilitate your research to find a suitable market, or to recycle an article to other buyers, these groups have been broken down further, according to subject. Consumer magazines appear in fourteen sub-groups: arts and cultural; business; city and entertainment; the environment; feminist; general interest; home and hobby; lifestyle; news, opinions, and issues; special interest; sports and outdoors; travel and tourism; women's; and youth and children's. Trade publications are divided into twenty-one sub-sections according to the professions or trades they serve. A section of prominent business journals is included in Chapter 1 in order to describe in greater detail the market they offer, but many comparable business publications retain a simplified listing in Chapter 3.

Inevitably, however, these classifications are somewhat arbitrary and have a tendency to overlap. Even the distinction between consumer and trade publications is sometimes difficult to delineate. Some "trade" periodicals – the book industry's *Quill & Quire*, for instance – have such a general popularity that they are considered consumer magazines.

Manuscripts

As a freelance writer, your manuscript is your product, and it should have a professional, uncluttered appearance. That means it ought to be as grammatically correct as you can make it and without any spelling mistakes. The more editorial work the publisher has to do on your article or book, the more expensive and time-consuming it becomes to produce; consequently, the less attractive it becomes.

A manuscript should be presented on standard 8½-by-11-inch, 20-pound, white bond paper. Your work should be computer-generated, so later it can be formatted from your electronic files. The font you select must be easily readable; italic or sans-serif typefaces should not be used as your primary font. The manuscript must be double-spaced and the margins at least one inch wide; this gives an editor space in which to write suggestions, queries, and editorial notations. The main body of text should be justified to the left-hand margins, and each page must be numbered.

The first page of your manuscript should prominently display the title of your work followed by your name. In one corner put your name again with your mailing address, telephone and fax numbers, and e-mail address. It is also a good idea (but not necessary) to include on this sheet a copyright notice (© Mary Smith) and the word count. To begin each chapter, start partway down the page with the chapter number and its title, if any.

A manuscript should not be bound or stapled; this impedes the editorial process. For a book-length manuscript, simply fasten it with elastic bands and support it between two sheets of cardboard, front and back, or better still, place it in a box. A magazine article can be secured with paper clips. Never send a publisher the only copy of your work.

If you are submitting your article in response to an editor's invitation or if you have signed a contract with a book publisher, it is likely you will be asked for a copy of your work on disk as well. Inquire as to what program and format is required. Microsoft Word is usually a safe bet. You may need to submit each article or chapter of a book in a separate file, but this varies from publisher to publisher.

Style

By style, most book and magazine editors mean the conventions of spelling, punctuation, and capitalization. There is, of course, no universally accepted manual for style because it varies from periodical to periodical, publishing house to publishing house, fiction to non-fiction, from genre to genre, and from discipline to discipline. Writers should remember, however, that style is an integral part of their craft, and by showing a blatant disregard for it, they can quite inadvertently prejudice an editor against their work.

Writers are expected to observe at least some of the basic house rules, and these should be obvious in what has already been published by those magazines and book-publishing houses for which they aspire to write. If they are not, the writer is always wise to find out as much as possible about what these rules are, and what stylistic traits – as idiosyncratic as many may appear to be – are preferred.

Canadian newspapers generally follow the *Canadian Press Stylebook* (which also contains some good tips on reporting), and magazines tend to develop their own standards and preferences from one authoritative source, or a compilation of several. Book publishers, however, usually adhere to well-known manuals. A selection of the best style and resource books is provided at the end of this book. Very often, a publishing house has compiled its own guide to house style, and the aspiring writer should never be afraid to ask for a copy of this.

Sending Out Queries and Submissions

It is crucial to research which magazine, newspaper, or book publisher is the best fit for your idea or manuscript. The listings in *The Canadian Writer's Market* are designed to help you determine the best publisher for your writing. In addition, read back issues of periodicals and newspapers, and study book publishers' catalogues to make sure you will not be wasting either your time or that of the editor. It's a mark of a professional to know what market in which to place your work.

Unless specifically told to do so, it is unwise to send queries or submissions by fax or e-mail. If e-mail is acceptable, resist the urge to become more informal or to take less care with your correspondence.

Of course, once you are ready to submit your writing, or even just send queries about it, you must maintain accurate records. Keep a list of dates that manuscripts or query letters were sent out, what publishers they were sent to, the date the editor responded, his or her comments, whether or not the work was sold, and, if you are fortunate, the payment particulars.

Simultaneous Submissions

There is nothing wrong with sending the same article, proposal, or book manuscript to more than one potential market at the same time. It is your work, after all, so you can do with it whatever you please. But unless you are sending off material simultaneously to magazines that are happy to buy second, third, or fourth rights (which we discuss later), you could run into problems.

The practice can sometimes be unethical. Busy magazines need at least a month to assess an idea or a manuscript properly, sometimes more. During this time, several people may be assigned the job of writing an informed critique explaining to the writer and the senior editor how the manuscript or article is effective, how it isn't, and what revisions may be necessary

In publishing houses, this work takes considerably longer and is correspondingly more expensive. Judging a promising book proposal or an intriguing manuscript of two or three hundred pages usually means that an editor must set aside present work. If the editor is busy, an assistant or an outside reader might be engaged to do this job instead. Readers may be hired for their specialized expertise, to judge whether a writer has covered his or her chosen subject, be it fact or fiction, well and accurately. If an idea or manuscript appears tempting, the publisher may recruit market researchers to assess its sales potential. By sending the same material to several houses, the writer may automatically involve them all in the expense of assessing something only one of them would eventually be able to acquire.

Indeed, to established writers, the idea of simultaneous submissions is distasteful. Knowing how overworked editors can be, they give them reasonable time to respond – about six weeks for a magazine and three months or longer for a publishing house. If after that they have heard nothing, they fire off a reminder, then turn immediately to other productive work. The publishing business is notorious for its slowness, and, unfortunately, this is something all writers have to accept.

Postage

All publishers are under pressure to reduce costs wherever possible. Postage rates have soared in recent years, and so for any business that relies heavily on our mail system, they represent a bigger expense than ever. It should now be taken for granted that if you want your manuscript returned, you must include a self-addressed, stamped envelope (SASE) so that it will not incur any cost to the publisher. Increasingly, publishers will assume that you do not want your material back if an SASE is not included, and will simply throw it away.

Magazine and book editors stress this point again and again, and writers ignore it at their peril. If submitting to U.S. publishers, enclose international postage coupons or keep a supply of American stamps. You can order them online at http://shop.usps.com.

Rejection

Authors must learn to cope with rejection. First-timers might draw comfort from the knowledge of how many great writers could have papered their walls with publishers' rejection letters received early in their careers. Faulkner's great work *The Sound and the Fury* was rejected thirteen times before finding a publisher, as, coincidentally, was William Kennedy's Pulitzer Prize–winning *Ironweed*. On an altogether different scale, big-selling English crime writer John Creasey is said to have received no fewer than 744 rejections during his career!

Since editors usually don't have time to issue more than a standard rejection note, take heart if the rejection is sugared with qualified praise or, better still, specific constructive criticism. Chances are the editor is not simply letting you down gently but genuinely sees value in your work. Be open to suggestions, and rework your manuscript according to the advice. Take note of the editor's name and resubmit your improved work to the same person.

Copyright

Copyright means the sole right to reproduce – or allow others to reproduce – a literary or artistic work. If you own a copyright, you are solely responsible for ensuring it is not infringed, and if you use work that belongs to another, you must respect his or her copyright rights. Therefore, as a freelance writer, you must have at least a general understanding of this area of law.

Here are some of the most frequently posed questions about copyright, with general answers:

What types of work are protected by copyright law?

According to the Copyright Act, writing is protected by copyright law "if the author has used labour, skill, and ingenuity to arrange his or her ideas." It may include poetry, novels, non-fiction works, compilations of literary works, catalogues, tables, reports, translations of these works, computer programs, unpublished writing, letters, e-mail, speeches, and song lyrics. Photographs and artwork are also protected by copyright.

When does copyright protection begin?

It begins upon creation rather than on publication.

Is every piece of written work copyrighted?

No. In Canada, copyright on a work lasts for the life of the author plus fifty years. In the United States, it lasts for the life of the author plus seventy years. After that, the work falls into the public domain and may be legally copied at will.

How can I tell who the rightful owner of a copyright is?

In the first few pages of a book or magazine there is a copyright notice. Typically it will read, "Copyright Josephine Blow, 2007" or "© Joseph P. Blow & Sons, Publishers, 2007." In Canada, the use of the symbol "©" is not required to establish copyright, but it is recommended. If you hold the copyright, you may use this symbol even if you have not registered your work with the Copyright Office.

The publisher's address will usually be printed above or below the copyright notice. Even if the copyright is held in the author's name, it is generally the publisher who has the right by contract to authorize reprints of excerpts. If, however, the author has retained these rights exclusively, which may sometimes be the case, he or she can be contacted through the publisher.

If you have difficulty contacting the copyright owner, try searching the Canadian Copyrights Database at the Canadian Intellectual Property Office (http://strategis.ic.gc.ca/sc_mrksv/cipo/cp/cp_main-e.html). Sometimes copyright is held by collectives who administer the copyrights for their clients. A list of these collectives is available at www.cb-cda.gc.ca/societies/index-e.html.

How does copyright infringement occur?

Usually through carelessness or ignorance. Few writers deliberately set out to steal something that doesn't belong to them. They either quote too much of someone else's work without first seeking permission to do so, or use previously written words without making a sufficient effort to rework them.

What is too much of someone else's work?

The answer to this isn't easy. It depends on several factors, principally the quantity and quality of the portion taken and whether its use will detract from the impact and/or the marketability of the original. No one minds if a writer uses a line or two from a book and indicates their source; to reproduce three or four key paragraphs without permission, however – even with an attribution – could lead to problems.

Some book publishers have established a guideline whereby permission is applied for if 100 or more words are borrowed from a single source. But, as previously stated, this is not a hard and fast rule. If the material is a key component of the original, permission may be necessary for far fewer words. Permission is required for the use of even one line of a song lyric or two lines from a short poem.

When it is determined that permission is necessary, the writer should contact the copyright holder to ask for the right to reproduce the work, quoting the extract(s) he or she wants to use in full, giving a true indication of context, details of the format (a magazine article, script, or book), size of audience or print run, the territory in which the periodical or book will be published, and the price of the publication. A neophyte writer wanting to use 100 words for publication in a small magazine probably will not be charged what a name writer would be expected to pay for a similar-sized extract in an article for one of the big players.

How can I copyright my work?

According to the Copyright Act of Canada, the act of creating the work is enough to establish copyright.

If, however, you feel there is a chance that one day the ownership of your manuscript may be in dispute or you want to be extra cautious, you may register it for a fee with the Copyright Office. If your work is registered in this way, you would be in a much stronger position if the case ever went to court. It would be up to the other party to prove that you are not the creator of your work.

You can also mail a copy of your manuscript to yourself in a registered package containing the date of creation. This will provide you with a dated receipt. Store the unopened package and its receipt in a safe place in case the manuscript's rightful ownership ever becomes a legal issue.

Does a Canadian copyright protect me worldwide?

Yes, throughout most of the world, in those countries that are signatories of the Berne Copyright Convention or the Universal Copyright Convention, which are most nations.

Can an idea be copyrighted?

No, ideas are considered part of the public domain. If, however, you worked on developing a central character and the plot of a novel, you are considered a co-author of that work even if you did not actually write it.

Can news items or real-life events be protected under copyright?

No, they are similar to ideas in that no one has exclusive rights to them; they are part of the public domain. It is the *presentation* of those facts, however, that is covered by copyright.

If I work for a newspaper or magazine, who owns the copyright on my work?

Usually, if you are employed by a company, it automatically owns the copyright of everything that is published by it in the course of your work. The article cannot be reproduced or re-sold in any form without permission first being obtained. Often, newspapers generously allow articles, or portions of them, to be reprinted without charge.

Can a magazine editor steal the idea contained in my story proposal and assign it to someone else to write?

Yes, because ideas are in the public domain and cannot be protected by copyright law. For this reason, it is useless to write "copyright" on your proposal. But reputable magazines and publishing houses won't take your idea. They stay in business because their editors are ethical.

What does "fair dealing" mean in regard to copyright?

The Copyright Act allows for quotes to be used without permission for purposes of criticism, review, and private, unpublished study or research. There are no limits stipulated on the number of words that can be used without permission; the courts are the only arbiter.

Should I copyright the book I have been contracted to write before sending it to the publisher?

No. All publishers will copyright your work for you, under either their name or yours, depending on the terms of the contract you have signed. They will also register it for you at the National Library in Ottawa as an original Canadian work.

Does copyright still apply when work is reproduced on the Internet?

Yes, although this can be very difficult to monitor. It is suggested that you put a copyright notice on all your work that appears on the Internet. If you use a quotation taken from a web site, you will need permission if it is a significant part of the entire piece.

For specific information on copyright as it applies to periodical publishing, see Chapter 1.

Libel

Defamation is an untrue statement about a person that harms his or her reputation. A person's reputation is deemed to be his or her property, which he or she has the right to protect. It is considered to have been harmed if as a result of a statement, that person is now hated, disrespected, or held in low esteem. If the defamation is spoken, it is slander; if it is written, it is libel. Someone who defames another may be sued in civil court.

Libel does not have to be malicious or intended in order to be proven. Negligence on behalf of the author is no defence. But if a damaging statement is proven to be true, whether the subject's reputation was sullied or not, it is not libellous. In English Canada, only the living can sue for libel; in Quebec, an action can be brought by a descendant if the libel defamed him or her.

Writers should understand enough about Canadian libel law to protect both themselves and their publishers against court action. This is absolutely necessary since nearly all publishers' contracts provide for indemnification for the publisher in cases where a person maligned in a manuscript resorts to a lawsuit.

Many writers hold the mistaken belief that the use of fictitious names, or a statement saying that any resemblance between the characters in the book and living persons is purely coincidental, will automatically protect them from the possibility of a libel suit. This assumption is wrong. If the average reader associates a character described in a manuscript with an actual person, and the description reflects unfavourably on that person's reputation or integrity, there is always the danger of libel. The apparent intention to libel a person, even in fiction, could be interpreted by legal minds as a personal attack and could possibly lead to an action.

Fair and honest statements on matters of public interest, as long as they are true, are permitted. An author who comments on current affairs or writes a biography is allowed to express honest opinions or fair criticism of someone's works or accomplishments because this is usually in the public interest and serves to promote a useful purpose. Fair comment extends to criticism of books, magazines, articles, plays, and films.

In a situation where a libel suit is possible, newspapers and magazines have a distinct advantage over book publishers due to their frequency of publishing. Sometimes a timely retraction is enough to avert a court case, or at least lower damages.

Taxes

In Canada, the Income Tax Act is good to writers, allowing you to deduct legitimate work expenses from your taxable income. In return, you are trusted to show all your earnings, particularly fees that are unsupported by T4, T4a, or T5 slips from magazines and publishing houses that have printed your work.

Basically, writers come under three classifications:

- Salaried employees who supplement their incomes by earning a little extra money as occasional freelance writers.
- Part-time writers whose major income comes from another job that will almost certainly be cast aside the moment writing becomes more profitable.

- Totally self-employed, full-time writers not on any payroll who are expected to file honest returns mindful that no income taxes have been deducted at source.

Writers with other jobs need only attach to their income tax returns a statement summarizing writing income and expenses, and to show whether this extra work resulted in a profit or a loss. Any profit must be added to that taxable income earned from the other job. Losses, however, may be used to reduce it.

Writers living entirely from their craft must keep many more details: a list of all income and its sources, and receipts and vouchers to support expenses. Maintaining proper financial records not only serves as a reminder of cash that has flowed both in and out, but also helps to reduce problems that might be encountered should a tax return be audited.

Legitimate business expenses are allowable deductions from a freelance writer's gross income. Letterhead, envelopes, manuscript paper, labels, file folders, and other office supplies, including pens, pencils, erasers, and paperclips, can be deducted. The price of photocopying, copyright costs, reference books, other research materials, subscriptions to magazines and newspapers, union dues, dues in writers' organizations, bank charges (if you maintain a separate account for your writing business), the cost of secretarial help, and any payment for research assistance are also deductible. Business telephone, fax, and Internet costs can be written off, as can postage and courier expenses. If you take a course related to your writing or attend up to two professional conventions per year, they are also allowable deductions.

The purchase price of a computer, printer, and other expensive office equipment can not be deducted all in one year; rather, the Canada Revenue Agency (CRA) stipulates at what rate each item can be written off. But related expenses, such as computer paper, manuals, ink cartridges, software, and equipment repairs are permitted deductions in the year they are purchased, as are the cost of other essential devices used in your work; for example, a tape recorder and tapes with which to record interviews.

An area of tax deduction often overlooked is the depreciation of office furniture and equipment. Both may be written off according to a fixed percentage determined by the income tax regulations. A computer may be depreciated by 30 to 45 per cent under the declining-balance method of depreciation. The same tax saving may be applied to printers, modems, fax machines, cameras, tape recorders, filing cabinets, desks, chairs, and telephone answering machines. It is permissible to defer depreciation deductions to a future year when the business will be more profitable.

Travel is also an allowable expense, whether it is to visit a publisher or to gather research for an article, be it by bus, subway, car, or plane. The non-fiction writer may have to interview people in a different town or find other resource information there; the cost of hotels, transportation, and generally 50 per cent of the price of meals and entertainment are deductible.

Keep track of how much time you use your vehicle for business and the distance you travel, for this is a legitimate write-off, as are payments for gas, oil, insurance, lease fees, interest on a car loan, maintenance, and repairs. CRA also allows you to claim depreciation on your vehicle, if you own it.

If you are a freelance writer working in a commercial office space, you may claim its rent as an expense. If you work from an office in your home, you are permitted to write off a reasonable portion of your living space. A writer using one room as an office in a four-room apartment, for example, may claim one-quarter of the rent or mortgage interest, property taxes, home insurance, maintenance and repairs, and utilities. You can deduct 100 per cent of telephone expenses if it's a separate business line.

For more complete information on income tax and the freelance writer, obtain a copy of the *Business and Professional Income Tax Guide*, a manual published by CRA.

If you have your own business, you must also be aware of the Goods and Services Tax (GST), or Harmonized Sales Tax (HST) in Newfoundland and Labrador, Nova Scotia, and New Brunswick. When your taxable sales of goods or services exceed $30,000 per year, you must register to file GST/HST returns. An option for some businesses with total sales under $200,000 is to use the "quick method" of calculating the amount owing as a percentage of total sales, instead of tracking the actual GST/HST paid out and collected throughout the year. A guide is available at www.ccra-adrc.gc.ca or at local CRA Tax Services offices.

Writers' Organizations

Writing is an isolating occupation, so it is good for morale as well as immensely practical to tap into one or more of the many writers' groups that exist in your community (a list of associations is provided in Chapter 10).

For professional writers with at least one published book behind them, valuable support is available from the Writers' Union of Canada, which offers members an impressive array of resources, including assistance with contracts and dealing with grievances with publishers, a manuscript evaluation service, your own web page on their web site, a quarterly newsletter, and a range of practical publications free of charge. The professional guides that may be ordered from the union by non-members for a small cost are *Anthology Rates and Contracts, Income Tax Guide for Writers, Author and Editor, Author and Literary Agent, From Page to Screen, Writers' Guide to Canadian Publishers, Incorporation for Writers, Glossary of Publishing Terms, Ghost Writing, New Technologies,* and *Writers' Guide to Grants.* At a higher cost, their *Contracts Self-Help Package* includes a model trade-book contract and *Help Yourself to a Better Contract.* Above all, the Writers' Union of Canada gives its members the opportunity to share their concerns and experiences with fellow writers, providing a forum for collective action to support their interests.

Many of these services are also available to members of the Canadian Authors Association, which has branches across the country. Founded in Montreal in 1921, the CAA has represented the interests of Canadian writers on many fronts, from championing improved copyright protection and the Public Lending Right to helping individual writers improve their contracts with publishers. (The Public Lending Right provides published writers with income from books held in libraries by compensating them according to how often their books are borrowed. In 2006, 14,972 writers, translators, and illustrators received over $9 million.) The CAA publishes *The Canadian Writer's Guide,* a handbook for freelance writers; it administers several major literary awards (see Chapter 7); and local branches hold writing classes and workshops.

The Writers' Trust of Canada is another national non-profit service organization mandated to advance and nurture Canadian writers and writing. Since 1976, working with an ever-changing pool of corporate partners, it has done just that in a number of practical and creative ways. It sponsors several major writing awards (see Chapter 7), supports the Woodcock Fund to provide bridge funding for established writers facing financial crises, and celebrates the importance of Canadian literature through the annual Politics and the Pen gala and the Great Literary Dinner.

Specialist writers' organizations, too, offer resources and support to writers in their field. The Canadian Society of Children's Authors, Illustrators and Performers (CANSCAIP), through its newsletter, regular meetings, and other organized activities, offers practical advice, moral support, and useful contacts to writers of children's books. Members are listed on their web site and in an annual directory. The Canadian Children's Book Centre also provides writers and illustrators of children's books with a range of resources and services. The centre has a comprehensive reference library of children's books, and promotes children's writers and titles through author tours, book readings, and their quarterly newsletter, *CAN-SCAIP News*.

For freelancers who write for magazines, newspapers, television, advertising agencies, and more, an excellent way to keep abreast of changes and developments in the industry is to join the Professional Writers Association of Canada. PWAC membership entitles you to a subscription to their informative newsletter, *PWAContact*, a comprehensive listing in their database; a copyright information kit; a mentoring program; and the opportunity to exchange market information and make important contacts with other writers. PWAC also sells a book called the *PWAC Guide to Roughing It in the Market* ($24.60 for non-members).

American Markets

The English-speaking Canadian who has begun to sell with some consistency in this country should not ignore the colossal market in the United States.

The American annual *Writer's Market* (see Chapter 11, Resources) contains 4,000 listings for book publishers, consumer magazines, trade journals, and literary agents in the United States.

It also gives the names and addresses of editors, and sets out their requirements: what they expect from a manuscript in content and length, and how long it takes them to report back to a writer with a decision on whether or not they will publish.

Two U.S. monthly magazines are also indispensable to Canadian writers seeking new markets south of the border: *Writer's Digest* (the publisher of the *Writer's Market*), for practical-minded free-lancers, and *The Writer*, for those with more literary tastes. These journals not only keep readers informed about markets and trends, but provide both a stimulus and a constant flow of fresh ideas. In addition, Writer's Digest Books publishes an astonishing array of practical books for writers, from guides to writing genre fiction to manuals on magazine-article writing.

Remember that just as you have to research magazines or book publishers in Canada before you send out a query letter or manuscript, it is imperative that you study the American market as well. Nearly all publishers have their own special character and narrow, specific needs.

But the enormous selection of American publishers in no way diminishes the difficulty of breaking into their huge market. Ask yourself why a U.S. publisher would be interested in your story, unless it is on a theme that has broad appeal to both nations. If it is a specifically Canadian story, there must be a compelling reason why Americans should care. Some Canadian stories will, of course, have an obvious, natural tie-in with American events. A perceptive article on NAFTA from a Canadian perspective might attract the interest of a U.S. business magazine. As a Canadian writer, you will have to work hard to penetrate the American market, especially with ideas for their consumer magazines.

Most Canadians who have consistently sold their writing in the United States do so thanks to the opportunities provided by the vast collection of American trade publications. Canada is closely related to the United States through common trade channels and by having similar concerns about world politics and business. The moment American equipment and/or expertise is brought to bear on a Canadian building site, for example, there could legitimately be the makings of a story for an American trade or professional magazine. Sometimes there may also be a story in how Canada sees, or deals with, problems specific to both countries.

But there is yet another hurdle to beat. Many American trade magazines are staff-written. This means that a staff writer will travel to Canada to cover an American story rooted here, so a manuscript from a Canadian freelancer must be exceptionally strong to win a place. The odds can be beaten, though. After accepting a few manuscripts from a Canadian contributor, the editor of an American trade magazine might be willing to publish a monthly feature written by a Canadian on the Canadian viewpoint: what his or her country thinks about mutual problems and issues, and what solutions it can offer.

It is well worth trying to secure a foothold in the American market for purely economic reasons. After all, it is still extremely difficult for Canadians to make a satisfactory living by writing exclusively for magazines and publishing houses in their own country, which explains why most writers combine the crafting of poetry, novels, magazine articles, or non-fiction with other work. The situation may change, though. Writing opportunities for Canada's writers have certainly increased since this book first appeared, and let's hope the trend continues. As it does, *The Canadian Writer's Market* will be there to guide and inform you with a richer list of resources than ever.

1

CONSUMER MAGAZINES

Writing for magazines can be both lucrative and fulfilling for the freelance writer. As you will see in the list below, pay rates vary widely, from a top figure of $1 per word down to zero. It can be argued, however, that even if you receive no payment for your work, just being published is an important step in the development and growth of your career.

In order to be a valuable marketing tool, *The Canadian Writer's Market* provides thumbnail sketches for each consumer magazine to briefly explain what types of articles it publishes. This is useful because so many magazines have names that give little indication of what they really are, who reads them, and, consequently, the kinds of articles or stories they buy. No one would ever guess, for instance, that an Ottawa magazine called *Summit* is not for mountain climbers but is a forum for public-sector purchasing. Or that, far from being a farm publication, as one might first suspect, *Grain* is a spunky little literary publication that has been produced quarterly in Regina since 1973.

The term *publication* is often used throughout this book because, strictly speaking, many of its listings are not really magazines as we have come to know them. Some are tabloid newspapers, some simple, one-colour, staple-bound periodicals that feed the needs, sometimes sporadically, of a small group of loyal readers, some are online magazines. Others, however, are magazines in the truest sense: glossy, highly professional consumer or trade journals that boast respectable circulations. The word *publication*, then, seems to safely cover all listings, both large and small.

Much more important to the freelance writer is that many of these publications provide opportunities both for established freelancers wanting to break fresh ground and for neophyte writers seeking to have their work published. Each one listed accepts outside contributions with varying frequency and for equally varying fees.

When writing for magazines, it is usual to present the idea for an article to the editor before you have completed the piece. Of course, you should do some initial research on the story so that you can decide on its focus and direction, and are able to write a compelling pitch to the magazine in your query letter. Large magazines plan their editorial content up to a year in advance. Therefore, if you have an article idea relating to a specific holiday, season, event, or anniversary, you must query the editor this far ahead.

Try to expand one article idea into several. Be alert as to how you can use the research for one story to provide the bases for other different but related pieces. For instance, background information for an article on city gardens for a general-interest consumer magazine could be utilized for a story on the gardening-centre phenomenon sold to a business journal or used for a more technical piece aimed at a trade publication.

For feature articles, editors tend to call on freelancers they have worked with before and know to be accurate and reliable. To break into this somewhat closed system, you may have to start by writing smaller pieces for a particular publication, then, after proving yourself, work your way up to the major stories. Along the way, try to establish relationships with the editors to whom you sell your work.

Researching Target Magazines

It is a waste of everyone's time to send a query letter to a gardening periodical if you are proposing to write about fly fishing. By using the list below, research what magazines publish the type of article you are proposing. Get the name of the editor or contact person. Note the frequency of publication; those magazines that publish more often require the most articles.

Read copies of the publications that are likely candidates for your story, and become familiar with their content and focus. It may be helpful to look at a magazine from the editor's point of view. His or her focus is to keep the readers resubscribing and keep them buying the advertisers' products. From this perspective, it's obvious that your article must appeal to the reader that the publication targets through its editorial and advertising focus. Use this information to either adjust the slant of your article or to determine that this is or is not a magazine to approach with your idea.

Another way to ascertain what magazines to query is to look at their mastheads and compare personnel names with the names of those who wrote each article. You may discover that a staff writer always pens the type of article or column you are intending to write. In these circumstances, it is unlikely that the editor will hire an outsider for these stories.

Find out if your target magazine has an editorial calendar or if it runs special or theme issues for which you could write a piece. The *CARD* directory and its annual supplement, *Publication Profiles*, sometimes list these. Also check a periodical's web site for information about forthcoming issues.

Once you understand what a magazine requires in terms of content, you must determine what its editor wants regarding format. Check the web site for guidelines or request them before you send a query letter, and follow them exactly. For example, it would be futile to offer an editor a 3,000-word article if the publication never publishes more than 2,000.

Payment Policy

Check the following listings to determine if payment for articles is due on acceptance or on publication, and always confirm this before reaching an agreement. Although you may be delighted to be published either way, you should understand the two schedules of compensation.

While payment on acceptance is much less common, it is preferable for the writer because even if the magazine decides not to publish your article or goes out of business, you will still receive the amount owing. By waiting until after the publication of your work to receive compensation, you run the risk of long delays or even the return of your work due to policy changes, a turnover of editorial staff, or a business setback.

The Query Letter

The query letter is usually the vehicle for a freelancer's initial contact with a magazine, as most editors prefer not to receive unsolicited articles. Query by phone only if the article you are proposing is time sensitive or if a magazine specifically invites telephone queries. It has been estimated that in order to sell one article, you must be prepared to send out ten queries.

No matter how ingenious your article (or idea) may be, if your query letter to an editor is not equally compelling, your work will not likely see the published page. It must be professional, well written, and convincing. As it's often the only means by which you can break into a new market, the query letter is a key factor in becoming a successful freelance writer.

Choose unadorned, business-like stationery on which you have included your name, address, telephone and fax numbers, and e-mail address. Address your letter to a specific person, using Mr. or Ms. Your correspondence must be typed, using an easily read font, and single-spaced. Mail your query (do not fax or e-mail it unless a magazine indicates otherwise) and enclose an SASE.

Since the query letter may be the only opportunity an editor has had to see your writing, it is crucial that the style of your letter attracts his or her attention and indicates you are a proficient journalist. Begin with an attention-grabbing intro and write in the style of your proposed article. If, for example, you want to write a humorous piece, your query must reflect that, leaving the editor in no doubt that you are up to the job.

Keep your letter to one page in length. In it you must provide a captivating, but brief, synopsis of the article you are proposing. Include your research plans and indicate what section of the magazine it would be most appropriate for. Then inform the editor why you are the person best suited to write this piece. Mention any first-hand knowledge or special interest you might have in the subject area you wish to write about. Indicate your publishing background and include the clippings most relevant to the magazine you are targeting.

Tell the editor what rights you are offering and if the article has appeared elsewhere. Provide the most accurate word count you can and the approximate delivery date. Also, mention any photos you can provide to accompany the piece (but do not send them at this time). Remember to check your spelling and grammar carefully before you send the letter.

Photographs

Photographs are another means by which you can increase the saleability of your article and earn extra money as well. By reviewing previous issues of your target publications, you will know whether they publish colour or black-and-white photos, or if they accept photos at all.

Describe in your query letter the photos you can provide. If interested, the editor will tell you the specifications the magazine requires. Before mailing off any pictures, make sure you have duplicates and print your name, address, and copyright notice on each slide or print. Captions may be typed and attached to photos individually, or several captions could be printed on a page and numbered to correspond to each image. Alternatively, your editor may prefer scanned photos and captions sent by e-mail.

Sidebars

Sidebars can be a means to help sell your article and boost your income. Also called boxes or bars, and often shaded to set them off from the rest of the text, these supplemental information bytes contain information germane to, but not intrinsically part of, the primary article. For example, if you are writing about the recording business in Canada, a sidebar might highlight the experiences of one specific record company; alternatively, a sidebar accompanying a piece about the challenges faced by XYZ Recording Company could give a broad overview of the entire industry.

Discuss the possibility of one or more sidebars with the editor; if accepted, they should earn you extra money. When preparing your manuscript, make sure sidebars are clearly marked so an editor knows they are not part of the main text.

Copyright and Contracts

Understanding how rights to published works are categorized is an important factor in making a living as a freelance writer. Before signing a contract or making a verbal agreement with a magazine or newspaper editor, you may wish to contact a lawyer specializing in this field. Nevertheless, you should still have a basic knowledge of what obligations and opportunities exist when you sell the rights to your work.

1) All rights: When you sell all rights to an article, it can be sold only once. You can, however, reuse the idea for the original work, as long as you completely rewrite and restructure the article and make it significantly different from the original by, for example, using new data, fresh quotes, a different focus, and by arriving at a contradictory conclusion.

2) First rights: First rights allow the periodical to publish your work once. After it has appeared in print, you are permitted to resell that same article as many times as you wish.

3) Second (or reprint) rights: These are the rights you are permitted to sell after your article has appeared in the publication that bought the first rights.

4) North American rights: This gives the publication the right to publish an article to be read by an audience across the continent.

5) Canadian rights: With these rights, the magazine has permission to publish a work that will be read only within the country.

6) Serial rights: This gives the publication the right to publish a work in a sister publication without having to pay extra for it.

In addition to specifying which of the above rights you are selling, the magazine or newspaper should inform you which electronic rights are included in the sale. If not, you could receive a hard lesson by discovering your work on the Internet, on a commercial database, or on a CD-ROM without compensation.

When buying first rights, some companies now insist on acquiring second rights and electronic rights for no additional fee or for a small payment at best. Do not sign away additional rights without consulting a legal specialist; you may lose a lucrative source of income. Always aim to retain as many rights as possible. Contact the Canadian Authors Association, the Periodical Writers Association of Canada, or the Writers' Union of Canada for more information.

Online Publications

When you are considering what publications to target, don't forget that publishing opportunities now exist in cyberspace. E-zines are proliferating on the Internet due in part to the lower costs of production. In addition, writers are required for online press releases, newsletters, and the larger web sites. While many electronic publishers do not pay writers, their sites may provide a good starting point to get your work in print.

As with hard-copy magazines, a query letter should be your first introduction to the editor. For this format, an e-mail query is required. Resist the urge toward informality; as is the case when you write to regular publications, you should correspond in a professional manner, showing the editor your best work.

The electronic medium fosters impatience in its users, so tailor the writing style of your article accordingly. Use shorter paragraphs and consider using subheads and sidebars. Long, dense articles appear daunting and tedious on a computer screen.

Arts & Cultural

Ascent: Aspirations for Artists Magazine
1560 Arbutus Drive, Nanoose Bay, BC V9P 9C8
Phone: (250) 468-7313
E-mail: ascentaspirations@shaw.ca
Web site: www.ascentaspirations.ca
Contact: David Fraser, editor
Published quarterly
　　Established 1997. A quality electronic publication specializing in poetry, short fiction, essays, and visual art, *Ascent* is dedicated to encouraging aspiring poets and fiction writers. Accepts all forms of poetry on any theme, but should be unique and touch the reader emotionally with relevant human, social, and philosophical imagery. "Does not want poetry that focuses on mainstream, overtly religious verse." Has published poetry by Janet Buck and Taylor Graham. Accepts about 20% of the poems submitted and publishes about 10 poems/issue. Submit 1 to 5 poems at a time. Accepts previously published poems and simultaneous submissions. Accepts e-mail submissions (prefers electronic submissions within the body of the e-mail or as an attachment in Word); no disk submissions. Time between acceptance and publication is 3 months. Occasionally publishes theme issues; a list of upcoming themes is available on the web site. Acquires one-time rights. "Write with passion for your material. In terms of editing, always proofread to the point where what you submit is the best it possibly can be. Never be discouraged if your work is not accepted; it may be just not the right fit for the current publication."

Azure
460 Richmond Street W., Suite 601, Toronto, ON M5V 1Y1
Phone: (416) 203-9674　Fax: (416) 203-9842
E-mail: azure@azureonline.com
Web site: www.azureonline.com
Contact: Nelda Rodger, editor
Circulation: 20,000
Published 8 times a year

A design review covering graphic, interior, and industrial design, architecture, landscape architecture, and contemporary art in Canada and abroad. Directed toward designers, architects, and the visually aware. Design projects and products are selected with an eye to technical and design innovation, aesthetics, and functionality. Fees vary depending on the department and are paid on publication. Unsolicited submissions not encouraged. Guidelines available.

B.C. BookWorld

3516 West 13th Avenue, Vancouver, BC V6R 2S3
Phone: (604) 736-4011 Fax: (604) 736-4011
E-mail: bookworld@telus.net
Contact: David Lester, editor
Circulation: 100,000
Published quarterly

Covers books written by B.C. authors and books about B.C. Circulated by more than 700 distributors. Preferred length 500 to 750 words. Pay rates vary depending on project, but most writing is in-house, so phone or write first. This is not a trade publication or a review periodical; it's a populist, tabloid-format newspaper.

Blackflash: Lens Site Scene

P.O. Box 7381, Station Main, Saskatoon, SK S7K 4J3
Phone: (306) 374-5115
E-mail: editor@blackflash.ca
Web site: www.blackflash.ca
Contact: Lissa Robinson, managing editor
Circulation: 1,600
Published 3 times a year

Focuses on critical writing about lens-based and new-media art production. Pays $200 to $350 on publication for 1,000 to 2,500 words. Accepts proposals/outlines only. Guidelines available on web site.

Border Crossings

70 Arthur Street, Suite 500, Winnipeg, MB R3B 1G7
Phone: (204) 942-5778 Fax: (204) 949-0793
E-mail: bordercrossings@mts.net
Web site: www.bordercrossingsmag.com

Contact: Meeka Walsh, editor
Circulation: 5,500
Published quarterly

An interdisciplinary arts review with an educated national and international audience, featuring articles, book reviews, artist profiles, and interviews covering the full range of the contemporary arts in Canada and beyond. Subjects include architecture, dance, fiction, film, painting, photography, poetry, politics, and theatre. Pays a negotiated fee on publication. "Use the magazine as your guide when formulating submissions, but query first by letter or phone."

Broken Pencil
P.O. Box 203, Stn. P, Toronto, ON M5S 2S7
Phone: (416) 204-1700
E-mail: editor@brokenpencil.com
Web site: www.brokenpencil.com
Contact: Lindsay Gibb, editor
Circulation: 5,000
Published quarterly

Broken Pencil is one of the few magazines in the world devoted exclusively to underground culture and the independent arts. It features reviews and articles about zines, politics, film, music, and other zaniness from an alternative perspective. Pays $50 to $400 on publication for articles and fiction 500 to 2,500 words. "Please read the magazine before submitting. Only the knowledgeable and unconventional need apply." Guidelines available.

Canadian Art
51 Front Street E., Suite 210, Toronto, ON M5E 1B3
Phone: (416) 368-8854, ext. 101   Fax: (416) 368-6135
E-mail: info@canadianart.ca
Contact: Richard Rhodes, editor
Circulation: 20,000
Published quarterly

Covers visual arts in Canada in a lively and opinionated way. Includes articles on painting, sculpture, film, photography, and video, with critical profiles of new artists and assessments of established art-world figures. Reviews are 500 words and features 2,000 to 3,000 words. Pays on publication $200 for 500 words, up to $1,500 for 3,000 words. Query first. No unsolicited submissions.

Canadian Screenwriter
366 Adelaide Street W., Suite 401, Toronto, ON M5V 1R9
Phone: (416) 979-7907 Fax: (416) 979-9273
E-mail: editor@wcg.ca
Web site: www.wgc.ca/magazine
Contact: Barb Farwell, editor
Circulation: 4,000
Published 3 times a year

A magazine for professionals in the Canadian film and television industry and for those who want to break into those fields. It is sent to all members of the Writers Guild of Canada as well as to film and television industry representatives, government agencies, and the media. Long features are 2,000 to 2,500 words; short features 1,200 to 1,500 words. Pays 50¢/word on acceptance. Guidelines available. "We have an editorial board that decides on the content of the magazine. Queries are welcome as well."

Canadian Theatre Review
School of Literatures and Performance Studies in English, Massey
   Hall, University of Guelph, Guelph, ON N1G 2W1
Phone: (519) 824-4120, ext. 3882 Fax: (519) 824-0560
E-mail: preynen@uoguelph.ca
Web site: www.utpjournals.com
Contact: Phyllis Reynen
Published quarterly

Publishes playscripts, essays of interest to theatre professionals, and interviews with playwrights, actors, directors, and designers. Issues are thematic and contain at least one complete playscript, insightful articles, and informative reviews. Pay scale and guidelines available on request.

Canadian Writer's Journal
P.O. Box 1178, New Liskeard, ON P0J 1P0
Phone: (705) 647-5424 or 1-800-258-5451 Fax: (705) 647-8366
E-mail: cwj@cwj.ca
Web site: www.cwj.ca

Contact: Deborah Ranchuk, editor
Published bimonthly

A digest-size quarterly that is a useful source of ideas on professional, motivational, and marketing aspects of the profession of writing. Emphasis on short how-to articles for both apprentice and professional writers. Also opinion pieces, book reviews, and short poems. Pays on publication $7.50/page (approximately 450 words). Contributor copies sent for each item published. "Queries or complete manuscripts welcome. Writers should present specifics rather than generalities and avoid overworked subjects such as overcoming writer's block, handling rejection, etc." Read guidelines.

Chart Magazine
41 Britain Street, Suite 200, Toronto, ON M5A 1R7
Phone: (416) 363-3101 Fax: (416) 363-3109
E-mail: chart@chartattack.com
Web site: www.chartattack.com
Contact: Nada Laskovski, co-publisher
Circulation: 40,000
Published 10 times a year

Covers new music for a high school/university audience, including Canadian bands, independent/alternative music, campus radio, pop-culture reviews, and articles. Pays on publication; rates vary depending on project. Guidelines available. "Generally ideas are worked through with editor(s). We rarely accept/publish completed articles as is."

Cinema Scope
465 Lytton Boulevard, Toronto, ON M5N 1S5
Phone: (416) 889-5430 Fax: (416) 977-1158
E-mail: info@cinema-scope.com
Web site: http://cinema-scope.com
Contact: Mark Peranson, publisher/editor
Circulation: 41,700
Published quarterly

Publishes interviews, features, and essays on film and video. *Cinema Scope* is geared to cinephiles looking for an intelligent forum on world cinema. Submissions are eagerly encouraged.

Coda, Journal of Jazz and Improvised Music
161 Frederick Street, Toronto, ON M5A 4P3
Phone: (416) 868-1958 Fax: (416) 868-1958
E-mail: editor@coda1958.com
Web site: www.coda1958.com
Contact: Daryl Angier, editor
Circulation: 3,000
Published bimonthly
  Specializing in jazz for over 45 years. Publishes articles on historical subjects as well as current music. "It takes jazz very seriously." Fees negotiated and paid on publication. "The magazine requires genuine expertise in the area of jazz/improvised music under discussion."

Color
321 Railway Street, Suite 105, Vancouver, BC V6A 1A4
Phone: (604) 873-6699
E-mail: sandro@colormagazine.com
Web site: www.colormagazine.com
Contact: Sandro Grison, editor-in-chief
Circulation: 20,000
Published quarterly
  A skateboarding and contemporary art quarterly that is heavy on design, art, and graphics with beautiful photography. Distributed in Canada, the U.S., Australia, and more. Pays 10¢/word on publication for articles from 700 to 1,000 words. Guidelines available.

The Dance Current
55 Mill Street, Suite 312, Toronto, ON M5A 3C4
Phone: (416) 588-0850
E-mail: editor@thedancecurrent.com
Web site: www.thedancecurrent.com
Contact: Megan Andrews, publisher/founding editor
Circulation: 1,150
Published 9 times a year
  Provides insight into professional dance, art, and culture for artists, dance professionals, students, and the general public. Articles 500 to 1,800 words. Fees are honoraria, paid on publication, and vary depending on the project. Guidelines available.

Dance International
677 Davie Street, Level 6, Vancouver, BC V6B 2G6
Phone: (604) 681-1525 Fax: (604) 681-7732
E-mail: danceint@direct.ca
Web site: www.danceinternational.org
Contact: Maureen Riches, managing editor
Circulation: 4,000
Published quarterly
   Provides a forum for lively and critical commentary on the best in national and international dance, classical and contemporary, including features, reviews, reports, and commentaries. Preferred length 1,250 to 2,000 words. Pays on publication $100 to $150 for features, $100 for commentaries, $85 for reviews, and $125 for notebook. Guidelines available.

Espace
4888 St-Denis, Montreal, QC H2J 2L6
Phone: (514) 844-9858 Fax: (514) 844-3661
E-mail: espace@espace-sculpture.com
Web site: www.espace-sculpture.com
Contact: Serge Fisette, editor
Circulation: 1,400
Published quarterly
   Canada's only sculpture publication, *Espace* presents a critical tool for the understanding of contemporary sculpture. Preferred length for articles is 900 to 1,000 words. Pays $60/page on publication. Guidelines available.

Front
303 East 8th Avenue, Vancouver, BC V5T 2S1
Phone: (604) 876-9343 Fax: (604) 876-4099
E-mail: frontmagazine@front.bc.ca
Web site: http://front.bc.ca/frontmagazine
Contact: Andreas Kahre editor
Circulation: 5,000
Published 5 times a year
   Front is a journal of contemporary art and culture with a mandate to publish original work by emerging and established Canadian and international artists. Publishes prose, poetry, fiction, and

performance documents. Each issue has a theme. Text can be up to 2,500 words. Pays $25/page. Guidelines on web site.

Fuse Magazine
401 Richmond Street W., Suite 454, Toronto, ON M5V 3A8
Phone: (416) 340-8026
E-mail: content@fusemagazine.org
Web site: www.fusemagazine.com
Contact: editorial committee
Circulation: 3,000
Published quarterly
    Addresses all aspects of contemporary art production, both nationally and internationally. Provides thorough coverage of art and its cultural climate, with a special emphasis on issues relating to cultural differences in terms of class, race, and gender. Encourages writers to submit proposals and accepts unsolicited manuscripts. Features are 4,500 to 6,000 words; reviews about 1,500 words; columns 1,500 to 2,500 words; interviews 2,000 to 3,000 words. No fiction. Pays 10¢/published word on publication; $150 for art and book reviews; $250 for artist projects. Guidelines on web site.

Galleries West
P.O. Box 5287, Banff, AB T1L 1G4
Phone: 1-866-415-3282
E-mail: editor@gallerieswest.ca
Web site: www.gallerieswest.ca
Contact: Jill Sawyer, editor
Published 3 times a year
    Galleries West strives to heighten awareness of the visual arts scene in Western Canada. Feature articles profile prominent artists. Query the editor with story ideas.

Inuit Art Quarterly
2081 Merivale Road, Ottawa, ON K2G 1G9
Phone: (613) 224-8189 Fax: (613) 224-2907
E-mail: iaq@inuitart.org
Web site: www.inuitart.org
Contact: James Sinclair, assistant editor

Circulation: 3,000
Published quarterly
   Devoted exclusively to Inuit art and covering issues important to academics, curators, dealers, collectors, artists, and art enthusiasts. This is the only magazine in the world dedicated to Inuit art. Carries feature articles, profiles, interviews, news and reviews, and reader commentary. Most articles (1,000 to 5,000 words) pay $200 to $1,000 (no fixed rate) on publication. "Please contact us for contributor's guidelines before submitting an article for consideration. A knowledge of Inuit art is essential."

Kiss Machine
P.O. Box 108, Stn. P, Toronto, ON M5S 2S8
E-mail: info@kissmachine.com
Web site: http://kissmachine.org
Contact: Emily Pohl-Weary, editor
Published quarterly
   A foray into independent art, literary culture, and political views. Each issue features two seemingly discordant themes. Publishes poetry, short and not-so-short fiction, and non-fiction. See web site for upcoming themes and deadlines. "The tiniest hint that you're addressing our upcoming theme will likely be enough to tempt our palates."

Legacy
9667 – 87 Avenue, Edmonton, AB T6C 1K5
Phone: (780) 439-0705 Fax: (780) 439-0549
E-mail: legacy@legacymagazine.ab.ca
Web site: www.legacymagazine.ab.ca
Contact: Barbara Dacks, publisher
Circulation: 12,000
Published quarterly
   Contains stories about the ways in which Albertans create, celebrate, and preserve their cultural heritage, past and present. Includes articles on visual arts, performing arts, architecture, music, poetry, educational programs, destinations, and challenging ideas, as well as book reviews and profiles. Does not respond to telephone inquiries. Send a query letter and brief résumé by mail or e-mail.

Columns generally 300 to 700 words; features from 1,200 to 2,200 words. Pays $150 to $1,000 and a complimentary copy of the issue. Guidelines available on web site.

Maisonneuve Magazine

400 de Maisonneuve W., Suite 655, Montreal, QC H3A 1L4
Phone: (514) 482-5089 Fax: (514) 482-6734
E-mail: submissions@maisonneuve.org
Web site: www.maisonneuve.org
Contact: Deborah Brewster, circulation manager
Circulation: 9,000
Published quarterly

Maisonneuve is a general-interest arts and culture publication aimed at curious-minded, media-savvy cultural consumers. Pays about 10¢/word on acceptance for articles 1,000 to 5,000 words. "Please send all submissions to submissions@maisonneuve.org." Guidelines available.

Masthead

1606 Sedlescomb Drive, Suite 8, Mississauga, ON L4X 1M6
Phone: (905) 625-7070 Fax: (905) 625-4856
E-mail: wshields@masthead.ca
Web site: www.mastheadonline.com
Contact: William Shields, editor
Circulation: 2,800
Published bimonthly

Offers news and feature coverage of Canada's periodical publishing industry. Fees are negotiable and paid 30 days after invoiced for articles of 150 to 2,500 words. "If you've got insight into Canada's periodical publishing industry, let's get writing!" Guidelines available.

Mix: A Declaration of Creative Independence

401 Richmond Street W., Suite 446, Toronto, ON M5V 3A8
Phone: (416) 506-1012 Fax: (416) 506-0141
E-mail: editor@mixmagazine.com
Web site: www.mixmagazine.com
Contact: Claudia McKoy, editor
Circulation: 4,000
Published quarterly

A national magazine that covers the work of younger and emerging Canadian artists, including painting, sculpture, installations, video, performance art, radio and television, dance, and new media. Articles 1,000 to 2,500 words. Pays on publication 20¢/word. Contact editor with article ideas.

Montage

111 Peter Street, Suite 402, Toronto, ON M5V 2H1
Phone: (416) 482-6640 Fax: (416) 482-6639
E-mail: montage@dgc.ca
Web site: www.dgc.ca
Contact: Cindy Goldrick, director of communications
Circulation: 8,000
Published twice a year

Montage is dedicated to showcasing the cutting edge creativity in Canada's vital and vibrant film and television industries. Articles 1,500 to 2,500 words. Pays 25¢/word on publication.

Musicworks: Explorations in Sound

401 Richmond Street W, Suite 358, Toronto, ON M5V 3A8
Phone: (416) 977-3546
E-mail: sound@musicworks.ca
Web site: www.musicworks.ca
Contacts: Gayle Young and David McCallum, editors
Circulation: 3,000
Published 3 times a year

Distributed with an audio component – CDs – to illustrate articles and interviews covering a broad range of contemporary classical and experimental music. Also ethnic music and sound related to dance and visual art. Features are 1,000 to 3,500 words. Fees depend on length, complexity, and other factors. Pays on publication. Welcomes inquiries. Guidelines available.

On Site Review

1326 – 11 Avenue S.E., Calgary, AB T2G 0Z5
Phone: (403) 266-5827
E-mail: editor@onsitereview.ca
Web site: http://onsitereview.ca
Contact: Stephanie White, editor

Circulation: 500
Published twice a year
A magazine devoted to architecture created by, written about, and photographed by young Canadian architects. Readers include practising architects, students, and interested lay people. Notes 100 to 150 words; letters 200 to 300 words; reports and reviews 500 words; articles 800 to 1,000 words. Articles accepted in English or French. Cannot pay but welcomes submission inquiries. "Wants sophisticated ideas in accessible language. Architectural or design training useful." Guidelines available.

On Spec
P.O. Box 4727, Edmonton, AB T6E 5G6
Phone: (403) 413-0215 Fax: (403) 413-1538
E-mail: onspec@onspec.ca
Web site: www.onspec.ca
Contact: Diane Walton, managing editor
Circulation: 1,100
Published quarterly
Specializes in science fiction, fantasy, and horror. Publishes short stories and poetry from 100 to 6,000 words. Payment on acceptance: stories less than 3,000 words earn $100; longer stories pay $180; poetry $20 to $50. "We do not read e-mailed or faxed submissions, and we do not buy stories or poetry that have appeared in print or on the Internet. Non-fiction and artwork by commission only. Send an SASE for guidelines."

Opera Canada
366 Adelaide Street E., Suite 244, Toronto, ON M5A 3X9
Phone: (416) 363-0395 Fax: (416) 363-0396
E-mail: editor.operacanada@sympatico.ca
Contact: Wayne Gooding, editor
Circulation: 3,400
Published 5 times a year from September to June
Devoted for 40 years to Canadian opera. Reviews international performances, interviews Canada's best singers, and addresses opera-related cultural issues. Reviews up to 350 words; features 1,200 to 2,000 words. Accepts submissions and submission inquiries. Pays $300 to $400 on publication for features; short features $175;

reviews $25. "A knowledge of opera is central for anyone wishing to write for the magazine."

Parachute

4060 St. Laurent Boulevard, Suite 501, Montreal, QC H2W 1Y9
Phone: (514) 842-9805 Fax: (514) 842-9319
E-mail: c.pontbriand@parachute.ca or info@parachute.ca
Web site: www.parachute.ca
Contact: Chantal Pontbriand, editor
Circulation: 4,000
Published quarterly

A bilingual magazine offering readers in-depth articles on the theory and practice of art today: interviews with artists and interdisciplinary articles on the visual arts, including video, performance, installation, cinema, photography, theatre, and dance. Each issue is thematic. Pays on publication $200 for reviews and issues column (to a maximum of 1,000 words), and up to $500 for articles and interviews (2,500 to 3,500 words). Guidelines available.

The Peer Review

21 Sussex Avenue, St. George Campus, University of Toronto,
  Toronto, ON M5S 1J6
Phone: (416) 946-7772
E-mail: info@thepeerreview.ca
Web site: www.thepeerreview.ca
Contact: Jeremy Nelson, editorial director
Circulation: 18,000
Published 3 times a year

Most interested in the work of graduate students post doctorate fellows. New writers are most likely to be accepted for the academentia or research sections of the publication.

POV Magazine

215 Spadina Avenue, Suite 126, Toronto, ON M5T 2C7
Phone: (416) 599-3844 Fax: (416) 979-3936
E-mail: pov@docorg.ca
Contacts: Barri Cohen, publisher; Marc Glassman, editor
Published quarterly

POV (Point of View) covers the art and business of indie docs and culture. Writers from across Canada share lively perspectives on independently produced documentary, animated, short, experimental, and feature films. Fees are 15¢/word – 20¢/word for established writers – and are paid on publication for 700 to 2,000 words.

Prairie books Now

100 Arthur Street, Suite 404, Winnipeg, MB R2M 4P2
Phone: (204) 947-2762 Fax: (204) 956-4689
E-mail: pbn@autobahn.mb.ca
Web site: www.bookpublishers.mb.ca/PBN
Contact: Carlene Rummery, executive editor
Circulation: 55,000
Published 3 times a year

PbN is a non-scholarly tabloid focusing on books and writers across Manitoba, Saskatchewan, and Alberta. Stories 500 to 800 words. Pays $100 to $175 on publication. "Interested freelancers are asked to submit a C.V. and writing samples to the executive editor." Contact the executive editor for guidelines.

Prefix Photo

401 Richmond Street W., Suite 124, Toronto, ON M5V 3A8
Phone: (416) 591-0357 Fax: (416) 591-0358
E-mail: info@prefix.ca
Web site: www.prefix.ca
Contact: Chantal Rousseau, operations manager
Circulation: 2,500
Published twice a year

Prefix Photo is a magazine that features critical essays on contemporary photography, media, and digital art. The market includes photographers, artists, students, educators, and a general readership. Articles from 2,600 to 3,900 words. Pays $750/article, one-third on acceptance and two-thirds on publication. Guidelines available.

Quill & Quire

111 Queen Street E., 3rd Floor, Toronto, ON M5C 1S2
Phone: (416) 364-3333 Fax: (416) 595-5415
E-mail: dweiler@quillandquire.com
Web site: www.quillandquire.com

Contact: Derek Weiler, editor
Circulation: 5,000
Published monthly
The news journal of the Canadian book trade for booksellers, librarians, educators, publishers, and writers. Prints news, reviews, lists of recently published and upcoming books, and profiles of authors and publishing houses. Includes the biannual supplement *Canadian Publishers Directory*. (Also publishes the compendious sourcebook of the publishing industry, *The Book Trade in Canada*.) Publishes short (300- to 1,200-word) and long (up to 3,000-word) news and feature stories about the business of writing, publishing, and bookselling in Canada. Author profiles are 1,800 to 3,000 words. Pays $90 for brief book reviews (350 words) and $300 for feature reviews (800 to 1,000 words). E-mail queries to editor first.

Storyteller: Canada's Short Story Magazine
3687 Twin Falls Place, Ottawa, ON K1V 1W6
Phone: (613) 822-9734
E-mail: info@storytellermagazine.com
Web site: www.storytellermagazine.com
Contact: Terry Tyo, publisher
Published quarterly
Features popular fiction of all types and genres. Each issue is an eclectic mix. Prefers stories with Canadian content and should be 2,000 to 6,000 words. No electronic or faxed submissions. Pays ½¢/word on publication and 2 copies of the magazine. "If you're sending us genre, make sure it's accessible to a general reader. Whatever you send us, it should pack an emotional wallop and have a discernable beginning, middle, and end." Guidelines available on web site.

Vallum Magazine
P.O. Box 48003, Montreal, QC H2V 4S8
Phone: (514) 278-4999 Fax: (514) 278-4999
E-mail: vallummag@sympatico.ca (queries only)
Web site: www.vallummag.com
Contacts: Joshua Auerbach and Eleni Zisimatos Auerbach, editors
Circulation: 2,500
Published twice a year

Vallum publishes poems, essays, interviews, and reviews on poetry. "Our mission is to bring together emerging voices and established writers from Canada, the U.S., and beyond. We are interested in original work that's fresh and edgy, something that reflects the contemporary experience. Open to diverse styles." Pays an honorarium and/or 1-year subscription. "Please send material for consideration, preferably with cover letter and an SASE or ING. No previously published texts or simultaneous submissions. Do not submit by fax or e-mail. Guidelines and upcoming themes available on web site."

Vernissage: The Magazine of the National Gallery of Canada

P.O. Box 427, Stn. A, Ottawa, ON K1N 9N4
Phone: (613) 990-0532 Fax: (613) 990-7460
E-mail: iparisien@gallery.ca
Web site: www.nationalgallery.ca/english/default_3222.htm
Contact: Ivan Parisien, editor-in-chief
Circulation: 15,000
Published quarterly

Browse rich images, eavesdrop on artists and curators, and look behind the scenes at fascinating details of art history. Articles from 1,200 to 1,400 words. Fees are negotiated and paid on acceptance.

Visual Arts News

1113 Marginal Road, Halifax, NS B3H 4P7
Phone: (902) 455-6960 Fax: (902) 422-0881
E-mail: vanews@visualarts.ns.ca
Web site: www.visualartsnews.ca
Contact: Sue Carter Flinn, editor
Published 3 times a year

The only magazine dedicated to contemporary visual art in Nova Scotia. Also covers national and international art events. Features are 1,000 to 3,000 words; exhibition reviews 55 to 750 words; artist profiles 500 to 1,500 words. Fees vary from $100 to $150/article, paid on acceptance.

Business

Atlantic Business Magazine

P.O. Box 2356, Stn. C, St. John's, NL A1C 6E7

Phone: (709) 726-9300 Fax: (709) 726-3013

E-mail: dchafe@atlanticbusinessmagazine.com

Web site: www.atlanticbusinessmagazine.com

Contact: Dawn Chafe, editor

Circulation: 30,000

Published bimonthly

Publishes stories about business activities unique to, or specifically focused on, Atlantic Canada. "We have a positive mandate to highlight the character and determination of Atlantic Canadians and the success of their economic initiatives in the global marketplace." Pays on publication 25¢/word for 1,200- to 2,500-word articles printed in the magazine with an additional 5¢/word for the online publication. "View recent copies online for sample of our style. Also, when pitching a story, writers new to us should reference previous published material." Guidelines available.

Backbone Magazine

1676 Wembury Road, Mississauga, ON L5J 4G3

Phone: (604) 986-5352 Fax: (604) 986-5309

E-mail: pwolchak@backbonemag.com

Web site: www.backbonemag.com

Contact: Peter Wolchak, editor

Circulation: 105,000

Published bimonthly

A national magazine that publishes articles on business, technology, and lifestyle. It delivers in-depth analysis and insight into the real benefits of e-commerce, online revenue strategies, and technological innovations that affect the way we live and do business. Articles from 300 to 2,000 words. Pays on publication 50¢/word. Guidelines available.

BCBusiness

4180 Lougheed Highway, 4th Floor, Burnaby, BC V5C 6A7

Phone: (604) 205-1701 Fax: (604) 299-9188

E-mail: ttjaden@canadawide.com
Web site: www.bcbusinessmagazine.com
Contact: Tracy Tjaden, editor
Circulation: 26,000
Published monthly

A regional business publication covering real estate, telecommunications, personal finance, management trends and technology, and lifestyle. Directed toward business owners, managers, entrepreneurs, and professionals. Pays about 60¢/word on publication for features of 1,500 to 4,000 words. "No industry overviews, please. Read at least 6 back issues before querying." Query by e-mail.

Canadian Business

1 Mount Pleasant Road, 11th Floor, Toronto, ON M4Y 2Y5
Phone: (416) 764-1200 Fax: (416) 764-1255
Web site: www.canadianbusiness.com
Contact: Kristina Smith, editorial assistant
Published monthly in June, July, August; rest of the year published
   bimonthly

Articles are 100 to 2,000 words. Fees are negotiated and paid on acceptance.

Canadian MoneySaver

P.O. Box 370, Bath, ON K0H 1G0
Phone: (613) 352-7448 Fax: (613) 352-7700
E-mail: moneyinfo@canadianmoneysaver.ca
Web site: www.canadianmoneysaver.ca
Contact: Dale Ennis, publisher/editor-in-chief
Circulation: 42,700
Published 9 times a year

A national consumer finance magazine offering articles (800 to 2,000 words) on such current topics as personal finance, tax, investment techniques, retirement planning, consumer purchases, small business practices, and discount services. "Contributors have the opportunity to participate in national and offshore conferences, and propose other writing projects." Cannot pay but welcomes submission inquiries. Guidelines available. An online edition is also published.

Contact Magazine

310 Front Street W., Suite 800, Toronto, ON M5V 3B5
Phone: (416) 408-2685, ext. 241, or 1-888-267-2772 Fax: (416) 408-2684
E-mail: bruffell@cpsa.com
Web site: www.cpsa.com
Contact: Brett Ruffell, editor
Circulation: 28,000
Published quarterly

The number-one source for sales and marketing professionals in Canada. Provides up-to-date information on what's new and important in sales and marketing. Articles 700 to 1,200 words. Some articles are unpaid; others receive approximately 70¢/word on acceptance. Guidelines available.

Corporate Knights

215 Spadina Avenue, Suite 121, Toronto, ON M5T 2C7
Phone: (416) 203-4674 Fax: (416) 979-3936
E-mail: info@corporateknights.ca
Web site: www.corporateknights.ca
Contact: Toby Heaps, editor
Published 5 times a year

Founded in 2002, Corporate Knights Inc. is an independent Canadian-based media company that publishes the world's largest circulation magazine with an explicit focus on corporate responsibility. The mission of the company is to humanize the marketplace. Fees are negotiated and paid on publication for articles from 800 to 2,500 words. "*Corporate Knights* encourages anyone with a good idea to e-mail us one paragraph outlining the idea and why you are the one to write the article." Guidelines available.

Country Guide

P.O. Box 9800, Winnipeg, MB R3C 3K7
Phone: (204) 944-5754 Fax: (204) 942-8463
E-mail: jay@fbcpublishing.com
Web site: www.agcanada.com
Contact: Jay Whetter, editor
Circulation: 40,000
Published monthly

A magazine for farmers or others in the agriculture business with articles that focus on farm business, including features on leading farmers, new agricultural products, and marketing, accounting, and legal tips. Articles 800 to 1,600 words. Pay varies from $175 to $350/article, paid on publication. "Pitch an idea, not a story. If the editor likes the idea, he will ask for the story."

The Far North Oil & Gas Review
4920 – 52nd Street, Suite 800, Yellowknife, NT X1A 3T1
Phone: (867) 920-4343, ext. 316 Fax: (867) 873-9876
E-mail: darren@uphere.ca
Web site: www.fnog.ca
Contacts: Darren Campbell, managing editor; Jake Kennedy, editor
Circulation: 10,000
Published quarterly
Covers news, politics, business, and other issues related to northern oil and gas development. Reaches a northern audience of Aboriginals and non-Aboriginals, the Canadian oil and gas industry in Calgary, and the related corporate offices in Houston, Dallas, and Toronto. The magazine deals with issues specific to the north and some general information issues. "Freelancers should be knowledgeable about northern issues and Aboriginal issues as they pertain to the north. Freelancers should also have a basic understanding of the Canadian oil patch and related technical issues. Copies of the magazine available upon request." Articles 2,500 to 4,000 words. Fees are negotiated, and the magazine pays on acceptance.

The Insurance Journal
321 rue de la Commune W., Suite 100, Montreal, QC H2Y 2E1
Phone: (514) 289-9595
E-mail: newsdesk@insurance-journal.ca
Web site: www.insurance-journal.ca
Contact: Donna Glasgow, editor-in-chief
Circulation: 20,000
Published 10 times a year
The Insurance Journal is Canada's leading news magazine for financial advisors. Covers news and developments in the life insurance and mutual fund industries. Articles 300 to 1,000 words. Fees

are negotiated and paid on acceptance. "If you are interested in business news writing, send us an e-mail. We also have a French-language sister publication, *Le Journal de l'assurance*."

Ivey Business Journal
179 John Street, Suite 501, Toronto, ON M5T 1X4
Phone: (416) 598-1741 Fax: (416) 598-0669
E-mail: sbernhut@ivey.uwo.ca
Web site: www.iveybusinessjournal.com
Contact: Stephen Bernhut, editor
Published bimonthly
   A long-established business journal, now published online only, that is directed toward senior managers, with a mission to improve the practice of management. Articles from 2,000 to 2,500 words. Contributors are unpaid. Inquiries welcome. Guidelines available on web site.

Progress Magazine
1660 Hollis Street, Suite 1203, Halifax, NS B3J 1V7
Phone: (902) 494-0999 Fax: (902) 494-4483
E-mail: editorial@progresscorp.com
Web site: www.progresscorp.com
Contact: Pamela Scott Crace, editor
Circulation: 26,500
Published 10 times a year
   Progress focuses on wealth creation through profitable business growth. Its audience comprises business and community leaders in Atlantic Canada and Maine. Articles are from 750 to 3,000 words. Fees vary depending on project and are paid within 60 days of acceptance. Guidelines available.

RealScreen
366 Adelaide Street W., Suite 500, Toronto, ON M5V 1R9
Phone: (416) 408-2300 Fax: (416) 408-0870
E-mail: bchristie@brunico.com
Web site: www.realscreen.com
Contact: Brendon Christie, editor
Circulation: 8,700
Published 5 times a year

An international publication about the business of international, non-fiction film and television. Written for producers, distributors, broadcasters, and suppliers. Contact editor with story ideas. Fees vary depending on project. Writers must have previous experience writing for this industry.

ShareOwner
4 King Street W., Suite 806, Toronto, ON M5H 1B6
Phone: (416) 484-9400 Fax: (416) 595-0400
E-mail: john.bart@shareowner.com
Web site: www.shareowner.com
Contact: John Bart, publisher/editor
Circulation: 10,000
Published bimonthly

A publication targeted on investment education for individual investors and investment clubs. Fees are negotiated and paid on acceptance. "Writers with personal experience owning stocks and funds are encouraged to contact the publisher."

SOHO Business Report
439A Marmont Street, Coquitlam, BC V3K 4S4
Phone: 1-888-936-5815 Fax: (604) 936-5805
E-mail: submissions@sohobusinessreport.com
Web site: www.sohobusinessreport.com
Contact: Melanie Jackson, editor-in-chief
Circulation: 40,000
Published quarterly

Formerly the *Home Business Report*. A magazine to link home-based businesses across the country, providing a network for sharing experiences, including advice for launching new businesses and support for those that are struggling. Regional reports 900 to 1,000 words. Pay rates depend on assignment; sometimes cannot pay. Guidelines available on web site.

Summit: Canada's Magazine on Public Sector Purchasing
263 Holmwood Avenue, Suite 100, Ottawa, ON K1S 2P8
Phone: (613) 688-0762 Fax: (613) 688-0763
E-mail: info@summitconnects.com or editor@summitconnects.com
Web site: www.summitconnects.com

Contact: Anne Phillips, editor
Circulation: 20,000
Published 7 times a year

For public-sector purchasers at the decision-making and policy levels of all municipal and provincial governments and the federal government. Stories on policy matters and how-to articles. Articles 1,000 to 1,500 words. Pays on publication 75¢/published word (20% of the proposed published word count is the kill fee). "Please confirm the potential for publication before submitting your article by calling or e-mailing the contact listed. Articles must be of interest to public sector purchasers and topics may include new technology, greening issues, energy, infrastructure, policy, contracting, legal, and human resources." Guidelines available.

Trade & Commerce
1700 Church Avenue, Winnipeg, MB R2X 3A2
Phone: (204) 632-2606 Fax: (204) 694-3040
E-mail: wtcommerce@wpgsun.com
Web site: www.tradeandcommerce.com
Contact: Laura Jean Stewart, editor
Circulation: 10,000
Published quarterly

Profiles companies and communities with an emphasis on their contribution to the economy or economic-development activity. Pays 28¢ to 40¢/word on acceptance for 1,200 to 2,500 words. Works with freelance writers all over Canada and the United States. Guidelines available.

City & Entertainment

Avenue
1210 – 20 Avenue S.E., Suite 105, Calgary, AB T2G 1M8
Phone: (403) 232-7703 Fax: (403) 240-9059
E-mail: jgray@redpointmedia.ca
Web site: www.redpointmedia.ca
Contact: Jennifer Gray, editor
Circulation: 40,000
Published 10 times a year

A city lifestyle magazine for Calgary with well-rounded coverage of the arts, food, fashion, design, the outdoors, and issues shaping the city. Articles 1,200 to 2,000 words. Fees vary depending on the project and are paid on publication. "We welcome queries from new writers for stories with relevance to Calgary residents or readers who are curious about Calgary." Guidelines available.

Barrie Life & Times, South Simcoe Life & Times, North Simcoe Life & Times

92 Caplan Avenue, Suite 509, Barrie, ON L4N 0Z7
Phone: (705) 719-7901 Fax: (866) 772-0893
E-mail: cb@life-and-times.ca
Web site: www.life-and-times.ca
Contact: Catherine Beauvais, owner/publisher
Circulation: 6,000–25,000
Published monthly

Good news papers only that focus on people, past and future events, and fundraising. The readership includes a faithful following of those aged 55 and up. Articles from 100 to 450 words. "Depending on the assignment, we may be able to negotiate fees. Currently, most of our contributions come from businesses looking for exposure." Submission inquiries welcome. Guidelines are available.

City Palate

722 – 11 Avenue S.W., Calgary, AB T2R 0E4
Phone: (403) 282-5376 Fax: (403) 282-9231
E-mail: yabbie@telusplanet.net
Web site: http://citypalate.ca
Contact: Kathy Richardier, editor
Circulation: 38,000
Published bimonthly

City Palate celebrates Calgary's food culture. Highlights local people in the food industry through articles both by and about them. Also includes food and drink articles on the basis of seasonality and what's happening in the culinary universe with, as often as possible, a local focus. Welcomes editorial queries in writing, either by fax or e-mail.

The Coast: Halifax's Weekly
5435 Portland Place, Halifax, NS B3K 6R7
Phone: (902) 422-6278 Fax: (902) 425-0013
E-mail: coast@thecoast.ca
Web site: www.thecoast.ca
Contacts: Mike Fleury, news editor; Tara Thorne, arts editor
Circulation: 23,500
    Established 1993. A free, locally owned, alternative weekly newspaper serving Metro Halifax that publishes short news stories and arts profiles as well as magazine-style features. *The Coast*'s goal is to be provocative and entertaining. Pays 10¢ to 20¢/word on acceptance for 500 to 3,000 words. Rate depends on complexity of topic and is negotiated up front. Guidelines available.

East of the City
130 Commercial Avenue, Ajax, ON L1S 2H5
Phone: (905) 426-4676 Fax: (416) 426-6598
E-mail: tmckee@durhamregion.com
Contact: Tamara McKee, editor
Circulation: 25,000
Published bimonthly
    Shines the spotlight on the culture in Durham Region, east of Toronto, and includes stories on home décor, gardening, health, and the personalities who call this area home. Readers are upscale, aged 35 and up, with household incomes of at least $150,000. Pay rates vary from $75 to $150, paid on publication, for articles of 800 to 1,500 words.

eye Weekly
625 Church Street, 6th Floor, Toronto, ON M5V 2G5
Phone: (416) 596-4393 Fax: (416) 504-4341
Web site: www.eyeweekly.com
Contact: Alan A. Vernon, editorial director
Circulation: 113,000
    Toronto's definitive source of alternative cultural commentary, with extensive arts and entertainment coverage, and listings. "We welcome submissions but are not responsible for unsolicited material." Fees vary and are paid on publication.

Famous

102 Atlantic Avenue, Suite 100, Toronto, ON M6K 1X9
Phone: (416) 539-8800 Fax: (416) 539-8511
E-mail: mweisz@fpmedia.ca
Contact: Marni Weisz, editor
Circulation: 650,000
Published monthly

An in-theatre magazine for Cineplex Theatres. Content focuses on movies, music, books, video games, and DVDs. Articles 600 to 1,400 words. Pays 50¢/word.

Fast Forward Weekly

1210 – 20 Avenue S.E., Suite 206, Calgary, AB T2G 3G2
Phone: (403) 244-2235 Fax: (403) 244-1431
E-mail: idoig@ffwd.greatwest.ca
Web site: www.ffwdweekly.com
Contact: Ian Doig, editor
Circulation: 35,000

Calgary's news and entertainment weekly. "The best way to get an article published in *Fast Forward* is to submit your ideas via mail or e-mail, along with some background information, credentials, and any writing samples you may have."

Focus

P.O. Box 5310, Victoria, BC V8R 6S4
Phone: (250) 388-7231 Fax: (250) 383-1140
E-mail: focusedit@shaw.ca
Web site: www.focusonline.ca
Contact: Leslie Campbell
Circulation: 35,000
Published monthly

Celebrates Victoria's creative and community spirit with diverse, intelligent editorial coverage. Publishes investigative features (2,000 to 3,000 words) and profiles (1,500 words). Please query first.

The Georgia Straight

1701 West Broadway, Vancouver, BC V6J 1Y3
Phone: (604) 730-7000 Fax: (604) 730-7010

E-mail: contact@straight.com
Web site: www.straight.com
Circulation: 125,000
Published weekly
    The Georgia Straight is Vancouver's premier news and entertainment weekly. Length of articles and fees vary. Paid on publication.

Niagara Life
3550 Schmon Parkway, Suite 1, Thorold, ON L2V 4Y6
Phone: (905) 641-1984   Fax: (905) 641-0682
E-mail: gtodd@niagaralifcmag.ca
Web site: www.niagaralifemag.com
Contact: Gail Atkinson Todd, managing editor
Circulation: 45,000
Published bimonthly in Niagara, 3 times a year for Toronto-
    Burlington
    A lifestyle magazine of the Niagara region, covering such topics as food, wine, art, fiction, travel, and events via issue themes of business, home and garden, health and wellness, design and décor, golf, travel and leisure, and holidays. Named "Niagara's premier magazine" by the *Buffalo News*. Articles 500 to 1,000 words. Pays on publication for Niagara-based themed features, profiles, and music, as well as book and play reviews. Fees are negotiated for submissions of copy, photography, and art. E-mail the editor.

NOW Magazine
189 Church Street, Toronto, ON M5B 1Y7
Phone: (416) 364-1300   Fax: (416) 364-1168
E-mail: news@nowtoronto.com or
    entertainment@nowtoronto.com
Web site: www.nowtoronto.com
Contacts: Ellie Kirzner (ellie@nowtoronto.com), senior news
    editor; Susan Cole (susan@nowtoronto.com), senior entertainment editor
Circulation: 109,000
Published weekly
    A news, entertainment, and listings magazine covering Toronto-region news, music, film, theatre, fashion, and the arts. Story length

from 400 to 2,000 words. Most work is assigned. Uses very few out-of-town writers. Toronto-region news submissions with an alternative perspective have best chance. Rates vary. Pays on publication. All fees negotiable. Inquiries welcome.

Ottawa Magazine
226 Argyle Avenue, Ottawa, ON K2P 1B9
Phone: (613) 230-0333 Fax: (613) 230-4441
E-mail: sbrown@stjosephmedia.com
Web site: www.ottawamagazine.com
Contact: Sarah Brown, editor
Circulation: 40,000
Published 8 times a year
Targeted at upwardly mobile Ottawans between the ages of 35 and 50. Pays 50¢/word on acceptance for articles 800 to 3,500 words.

Riverside Quarterly
276 Carlaw Avenue, Studio 204, Toronto, ON M4M 3L1
Phone: (416) 466-1815 Fax: (416) 466-1719
E-mail: info@rqmag.com
Web site: www.rqmag.com
Circulation: 10,000
Provides a wide spectrum of educational and entertaining literary stories focused on life in Toronto's historical East End. Covers a balance of old and new. Articles from 500 to 1,200 words. Query first by letter to submissions department. Pays within 60 days of publication $85 to $175 for feature articles with photos.

Scene
195 Dufferin Avenue, Suite 602, London, ON N6A 1K7
Phone: (519) 642-4780 Fax: (519) 642-0737
E-mail: bret@scenemagazine.com
Web site: www.scenemagazine.com
Contact: Bret Downe, publisher/editor-in-chief
Circulation: 19,000
Published 25 times a year
London's entertainment, arts, and news paper. Articles 500 to 750 words. Pays $50/article on acceptance. Guidelines available.

Toronto Life
111 Queen Street E., Suite 320, Toronto, ON M5C 1S2
Phone: (416) 364-3333 Fax: (416) 861-1169
E-mail: editorial@torontolife.com
Contact: John Macfarlane, editor
Circulation: 91,000
Published monthly
    Established 1966. A city magazine that tells readers how Toronto works, lives, and plays. Examines city politics, society, business, entertainment, sports, food and restaurants, and shopping in a unique mix of reporting and service journalism. Also publishes city guides. Draws on a stable of experienced writers and rarely accepts outside submissions. Pays on acceptance between $500 and $5,000 for 100 to 6,000 words, depending on assignment. "Submissions should have a strong Toronto orientation. Story suggestions should be submitted in writing in the form of a 1-page proposal." Guidelines available.

TV Week
4180 Lougheed Highway, 4th Floor, Burnaby, BC V6B 6A7
Phone: (604) 299-7311 Fax: (604) 299-9188
E-mail: tvweek@canadawide.com
Web site: www.canadawide.com
Contact: Brent Furdyk, editor
Circulation: 100,000
Published weekly
    A television and entertainment guide. Pays 40¢/word on publication for stories of 600 to 1,300 words.

Uptown Magazine
1465 St. James Street, Winnipeg, MB R3H 0W9
Phone: (204) 949-4370 Fax: (204) 949-4376
E-mail: john.kendle@uptownmag.com
Web site: www.uptownmag.com
Contact: John Kendle, editor
Circulation: 20,000
Published weekly
    An arts, entertainment, and news weekly for readers 15 to 50. Articles 500 to 1,000 words. Pay rates vary and are paid on publication. Contact editor regarding submissions.

Vancouver Magazine
2608 Granville Street, Suite 500, Vancouver, BC V6H 3V3
Phone: (604) 877-7732 Fax: (604) 877-4823
E-mail: mail@vancouvermagazine.com
Web site: www.vancouvermagazine.com
Contact: Gary Stephen Ross, editor-in-chief
Circulation: 48,000
Published 11 times a year
   The city magazine of the new Vancouver – its people, stories, and ideas – focusing on urban culture and current affairs. Articles must be Vancouver specific. Most stories are 1,500 words; no poetry or fiction. Query first. Read the magazine before submitting. Guidelines available.

Vue Weekly
10303 – 108 Street, Edmonton, AB T5J 1L7
Phone: (780) 426-1996 Fax: (780) 426-2889
E-mail: carolyn@vueweekly.com
Web site: www.vueweekly.com
Contact: Carolyn Nikodym, managing editor
Circulation: 30,000
Published weekly
   An alternative arts and entertainment weekly with a focus on Edmonton and Alberta. Pays on publication 8¢ to 12¢/word for articles of 400 to 1,500 words. "We welcome a variety of pitches, focusing on alternative news and A&E. Please check out our web site to get a feel for what we do. No fiction or poetry, please."

The Environment

Alternatives Journal: Canadian Environmental Ideas and Action
Faculty of Environmental Studies, University of Waterloo, Waterloo, ON N2L 3G1
Phone: (519) 888-4442 Fax: (519) 746-0292
E-mail: editor@alternativesjournal.ca
Web site: www.alternativesjournal.ca

Contact: Nicola Ross, executive editor
Published quarterly
A long-standing leader in environmental journalism. Articles provide a blend of practical information and analysis from across Canada and abroad. "Environment is defined in the broadest sense. Readers include environmental professionals and academics, activists, concerned citizens, and students." Feature-length articles (1,500 to 3,000 words) are peer reviewed. Also publishes reports (500 to 1,200 words) and notes (up to 500 words). Pay rates negotiable. Guidelines available on web site.

Common Ground
4381 Fraser Street, Suite 204, Vancouver, BC V5V 4G4
Phone: (604) 733-2215 Fax: (604) 733-4415
E-mail: editor@commonground.ca
Contact: Joseph Roberts, publisher/senior editor
Circulation: 768,000
Published monthly
Aims to inform, inspire, and educate readers about health, wellness, ecology, personal growth, travel, professional development, and creativity. Prefers Canadian authors. Rarely accepts fiction or poetry. Pays 10¢/published word on publication for articles from 600 to 1,500 words.

Green Teacher
95 Robert Street, Toronto, ON M5S 2K5
Phone: (416) 960-1244 Fax: (416) 925-3474
E-mail: info@greenteacher.com
Web site: www.greenteacher.com
Contact: Tim Grant, co-editor
Circulation: 7,200
Published quarterly
A magazine by and for educators that aims to provide ideas, inspiration, and classroom-ready materials to help all educators (including parents) promote environmental and global awareness among young people, preschool to college, in school and in the community. Articles 1,200 to 3,800 words. All writers are volunteers; they receive a complimentary 1-year subscription. Submissions welcome. Guidelines available on web site.

Harrowsmith Country Life

3100 de la Concorde E. Boulevard, Suite 213, Laval, QC H7E 2B8
Phone: (514) 327-4464 Fax: (450) 665-2974
Web site: www.harrowsmithcountrylife.ca
Contact: Tom Cruickshank, editor
Circulation: 125,000
Published bimonthly

A magazine for a thoughtful, critical audience interested in all aspects of country living. Subject areas most frequently covered include rural issues, home improvement, gardening, energy and ecology, and innovative architecture. Canadian themes essential. Welcomes written inquiries by mail or fax; no e-mail queries accepted. Pays a negotiated rate on acceptance for 1,000 to 1,500 words; rate varies according to complexity and writer's experience.

Nature Canada

85 Albert Street, Suite 900, Ottawa, ON K1P 6A4
Phone: (613) 562-3447 Fax: (613) 562-3371
E-mail: info@naturecanada.ca
Web site: www.cnf.ca
Contact: Chris Sutton, manager, communications
Circulation: 20,000
Published quarterly

Mailed to supporters of Nature Canada, a non-profit conservation organization. Also, an electronic newsletter, *The Nature Nation*, is issued monthly. *Nature Canada* magazine is aimed at people interested in learning about and protecting nature. Focuses on conservation issues related to protected federal areas, endangered species, and important bird areas. Features 500 to 1,200 words. Rates vary and are paid on publication. "Stories in the print and electronic newsletters focus strongly on Nature Canada programs. General interest stories must be relevant to our programs." Guidelines available.

The Sustainable Times

1225 Prospect Bay Road, Prospect, NS B3T 2A6
Phone: (902) 850-2510
E-mail: times@chebucto.ns.ca

Web site: www.sustainabletimes.ca
Contact: Sean Kelly, managing editor
   An Internet magazine focusing on ecology, green economics, international development, and fair trade. Published by CUSO. "We believe economics should be guided by environmental protection and fairness, not just profit." Send initial query rather than complete article. Guidelines available.

Feminist

Herizons
P.O. Box 128, Winnipeg, MB R3C 2G1
Phone: (204) 774-6225 Fax: (204) 786-8038
E-mail: editor@herizons.ca
Web site: www.herizons.ca
Circulation: 4,000
Published quarterly
   A feminist periodical focusing on women's issues and the women's movement. Features 1,000 to 3,000 words. Pays 20¢/word on publication. Send query and sample of previous published work written from a feminist perspective. Guidelines available on web site.

Women & Environments International Magazine
c/o I.W.S.G.S. New College, University of Toronto, 40 Willcocks
   Street, Toronto, ON M5S 1C6
Phone: (416) 978-5259 Fax: (416) 946-5561
E-mail: we.mag@utoronto.ca
Web site: www.weimag.com
Contact: editorial board
Published twice a year
   A co-operative forum for discussion, review, and research on women's built, natural, social, and political environments for feminists, academics, and a broad base of grassroots groups. Features 1,500 to 2,500 words. Shorter pieces, book and film reviews, poetry, and artistic expressions are welcome. Contributors are not paid. "Clear language is essential – no academic jargon, please. We

are cross-cultural and international. All issues are theme related. For the next 2 years, we aim to publish issues on women, communities, health, mobility, governance, spirituality, social change, and violence." Guidelines available.

General Interest

Alberta Views
320 – 23 Avenue S.W., Suite 208, Calgary, AB T2S 0J2
Phone: (403) 243-5334 Fax: (403) 243-8599
E-mail: avadmin@albertaviews.ab.ca
Web site: www.albertaviews.ab.ca
Contact: Gillian Steward, publisher
Circulation: 20,000
Published 10 times a year
   Publishes commentary and analysis that explores political, social, and cultural life in Alberta in order to stimulate public discussion. Articles are from 700 to 3,000 words. Pays 50¢/word on acceptance. Guidelines available.

The Beaver
167 Lombard Avenue, Suite 478, Winnipeg, MB R3B 0T6
Phone: (204) 988-9300 Fax: (204) 988-9309
E-mail: editors@historysociety.ca
Web site: www.thebeaver.ca
Contact: Doug Whiteway, editor
Circulation: 48,000
Published bimonthly
   A market since 1920 for lively, well-researched, informative, expository articles on Canadian history. "We welcome popularly written features on Canadian history, particularly those based on unpublished or new material, written from a non-traditional point of view or a new interpretation of significant events or people." Interested in submissions from all parts of the country. Pays a varying rate (depending on research necessary and writer's experience) on acceptance for articles of 800 to 3,000 words. "Writers should thoroughly acquaint themselves with the magazine by reading back issues." Guidelines available on web site.

Beyond Ordinary Living

P.O. Box 21033, Paris, ON N3L 4A5
Phone: 1-877-442-3449 Fax: (519) 442-4023
E-mail: editors@beyondordinaryliving.com
Web site: www.beyondordinaryliving.com
Contact: Ethel Rowntree, publisher/editor
Published bimonthly

Carries inspirational, thought-provoking stories of Canadians making a difference, motivational and transformational articles, and profiles of well-known individuals whose faith has inspired or influenced their contribution to society. First-person accounts from 500 to 1,200 words are generally unpaid; interviews and profiles from 1,200 to 1,500 words receive 10¢/word or more on publication. Guidelines on web site.

Canadian Stories

P.O. Box 232, Fergus, ON N1M 2W8
Phone: (519) 787-2451 Fax: (519) 787-2451
E-mail: ejanzen345@sympatico.ca
Web site: www.canadianstories.net
Contact: Ed Janzen, publisher/editor
Published bimonthly

A collection of Canadian folk stories, old and recent, memories, memoirs, and historical articles. Readers are mostly middle aged and seniors. Preferred length of articles 200 to 1,200 words. Cannot pay but welcomes submission inquiries. Contributors are from across Canada and are mostly first-time writers. See web site for examples and guidelines.

Nuvo Magazine

3055 Kingsway, Vancouver, BC V5R 5J8
Phone: (604) 899-9380 or 1-877-205-6886 Fax: (604) 899-1450
E-mail: editorial@nuvomagazine.com
Web site: www.nuvomagazine.com
Contact: Jim Tobler, editor
Circulation: 46,000
Published quarterly

Canada's culture, style, and celebrity magazine with a unique perspective on Canadian culture. Includes stories on film, music, food and wine, sports, travel, fashion, beauty, architecture, design, and celebrities. "Please pick up a copy of *Nuvo* and visit our web site before making your submission. E-mail queries only; no telephone queries are accepted." Guidelines available on web site.

Our Canada

1100 René Levesque Boulevard W., Montreal, QC H3B 5H5
Phone: (514) 940-7205
E-mail: simon.mcdermott@rd.com
Web site: www.ourcanada.ca
Contact: Simon McDermott, associate editor
Circulation: 260,000
Published bimonthly
The tagline for this magazine is "Our country, your stories." Publishes reader-contributed stories of Canadian life. Writers should check departments in the magazine. Stories 200 to 1,000 words. Fees vary depending on the project and are paid on publication. "Tell us your stories. Send us your photos. Read the magazine for a clear idea of what we publish." Guidelines available.

Reader's Digest

1100 René Levesque Boulevard W., Montreal, QC H3B 5H5
Phone: (514) 940-0751   Fax: (514) 940-3637
E-mail: editor@readersdigest.ca
Web site: www.readersdigest.ca
Contact: editorial department
Circulation: 921,000
Published monthly
This mass-interest magazine is among the freelancer's most lucrative potential markets. Carries articles on everything from nature, science, and politics to drama, self-improvement, and people, prominent or otherwise. All pieces contain advice, an experience, or a philosophical message of value to the magazine's 4 million readers. No fiction or poetry. Commissions original articles and adaptations of Canadian subjects of between 3,500 and 5,000 words. Pays $200/anecdote. Also buys material previously published in books, magazines, or newspapers. Buys global rights and pays on acceptance for original articles, one-time or global rights for previously published "pickups." No unsolicited manuscripts.

Send letter of inquiry with a 2-page outline. Guidelines available on web site.

Toro

119 Spadina Avenue, Suite 502, Toronto, ON M5V 2L1
Phone: (416) 785-9446 Fax: (416) 785-9434
E-mail: info@toromagazine.ca or submissions@toromagazine.ca
Web site: www.toromagazine.ca
Contact: Dave Morris, associate editor
Circulation: 220,000
Published 8 times a year
A general interest magazine for men. Articles 150 to 6,000 words. Fees, which are paid on acceptance, are negotiated and vary depending on the project. "If a writer hasn't worked with us before or is unknown to the editors, we always suggest sending in clips along with his or her pitches." Guidelines available on web site.

Up Here Magazine

4920 – 52 Street, Suite 800, Yellowknife, NT X1A 3T1
Phone: (867) 766-6710 Fax: (867) 873-9876
E-mail: jasmine@uphere.ca
Web site: www.uphere.ca
Contact: Jasmine Bukak, senior editor
Circulation: 25,000
Published 8 times a year
· A lively, informative magazine about travel, wildlife, arts, culture, lifestyles, and especially the people of Canada's far northern regions. Articles 2,200 to 2,500 words (maximum 3,500 words). Fees negotiable and paid on publication. "We strongly prefer written queries that present a well-focused story and, if not samples, then suggested leads for accompanying photography. Complete manuscripts with photos are okay, but please be aware we cannot be responsible for unsolicited material. We're looking for solid reporting and research, and top-notch photos. Always tell your story through the people involved." Guidelines available.

Your Workplace

23 Queen Street, Kingston, ON K7K 1A1
Phone: (613) 549-1222

E-mail: editor@yourworkplace.ca
Web site: www.yourworkplace.ca
Contact: Elizabeth Colon, office assistant
Circulation: 100,000
Published 8 times a year
   Provides inspiration for work and life, healthy workplaces, the
work-life balance, trends, safety, and employee concerns. Articles
700 to 1,600 words. Pays 20¢/word on publication. Welcomes sub-
mission queries. Guidelines available.

Home & Hobby

Antique and Collectibles Showcase
P.O. Box 1626, Holland Landing, ON L9N 1P2
Phone: (905) 853-9191 Fax: (905) 853-9141
E-mail: asceditor@rogers.com
Web site: www.antiqueandcollectiblesshowcase.ca
Contact: Judy Penz Sheluk, editor
Circulation: 60,000
Published bimonthly
   Theme-based issues feature antiques and collectibles in respect
to the holiday season, celebrating Canada, and back to school.
Articles from 750 to 1,500 words. Fees vary from $75 to $200 on
publication, the average pay being $100 to $150. Guidelines avail-
able on web site. "Read the guidelines. Read the magazine. Your
pitch should be professional."

The Canadian Amateur
720 Belfast Road, Suite 217, Ottawa, ON K1G 0Z5
Phone: (613) 244-4367 Fax: (613) 244-4369
E-mail: tcamag@yahoo.ca
Web site: www.rac.ca
Contact: Alan Griffin, editor
Published bimonthly
   Provides radio amateurs, those interested in radio communica-
tions and electronics, and the general public with information
related to the science of telecommunications. Welcomes technical

and non-technical articles. Some articles may be published in both English and French. Cannot pay. Guidelines on web site.

Canadian Coin News
103 Lakeshore Road, Suite 202, St. Catharines, ON L2N 2T6
Phone: (905) 646-7744 Fax: (905) 646-0995
E-mail: bret@trajan.com
Web site: www.canadiancoinnews.com
Contact: Bret Evans, editor
Circulation: 11,000
Published biweekly
 A tabloid magazine for Canadian collectors of coins and paper money. Query first by e-mail or phone. Pays a month after publication. Fees negotiable.

Canadian Gardening
25 Sheppard Avenue W., Suite 100, Toronto, ON M2N 6S7
Phone: (416) 733-7600 Fax: (416) 227-8298
E-mail: editor@canadiangardening.com
Web site: www.canadiangardening.com
Contact: Aldona Satterthwaite, editor-in-chief
Circulation: 152,000
Published 8 times a year
 A magazine geared toward the avid home gardener. Carries people-oriented feature articles on home gardens, garden design, and tips and techniques on gardening in the Canadian climate. Features are 500 to 1,500 words. Fees vary and are paid on acceptance. "We prefer story ideas and outlines to unsolicited, finished stories." Guidelines available on web site.

Canadian Home & Country
340 Ferrier Street, Suite 210, Markham, ON L3R 2Z5
Phone: (905) 475-8440 Fax: (905) 475-9246
E-mail: editorial@canadianhomeandcountry.com
Web site: www.canadianhomeandcountry.com
Contact: Rebecca Zamon, assistant editor
Circulation: 140,000
Published 8 times a year

A magazine for lovers of country living and country style. Contains feature stories (600 to 850 words) about country houses, historic houses, artisans, entertaining, decorating, and antiques. Fees vary according to project and are paid on publication. Query first. "When pitching, queries should be accompanied by relevant scouting photos." Guidelines available.

Canadian Homes and Cottages
2650 Meadowvale Boulevard, Unit 4, Mississauga, ON L5N 6M5
Phone: (905) 567-1440 Fax: (905) 567-1442
E-mail: editorial@homesandcottages.com
Web site: www.homesandcottages.com
Contact: Steven Chester, managing editor
Circulation: 79,000
Published bimonthly
Canada's largest residential building magazine for consumers as well as building trades. Provides thought-provoking and innovative ideas and technical information to help Canadians build or renovate their homes and cottages. Articles 600 to 1,200 words. Fees vary according to complexity, but average is $300. All articles are assigned. Pays on acceptance. "We have consumer and trade editions. We write about architecture and design, but not decorating; hard landscaping, but not gardening; cottage renovation and construction, but not cottage lifestyles." Guidelines available.

Canadian House & Home
511 King Street W., Suite 120, Toronto, ON M5V 2Z4
Phone: (416) 593-0204 Fax: (416) 591-1630
E-mail: cheditorial@hhmedia.com
Web site: www.houseandhome.com
Contacts: Trish Snyder or Danny Sinopoli, senior features
    editors
Circulation: 250,000
Published monthly
Focuses on creative home decoration and design. Inspires and teaches through pictorial essays and how-to articles featuring Canadian designers, architects, and artisans. Fees vary depending on project and are paid on acceptance. "Stories are usually assigned based on acceptance of visuals. Always include colour

photos with submissions. Submit story proposals only, not completed manuscripts."

Canadian Stamp News

103 Lakeshore Road, Suite 202, St. Catharines, ON L2N 2T6
Phone: (905) 646-7744 Fax: (905) 646-0995
E-mail: bret@trajan.com
Web site: www.canadianstampnews.ca
Contact: Bret Evans, managing editor
Circulation: 5,000
Published biweekly
   A tabloid magazine serving Canadian philatelists and enthusiasts around the world who collect Canadian stamps. Query first by e-mail or phone. Pays two months after publication. Fees negotiable.

Canadian Woodworking Magazine

R.R. #3, Burford, ON N0E 1A0
Phone: (519) 449-2444 Fax: (519) 449-2445
E-mail: fulcher@canadianwoodworking.com
Web site: www.canadianwoodworking.com
Contact: Linda Fulcher, publisher
Circulation: 30,000
Published bimonthly
   A special-interest publication with articles, editorials, photos, and ads for the hobbyist woodworker, beginner to advanced. Looking for articles on practical woodworking projects for the home workshop. Pays $50 to $150 on publication for articles of 500 to 1,000 words.

Dream House Magazine

873 Beatty Street, Suite 106, Vancouver, BC V6B 2M6
Phone: (604) 681-3463 Fax: (604) 681-3494
E-mail: tracey@dreamhousemag.com
Web site: www.dreamhousemag.com
Contact: Tracey Ellis, editor
Circulation: 30,000
Published bimonthly
   Western Canada's premier fine home and lifestyle magazine. Stories run from 500 to 800 words. Fees are about 25¢/word or

$200/article, paid within 30 days of publication. "Kill fees paid at half rate if story doesn't run within 6 issues." Guidelines available.

Gardens West
P.O. Box 2680, Vancouver, BC V6B 3W8
Phone: (604) 879-4991 Fax: (604) 879-5110
E-mail: grow@gardenswest.com
Web site: www.gardenswest.com
Contact: Mike Barter, production manager
Circulation: 37,000
Published 9 times a year
A magazine that is fun and informative, *Gardens West* nurtures novice and expert home gardeners. Articles are from 800 to 1,000 words. Fees vary depending on project and are paid on publication. "Make sure to read a couple of recent issues to learn the style and type of articles we accept."

Home Digest
115 George Street, Unit 604, Oakville, ON L6J 0A2
Phone: (905) 844-3361 Fax: (905) 849-4618
E-mail: homedigesteditor@sympatico.ca
Web site: www.home-digest.com
Contact: William Roebuck, editor
Published 5 times a year
Carries articles devoted to food and wine, health, household hints, fitness, family activities, Toronto-area events, home decoration and renovation, raising children, and keeping pets. Aimed at mid- to upper-income Canadians. Stories 300 to 800 words; short service, human interest, and humour items are 50 to 200 words. Pays 10¢/word on publication.

Homes & Living Magazine
873 Beatty Street, Suite 106, Vancouver, BC V6B 2M6
Phone: (604) 681-3463 Fax: (604) 681-3494
E-mail: tracey@dreamhousemag.com
Web site: www.dreamhousemag.com
Contact: Tracey Ellis, editor
Circulation: 30,000
Published twice a year

Western Canada's premier fine home and lifestyle magazine, affiliated with *Dream House Magazine*. Stories run from 500 to 800 words. Fees are about 25¢/word or $200/article, paid within 30 days of publication. "Kill fees paid at half rate if story doesn't run within 6 issues." Guidelines available.

Ontario Gardener Living Magazine
219 Dufferin Street, Suite 201C, Toronto, ON M6K 3J1
Phone: (416) 963-3934 Fax: (416) 963-5929
E-mail: shaunad@localgardener.net
Web site: www.localgardener.net
Contact: Shauna Dobbie, publisher/editor
Circulation: 18,000
Published 8 times a year
   A magazine with informative, entertaining articles for passionate gardeners across Ontario. Articles 200 to 1,000 words. Pays $70 to $350 on publication, depending on the project. "Please call or e-mail for guidelines."

Photo Life
1 Dundas Street W., Suite 2500, P.O. Box 84, Toronto, ON M5G 1Z3
Phone: 1-800-905-7468 Fax: 1-800-664-2739
E-mail: write@photolife.com
Web site: www.photolife.com
Contact: Sonia Roy, assistant editor
Published bimonthly
   Established 1976. Delivers serious information to photographers from beginners to advanced in a readable way. Articles 600 to 1,500 words. Fees are negotiated and paid on publication. *Photo Life* offers the opportunity for photographers to have their work published. "All photography-related articles are welcome. Submission guidelines are available at our web site."

Style at Home
25 Sheppard Avenue W., Suite 100, Toronto, ON M2N 6S7
Phone: (416) 218-3685 Fax: (416) 218-3632
E-mail: letters@styleathome.com
Web site: www.styleathome.com
Contact: Gail Johnston Habs, editor

Circulation: 235,000

Published 12 times a year

A glossy magazine featuring Canadian home-décor stories, news, products, and trends. Rates vary with project and writer, but pays up to $1/word on acceptance for stories of 300 to 700 words. "Please read several issues of *Style at Home* before presenting queries." Guidelines available.

Upper Canadian

13 Nelles Boulevard, Grimsby, ON L3M 3P9

Phone: (905) 945-5757 Fax: (905) 945-4740

E-mail: inquiries@theuppercanadian.com

Web site: www.theuppercanadian.com

Contact: J. Herbert Bond, editor

Circulation: 4,500

Published bimonthly

Since 1980, the authoritative voice covering Canadian antiques, fine art, and folk art. Trusted by collectors, and valued by dealers, auctioneers, and the trade. Articles 600 to 1,000 words. Fees vary and are paid on publication. "We particularly appreciate writers with a passion for antiques, art, and/or collecting." Guidelines available.

Lifestyle

Access Magazine

79 Portsmouth Drive, Toronto, ON M1C 5C8

Phone: (416) 335-0747 Fax: (416) 335-0748

E-mail: keith@accessmag.com

Web site: www.accessmag.com

Contact: Keith Sharp, publisher

Circulation: 115,000

Published bimonthly

A lifestyle/entertainment magazine focusing on music, film, video, fashion, travel, and other lifestyle topics. Articles 1,000 to 1,500 words. Pays 25¢/word on publication. Guidelines available.

Alive Magazine
7432 Fraser Park Drive, Burnaby, BC V5J 5B9
Phone: (604) 435-1919   Fax: (604) 435-4888
E-mail: editorial@alive.com
Web site: www.alive.com
Contact: Terry-Lynn Stone, editor-in-chief
Circulation: 187,000
Published monthly
　　A national magazine for health-conscious Canadians featuring articles on whole-foods nutrition, alternative medicine, and the environment. Articles of 800 to 1,000 words by health researchers and professionals. Pays 25¢/word on publication. "Always query. Do not send unsolicited articles or manuscripts." Guidelines available.

Ascent – Yoga for an Inspired Life
837 Gilford Street, Montreal, QC H2J 1P1
Phone: (514) 499-3999   Fax: (514) 499-3904
E-mail: managing_editor@ascentmagazine.com
Web site: www.ascentmagazine.com
Contact: Anurag Dhir, managing editor
Published quarterly
　　A magazine of yoga and engaged spirituality that publishes thoughtful and lively articles exploring how spiritual values are brought to life in the everyday. Each issue has a theme (listed on web site). Features are 2,000 to 3,500 words; interviews 1,800 to 2,500 words; other articles 1,000 to 2,000 words. Pays 10¢ to 20¢/published word on publication. "We prefer to work with writers from the query stage onward. We rarely accept unsolicited submissions." Guidelines available.

Best Wishes
65 The East Mall, Toronto, ON M8Z 5W3
Phone: (416) 537-2604   Fax: (416) 538-1794
E-mail: susanp@parentscanada.com
Web site: www.parentscanada.com
Contact: Susan Pennell-Sebekos, editor
Circulation: 100,000
Published twice a year

Given to new parents in hospitals and other medical outlets. Articles cover topics relevant to parenting a baby from birth to 6 months of age and are written by Canadian healthcare professionals. Articles 1,000 to 2,000 words. Rates vary and are paid on acceptance.

Beyond Fitness

3535 Saint-Charles Blvd., Suite 502, Kirkland, QC H9H 5B9
Phone: (514) 697-5888 Fax: (514) 693-0833
E-mail: beyondfit@bellnet.ca
Contact: Laura Warf, editor-in-chief
Circulation: 150,000
Published bimonthly

A free magazine available in gyms and fitness clubs across the country. Articles from 750 to 1,200 words on physical and spiritual fitness, nutrition, pilates, etc. Pays $200/article on publication. Guidelines available.

Canadian Family

111 Queen Street E., Suite 320, Toronto, ON M5C 1S2
Phone: (416) 364-3333, ext. 3131
E-mail: editor@canadianfamily.ca
Web site: www.canadianfamily.ca
Circulation: 125,000
Published 8 times a year

Includes stories on parenting, family life, education, health, décor, fashion, beauty, and contemporary parenting issues. Pays on average $1/word for articles 100 to 1,500 words. Paid on acceptance. "Please study the new, relaunched version of our magazine. We are not like the old *Canadian Family*. Writers must excel at engaging, conversational copy and not write in a pedantic or arcane style. We're fun, hip, savvy, and supportive. Always include clips." Guidelines available with an SASE.

City Parent

467 Speers Road, Oakville, ON L6K 3S4
Phone: (905) 815-0017 Fax: (905) 337-5571
E-mail: cityparent@haltonsearch.com
Web site: www.cityparent.com
Contact: Jane Muller, editor

Circulation: 170,000
Published monthly
   A magazine for families with children under age 14. Serves the Greater Toronto Area, Halton, Hamilton, and Niagara. Includes information on new products, arts and entertainment, and reviews as well as informative articles. Articles 450 to 1,000 words. Pays about 10¢/word on publication, depending on research and quality.

Cottage Life
54 St. Patrick Street, Toronto, ON M5T 1V1
Phone: (416) 599-2000 Fax: (416) 599-0800
E-mail: editorial@cottagelife.com
Web site: www.cottagelife.com
Contact: Penny Caldwell, editor
Circulation: 70,000
Published 6 times a year
   An award-winning magazine directed toward those who own and spend time at cottages on Ontario's lakes. Examines and celebrates the history, personalities, and issues of cottaging. Also provides practical advice to help readers keep their cottages, docks, and boats in working order. Pays on acceptance for articles of 150 to 3,000 words; pay rates vary depending on project. Query all ideas before submission. "Our guidelines are available on the 'contact us' section of our web site. Also, our online searchable index can help free-lancers know what stories have recently been published."

The Cottager
P.O. Box 40, Victoria Beach, MB R0E 2C0
Phone: (204) 756-8381 Fax: (204) 756-2662
E-mail: cottager@granite.mb.ca
Web site: www.cottager.com
Contact: Connie Oliver, editor
Circulation: 10,000
Published quarterly
   The Cottager is dedicated to present and future cottage owners in Manitoba and northwestern Ontario. Pays 20¢ to 30¢/word on publication for articles from 800 to 1,200 words. Guidelines available on web site.

The Country Connection

P.O. Box 100, Boulter, ON K0L 1G0
Phone: (613) 332-3651
E-mail: editor@pinecone.on.ca
Web site: www.pinecone.on.ca
Contact: Gus Zylstra, publisher/managing editor
Circulation: 2,000
Published quarterly

A nature-friendly magazine for the discerning reader, with a focus on green travel, heritage, nostalgia, nature, the environment, and the arts. Articles 1,000 to 1,500 words. Submit article ideas and short fiction. Pays on publication 10¢/word for electronic submissions and 7¢/word for handwritten or typed submissions. "Visit our web site for detailed requirements for upcoming issues."

The Country Register of Manitoba and Saskatchewan

107 Louisa Avenue, P.O. Box 850, Kipling, SK S0G 2S0
Phone: (306) 736-2441   Fax: (306) 736-8389
E-mail: countryregister@sasktel.net
Web site: www.countryregister.com
Contact: Marj Kearns, co-publisher
Circulation: 23,000
Published bimonthly

Publishes stories up to 300 words on crafts, gifts, hobbies, and tourism. Cannot pay but welcomes submission inquiries. Guidelines available.

CSANews

180 Lesmill Road, North York, ON M3B 2T5
Phone: (416) 441-7000   Fax: (416) 441-7020
E-mail: csawriteus@snowbirds.org
Web site: http://snowbirds.org
Contact: Chris Bradbury, president
Circulation: 75,000
Published quarterly

The publication of the Canadian Snowbirds Association. Covers seniors' travel, government lobbying, financial and retirement issues, and insurance. Articles from 600 to 1,200 words. Fees vary depending on project and are paid on publication.

Downhome

43 James Lane, St. John's, NL A1E 3H3
Phone: (709) 726-5113 Fax: (709) 726-2135
E-mail: editorial@downhomelife.com
Web site: www.downhomelife.com
Contact: Leslie McNab, managing editor
Circulation: 40,000
Published monthly

Downhome's mandate is to share with the world the best of everything Atlantic Canada has to offer. "From the outdoors to the arts, from the people to their values, we celebrate the downhome lifestyle of Canada's East Coast." Articles from 1,200 to 1,600 words. Fees vary depending on the project and are paid on publication. "*Downhome* is the largest paid-circulation magazine in Atlantic Canada. We prefer queries to whole manuscripts. Please read the magazine before pitching." Guidelines available.

Elevate

365 Bloor Street E., Suite 1902, Toronto, ON M4W 3L4
Phone: (416) 869-3131 Fax: (416) 869-3008
E-mail: info@elevatemagazine.com
Web site: www.elevatemagazine.com
Contact: Chantel Simmons, publisher/editor-in-chief
Circulation: 35,000
Published 5 times a year

Elevate is Canada's leading anti-aging, wellness, and enhancement magazine. Accepts queries for all sections of the publication. Pays 50¢/word. "Please send a brief query including the topic you want to write about, a sample paragraph, proposed interviewees, and proposed word count."

Expecting

65 The East Mall, Toronto, ON M8Z 5W3
Phone: (416) 537-2604 Fax: (416) 538-1794
E-mail: susanp@parentscanada.com
Web site: www.parentscanada.com
Contact: Susan Pennell-Sebekos, editor
Circulation: 100,000
Published twice a year

A digest-sized parental magazine distributed to expectant parents in doctors' offices and prenatal classes. All articles must be written by Canadian healthcare professionals and deal with topics relevant to pregnancy. Articles 1,000 to 2,000 words. Fees vary and are paid on acceptance.

Fab Magazine
Phone: (416) 925-5221
E-mail: editor@fabmagazine.com
Web site: www.fabmagazine.com
Contact: Steven Bereznai, editor-in-chief
Circulation: 31,000
Published 26 times a year

Culture and lifestyle get a fierce gay spin in *Fab*, Ontario's gay scene report. Articles 180 to 1,500 words. Pays on publication.

50 Plus Magazine
27 Queen Street E., Toronto, ON M5C 2M6
Phone: (416) 363-5562   Fax: (416) 363-7394
E-mail: b.baker@kemur.ca
Web site: www.carp.ca
Contact: Bonnie Baker Cowan, editor
Circulation: 250,000
Published 9 times a year

The official voice of Canada's Association for the 50-Plus and a leading magazine for the over-50s. Accepts a limited number of freelance articles each year. Pays 60¢/word on acceptance for articles of 500 to 2,000 words. "Send query and writing samples. Please don't phone." Guidelines available.

Going Natural/Au naturel
P.O. Box 81128, FGPO, Ancaster, ON L9G 4X1
Phone: (905) 304-4836   Fax: (416) 410-6833
E-mail: information@fcn.ca or editor@fcn.ca
Web site: www.fcn.ca/GN.html
Contact: Paul Rapoport, editor
Circulation: 2,300
Published quarterly

Features information and news for anglophone and francophone naturists (nudists) in Canada, the rest of North America, and the world. Also useful for future naturists. "Aims for an acceptance of the entire human body, of all ages and shapes, without shame or penalty (in non-erotic contexts)." Articles should not exceed 1,100 words. Fees vary depending on project and are paid on publication. "Must be comfortable with at least the concept of non-sexualized nudity and preferably the practice as well!" Guidelines available.

Good Times

2001 University Street, Suite 900, Montreal, QC H3A 2A6
Phone: (514) 499-0491 Fax: (514) 499-3078
E-mail: editor@goodtimes.ca
Web site: www.goodtimes.ca
Contact: Murray Lewis, editor-in-chief
Circulation: 150,000
Published 11 times a year
Addresses the concerns of retired Canadians and those planning retirement. Topics include financial and retirement planning, health, nutrition, and fitness; lifestyles; better living and wellbeing; relationships; celebrity profiles; and leisure activities. Welcomes inquiries that note areas of expertise and suggestions along with writing samples. Articles 1,200 to 2,000 words. Buys first rights and pays a negotiated rate per word. E-mail queries are best.

Health 'n Vitality

3535 St. Charles, Suite 502, Kirkland, QC H9H 5B9
Phone: (514) 697-5888 Fax: (514) 693-0833
E-mail: magpie@videotron.ca
Contact: Kate Tompkins, editor
Circulation: 200,000
Published bimonthly
Contains articles that educate consumers about alternative health. Distributed through health-food stores in Canada and the United States. Articles are from 800 to 1,200 words. Pays $200/article on publication. Submission guidelines available.

Inuktitut Magazine
170 Laurier Avenue W., Suite 510, Ottawa, ON K1P 5V5
Phone: (613) 238-8181 or 1-866-262-8181 Fax: (613) 234-1991
E-mail: coms@itk.ca
Web site: www.itk.ca
Contact: Stephen Hendrie, managing editor
Circulation: 13,000
Published 3 times a year
   Presents the heritage of Inuit culture, language, and society. *Inuktitut* is distributed in Inuit communities in Labrador, Nunavik, Nunavut, and the Northwest Territories. Stories are published in Inuktitut, English, and French. All articles are assigned, so query first. Stories are generally 1,500 words or less. Pays a minimum of 50¢/word for the length of story commissioned. Guidelines on web site.

Island Parent Magazine
830 Pembroke Street, Suite A-10, Victoria, BC V8T 1H9
Phone: (250) 388-6905 Fax: (250) 388-6920
E-mail: editor@islandparent.ca
Web site: www.islandparent.ca
Contact: Sue Fast, editor
Circulation: 20,000
Published monthly
   A resource publication for Vancouver Island families. Regular features include a calendar of events, new parents pages, parenting advice, book reviews, a food column, arts and entertainment, nature education, recreation, finance, and family fun. Articles 750 to 1,500 words. Pays $25/article on publication. Guidelines available at www.islandparent.ca/writers.php. "Most of our submissions are from Vancouver Island residents."

Kerby News
1133 – 7 Avenue S.W., Calgary, AB T2P 1B2
Phone: (403) 705-3229 Fax: (403) 705-3211
E-mail: editor@kerbycentre.com
Web site: www.kerbycentre.com
Contact: Barry Whitehead, editor

Circulation: 25,000
Published monthly
A publication targeted at those 50 years of age and over who live in southern Alberta. Covers financial planning, seniors' events, local and federal news, and stories on healthy eating, fitness, and travel. Accepts submissions from older writers. Articles 500 to 800 words. Cannot pay but welcomes submission inquiries.

Lethbridge Living

P.O. Box 22005, Henderson Lake P.O., Lethbridge, AB T1K 6X5
Phone: (403) 329-1008 Fax: (403) 329-0264
E-mail: oordt@shaw.ca
Contacts: Martin Oordt, publisher/editor; Mary Oordt, publisher/managing editor
Circulation: 15,000
Published quarterly
A lifestyle magazine focusing on the concerns and interests of the people of Lethbridge and southwestern Alberta. Pays 23¢/word on publication for articles of 350 to 1,200 words. "Writing samples are required. Preference is given to writers from our distribution area." Guidelines available.

Montreal Families

5764 Monkland Avenue, Suite 118, Montreal, QC H4A 1E9
Phone: (514) 487-8881 Fax: (514) 487-4420
E-mail: editorial@montrealfamilies.ca
Contact: Kelly Wilton, editor
Circulation: 30,000
Published monthly
A free, pickup parenting magazine. Fees are negotiated and paid on publication for stories of 500 to 750 words.

Natural Life

264 Queens Quay W., Suite 508, Toronto, ON M5J 1B5
Phone: (416) 260-0303
E-mail: natural@life.ca
Web site: www.naturallifemagazine.com
Contact: Wendy Priesnitz, editor

Circulation: 35,000

Published bimonthly

Provides information and inspiration about healthy, sustainable living, including articles on natural health, healthy homes, and renewable energy. Articles 1,000 to 1,500 words. Cannot pay but welcomes submission inquiries. "Please read the magazine first. Prefer queries by e-mail, not complete articles. Lots of back issues on web site." Guidelines available on web site.

Okanagan Life Magazine

1753 Dolphin Avenue, Suite 10, Kelowna, BC V1Y 8A6

Phone: (250) 861-5399 or 1-888-311-1119   Fax: (250) 868-3040

E-mail: editorial@okanaganlife.com

Web site: www.okanaganlife.com

Contact: Dona Sturmanis, associate editor

Circulation: 25,000

Published 10 times a year

A regional magazine featuring articles for affluent, active, and educated readers on homes, cuisine, fashion, and lifestyle. Pays 20¢ to 25¢/assigned word within 30 days of publication for articles of 1,500 to 3,000 words. Query first by e-mail or post. Guidelines available on web site.

The Prime Times

1465 St. James Street, Winnipeg, MB R3H 0W9

Phone: (204) 949-4816   Fax: (204) 949-4818

E-mail: bernice.pontanilla@canstarnews.com

Contact: Bernice Pontanilla, editor

Circulation: 10,000

Published biweekly

A tabloid-sized publication containing news, features, and games of interest to people over 50 years old. Articles 500 to 750 words. Pay rates vary and are paid on publication.

Saltscapes

40 Alderney Drive, Suite 501, Halifax, NS B2Y 2N5

Phone: (902) 464-7258   Fax: (902) 464-5755

E-mail: jgourlay@saltscapes.com

Web site: www.saltscapes.com

Contact: Jim Gourlay, editor-in-chief
Circulation: 35,000
Published 7 times a year
Focuses on the people and places of Atlantic Canada. Feature articles 1,200 to 1,800 words. Rates vary according to project and are paid on publication. Guidelines available on web site.

Senior Living Vancouver Island / Senior Living Vancouver
1581-H Hillside Avenue, Suite 153, Victoria, BC V8T 2C1
Phone: (250) 479-4705 Fax: (250) 479-4808
E-mail: editor@seniorlivingmag.com
Web site: www.seniorlivingmag.com
Contact: Bobbie Jo Sheriff, editor
Circulation: 25,000
Published monthly
The focus of these two publications is the 50-plus demographic. Features profiles of seniors and seniors' groups that are inspirational and very community oriented. Articles from 750 to 1,200 words and must be about people or groups in the published area. Pays $30 to $75 on publication. "Also publishes articles on health, finance, and legal issues pertinent to seniors." Guidelines available on web site.

Sposa
55 York Street, Suite 202, Toronto, ON M5J 1R7
Phone: (416) 364-5899 Fax: (416) 364-5996
E-mail: editor@sposa.com
Web site: www.sposa.com
Circulation: 50,000
Published twice a year
The world's first reality-based wedding magazine, featuring witty, provocative articles about love and marriage from a global perspective. "Wit and humour much appreciated." Articles 800 to 1,000 words. Fees vary and are paid on acceptance. Guidelines available.

Synchronicity, the Magazine
P.O. Box 63118, 2604 Kensington Road N.W., Calgary, AB T2N 4S5
Phone: (403) 270-9544 Fax: (403) 270-7407
E-mail: editor@synchronicitymagazine.ca

Web site: www.synchronicitymagazine.ca

Published bimonthly

An alternative magazine with a body-mind-spirit focus, available free on stands in Alberta and the interior of B.C. Cover features are up to 3,000 words; feature stories about 900 to 1,600 words; short pieces from 350 to 900 words. An honorarium is paid on publication. "We recommend that writers obtain copies of the magazine to discover if this is their kind of writing. We encourage submission inquiries." See the web site for future themes and guidelines.

TCHAD Magazine

219 Dufferin Street, Suite 102B, Toronto, ON M6K 3T1

Phone: (416) 539-0222 Fax: (416) 539-0221

E-mail: editorial@tchadmag.com

Web site: www.tchadmag.com

Contact: Anne Campbell, senior writing editor

Circulation: 10,000

Published bimonthly

An informative guide for those living the metropolitan lifestyle. Includes interesting articles, savvy columns, and rich photography. Pays $100 or more on acceptance for articles of 750 to 1,000 words. "Our main focus is how our male and female readers can maintain a metropolitan lifestyle and keep informed."

Today's Parent Baby & Toddler

1 Mount Pleasant Road, 8th Floor, Toronto, ON M4Y 2Y5

Phone: (416) 764-2829

Contact: Holly Bennett, editor

Circulation: 175,000

Published twice a year

A consumer magazine for parents with children up to the age of 3. It is distributed as a special edition of *Today's Parent* through doctors' offices and to new subscribers of *Today's Parent* who have babies. Supportive articles focus on health, childcare, development, parenting, and family-life issues. Does not publish poetry or fiction. "Because we promote ourselves as a Canadian magazine, we use only Canadian writers." Word length and fees vary depending on the complexity of the story, usually 500 to 2,500 words. Pays 75¢ to

$1/word on acceptance. Query in advance with samples of published work. Guidelines available.

Today's Parent Pregnancy & Birth

1 Mount Pleasant Road, 8th Floor, Toronto, ON M4Y 2Y5
Phone: (416) 764-2829
Contact: Holly Bennett, editor
Circulation: 200,000
Published 3 times a year

Provides support, information, advice, and encouragement to expectant and new parents. Articles are directed toward promoting healthy pregnancy and an active role in the birth and early care of the child. Encourages informed consumer choice, breastfeeding, and gentle parenting. Pays 75¢ to $1/word on acceptance for articles from 500 and 2,500 words (less for personal stories). Rates depend on the complexity and research demands of the article. "Most editorial is provided by our regular freelancers. We are especially interested in writers with backgrounds in childbirth issues." Guidelines available.

Today's Parent Toronto

1 Mount Pleasant Road, Toronto, ON M4Y 2Y5
Phone: (416) 764-1926 Fax: (416) 764-2894
E-mail: tiziana.roberts@tpg.rogers.com
Web site: www.torontofamilies.ca
Contact: Tiziana Roberts, publisher
Circulation: 70,000
Published monthly

Readers are busy, Greater Toronto–area parents of children, newborn to 14 years old. Content must be local. Pay ranges from $150 to $400 for articles of 500 to 1,200 words. Paid on acceptance.

Urban Male Magazine (UMM)

131 Bank Street, Suite 300, Ottawa, ON K1P 5N7
Phone: (613) 723-6216 Fax: (613) 723-1702
E-mail: editor@umm.ca
Web site: www.umm.ca
Contact: Nash Gangji, director of operations
Circulation: 95,000
Published quarterly

UMM covers any issues of interest to Canadian men, including sports, health, travel, adventure, cars, fashion, fitness, DIY, beautiful women, humour, social and political issues, and especially any ideas focusing on Canadian people, issues, or icons. Features are generally 2,000 to 3,000 words; interviews usually about 1,300 words. Accepts smaller miscellaneous pieces for the front of the magazine. Pays 20¢/word, payable 45 days after publication. "Originality in focus and style are key to catching our attention, as is a query that has had thought and care put into it. *UMM* welcomes submissions from freelancers who specialize in the topic of the article they are submitting."

Send queries to the director of operations by mail or preferably e-mail, with an outline of the proposed article and a sample paragraph. Include any relevant credentials and writing samples.

Weddings & Honeymoons

65 Helena Avenue, Toronto, ON M6G 2H3
Phone: (416) 653-4986   Fax: (416) 653-2291
E-mail: barwed@interlog.com
Web site: www.weddingshoneymoons.com
Contact: Joyce Barslow, editor-in-chief
Circulation: 30,000
Published annually in print; quarterly online

Canada's how-to magazine for brides to be, serving the mainstream wedding marketplace. Articles and columns include the elements required for planning and budgeting a wedding: fashion and accessories, beauty, ceremonies, receptions, menus and cakes, flowers, photography, and gifts, as well as newlywed information regarding homes, finance, and other real life matters. Main sections include "Romance Travel" – featuring romantic places for proposals, destination weddings and honeymoons – and "Wines of the World" – featuring wines and spirits for weddings, and winery weddings. Stories range from between 50 to 500 words. Articles and photos are considered for credits. Pays a negotiated rate of $50 to $150. A free glossy magazine, *Weddings & Honeymoons* is distributed to major retail outlets and can be downloaded from www.weddingshoneymoons.com. Include an SASE for return of material.

Wellness Options
P.O. Box 160, Stn. D, Toronto, ON M1R 5B5
Phone: (416) 502-9600 Fax: (416) 502-0699
E-mail: info@wellnessoptions.ca
Web site: www.wellnessoptions.ca
Contact: Lillian Chan, editor
Circulation: 30,000
Published bimonthly
    A consumer health magazine that provides full journal references and information sources. It explains health conditions from multiple disciplines and perspectives, reports the latest research, reviews physical and nutritional wellness trends, and covers mental, emotional, and fitness topics. Fees vary and are paid on publication. "We need full references as in scientific journals."

Westcoast Families
13988 Maycrest Way, Suite 140, 2nd Floor, Richmond, BC V6V 3C3
Phone: (604) 249-2866 Fax: (604) 247-1331
E-mail: info@westcoastfamilies.com
Web site: www.westcoastfamilies.com
Contact: Michelle Froese, managing editor
Circulation: 50,000
Published monthly
    A newspaper geared to parents of children and teens. An information source and guide to fun for families in the Vancouver area. Articles 650 to 850 words. Rates vary according to project and are paid on publication. "Please do not submit humorous essays. All submissions must be relevant to Canadians; local content preferred. No phone calls, please." Guidelines available.

Western Living
2608 Granville Street, Suite 560, Vancouver, BC V6H 3V3
Phone: (604) 877-7732 Fax: (604) 877-4838
E-mail: wlmail@westernlivingmagazine.com
Web site: www.westernlivingmagazine.com
Contact: Jim Sutherland, editor
Circulation: 185,000
Published 10 times a year

A general interest and lifestyle magazine with a special emphasis on the home. The largest regional magazine in Canada. Regular features cover personalities and trends, regional and international travel, food and recipes, and homes and design, all with a Western Canadian focus. Article lengths and pay rates vary; contact by phone or e-mail with queries or to pitch a story.

The Western Producer

P.O. Box 2500, 2310 Millar Avenue, Saskatoon, SK S7K 2C4
Phone: (306) 665-3544 Fax: (306) 934-2401
E-mail: newsroom@producer.com
Web site: www.producer.com
Contact: Terry Fries, news editor
Circulation: 70,000
Published weekly

Publishes news and feature stories of interest to Western Canadian farmers, ranchers, and rural dwellers. Articles 500 to 800 words. Fees vary depending on project and are paid on publication. Guidelines available.

What's Up Kids? Family Magazine

496 Metler Road, Ridgeville, ON L0S 1M0
Phone: (905) 892-7970 Fax: (905) 892-6673
E-mail: paul@whatsupkids.com
Web site: www.whatsupkids.com
Contact: Paul Baswick, editor-in-chief
Circulation: 200,000
Published bimonthly

Focuses on issues relating to families, including discipline, diet, and health. No fiction or poetry. Articles 800 to 1,800 words. Payment made on publication; fees vary depending on length. Query first; length of article will be assigned by editor. Guidelines available.

WHGroom

65 Helena Avenue, Toronto, ON M6G 2H3
Phone: (416) 653-4986 Fax: (416) 653-2291
E-mail: barwed@interlog.com
Web site: www.weddingshoneymoons.com
Contact: Joyce Barslow, editor-in-chief

Circulation: 30,000
Published annually in print; quarterly online
  Canada's only magazine for grooms to be. Articles and columns include the elements required for planning and budgeting a wedding: engagement rings, fashion and accessories, grooming, ceremonies, receptions, food and cakes, limousines, flowers, photography, and gifts, as well as newlywed information regarding homes, finance, and other real life matters. Main sections include "Romance Travel" – featuring romantic places for proposals, destination weddings and honeymoons – and "Wines of the World" – featuring wines and spirits for weddings, and winery weddings. Stories range from between 50 to 500 words. Articles and photos are considered for credits. Pays a negotiated rate of $50 to $150. A free glossy magazine, *WHGroom* is distributed to major retail outlets and can be downloaded from www.weddingshoneymoons.com. Include an SASE for return of material.

Xtra!
491 Church Street, Suite 200, Toronto, ON M4Y 2C6
Phone: (416) 925-6665 Fax: (416) 925 6503
E-mail: info@xtra.ca
Web site: www.xtra.ca
Contact: Paul Gallant, managing editor
Circulation: 45,000
Published biweekly
  Toronto's gay and lesbian periodical with news, analysis, op-ed pieces, and stories on arts and entertainment. Articles 400 to 800 words. Pays about 10¢/word on publication. "No submissions on spec. Pre-assigned stories only. Queries and story pitches welcome." Guidelines available.

News, Opinions, & Issues

Adbusters Magazine
1243 West 7th Avenue, Vancouver, BC V6H 1B7
Phone: (604) 736-9401 Fax: (604) 737-6021
E-mail: editor@adbusters.org
Web site: www.adbusters.org

Contact: Kalle Lasn, editor
Circulation: 120,000
Published bimonthly

Established 1989. A combative, uncompromising commentator on the politics of media control and environmental strategy. Pay rates vary for 100 to 1,500 words. Contact editor first if planning a lengthy submission. Guidelines available on web site.

The Advocate

1600 Cathedral Place, 925 West Georgia Street, Vancouver, BC
V6C 3L2
Phone: (604) 685-3456　Fax: (604) 669-1620
E-mail: tswoods@lawsonlundell.com
Web site: www.vancouverbar.ca/advocate
Contact: Thomas S. Woods, editor
Circulation: 11,000
Published bimonthly

Published by the Vancouver Bar Association, *The Advocate* carries substantive, procedural, and other articles on legal subjects of interest to the legal profession and the judiciary, mainly in B.C. Articles are 2,000 to 10,000 words. Contributors are rarely paid.

Alberta Sweetgrass

13245 – 146th Street, Edmonton, AB T5L 4S8
Phone: (780) 455-2700 or 1-800-661-5469　Fax: (780) 455-7639
E-mail: sweetgrass@ammsa.com
Web site: www.ammsa.com
Contact: Debora Steel, editor
Circulation: 7,500
Published monthly

A community newspaper highlighting Aboriginal issues, programs, people, arts, culture, and advances in Alberta. Pays $3.00 to $3.60/column inch on publication for stories of 500 to 800 words (rate depends on sources, editing, photos, etc.). Query first. Not interested in poetry or fiction. Guidelines available on web site.

Anglican Journal

80 Hayden Street, Toronto, ON M4Y 3G2
Phone: (416) 924-9192, ext. 307　Fax: (416) 921-4452

E-mail: editor@national.anglican.ca
Web site: www.anglicanjournal.com
Contact: Leanne Larmondin, editor
Circulation: 210,000
Published 10 times a year
    Independently edited national publication of the Anglican
Church of Canada, established in 1875. Contains news and fea-
tures from across Canada and abroad. Subjects include news of all
denominations and faiths, and articles on a range of social and
ethical issues. Stories should be of interest to a national audience.
Length 600 to maximum of 1,200 words. Pays a base rate of
23¢/published word on publication. Initial inquiry recommended.
"Basic style is as for a daily newspaper. Use *CP Style Book* as a
guide." Guidelines available.

Behind the Headlines
205 Richmond Street W., Suite 302, Toronto, ON M5V 1V3
Phone: (416) 977-9000 Fax: (416) 977-7521
E-mail: bjohnstone@ciia.org
Web sites: www.ciia.org and
    www.canadianinternationalcouncil.org
Contact: Robert Johnstone, editor
Circulation: 1,500
Published bimonthly
    For members of the Canadian Institute of International Affairs,
libraries, and other institutions. Articles contribute to a deeper
understanding of international affairs and international gover-
nance. Length of articles from 6,000 to 7,000 words. Pays $500 per
article on acceptance.

Beyond Magazine
3408 3rd Street N.W., Calgary, AB T2K 0Z5
E-mail: readit@beyondmag.com
Web site: www.beyondmag.com
Contact: Karen, editor
Circulation: 5,000
Published 3 times a year
    Beyond delves into the questions and ideas that wake us up to
where we come from, who we are, and where we are going. It helps

readers reflect on their lives while inspiring them to be instruments of justice, compassion, beauty, and meaning. Collaborates with writers, poets, thinkers, activists, art lovers, philosophers, and readers to produce a well designed, thought provoking magazine. Articles 500 to 2,000 words. Fees vary depending on project and are paid on publication. Guidelines available on web site.

bout de papier

47 Clarence Street, Suite 412, Ottawa, ON K1N 9K1
Phone: (613) 241-1391 Fax: (613) 241-5911
E-mail: boutdepapier@pafso.com
Web site: www.pafso.com
Contact: Debra Hulley, managing editor
Circulation: 2,500
Published quarterly

Examines all aspects of Canadian foreign policy and life in the Foreign Service. Provides a unique first-hand insight into the conduct and evolution of Canadian diplomacy. Articles are published in the language of submission. Features articles, interviews, book reviews, and commentaries from 1,000 to 2,800 words. Contributors are not paid. Welcomes submission inquiries from qualified writers.

Briarpatch

2138 McIntyre Street, Regina, SK S4P 2R7
Phone: (306) 525-2949
E-mail: editor@briarpatchmagazine.com
Web site: www.briarpatchmagazine.com
Contact: Dave Oswald Mitchell, editor
Circulation: 1,500
Published 10 times a year

"*Briarpatch* is helping to build a strong activist network by covering issues and stories that expose the evils of this world and highlighting the work of people trying to make the world a better place. We provide a publishing opportunity for writers in the social justice movement who are ignored by the mainstream media." Carries articles of 600 to 1,200 words, also short reviews of 300 words. Cannot pay, but submission inquiries are welcome.

Canadian Dimension
91 Albert Street, Suite 2E, Winnipeg, MB R3B 1G5
Phone: (204) 957-1519 Fax: (204) 943-4617
E-mail: gbergen@canadiandimension.com
Web site: www.canadiandimension.com
Contact: Glenn Bergen, associate publisher
Circulation: 3,000
Published bimonthly
   Established 1963. Publishes fact and analysis that bring Canada and the world into focus. Carries alternative information on issues concerning women, the labour movement, peace politics, Aboriginal peoples, the environment, economics, and popular culture. "*CD* is a magazine for people who want to change the world. We debate issues, share ideas, recount our victories, and evaluate our strategies for social change." Articles 600 to 2,000 words. Fees are negotiated and paid on publication. Send written query of no more than 1 page. Guidelines available on web site.

Canadian Lawyer
240 Edward Street, Aurora, ON L4G 3S9
Phone: (905) 841-6480 Fax: (905) 727-0017
E-mail: cleditor@clbmedia.ca
Web site: www.canadianlawyermag.com
Contact: Kirsten McMahon, managing editor
Circulation: 27,500
Published 11 times a year
   Sent to practising lawyers, judges, and corporate counsel, this is the magazine legal professionals from coast to coast turn to for news, trends, and issues that shape the profession. Fees vary depending on project and are paid on acceptance. Guidelines available.

Canadian Lawyer INHOUSE
240 Edward Street, Aurora, ON L4G 3S9
Phone: (905) 841-6480 Fax: (905) 727-0017
E-mail: cleditor@clbmedia.ca
Web site: www.canadianlawyermag.com
Contact: Kirsten McMahon, managing editor
Circulation: 10,000
Published 5 times a year

Canadian Lawyer INHOUSE is distributed as a supplement to *Canadian Lawyer* and is sent to corporate counsel, presidents, CFOs, and CEOs of large organizations across Canada. Fees vary depending on project and are paid on acceptance. Guidelines available.

Catholic Insight

P.O. Box 625, Adelaide Stn., Toronto, ON M5C 2J8
Phone: (416) 204-9601 Fax: (416) 204-1027
E-mail: reach@catholicinsight.com
Web site: www.catholicinsight.com
Contact: Alphonse de Valk, editor
Circulation: 3,570
Published 11 times a year

A journal of news and opinion on matters of religion, politics, society, and culture pertinent to Canada and the Catholic Church. "Most articles are pre-arranged for subject matter. Occasionally we accept an unsolicited freelance article." Length 740 to 1,400 words. Pays on publication from $150 to $350 for features, $135 for columns, and $75 for book reviews. Payment for interviews is negotiated.

Catholic New Times

80 Sackville Street, Toronto, ON M5A 3E5
Phone: (416) 361-0761 Fax: (416) 361-0796
E-mail: editor@catholicnewtimes.org
Web site: www.catholicpublisher/editor
Circulation: 4,100
Published biweekly

A magazine focused on faith and social justice from an ecumenical standpoint. Articles 700 to 2,000 words. Pays $5/100 words on publication. Guidelines available.

The Columbia Journal

P.O. Box 2633, MPO, Vancouver, BC V6B 3W8
Phone: (604) 266-6552 Fax: (604) 267-3342
E-mail: editor@columbiajournal.ca
Web site: www.columbiajournal.ca
Contact: Marco Procaccini, editor

Circulation: 16,000
Published bimonthly
   The Columbia Journal is a positive, progressive alternative to the conservative corporate press in B.C. Dedicated to inform, entertain, and advocate for the people of B.C. Encourages written contributions covering public issues. Seeks comment from social activist groups, labour unions, and environmental and religious organizations. Stories should be supportive of progressive actions and policies. Covers issues related to the environment, the economy, labour, human rights, social issues, human interest, the government, and B.C. politics.

Concordia University Magazine
1455 de Maisonneuve Boulevard W., FB 520, Montreal, QC
   H3G 1M8
Phone: (514) 848-2424, ext. 3826   Fax: (514) 848-2826
E-mail: howard.bokser@concordia.ca
Web site: http://magazine.concordia.ca
Contact: Howard Bokser, editor
Circulation: 80,000
Published quarterly
   The alumni magazine of Concordia University. It covers stories about Concordia alumni, the university, and education in Canada. Length 1,000 to 2,000 words. Pays $500 per feature on acceptance.

Education Canada
317 Adelaide Street W., Suite 300, Toronto, ON M5V 1P9
Phone: (416) 591-6300   Fax: (416) 591-5345
E-mail: glatour@cea-ace.ca
Web site: www.cea-ace.ca
Contact: Gilles Latour, business/circulation manager
Circulation: 4,000
Published quarterly
   Canada's premier award-winning publication for informed dialogue on education. Each issue provides readers with articles of educational significance that are readable, credible, and thought-provoking. The content is varied, with features and regular articles, columns, commentary, research reviews, case studies, and letters.

Cannot pay but welcomes inquiries. "Visit our web site for more details." Guidelines available.

Education Forum

c/o OSSTF, 60 Mobile Drive, Toronto, ON M4A 2P3
Phone: (416) 751-8300 Fax: (416) 751-3875
E-mail: clayton@osstf.on.ca
Web site: www.osstf.on.ca
Contact: M. Clayton, assistant editor
Circulation: 51,000
Published 3 times a year
  A publication dealing with issues of education. Features range from 1,800 to 2,000 words. Cannot pay but welcomes submission inquiries.

Education Today

439 University Avenue, 18th Floor, Toronto, ON M5G 1Y8
Phone: (416) 340-2540 Fax: (416) 340-7571
E-mail: et@opsba.org
Web site: www.opsba.org
Contact: Catherine Watson, editor
Circulation: 3,500
Published 3 times a year
  Delivers informed commentary on Ontario's public education system. Areas covered include governance, law, and the voice of students. Articles 500 to 1,500 words. Rates vary with project and are paid on acceptance. "Interested writers should submit a query to the editor. Editorial decisions are made by the editorial board." Guidelines available.

Faith Today

M.I.P. Box 3745, Markham, ON L3R 0Y4
Phone: (905) 479-5885 Fax: (905) 479-4742
E-mail: ft@efc-canada.com
Web site: www.faithtoday.ca
Contact: Gail Reid, managing editor
Circulation: 18,000
Published bimonthly

A general-interest magazine of feature articles for Canadian evangelicals, including how-to features and profiles of Canadian individuals and ministries. Query first; does not accept unsolicited manuscripts. Features 800 to 1,750 words. Pays on acceptance 25¢/word for features, 15¢/word for essays. Guidelines available on web site.

Geez Magazine
264 Home Street, Winnipeg, MB R3G 1X3
Phone: (204) 772-9610
E-mail: editor@geezmagazine.org
Web site: www.geezmagazine.org
Contact: Will Braun, editor
Circulation: 4,000
Published quarterly
Geez offers readers a lively dose of "holy mischief in an age of fast faith." Aimed at those on the fringes of faith, this ad-free magazine explores the religious and spiritual dimension of the big issues of our day. Articles 400 to 2,000 words. Pays $50 to $200 on publication. Guidelines available

Humanist Perspectives
P.O. Box 943, Duncan, BC V9L 3Y2
Phone: (250) 748-0962 Fax: (250) 746-6672
E-mail: editor@humanistperspectives.org
Web site: www.humanistperspectives.org
Contact: Gary Bauslaugh, editor
Circulation: 2,000
Published quarterly
Formerly *Humanist in Canada*. Explores contemporary topics from a humanistic viewpoint, reflecting the principle that human problems can be solved rationally without relying on belief in the supernatural. For non-believers with an interest in social issues. Cannot pay (provides author copies) but welcomes submission inquiries. "A good opportunity for writers with alternative, divergent, or thought-provoking views." Guidelines available on web site.

Law Times

240 Edward Street, Aurora, ON L4G 3S9
Phone: (905) 841-6481 Fax: (905) 727-0017
E-mail: lawtimes@clbmedia.ca
Web site: www.lawtimesnews.com
Contact: Gail J. Cohen, editor
Circulation: 12,000
Published weekly

Serves the Ontario legal market. Readership includes lawyers, judges, and law clerks. "If you have story ideas that would be relevant to *Law Times* readers, please feel free to send pitches to us by e-mail." Articles 800 to 1,200 words. Pays $175 to $275/article on publication. "We are always interested in pitches for news and features about or of interest to the legal community in Ontario."

Legion Magazine

86 Aird Place, Kanata, ON K2L 0A1
Phone: (613) 591-0116 Fax: (613) 591-0146
E-mail: magazine@legion.ca
Web site: www.legionmagazine.com
Contact: Dan Black, editor
Circulation: 350,000
Published bimonthly

A magazine for Canada's war veterans, RCMP members, forces personnel and their families, seniors, and the wider public. Carries news, views, and serious articles exploring Canada's military history, defence, veterans' affairs, health, and pensions. Offers humour and opinion columns, and also buys memoirs and nostalgia. Articles 600 to 2,500 words. Pays about $1,100 for 2,500 words (fee determined after final edit). "Please familiarize yourself with magazine and send an SASE with submission. Allow up to 6 months for response."

Life Learning

264 Queens Quay W., Suite 508, Toronto, ON M5J 1B5
Phone: (416) 260-0303
E-mail: editor@lifelearningmagazine.com
Web site: www.lifelearningmagazine.com
Contact: Wendy Priesnitz, editor

Circulation: 35,000
Published bimonthly
Focuses on how-to and inspirational stories about self-directed learning, unschooling, and natural parenting for a Canadian and U.S. audience. Articles 1,000 to 1,500 words. Cannot pay but welcomes submissions. Guidelines available on web site.

Living Light News
5306 – 89th Street, Suite 200, Edmonton, AB T6E 5P9
Phone: 1-800-932-0555 Fax: (780) 468-6872
E-mail: shine@livinglightnews.org
Web site: www.livinglightnews.org
Contact: Jeff Caporale, editor
Published 7 times a year
A tabloid-sized evangelical newspaper with positive, contemporary, family-oriented appeal for Christians and spiritual seekers. Send query first. Features 1,200 to 1,500 words; news stories that glorify God 250 to 1,200 words; also profiles and stories about ministries. Pays 10¢/word on publication for first rights, 5¢/word for reprint rights. Also pays for photos. "We are looking for writers who are evangelical Christians desiring to serve God through their writing. Our preference is on positive news that glorifies God or feature articles about well-known Christian celebrities and family-oriented subject matter." Guidelines available.

Maclean's
1 Mount Pleasant Road, 11th Floor, Toronto, ON M4Y 2Y5
Phone: (416) 764-1339 Fax: (416) 764-1332
E-mail: letters@macleans.ca
Web site: www.macleans.ca
Contact: Kenneth Whyte, editor-in-chief
Circulation: 3,100,000
Published weekly
Canada's most widely read news magazine. Examines news events, trends, and issues from a Canadian perspective. Has correspondents in 5 Canadian cities and a network of writers around the world. Staff writers and freelancers contribute to weekly sections on politics, business, entertainment, sports, leisure, education, health,

science, personal finance, justice, and technology. Pays a variable but competitive fee on publication.

Monday Magazine
818 Broughton Street, Victoria, BC V8W 1E4
Phone: (250) 382-6188   Fax: (250) 381-2662
E-mail: editorial@mondaymag.com
Web site: www.mondaymag.com
Contact: Alisa Gordaneer, editor
Circulation: 40,000
Published weekly
   An opinionated news and arts magazine for Victoria's progressive citizens. Cover stories 500 to 3,000 words; feature articles 850 to 1,500 words; also CD and book reviews. Fees are about 10¢/word and are paid on publication. Seeks intelligent, inquisitive, and investigative stories with a strong Victoria focus. "Query first for most stories. We also publish personal essays (850 to 1,000 words) on a variety of topics. Send entire essay for consideration. We respond within a month, but only to submissions we're planning to publish. We prefer e-mailed submissions and queries." Guidelines available on web site.

National
865 Carling Avenue, Suite 500, Ottawa, ON K1S 5S8
Phone: (613) 237-2925   Fax: (613) 237-0185
E-mail: national@cba.org
Web site: www.cba.org/national
Contact: Jordan Furlong, editor-in-chief
Published 8 times a year
   The member magazine of the Canadian Bar Association, *National* tracks trends and developments in the practice of law in Canada. Pays 75¢/word on acceptance for articles from 500 to 2,000 words.

New Socialist
P.O. Box 167, 253 College Street, Toronto, ON M5T 1R5
Phone: (416) 955-1581
E-mail: magazine@newsocialist.org
Web site: www.newsocialist.org

Contact: editorial committee
Published 5 times a year
   A new left publication that aims to make changes by helping to build unions and support social movements. Publishes articles and interviews about developments in Canada and elsewhere, strategies for social change, and debates on the left by activists and writers. Welcomes letters, articles, and illustrations. Unable to pay contributors, but offers free copies of the magazine.

New Internationalist
401 Richmond Street W., Suite 393, Toronto, ON M5V 3A8
Phone: (416) 588-6478 Fax: (416) 588-4285
Web site: www.newint.org
Contact: Wayne Ellwood, co-editor
Published 11 times a year
   An international periodical focusing on global issues such as health, environment, trade, aid, and poverty from a social justice perspective. Subscribers are aware, socially conscious, and liberal. Articles 250 to 1,500 words. Pays 35¢/word on publication.

Northword Magazine
P.O. Box 817, 1188 Main Street, Suite 4, Smithers, BC V0J 2N0
Phone: (250) 847-4600 or 1-866-632-7688 Fax: (250) 847-4668
Web site: http://northword.ca
Contact: Joanne Campbell, publisher
Circulation: 10,000
Published quarterly
   Northword "aims to put in print the wide range of voices, views, and opinions of people who have a connection with the top half of B.C." First send a story query, not a finished article. Rates vary and are paid within 30 days of receiving invoice.

Off-Centre Magazine
P.O. Box 1384, Vernon, BC V1T 6N7
Phone: (250) 558-3979 Fax: (250) 558-3912
E-mail: editor@off-centre.ca
Web site: www.off-centre.ca
Contact: Kelly Winston, editor

Circulation: 20,000
Published monthly
An independent arts, culture, and political magazine. Edgy, fun, witty, and hip. Articles 400 to 700 words. Pays 10¢/word on publication. "Looking for good political satire, provincial B.C. or national."

Our Times
P.O. Box 182, New Glasgow, NS B2H 5E2
Phone: (902) 755-6840 Fax: (902) 755-1292
E-mail: editor@ourtimes.ca
Web site: www.ourtimes.ca
Contact: Lorraine Endicott, managing editor
Circulation: 3,000
Published bimonthly
Published by a not-for-profit organization to promote workers' rights, unionization, and social justice. Many articles are contributed by union activists. Query first. Features are 1,500 to 3,000 words; opinions 850 words; notes and reviews 600 to 1,000 words. Pays between $100 and $300, usually on publication; $25 for small items. Guidelines available on web site.

Outlook Magazine
6184 Ash Street, Vancouver, BC V5Z 3G9
Phone: (604) 324-5101
E-mail: cjoutlook@telus.net
Web site: www.vcn.bc.ca/outlook
Contact: Carl Rosenberg, editor
Published bimonthly
An independent, secular Jewish publication with a socialist-humanist perspective. Contact the editor before completing an article. Articles 1,000 to 1,500 words.

Peace Magazine
P.O. Box 248, Stn. P, Toronto, ON M5S 2S7
Phone: (416) 588-8748
E-mail: mspencer@web.net
Web site: www.peacemagazine.org

Contact: Metta Spencer, editor-in-chief
Published quarterly
Welcomes submissions relating to peace, disarmament, weapons of mass destruction, conflict resolution, and political and military affairs in hot spots around the world. Articles 400 to 3,000 words. Cannot pay.

Policy Options
1470 Peel Street, Suite 200, Montreal, QC H3A 1T1
Phone: (514) 985-2461 Fax: (514) 985-2559
E-mail: imacdonald@irpp.org
Web site: www.irpp.org/po
Contact: L. Ian MacDonald, editor
Circulation: 3,000
Published 10 times a year
A bilingual magazine published by the Institute for Research on Public Policy, a national, independent, not-for-profit think tank. Carries analyses of public policy so as to encourage wide debate on major policy issues. Articles 1,500 to 4,000 words. Contributors are unpaid, but submission inquiries by qualified writers are welcome.

Queen's Alumni Review
Office of Marketing and Communications, Stewart-Pollock Wing, Fleming Hall, Room 307, Queen's University, Kingston, ON K7L 3N6
Phone: (613) 533-6000, ext. 74125 Fax: (613) 533-6828
E-mail: review@post.queensu.ca
Web site: www.alumnireview.queensu.ca
Contact: Ken Cuthbertson, editor
Circulation: 105,000
Published quarterly
Publishes news about and of interest to Queen's alumni, faculty, and friends of the university. Articles 250 to 2,500 words. Rates vary depending on project and are paid on acceptance. "We buy a limited amount of freelance material, but we are always in the market for well-written, timely articles. Would-be freelancers should study past issues before querying us." Guidelines available.

Ryerson University Alumni
350 Victoria Street, Toronto, ON M5B 2K3
Phone: (416) 979-5000, ext. 7000 Fax: (416) 979-5166
E-mail: ryemag@ryerson.ca
Web site: www.ryerson.ca/alumni/magazine
Contact: Dana Yates, editor
Circulation: 80,000
Published twice a year
  Published for alumni and friends of Ryerson by the Office of University Advancement. Articles 600 to 1,200 words. Pays 50¢/word on acceptance.

Saskatchewan Sage
13245 – 146 Street, Edmonton, AB T5L 4S8
Phone: (780) 455-2700 Fax: (780) 455-7639
E-mail: sage@ammsa.com
Web site: www.ammsa.com
Contact: Cheryl Petten, editor
Circulation: 1,500
Published monthly
  A community newspaper featuring news, arts and entertainment, reviews, and feature articles about and by Aboriginal people of Saskatchewan. No poetry or fiction. Pitch idea first. Most stories 500 to 800 words. Pays $3.00 to $3.60/column inch on publication. "Stories must be of provincial interest. Always query first, preferably by phone or e-mail. Guidelines available on Internet site."

Teach Magazine
258 Wallace Avenue, Suite 206, Toronto, ON M6P 3M9
Phone: (416) 537-2103 Fax: (416) 537-3491
E-mail: info@teachmag.com
Web site: www.teachmag.com
Contact: Wili Liberman, publisher
Circulation: 22,000
Published 5 times a year
  Explores pragmatic issues and ideas for educators of grades K through 12. Articles 1,200 to 1,500 words. Fees vary and are paid

on publication. "Please read the publication first, then send a query letter. E-mail is fine." Guidelines available.

This Magazine

401 Richmond Street W., Suite 396, Toronto, ON M5V 3A8
Phone: (416) 979-8400 Fax: (416) 979-1143
E-mail: queries@thismagazine.ca
Web site: www.thismagazine.ca
Contact: Jessica Johnston, editor
Circulation: 5,000
Published bimonthly

Canada's leading alternative magazine carrying investigative features and researched commentary on culture, politics, and the arts. Features of 2,000 to 4,000 words earn $200 to $400; pay for shorter items from 500 to 1,500 words is $50 to $150. Paid on publication. "We prefer clearly focused, thoroughly researched, and sharply written investigative articles on topics the mainstream media ignore. No unsolicited poetry, fiction, or drama." Send a query letter. Guidelines available on web site.

The United Church Observer

478 Huron Street, Toronto, ON M5R 2R3
Phone: (416) 960-8500 Fax: (416) 960-8477
E-mail: general@ucobserver.org
Web site: www.ucobserver.org
Contact: David Wilson, editor
Circulation: 65,000
Published 11 times a year

The national magazine of the United Church of Canada. Provides news of the church, the nation, and the world while maintaining an independent editorial policy. Prints serious articles on issues such as human rights, social justice, and Christian faith in action, and stories of personal courage – all with a Christian perspective. Also covers the religious dimensions of art, literature, and theatre. Articles 500 to 2,500 words. Fees are negotiated and paid on publication. Personal stories are paid at lower rates. "Should use news-feature treatment. Query first by fax or e-mail. Mostly staff written, but some freelance opportunities (also art and photography)." Guidelines available.

University Affairs
600 – 350 Albert Street, Ottawa, ON K1R 1B1
Phone: (613) 563-1236, ext. 228   Fax: (613) 563-9745
E-mail: pberkowi@aucc.ca
Web site: www.universityaffairs.ca
Contact: Peggy Berkowitz, editor
Circulation: 25,000
Published 10 times a year
Canada's main source of information on university education, published by the Association of Universities and Colleges of Canada. Publishes articles in both English and French. Covers major issues and trends in higher education and other articles of interest to professors and administrators. Stories from 300 to 2,000 words. Fees are a minimum of 50¢/word, paid on acceptance, but are higher for complicated features. "Please read the magazine and guidelines before submitting a story idea."

University of Toronto Magazine
21 King's College Circle, Toronto, ON M5S 3J3
Phone: (416) 946-7575   Fax: (416) 978-3958
E-mail: uoft.magazine@utoronto.ca
Web site: www.magazine.utoronto.ca
Contact: Scott Anderson, editor/manager
Circulation: 270,000
Published quarterly
Promotes the University of Toronto to its alumni, friends of the university, and the U. of T. community by publishing articles about alumni and campus news. U. of T. angle must be strong. Pays $1/word on acceptance for articles of 750 to 4,000 words.

The Walrus Magazine
19 Duncan Street, Suite 101, Toronto, ON M5H 3H1
Phone: (416) 971-5004   Fax: (416) 971-8768
E-mail: editorial@walrusmagazine.com
Web site: www.walrusmagazine.com
Contact: Ken Alexander, editor
Circulation: 42,000
Published 10 times a year

A general interest magazine with an international thrust. Features start at 3,000 words; field notes 800 to 1,000 words; columns 1,500 to 2,500 words. Pay rates vary depending on project and are paid on publication. "Please note that we do not accept unsolicited fiction or poetry submissions." Guidelines available.

Western Alumni Gazette

University of Western Ontario, Stevenson-Lawson Bldg., Room 335, London, ON N6A 5B8
Phone: (519) 661-2111, ext. 88467   Fax: (519) 661-3921
Web site: www.uwo.ca or http://communications.uwo.ca/alumni/
Contact: editor
Circulation: 145,000
Published 3 times a year
Written for Western alumni around the world. Pays on acceptance.

Windspeaker

13245 – 146 Street, Edmonton, AB T5L 4S8
Phone: (780) 455-2700   Fax: (780) 455-7639
E-mail: edwind@ammsa.com
Web site: www.ammsa.com
Contact: Debora Steel, editor
Circulation: 27,000
Published monthly
A national news magazine dealing with the issues and concerns of Aboriginal people in Canada from an Aboriginal perspective. Articles 800 to 1,000 words. Pays $3.00/published column inch on publication for single-source stories and $3.60/published column inch for multiple source stories. "Remember the perspective; remember the audience." Guidelines available.

Special Interest

Abilities

340 College Street, Suite 401, Toronto, ON M5T 3A9
Phone: (416) 923-1885   Fax: (416) 923-9829
E-mail: able@abilities.ca

Web site: www.abilities.ca
Contact: Jaclyn Law, managing editor
Circulation: 45,000
Published quarterly
Canada's lifestyle magazine for people with disabilities. Provides inspiration, information, and opportunities to people with disabilities. Articles/stories 500 to 2,000 words. A non-profit organization that pays honoraria to writers ranging from $50 to $300 on publication. "First-hand knowledge of disability is helpful. We are interested in new ideas, resources, or strategies that will empower our readers. Avoid telling them what they already know." Guidelines available online.

Burnt Toast
P.O. Box 56012, Ottawa, ON K1R 7Z0
Phone: (613) 236-0764
E-mail: burnt.toast@sympatico.ca
Web site: www.burnt-toast.ca
Contact: Cindy Deachman, editor
Circulation: 2,000
Published quarterly
A food magazine investigating eating from quirky and personal perspectives. "C'mon and eat, baby!" Articles are from 400 to 800 words. Pays on acceptance $50 per article. Submission guidelines available. "How about some fresh and fun stories about food? Let's throw this staid old world over, okay?"

Canadian Newcomer Magazine
222 Parkview Hill Crescent, Toronto, ON M4B 1R8
Phone: (416) 406-4719 Fax: (416) 757-7086
E-mail: cnmagstories@rogers.com
Web site: www.cnmag.ca
Contact: Dale Sproule, publisher
Circulation: 47,000
Published quarterly
Provides free information, advice, entertainment, and encouragement to new immigrants. The magazine is written in English, but the vocabulary is kept simple. Covers employment, housing, Canadian

lifestyles, health, finances, ethnic media, and education. Used as a teaching tool in many ESL schools in Toronto. Seeks articles from 250 to 1,000 words. It is best to query first, although unsolicited manuscripts will be considered. Payment is negotiated.

Canadian Teacher Magazine
1773 El Verano Drive, Gabriola, BC V0R 1X6
Phone: (250) 247-9093 Fax: (250) 247-9083
E-mail: dmumford@canadianteachermagazine.com
Web site: www.canadianteachermagazine.com
Contact: Diana Mumford, editor
Circulation: 14,000
Published 3 times a year

Canadian Teacher Magazine informs and entertains teachers both in and outside the classroom. Focuses on instructional strategies, classroom management, professional and personal development, and national and international education issues. For life after 3 P.M., *CTM* includes articles about holiday destinations, retirement options, and lifestyle choices. Articles from 800 to 1,000 words. Usually cannot pay but welcomes submission inquiries. Guidelines available.

Celtic Heritage Magazine
1657 Barrington Street, Suite 122, Halifax, NS B3J 2A1
Phone: (902) 425-4944 Fax: (902) 425-4910
E-mail: editorial@celticheritage.ns.ca
Web site: www.celticheritage.ns.ca
Contact: Alexa Thompson, editor
Circulation: 5,000
Published bimonthly

"We welcome articles that chronicle the unique history and achievements of the various Celtic groups that have settled in Canada, especially the accounts of those individuals not generally recorded in history books." Articles from 1,500 to 2,500 words. Pays on publication $75/article and $50/review (music, books, videos). "Please submit query by e-mail or in writing. Also please be on the lookout for new story ideas of national interest. Sample issue is available in PDF at the web site." Guidelines available.

Challenging Destiny

R.R. #6, St. Marys, ON N4X 1C8
E-mail: csp@golden.net
Web site: www.challengingdestiny.com
Contact: David M. Switzer, editor/publisher
Circulation: 200
Published quarterly
Established 1997; now an electronic magazine. Publishes all kinds of science fiction and fantasy short stories. Stories from 2,000 to 10,000 words. Pays 1¢/word on publication. "We're looking for interesting stories with believable characters. We like to see stories with religious or philosophical themes." Guidelines available.

C-ing Magazine

P.O. Box 61061, Calgary, AB T2N 3P9
Phone: (403) 282-0837
E-mail: editor@c-ingmagazine.ca
Web site: www.c-ingmagazine.ca
Contact: Colleen Hughes, managing editor
Published quarterly
Showcases quality photojournalism from a Canadian perspective. Main stories are from 700 to 800 words. Guidelines and deadlines on web site.

Digital Journal

P.O. Box 1046, 31 Adelaide Street E., Toronto, ON M5C 2K4
Phone: (416) 410-9675
E-mail: editor@digitaljournal.com
Web site: www.digitaljournal.com
Contact: Chris Hogg, editor-in-chief
Circulation: 20,000
Published quarterly
Established on the Internet in 1998 then evolved into a printed publication. The first newsstand magazine devoted to the ongoing convergence of information technology, lifestyle, and the arts. Readers are affluent, educated urban professionals, aged 18 to 49. Articles 600 to 850 words. Pays on publication per published word for articles; amount varies depending on project. Guidelines available on web site.

Divorce Magazine
2255B Queen Street E., Suite 1179, Toronto, ON M4E 1G3
Phone: (416) 368-8853 Fax: (416) 368-4978
E-mail: editors@divorcemag.com
Web site: www.divorcemagazine.com
Contact: Dan Couvrette, publisher
Circulation: 125,000
Published twice a year
   A self-help magazine for people experiencing separation, divorce, and remarriage. Articles 750 to 3,000 words. Fees are negotiated based on project and paid on publication. Guidelines available on web site.

Dog Sport
131 McElderry Road, Guelph, ON N1G 4J8
Phone: (519) 837-9257 or 1-866-364-7778 Fax: (519) 837-4976
E-mail: anne@dogsportmagazine.com
Web site: www.dogsportmagazine.com
Contact: Anne B. Douglas, editor
Published bimonthly
   The aim of *Dog Sport* is to provide dog-sport enthusiasts with practical ideas on how to improve the quality of their training and competing. Contact editor with article ideas. Does not accept unsolicited manuscripts.

Dogs in Canada
89 Skyway Avenue, Suite 200, Etobicoke, ON M9W 6R4
Phone: (416) 798-9778 Fax: (416) 798-9671
E-mail: info@dogsincanada.com
Web site: www.dogsincanada.com
Contact: Kelly Caldwell, editor-in-chief
Circulation: 45,000
Published monthly with an annual issue
   A reliable and authoritative source of information about dogs for a diverse readership from dog professionals to pet owners. Articles from 800 to 1,200 words. Fees vary and are paid on acceptance. Guidelines available.

The Driver
1315 Finch Avenue W., Suite 408, Toronto, ON M3J 2G6
Phone: (416) 398-2700 Fax: (416) 398-3272
E-mail: editor@thedrivermagazine.com
Web site: http://drivermagazine.ca
Circulation: 20,000
Published bimonthly
Serves drivers from 16 to 55, male and female. "Our articles are intended to inform, invigorate, and entertain." Features from 1,000 to 1,500 words; shorter pieces from 100 to 1,000 words. Pays between 10¢ to 15¢/word. Query first.

Exceptional Family
8160 Royden Road, Mount Royal, QC H4P 2T2
Phone: (514) 345-8330, local 182 Fax: (514) 345-1619
E-mail: submissions@exceptionalfamily.ca
Web site: www.exceptionalfamily.ca
Contact: Aviva Engel, editor
Published quarterly
Founded in 2005, *Exceptional Family* is a resource magazine for Canadian parents of exceptional children, with physical and cognitive disabilities, up to age 18. Maximum length for articles is 2½ pages, single-spaced. Query first. Cannot pay.

The Flag & Banner
1755 West 4th Avenue, Vancouver, BC V6J 1M2
Phone: (604) 736-8161 Fax: (604) 736-6439
E-mail: doreenb@flagshop.com or editor@flagshop.com
Web sites: www.flagshop.com and www.flagandbanner.html
Contact: Doreen Braverman, editor
Circulation: 14,000
Published twice a year
The Flag & Banner is a magazine for flag enthusiasts and the only magazine in the world dedicated to flags. Articles cover new national flags, flags in the news, and entertaining articles for hobbyists, vexillologists, and patriots. Distributed free of charge to schools and libraries. Pays $50 to $100 on acceptance for articles of 200 to 1,000 words. "Sometimes issues have a theme (for example, the Turin Olympic flag and Afghanistan flags)." Guidelines available.

Heritage
5 Blackburn Avenue, Ottawa, ON K1N 8A2
Phone: (613) 237-1066
E-mail: heritagecanada@heritagecanada.org
Web site: www.heritagecanada.org
Contact: Carolyn Quinn, director, communications
Circulation: 4,000
Published quarterly
    The magazine for members of the Heritage Canada Foundation, a charitable, non-profit organization. Also distributed to elected officials, both federal and provincial. Covers issues and activities in the field of preservation of heritage buildings. "Articles must address preservation issues or be about historic properties that have either been rehabilitated or are endangered." Articles 1,500 to 2,000 words. Payment is negotiable. Guidelines available.

Hub: Digital Living
775-B The Queensway, Toronto, ON M8Z 1N1
Phone: (416) 348-9666 Fax: (416) 348-9553
E-mail: erin@ppublishing.ca
Web site: www.hubcanada.com
Contacts: David Tanaka, editor; Erin Bell, managing editor
Circulation: 200,000
Published monthly
    A publication focusing on computers, consumer technology trends, and product reviews and news. Articles from 750 to 1,400 words. Pays $250 on publication. "We're looking primarily for freelancers who have expertise in specific areas of consumer tech; namely, Mac, PC, Linux, digital audio players, digital imaging, etc." Guidelines available.

Inside Motorcycles
P.O. Box 7100, Stn. B, Toronto, ON M5W 1X7
Phone: (416) 962-7223 Fax: (416) 962-7208
E-mail: editor@insidemotorcycles.com
Web site: www.insidemotorcycles.com
Contact: John Hopkins, editor
Circulation: 10,000
Published 10 times a year

Covers motorcycle racing and recreation with a Canadian perspective. Fees vary and are paid on publication.

The Leader Magazine
1345 Baseline Road, Suite 100, Ottawa, ON K2C 0A7
Phone: (613) 224-5131 Fax: (613) 224-3571
E-mail: smuehlherr@scouts.ca
Web site: www.scouts.ca/leader
Circulation: 35,000
Published 10 times a year

For Scouts Canada leaders. It encourages the development of youth and leaders through program-related articles on indoor and outdoor activities including camping, computers, and crafts for ages 5 to 26. Articles are 500 to 1,500 words. Does not pay, but welcomes submission inquiries. "Those who submit material should be active scouting members with program ideas to share." Guidelines available on web site.

Muse
280 Metcalfe Street, Suite 400, Ottawa, ON K2P 1R7
Phone: (613) 567-0099 Fax: (613) 233-5438
E-mail: ngratton@museums.ca
Web site: www.museums.ca
Contact: Naomi Gratton, editor
Circulation: 1,800
Published bimonthly

A source for features, news, and opinion pieces covering Canadian and international heritage institutions (museums, archives, libraries, zoos, etc.). Feature articles are 1,000 to 2,500 words; book reviews are 200 words maximum; musings are 750 words. Contributors receive copies of the issue in which their article appears. Guidelines on web site.

The Navigator Magazine
P.O. Box 29126, 197 Majors Path, St. John's, NL A1A 5B5
Phone: (709) 754-7977 Fax: (709) 754-6225
E-mail: admin@thenavigatormagazine.com
Web site: www.thenavigatormagazine.com

Contact: Jim Wellman, editor
Circulation: 10,000
Published monthly

The Navigator is the voice of the commercial fishing industry in Atlantic Canada. Articles from 1,000 to 1,500 words. Rates vary depending on project. Fees are negotiated in advance and paid on publication. Submission guidelines available.

Neo-opsis Science Fiction Magazine
4129 Carey Road, Victoria, BC V8Z 4G5
Phone: (250) 881-8893
E-mail: neoopsis@shaw.ca
Web site: www.neo-opsis.ca
Contact: Stephanie Johanson, art director/assistant editor
Circulation: 450
Published 2–3 times a year

Publishes stories written from the perspective of science fiction and fantasy, with informative articles on science and nature, humorous opinion pieces, book and movie reviews, and illustrations. "It is the intention of this publication to maintain a market for the works of science fiction writers and artists, and in that process to entertain and enlighten its readership." The target market is between the ages of 26 and 50. Preferred length of articles from 500 to 6,000 words. Pays on publication 1.5¢/word to a maximum of $125/story. Guidelines available on web site.

ON Nature
366 Adelaide Street W., Suite 201, Toronto, ON M5V 1R9
Phone: (416) 444-8419 Fax: (416) 444-9866
E-mail: victoriaf@ontarionature.org
Web site: www.ontarionature.org
Contact: Victoria Foote, editor
Circulation: 12,000
Published quarterly

ON Nature focuses on environmental issues, conservation, and "soft" travel within Ontario. Articles 300 to 3,000 words. Rates vary depending on project and are paid on acceptance. Guidelines available.

Promise

4180 Lougheed Highway, 4th Floor, Burnaby, BC V5C 6A7
Phone: (604) 299-7311 Fax: (604) 299-9188
E-mail: cwm@canadawide.com
Web site: www.canadawide.com
Contact: Sheila Hansen, editor
Circulation: 30,000
Published twice a year

Promise is the voice of St. Paul's Hospital Foundation. It's audience consists of donors and future donors to the hospital, plus hospital staff, patients, and visitors. Pays 50¢/word on publication for articles from 750 to 1,500 words. "The editorial content is directed by St. Paul's Hospital Foundation. Story assignments are given by the editor in consultation with foundation staff. Freelance queries are not accepted."

Provocative Magazine

P.O. Box 30104, 2141 Kipling Avenue, Etobicoke, ON M9W 4R8
Phone: (416) 207-1000
E-mail: info@dressresponsibly.com
Web site: www.dressresponsibly.com
Contact: Donna McPherson, production director/co-founder
Circulation: 20,000
Published quarterly

Caters to the Canadian and international fashion markets for men and women. Readership is ages 21 to 29 years of age whose lives revolve around fashion. "Our objective is to cater to the masses, setting up the right audience and the right promotional mix of high-impact advertising and content integration opportunities to produce successful campaigns. We are a part of a new era in technology, as we are a CD-ROM-enhanced magazine. Our editorials are focused on boutiques, designers, and trend forecasting." The length of articles and fees vary depending on the project. Paid on publication. "*Provocative Magazine* welcomes your comments, letters to the editor, or written submissions for consideration." Guidelines available.

Puppy&Dog Basics

65 The East Mall, Toronto, ON M8Z 5W3
Phone: (416) 537-2604 Fax: (416) 538-1794

E-mail: susanp@parentscanada.com
Web site: www.puppybasics.com
Contact: Susan Pennell-Sebekos, editor
Circulation: 126,000
Published twice a year

A publication that strives to provide its readers with all the information they need to make dog ownership the joyous experience it should be. Stories are written by veterinarians, animal behaviourists, or other experts in their field. Covers the latest in health, nutrition, training, socialization, safety, exercise, and care. Articles 1,000 to 2,000 words. Rates vary and are paid on acceptance.

Stitches: The Journal of Medical Humour
240 Edward Street, Aurora, ON L4G 3S9
Phone: (905) 727-0077 Fax: (905) 727-0017
E-mail: simon@stitchesmagazine.com
Contact: Simon Hally, editor
Circulation: 43,000
Published bimonthly

A magazine of humour and travel for practising physicians. Pays 35¢/word on publication for stories as short as 20 words and up to 3,000 words, but prefers 1,000 words or less. "Aspiring contributors are encouraged to request a free sample copy of the magazine. No story ideas, please; we need to see the story itself. We are eager to hear from genuinely funny writers."

UrbanBaby & Toddler Magazine
6060 Inverness Street, Vancouver, BC V5W 3P7
Phone: (604) 420-8760 Fax: (604) 420-8776
E-mail: info@urbanbaby.ca
Web site: www.urbanbaby.ca
Contact: Emma Lee, editor
Circulation: 40,000
Published quarterly

A publication targeted at expectant parents and parents with children under five years. Articles from 800 to 1,400 words. Fees vary and are paid on publication. Guidelines available.

Wedding Essentials

50 Nashoeme Road, Suite 104, Toronto, ON M1V 5J2
Phone: (416) 498-4996 Fax: (416) 498-5997
E-mail: mail@weddingessentials.ca
Web site: www.weddingessentials.ca
Contact: Brandon Jones, editorial director
Circulation: 15,000
Published twice a year

For newly engaged couples in Greater Toronto and surrounding areas who want a formal wedding and a great honeymoon. Pays 35¢/word on publication for articles from 900 to 1,500 words.

Wedding Essentials for Same-Sex Couples

50 Nashoeme Road, Suite 104, Toronto, ON M1V 5J2
Phone: (416) 498-4996 Fax: (416) 498-5997
E-mail: mail@weddingessentials.ca
Web site: www.weddingessentials.ca
Contact: Brandon Jones, editorial director
Circulation: 15,000
Published twice a year

A publication for gay men and lesbians who wish to get married in Ontario. Pays 35¢/word on publication for articles from 900 to 1,500 words.

Sports & Outdoors

Athletics

1185 Eglinton Avenue E., Suite 302, Toronto, ON M3C 3C6
Phone: (416) 426-7215 Fax: (416) 426-7358
E-mail: ontrack@eol.ca
Web site: www.otfa.ca
Contact: John Craig, editor
Circulation: 3,500
Published 8 times a year

Publishes in-depth stories and photographs on track and field and road running from grass roots to the Olympic level. Articles from 750 to 1,500 words. Rates vary; paid on publication.

Atlantic Boating News
162 Trider Crescent, Dartmouth, NS B3B 1R6
Phone: (902) 422-4990 Fax: (902) 422-4728
E-mail: editor@advocatemediainc.com
Web site: www.atlanticboatingnews.com
Contact: Joanne Elliott, editor
Circulation: 7,000
Published bimonthly
    Geared for the Atlantic Canadian marketplace, so stories focus on all aspects of recreational boating in that region. Pay varies and is paid on publication for 600 to 800 words. Photos should accompany submissions.

B.C. Outdoors Sport Fishing
1080 Howe Street, Suite 900, Vancouver, BC V6Z 2T1
Phone: (604) 606-4644 Fax: (604) 687-1925
E-mail: bcoutdoors@oppublishing.com
Web site: www.bcosportfishing.com
Contact: Ryan Pohl, editor
Circulation: 35,000
Published 7 times a year
    Publishes stories about fishing in B.C. and everything that goes along with it. "We are looking for original queries from knowledgeable writers who can write factual and entertaining articles on technique, resource management, and B.C.'s world famous fishing opportunities." Carries articles from 1,500 to 2,500 words. Pays $300 to $600/article on publication. "Rates are commensurate with experience and are determined by the editor." Guidelines available. "As with any publication, the best way to know what we are looking for is to read our magazine."

Below the Belt Boxing Magazine
1478 Pilgrims Way, Suite 1712, Oakville, ON L6M 3G7
Phone: (416) 336-1947
E-mail: okposio@hotmail.com
Web site: www.belowthebelt.tv
Contact: Dameon Okposio, publisher
Circulation: 500
Published quarterly

Features amateur and professional boxing coverage aimed at entertaining and educating fans of the sport. Will not be accepting freelance work in 2007, but will review that policy annually.

Camping Canada's RV Lifestyle Magazine
1020 Brevik Place, Suite 5, Mississauga, ON L4W 4N7
Phone: (905) 624-8218 Fax: (905) 624-6764
E-mail: jonathan@rvlifemag.com
Web site: www.rvlife.com
Contact: Jonathan Lee, editor
Circulation: 51,000
Published 7 times a year
Established 1971. Geared to readers who enjoy travel and camping. Readers vary from owners of towable trailers or motorhomes to young families and entry-level campers (no tenting). Half of the articles are written by freelancers. Publishes non-fiction articles on how-to, personal experience, and travel. Buys 20 to 30 manuscripts/year of 1,800 to 2,500 words. Send photos with submission. Occasionally accepts previously published submissions, if so noted. Pay varies; received on publication. Buys first North American serial rights. Byline given. Editorial lead time 3 months. Reports in 1 month on queries, 2 months on manuscripts. Sample copy free.

Canadian Biker
735 Market Street, Victoria, BC V8T 2E2
Phone: (250) 384-0333 Fax: (250) 384-1832
E-mail: edit@canadianbiker.com
Web site: www.canadianbiker.com
Contact: John Campbell, editor
Circulation: 11,000
Published 10 times a year
A general motorcycle magazine with an emphasis on cruiser-type motorcycles and touring articles with a Canadian slant. Other subjects include custom and vintage motorcycles, personality profiles, event coverage, and new model reviews (including sport, sport-touring, and dual-sport motorcycles). "Although freelance material is actively sought, potential contributors are strongly urged

to contact the editor before submitting if they wish to avoid disappointment." Features are 1,500 to 2,500 words; shorter stories for specific departments from 500 to 700 words. Pay rate is negotiated. "Articles paid according to quality rather than quantity and based on topic, frequency of contributions, and originality. Preference given to work sent on disk with hard copy and a minimum of two photos (captioned)." Guidelines available.

The Canadian Fly Fisher

389 Bridge Street W., Belleville, ON K8N 4Z2
Phone: (613) 966-8017 or 1-888-805-5608 Fax: (613) 966-4192
E-mail: info@canflyfish.com
Web site: www.canflyfish.com
Contact: Chris Marshall, editor
Published quarterly

Canada's only national fly fishing magazine, with information on Canadian fly fishing destinations, techniques, fly tying, etc. Stories must have a Canadian connection. Features range from 1,800 to 2,500 words, shorter pieces from 700 to 900 words, and occasionally very short filler items are used. Sidebars are appreciated. Enclose an SASE for queries and unsolicited manuscripts that are mailed, but e-mail queries are preferred. First-time writers must include a bio of 50 to 70 words. Responds to queries in at least 4 weeks. Pays from $150 to $300 for major features and super features with supporting photos and graphics, and between $100 and $200 for shorter pieces. Guidelines available on web site.

Diver Magazine

241 East 1st Street, North Vancouver, BC V7L 1B4
Phone: (604) 948-9937 Fax: (604) 948-9985
E-mail: mail@divermag.com
Web site: www.divermag.com
Contact: Virginia Cowell, editor
Circulation: 7,000
Published 8 times a year

For North American sport divers. Carries regular articles on travel destinations, snorkelling, and scuba and deep-water diving. Also covers marine life and underwater photography. Articles 500 to 1,000 words. Pays $2.50/column inch after publication. Check guidelines before submitting material.

Eastern Woods & Waters
40 Alderney Drive, Suite 501, Dartmouth, NS B2Y 2N5
Phone: (902) 464-3757 Fax: (902) 464-3755
E-mail: mhamilton@saltscapes.com
Web site: www.easternwoodsandwaters.com
Contact: Mark Hamilton, associate editor
Circulation: 17,700
Published bimonthly
    Eastern Canada's outdoor magazine dealing with every aspect of traditional outdoor pursuits – hunting, fishing, conservation, and the environment. Pays 30¢ to 40¢/word for articles of 1,200 to 2,500 words. "Credibility is our credo. Our writers are experienced outdoorspeople first. Please contact us for submission guidelines."

Explore: Canada's Outdoor Magazine
54 St. Patrick Street, Toronto, ON M5T 1V1
Phone: (416) 599-2000 Fax: (416) 599-0800
E-mail: explore@explore-mag.com
Web site: www.explore-mag.com
Contact: James Little, editor
Circulation: 30,000
Published bimonthly
    For people who enjoy outdoor recreational activities such as backpacking, mountain biking, canoeing, kayaking, skiing, and adventure travel. Most features run from 2,000 to 5,000 words. Payment depends on quality and length, and ranges from $1,000 and up. *Explore* also has sections for shorter stories, which generally run from 250 to 1,000 words. Payment depends on quality and length, and ranges from $125 and up. Fees are paid on acceptance. "Excellent photographs are essential for almost every *Explore* story, and though we generally use the work of full-time pros, we occasionally rely on a writer to provide appropriate photo support." Guidelines available on web site.

Get Out There Magazine
1 Aberfoyle Crescent, Suite 1200, Toronto, ON M8X 2X8
Phone: (416) 239-1590 Fax: (416) 840-4943
E-mail: info@getouttheremag.com
Web site: www.getouttheremag.com
Contact: Marissa Schroder, publisher
Circulation: 80,000
Published bimonthly
   Covers amateur sports with an outdoors focus. Articles from 500
to 750 words. Pays 40¢/word on publication. "Pitch letters and
writing samples are welcome."

The Hockey Reporter
91 Hemmingway Drive, Courtice, ON L1E 2C2
Phone: (905) 434-7409 Fax: (905) 434-1654
E-mail: hockeyreporter@istar.ca
Contact: Greg McDowell, managing editor
Circulation: 35,000
Published quarterly
   Covers the amateur hockey scene in Ontario. Fees are negotiated
and paid on publication for articles from 500 to 1,500 words.

Horse-Canada.com Magazine
P.O. Box 670, Aurora, ON L4G 4J9
Phone: (905) 727-0107 Fax: (905) 841-1530
E-mail: info@horse-canada.com
Web site: www.horse-canada.com
Contact: Lee Benson, managing editor
Published bimonthly
   Canada's family horse magazine for all breeds and disciplines
with emphasis on equine health and care. Includes a special pull-
out section for children who love horses. Accepts unsolicited mate-
rial. Preferred length 750 to 2,500 words. Guidelines available.

Horse Country
P.O. Box 203, 845 Dakota Street, Suite 23, Winnipeg, MB R2M 5M3
Phone: (204) 256-7467 Fax: (204) 257-2467
E-mail: horsecountry@mts.net
Web site: www.horsecountry.ca

Contact: Linda Hazelwood, publisher/editor
Circulation: 10,000
Published 8 times a year

Publishes stories for all ages on Canadian prairie horse people, on all disciplines of riding, and on all breeds of horses. Fees are negotiated for commissioned work and paid on publication. Articles are from 500 to 1,000 words. Welcomes submissions from emerging writers. "Unsolicited manuscripts are accepted but not returned. Send manuscripts by e-mail. Query letters or unsolicited manuscripts should state payment rate required, or it will be assumed they are gratis. Factual training and horse health articles are particularly sought."

Horses All

629 Evermeadow Road S.W., Calgary, AB T2Y 4W8
Phone: (403) 249-8770 Fax: (403) 249-8769
E-mail: cindym@horsesall.com
Web site: www.horsesall.com
Contact: Cindy Mark, editor
Circulation: 6,000
Published monthly

Horses All has featured equine news and information since 1979. Includes training and performance tips, stories on equine health, show results, humour, and fashion. Articles 500 to 1,500 words. Fees vary, but average about $100/story paid on publication. "Freelance writers must be knowledgeable horse people. Articles must be relevant to Canadian, Western Canadian, or Albertan readers. We do not publish fiction." Guidelines available.

Impact Magazine

2007 – 2nd Street S.W., Calgary, AB T2S 1S4
Phone: (403) 228-0605 Fax: (403) 228-0627
E-mail: louise@impactmagazine.ca
Web site: www.impactmagazine.ca
Contact: Louise Hodgson-Jones, editor
Circulation: 90,000
Published bimonthly

Western Canada's only fitness, performance, and sport magazine with editions in Calgary and Vancouver. Articles 600 to 1,000 words. Fees vary depending on the project and are paid on publication. Query by letter or e-mail before submitting. "We do not accept unsolicited articles." Guidelines available on web site.

Inside Track Motorsport News

P.O. Box 7100, Stn. B, Toronto, ON M5W 1X7
Phone: (416) 962-7223 Fax: (416) 962-7208
E-mail: editor@insidetracknews.com
Web site: www.insidetracknews.com
Contact: John Hopkins, editor
Circulation: 8,000
Published monthly
Aimed at Canadian motorsport racing fans. Includes race reports, features, news, and interviews. Articles 600 to 1,200 words. Fees vary and are paid on publication. "E-mail submissions preferred. Colour photos in JPG format at 300 DPI."

Kanawa: Canada's Paddling Magazine

1968 Haig Drive, Ottawa, ON K1G 2K1
Phone: (613) 521-7267
E-mail: kanawa@paddlingcanada.com
Web site: www.paddlingcanada.com
Contact: Judy Lord, editor
Published quarterly
Canada's foremost full-colour magazine for paddling on oceans, lakes, rivers, streams, or even creeks. "Many of our contributors are not professional writers or photographers but individuals who share a love of paddling and Canada's natural environment." Features 1,500 to 2,500 words; shorter articles 500 to 1,500 words. Cannot pay. Guidelines available on web site.

Ontario Golf

1074 Cooke Boulevard, Burlington, ON L7T 4A8
Phone: (905) 634-8003 Fax: (905) 634-7661
E-mail: tedbits@golfontario.ca
Web site: www.golfontario.ca
Contact: Ted McIntyre, editor
Circulation: 55,000
Published quarterly

The official publication of the Golf Association of Ontario with content of interest to all of Ontario's golf enthusiasts from features to travel, instruction to profiles, etc. Use celebrities who play golf on covers with question-and-answer interviews inside. Negotiated fees are paid for articles of 500 to 2,200 words. "We try to pay a month after submission. Stories are filed via e-mail. More than one Canadian golf writer has referred to *Ontario Golf* as the best golf magazine in Canada. Ours is a very slick publication with high standards for writing and photography." Guidelines available.

Ontario Out of Doors

1 Mount Pleasant Road, 7th Floor, Toronto, ON M4Y 2Y5
Phone: (416) 764-1657 Fax: (416) 764-1751
E-mail: matt.nicholls@ood.rogers.com
Web sites: www.fishontario.com and www.huntontario.com
Contact: Matt Nicholls, editor-in-chief
Circulation: 98,500
Published 10 times a year

Ontario's leading publication for outdoors enthusiasts. Specializes in how-to, where-to, and destination pieces on all aspects of hunting and fishing. Articles 600 to 2,000 words. Pays 50¢/word on either acceptance or publication, depending on the project. Guidelines available.

Ontario Sailor Magazine

91 Hemmingway Drive, Courtice, ON L1E 2C2
Phone: (905) 434-7409 Fax: (905) 434-1654
E-mail: sails@istar.ca
Web site: www.ontariosailormagazine.ca
Contact: Greg McDowell
Circulation: 8,000
Published 7 times a year

Covers the Great Lakes sailing scene in Canada and the U.S. Articles 500 to 1,500 words. Pay rates vary (start at $20/story) and are paid on publication. "Please query first. We accept freelance photos and prefer stories to be accompanied by a photo."

Outdoor Canada

25 Sheppard Avenue W., Suite 100, Toronto, ON M2N 6S7
Phone: (416) 733-7600 Fax: (416) 227-8296
E-mail: editorial@outdoorcanada.ca
Web site: www.outdoorcanada.ca
Contact: Bob Sexton, associate editor
Circulation: 93,000
Published 8 times a year

Canada's only national magazine about fishing, hunting, and related conservation issues. "Our readers are passionate about this country's natural heritage, and they want to get the most out of their outdoor experiences. That's why each issue contains a solid mix of how-to articles, service pieces, entertaining features, and in-depth reporting." Articles 100 to 3,000 words. Pays on acceptance 50¢ to $1/word. Fees are established upon assignment based on complexity and length of story. "We welcome query letters from professional writers (please do not submit unsolicited manuscripts). All story ideas must be designed solely to serve the interests and needs of our readers. Contributors are therefore encouraged to first review the magazine and familiarize themselves with its tone and specific editorial departments." Guidelines available.

Pacific Yachting

1080 Howe Street, Suite 900, Vancouver, BC V6Z 2T1
Phone: (604) 606-4644 Fax: (604) 687-1925
E-mail: editorial@pacificyachting.com
Web site: www.pacificyachting.com
Contact: Peter Robson, editor
Circulation: 19,000
Published monthly

A magazine that is all about recreational boats, boating, and the boating lifestyle. "We're looking for stories about cruising in B.C., how-to, adventure, and short 100- to 400-word news items." Preferred length for articles is 1,250 to 1,500 words. Pays $400 to $500 on publication for features, including photos. "Writers must be familiar with our special-interest viewpoint, language, and orientation. First-hand experience of subject is essential. Know our magazine, know the B.C. coast, and know boating." Guidelines available.

Real Fishing
940 Sheldon Court, Burlington, ON L7L 5K6
Phone: (905) 632-8679 Fax: (905) 632-2833
E-mail: jhughes@izumioutdoors.com
Web site: www.realfishing.com
Contact: Jerry Hughes, editor
Circulation: 20,000
Published quarterly

Real Fishing provides fishing tips and information about destinations and products geared to freshwater fishing in Canada. Pay rates vary, depending on the project, and are paid on publication. Guidelines available. "Articles should be relevant to Canadian anglers. Excessive product mentions are discouraged. Photos are required with stories."

Replay
79 Portsmouth Drive, Toronto, ON M1C 5C3
Phone: (416) 355-0747 Fax: (416) 355-0748
E-mail: keith@accessmag.com
Web site: www.replaymagazine.com
Contact: Keith Sharp, publisher
Circulation: 100,000
Published quarterly

A sports and entertainment magazine. Pays 25¢/word on publication for articles of 750 to 1,500 words.

RidersWest
100 – 7th Avenue S., Suite 100, Cranbrook, BC V1C 2J4
Phone: (250) 426-7253 Fax: (250) 426-4125
E-mail: info@kpimedia.com
Contact: Keith Powell, publisher
Circulation: 32,000
Published twice a year

Primarily a destinations-type magazine looking for first-person ATV travel adventure articles. Stories 500 to 800 words. Pays $85/story, which must have a photo to accompany it. Pays when story and photo are received and approved to run.

Ski Canada
117 Indian Road, Toronto, ON M6R 2V5
Phone: (416) 538-2293
E-mail: mac@skicanadamag.com
Web site: www.skicanadamag.com
Contact: Iain MacMillan, editor
Circulation: 42,000
Published 6 times a year
   Publishes a balanced mix of entertainment and information for both the experienced and the novice-intermediate skier. "Published from early autumn through winter (with one summer issue), *SC* covers equipment, travel, instruction, competition, fashion, and general skiing- and alpine-related news and stories. Query letters are preferred; unsolicited manuscripts rarely fit into a determined schedule. Replies will take time. Note: yearly editorial schedules are set at least 6 months before commencement of publishing season." Articles 400 to 2,500 words. Pays (within 30 days of publication) between $100 (news) and $500 to $800 (features), depending on length, research necessary, and writer's experience.

Sno Riders
100 – 7th Avenue S., Suite 100, Cranbrook, BC V1C 2J4
Phone: (250) 426-7253 Fax: (250) 426-4125
E-mail: info@kpimedia.com
Contact: Keith Powell, publisher
Circulation: 32,000
Published 3 times a year
   Primarily a destinations-type magazine looking for first-person snowmobile travel adventure articles. Stories 500 to 800 words. Pays $85/story, which must have a photo to accompany it. Pays when story and photo are received and approved to run.

WaveLength Magazine
1773 El Verano Drive, Gabriola, BC V0R 1X6
Phone: (250) 247-9093 Fax: (250) 247-9083
E-mail: diana@wavelengthmagazine.com
Web site: www.wavelengthmagazine.com
Contact: Diana Mumford, editor
Published quarterly

For paddlers, especially sea kayakers, and those interested in marine ecotourism and the marine environment, specifically on the West Coast. Articles from 1,000 to 1,500 words. Pays on publication $50 to $100, depending on length of article, $25 to $100 for photos. "Knowledge of kayaking (or canoeing) essential. Humour and good pictures are an asset." Guidelines available on web site.

Western Sportsman

1080 Howe Street, Suite 900, Vancouver, BC V6Z 2T1
Phone: (604) 606-4644 Fax: (604) 687-1925
E-mail: editor@westernsportsman.com
Web site: www.westernsportsman.com
Contact: David Webb, editor
Circulation: 20,000
Published bimonthly
Publishes articles on recreational fishing, hunting, and conservation from west of the Rockies to Manitoba. Stories 1,600 to 2,000 words. Pays on publication. Please query. Guidelines available.

Travel & Tourism

British Columbia Magazine

1803 Douglas Street, 3rd Floor, Victoria, BC V8T 5C3
Phone: (250) 356-5860 Fax: (250) 356-5896
E-mail: editor@bcmag.ca
Web site: www.bcmag.ca
Contact: Anita Willis editor
Circulation: 115,000
Published monthly
Portrays a fresh view of B.C., highlighting exotic and unknown features or a new angle to a familiar place or theme. Does not publish poetry or fiction. Reviews all proposals in December and January each year, and considers spec manuscripts throughout the year (although it's best to submit before March). Especially welcomes experienced writers who can provide excellent photos. Features are usually 1,500 to 2,500 words; shorter stories from 1,000 to 1,500 words; sidebars 200 to 500 words. Pays 50¢/word

on acceptance; higher rates for more complex research assignments. Guidelines on web site.

DreamScapes Travel and Lifestyle Magazine

642 Simcoe Street, S.S. 1, Niagara-on-the-Lake, ON L0S 1J0
Phone: (905) 468-4021 Fax: (905) 468-2382
E-mail: editor@dreamscapes.ca
Web site: www.dreamscapes.ca
Contact: Donna Vieira, editor
Circulation: 110,000
Published 8 times a year
Distributed to the highest income households in six key markets across Canada. See web site for publishing and editorial schedule. Articles from 500 to 1,200 words. Pays 35¢/word on publication; this fee covers both the printed magazine format and the online version. "Photos must accompany all editorials. We do not pay for them, although we do give a photo credit." Guidelines available.

enRoute

4200 Saint Laurent Boulevard, Suite 707, Montreal, QC H2W 2R2
Phone: (514) 844-2001 Fax: (514) 844-6001
E-mail: info@enroutemag.net
Web site: www.enroutemag.com
Circulation: 160,000
Published monthly
Air Canada's French-English inflight magazine. A general travel lifestyle publication featuring trends, travel, entertainment, social stories, fashion, and food. Aimed at a high-end market. Articles 200 to 1,500 words. Pays $1 per word on acceptance. Inquire first with ideas. Always enclose tearsheets. Guidelines posted at www.enroutemag.com.

Journeywoman: The Premier Travel Resource for Women

50 Prince Arthur Avenue, Toronto, ON M5R 1B5
Phone: (416) 929-7654
E-mail: editor@journeywoman.com
Web site: www.journeywoman.com
Contact: Evelyn Hannon, publisher/editor

An online international travel resource that publishes stories and tips focusing on the specific needs and interests of women travellers. Stories up to 900 words, with two additional sidebars and a 2- to 3-line bio. Pays a $35 honorarium for articles. Each published article is eligible for the Annual Journeywoman Travel Writing Competition, with two top prizes of $100 each.

99 North
4180 Lougheed Highway, 4th Floor, Burnaby, BC V5C 6A7
Phone: (604) 299-7311 Fax: (604) 299-9188
E-mail: clumsdon@canadawide.com
Web site: www.canadawide.com
Contact: Chris Lumsdon, editor
Circulation: 75,000
A magazine that covers tourism, adventure tourism, and experiential travel in the Sea-to-Sky corridor of British Columbia (Brittania Beach–Squamish–Whistler–Pemberton). Articles from 750 to 2,000 words. Fees are negotiated. "Ideas may be pitched to the editorial team at any time on a topic relating to tourism in the Sea-to-Sky region."

Outpost Magazine
425 Queen Street W., Suite 201, Toronto, ON M5V 2A5
Phone: (416) 972-6527 Fax: (416) 972-6645
E-mail: editor@outpostmagazine.com
Web site: www.outpostmagazine.com
Contact: Larry Frolick, editor
Circulation: 28,000
Published bimonthly
Outpost takes a more adventurous and realistic view of travel. All story ideas should be submitted by a query letter first. Features are 2,800 to 5,000 words; shorter pieces are used for other sections. Guidelines on web site.

Prairies North
P.O. Box 520, Norquay, SK S0A 2V0
Phone: (306) 594-2455 Fax: (306) 594-2119
E-mail: lionel@prairiesnorth.com

Web site: www.sasknaturally.com
Contact: Lionel Hughes, co-publisher/editor
Circulation: 22,000
Published quarterly
  Previously *Saskatchewan Naturally Magazine*, relaunched in 2004 as *Prairies North*. Stories feature the unique wildlife, people, and places of Saskatchewan, using stunning photos and fresh editorial content. Uses 5 feature articles/issue of 1,200 to 2,500 words. Pays on publication 25¢/word. Guidelines available.

RVWest
100 – 7th Avenue S., Suite 100, Cranbrook, BC V1C 2J4
Phone: (250) 426-7253 Fax: (250) 426-4125
E-mail: info@kpimedia.com
Contact: Keith Powell, publisher
Circulation: 30,000
Published bimonthly
  Primarily a destinations-type magazine looking for first-person RV travel adventure articles. Stories 500 to 800 words. Pays $85/story, which must have a photo to accompany it. Pays when story and photo are received and approved to run.

Snowbirds & RV Travelers
P.O. Box 99, Greenwood, BC V0H 1J0
Phone: (250) 445-2233 Fax: (250) 445-2243
E-mail: bctimes@direct.ca
Web site: www.rvsnowbirds.com
Contact: Reed Turcotte, publisher
Circulation: 10,000
Published quarterly
  Articles from 100 to 800 words. Fees are negotiated and paid on publication.

The Student Traveller
45 Charles Street E., Suite 200, Toronto, ON M4Y 1S2
Phone: (416) 966-2887 Fax: (416) 966-4043
E-mail: stutrav@travelcuts.com
Web site: www.travelcuts.com

Contact: Lisa Trainor, managing editor
Circulation: 130,000
Published twice a year
    A travel magazine geared specifically toward student, youth, and budget travellers. Pays 10¢/word on publication for articles 500 to 1,200 words and $25/published photo. Guidelines available.

Verge Magazine
1517B Schutt Road, R.R. #2, Palmer Rapids, ON K0J 2E0
Phone: (613) 758-9909
E-mail: contributing@vergemagazine.ca
Web site: www.vergemagazine.ca
Contact: Jeff Minthorn, publisher
Circulation: 10,000
Published 3 times a year
    This travel magazine focuses on overseas work, study, volunteering, and adventure travel options. The primary market is college and university students. Pays 10¢/word on publication for articles 500 to 2,500 words. Guidelines available.

**Westworld Alberta / Westworld B.C. / Westworld
    Saskatchewan**
4180 Lougheed Highway, 4th Floor, Burnaby, BC V5C 6A7
Phone: (604) 299-7311 Fax: (604) 299-9188
Web site: www.canadawide.com
Contact: Anne Rose, editor
Circulation: 1,115,000 (combined)
Published quarterly (*Westwood Alberta* published 5 times a year)
    A travel (regional, national, and international), active-lifestyle, and auto-club magazine. Pays 50¢ to $1/word on publication for articles of 500 to 2,000 words. Kill fees are 50%. "Writers should review back issues for style, tone, and focus of departments and features."

Where Calgary
125 – 9 Avenue S.E., Suite 250, Calgary, AB T2G 0P6
Phone: (403) 299-1888 Fax: (403) 299-1899
E-mail: info_calgary@where.ca
Web site: www.where.ca/calgary

Contact: Andrew Mah, editor
Circulation: 50,000
Published bimonthly
News of events and attractions for visitors in Calgary and Alberta, including local dining, shopping, and fine art. Cover stories highlight things to do and see. Pays about 50¢/word on acceptance. Word count and rates vary with project. "Query first with résumé and clips. Please don't send spec manuscripts, fiction, or poetry."

Where Toronto

111 Queen Street E., Toronto, ON M5C 1S2
Phone: (416) 364-3333, ext. 3078 Fax: (416) 594-3375
E-mail: editorial@where.ca
Web site: www.where.ca/toronto
Contact: Anne Gibson, editor-in-chief
Circulation: 63,000
Published monthly
Where Toronto is a destination magazine for affluent visitors that covers the best each month in entertainment, shopping, dining, and attractions. Articles 300 to 1,200 words. Pay rates vary depending on project and are paid on publication. "Most articles are written by the staff."

Where Vancouver

2208 Spruce Street, Vancouver, BC V6H 2P3
Phone: (604) 736-5586 Fax: (604) 736-3465
E-mail: infovancouver@where.ca
Web site: www.where.ca/vancouver
Contact: Sheri Radford, editor
Circulation: 50,000
Published monthly
A visitors' guide incorporating listings for shopping, dining, art, and entertainment. *Where Vancouver* is an intelligent magazine and city guide for the upscale traveller. Articles 800 to 1,000 words. Pay rates vary depending on project and are paid on acceptance. "Our need for freelance submissions is minimal. The most common mistake we see is ideas for features that would appeal to Vancouver residents but not to visitors."

Women's

Black Woman and Child
P.O. Box 47045, 300 Borough Drive, Toronto, ON M1P 4P0
Phone: (416) 689-2922 Fax: (416) 754-6821
E-mail: bwac@nubeing.com
Web site: www.nubeing.com
Published quarterly
Provides pregnancy and parenting information rooted in African culture. "The foundation of our magazine is the traditional spoken-word wisdom of African people and the undeniable spirit and knowledge of African mothers." Articles 750 to 1,500 words; feature articles generally about 2,000 to 2,500 words. Guidelines and submission deadlines on web site.

Chatelaine
1 Mount Pleasant Road, 8th Floor, Toronto, ON M4Y 2Y5
Phone: (416) 764-2421 Fax: (416) 764-2431
E-mail: editors@chatelaine.com
Web site: www.chatelaine.com
Contact: Maryam Sanati, deputy editor
Circulation: 700,000+
Published monthly
A high-quality, glossy magazine addressing the needs, interests, and preferences of Canadian women. Covers current issues, personalities, lifestyles, health, relationships, travel, and politics. Features of 1,000 to 2,500 words earn $1,250 and up; one-page columns start at $500. "For all serious articles, deep, accurate, and thorough research and rich details are required. Features on beauty, food, fashion, and home decorating are supplied by staff writers and editors only." Buys first North American serial rights in English and French (to cover possible use in French-language edition). Pays on acceptance. Query first with brief outline. Guidelines available on web site (type *guidelines* in search category).

The Compleat Mother
P.O. Box 38033, Calgary, AB T3K 5G9
Phone: (403) 255-0246

E-mail: angela@thecompleatmother.com
Web site: www.thecompleatmother.com
Contact: Angela van Son, publisher/editor
Circulation: 8,000
Published quarterly
   The magazine of pregnancy, birth, and breastfeeding, focusing on mothers from all walks of life. "We publish articles ranging from birth stories to experiences relating to weaning and everything in between." Cannot pay but welcomes submission inquiries. "Articles are considered if they are passionate, gutsy, hysterical, or brilliant. We also love to receive photos, drawings, cartoons, etc., to print alongside articles." Guidelines available.

Elle Canada
25 Sheppard Avenue W., Suite 100, Toronto, ON M2N 6S7
Phone: (416) 227-8210 Fax: (416) 733-7981
E-mail: editors@ellecanada.com
Circulation: 200,000
Published monthly
   Features stories on women's beauty, fashion, and lifestyle. Articles 300 to 1,200 words. Pays $1/word on acceptance.

Flare Magazine
1 Mount Pleasant Road, 8th Floor, Toronto, ON M4Y 2Y5
Phone: (416) 764-2863 Fax: (416) 764-2866
Web site: www.flare.com
Contact: Tracy Picha, managing editor
Circulation: 160,000
Published monthly
   A magazine for women aged 20 to 35, focusing on fashion, beauty, and style. Pays $1/word on acceptance for articles 600 to 1,200 words. Guidelines available.

Glow
1 Mount Pleasant Road, Toronto, ON M4Y 2Y5
Phone: (416) 764-2484 Fax: (416) 764-2488
E-mail: beth.thompson@glow.rogers.com
Web site: www.glow.ca
Contact: Beth Thompson, editor-in-chief

Circulation: 500,000
Published bimonthly
   Glow is a beauty and health magazine with a Canadian spin.
Articles are 1,000 to 1,500 words. Pays $1/word on publication. "A
good query letter is your best foot in the door. Be innovative and
smart to get the editor's attention." Guidelines available.

WeddingBells
111 Queen Street E., Suite 320, Toronto, ON M5C 1S2
Phone: (416) 364-3333 Fax: (416) 594-3374
E-mail: editorial@weddingbells.com
Web site: www.weddingbells.com
Contact: Kate Yorga, managing editor
Circulation: 105,000
Published twice a year
   Provides inspiration and planning tools for Canadian brides-to-
be. "Currently all editorial is handled in-house by staff."

Women's Post
2 Carlton Street, Suite 804, Toronto, ON M5B 1J3
Phone: (416) 964-5850 Fax: (416) 964-6142
E-mail: editor@womenspost.ca
Web site: www.womenspost.ca
Contact: Sarah Thomson, publisher
Circulation: 100,000
Published twice a month; weekly as of September 2007
   A newspaper targeting professional women between the ages of
25 and 55. Articles should be intimate, first-person narratives from
500 to 600 words. Pays approximately $75/story on publication.
Guidelines available.

Youth & Children's

Chirp
10 Lower Spadina Avenue, Suite 400, Toronto, ON M5V 2Z2
Phone: (416) 340-2700 Fax: (416) 340-9769
Web site: www.owlkids.com
Contact: Sarah Trusty, associate editor

Circulation: 80,000
Published 10 times a year

The "see and do" magazine for children aged 3 to 6. Publishes puzzles, games, rhymes, stories, and songs to entertain and teach preschoolers about animals, nature, letters, numbers, and more. No unsolicited manuscripts; query first. Prefers complete articles of 300 to 450 words (fees range between $100 and $350). Short poems (25 to 40 words) are paid $50.

The Claremont Review
4980 Wesley Road, Victoria, BC V8Y 1Y9
E-mail: bashford@islandnet.com or markskanks@sd63.bc.ca
Web site: www.theclaremontreview.ca
Contact: Lucy Bashford, managing editor
Circulation: 400
Published twice a year

TCR publishes youth fiction and poetry for ages 13 to 19. Pays with copies of the publication. Guidelines available.

Fashion18
111 Queen Street E., Suite 320, Toronto, ON M5C 1S2
Phone: (416) 364-3333 Fax: (416) 594-3374
E-mail: editorial@fashion18.com
Web site: www.fashion18.com
Contact: Kate Yorga, managing editor
Circulation: 90,000
Published quarterly

A fashion and beauty magazine that also covers celebrity news and fun stuff for Canadian teenaged girls. "Currently all editorial is handled in-house by staff."

Faze Magazine
4936 Yonge Street, Suite 2400, Toronto, ON M2N 6S3
Phone: (416) 222-3060 Fax: (416) 222-2097
E-mail: editor@fazeteen.com
Web site: www.fazeteen.com
Contact: Lorraine Zander, editor-in-chief
Circulation: 375,000
Published quarterly

Offers Canadian teenagers a look at real life issues, entertainment, global issues, health, personal style, careers, and technology. Strives to be both entertaining and empowering. Rates vary depending on project and are paid on publication. Guidelines available.

Fun Times Magazine

777 Hornby Street, Suite 1600, Vancouver, BC V6Z 2T3
Phone: (604) 687-7911 Fax: (604) 608-4411
E-mail: marina.goric@ddbkiathink.com
Web site: www.funtimesgiveaways.com
Contact: Marina Goric, account executive
Circulation: 3 million
Published 8 times a year

Fun Times is McDonald's branded magazine catering to kids from 6 to 11 years old. It reflects real kids, what they're into, and their pal Ronald McDonald. Stories 10 to 75 words. Fees vary depending on project and are paid on acceptance. "Your writing must have a sense of fun, wackiness, creativity, and education – while working under the McDonald's guidelines." Guidelines available.

Kayak: Canada's History Magazine for Kids

167 Lombard Avenue, Suite 478, Winnipeg, MB R3B 0T6
Phone: (204) 988-9300 Fax: (204) 988-9309
E-mail: editor@kayakmag.ca
Web site: www.kayakmag.ca
Contact: Jill Foran, editor
Circulation: 3,000
Published bimonthly

Aimed at children 7 to 11 years of age, *Kayak* is a fun, engaging, sometimes irreverent but always informative voyage of discovery into Canada's past. Articles from 50 to 150 words. Fees vary depending on project and are paid on acceptance. Guidelines available.

Know: The Science Magazine for Curious Kids

3960 Quadra Street, Suite 501, Victoria, BC V8X 4A3
Phone: (250) 477-5543 or 1-888-477-5543 Fax: (250) 477-5390
E-mail: info@knowmag.ca
Web site: www.knowmag.ca
Contact: Adrienne Mason, managing editor

Circulation: 8,000
Published bimonthly

A science magazine for children aged 6 to 9. "Our approach is that science is all around us, and we help answer some of the how, what, and why questions that all children who are naturally curious ask." Stories 50 to 500 words. Pay rates vary depending on project from about 30¢ to 40¢/word, paid on publication. "Most articles are assigned; however, we would like to hear from non-fiction writers who are interested in working with us. We do accept unsolicited poetry and fiction (related to theme) up to 500 words." Guidelines available at web site.

OWL

10 Lower Spadina Avenue, Suite 400, Toronto, ON M5V 2Z2
Phone: (416) 340-2700 Fax: (416) 340-9769
E-mail: editor@owlkids.com
Web site: www.owlkids.com
Contact: Craig Battle, editor
Circulation: 75,000
Published 10 times a year

A general interest magazine for 9- to 13-year-olds. Entertains and informs on the topics and issues that concern them. Topics include everything from sports to the environment, and pop culture to peer relationships. Pays $500 and up on publication for 600 to 800 words. Prefers submission inquiries; no unsolicited manuscripts. Strongly recommends writers check back issues (available in libraries) for a sense of *OWL*'s approach.

Yes Magazine

3960 Quadra Street, Suite 501, Victoria, BC V8X 4A3
Phone: (250) 477-5543 or 1-888-477-5543 Fax: (250) 477-5390
E-mail: editor@yesmag.ca
Web site: www.yesmag.ca
Contact: Jude Isabella, managing editor
Circulation: 22,000
Published bimonthly

A science magazine for kids aged 9 to 14. "We cover all the sciences. Each issue features a theme." Stories 100 to 800 words. Fees are about $70/article, paid on acceptance. Guidelines available at web site.

Youthink Magazine
1275 West 6th Avenue, Suite 206, Vancouver, BC V6H 1A6
Phone: (604) 732-6397 Fax: (604) 732-6390
E-mail: janine@youthink.ca
Web site: www.youthink.ca
Contact: Janine Verreault, managing editor
Circulation: 55,000
Published monthly

Youthink is distributed through high schools and businesses in B.C. and is written entirely by students. There is a heavy focus on entertainment, particularly music. Articles 250 to 600 words. Cannot pay but welcomes inquiries. "Only high school students are eligible to submit articles, poem, artwork, and photography, etc."

2

LITERARY & SCHOLARLY
PUBLICATIONS

It's ironic that literary and scholarly journals, which are among the most prestigious outlets for a writer's work, can least afford to pay their contributors. Many journals rely on funding from arts councils, or from academic or professional sources, and still run at a loss. They have relatively small subscription lists, perhaps two or three unpaid or part-time staff, and attract little or no advertising support. They can rarely afford to pay their contributors much, and in many cases, modest funding and low revenues preclude payment altogether, or limit it to small honoraria or free copies.

Writers would be unwise to look to this sector of publishing as a significant source of income. Qualified writers would be just as unwise to neglect it because of this. Publishing your work in a distinguished literary or scholarly journal can add immeasurably to your reputation and may well open up other publishing opportunities. This chapter lists many of Canada's most notable journals and literary magazines. Use the information presented in each entry to help you choose the most appropriate publications to approach.

Contributors to scholarly journals are frequently graduate students, salaried academics, or professionals who draw on current areas of research. For graduate students, journal publication is often an essential element of their professional development. The successful applicant for a university teaching position, for instance, will usually have a substantial publishing history.

Before you make your submission, familiarize yourself thoroughly with the journal to which you hope to contribute. Editors take a dim view of submissions from writers who are obviously unfamiliar with their publication. Study several recent issues, or better still, subscribe. Learn what you can of the editors' approaches and points of view, and the kind of work they favour. Determine who their readers are. If they have a web site, be sure to visit it.

Always request writers' guidelines or read them online, and follow these closely to ensure you meet the editors' needs. Remember to include an SASE whenever you expect a response. Refereed journals will require several copies of your submission. Scholarly articles will need to be accompanied by full documentation. Fiction, poetry, reviews, and criticism must be carefully targeted and professionally presented. The extra care and attention will pay dividends.

Acadiensis: Journal of the History of the Atlantic Region

University of New Brunswick, P.O. Box 4400, Fredericton, NB
   E3B 5A3
Phone: (506) 453-4978 Fax: (506) 453-5068
E-mail: acadnsis@unb.ca
Web site: www.lib.unb.ca/texts/acadiensis
Contact: Bill Parenteau, editor
Circulation: 850
Published twice a year

Includes original academic research, review articles, documents, notes, and a running bibliography compiled by librarians in the four Atlantic provinces. "Canada's most ambitious scholarly journal" – Michael Bliss, *Journal of Canadian Studies*. Articles published in English and in French. Cannot pay but welcomes submission inquiries. Guidelines available.

Alberta History

95 Holmwood Avenue N.W., Calgary, AB T2K 2G7
Phone: (403) 289-8149 Fax: (403) 289-8144
E-mail: potaina@shaw.ca
Contact: Hugh Dempsey, editor
Circulation: 1,200
Published quarterly

Publishes articles on Alberta history from 3,000 to 5,000 words to a mostly province-wide audience. Cannot pay, but welcomes submission inquiries. Guidelines available.

The Antigonish Review
St. Francis Xavier University, P.O. Box 5000, Antigonish, NS
    B2G 2W5
Phone: (902) 867-3962 Fax: (902) 867-5563
E-mail: tar@stfx.ca
Web site: www.antigonishreview.com
Contact: Bonnie McIsaac, office manager
Circulation: 1,000
Published quarterly
    A creative literary review featuring poetry, fiction, reviews, and critical articles using original graphics to enliven the format. Directed at a general audience. Preferred length 2,000 to 3,000 words. Pays on publication $100/article or essay, $50/fiction or book review, and copies of the publication for poetry. Rights remain with author. Guidelines available at web site.

Arc Poetry Magazine
P.O. Box 81060, Ottawa, ON K1P 1B1
E-mail: editor@arcpoetry.ca
Web site: www.arcpoetry.ca
Contact: Anita Lahey, editor
Circulation: 1,000
Published twice a year
    Publishes poetry from Canada and abroad, as well as reviews, interviews, and articles on poetry and poetry related subjects. No fiction or drama. Poetry submissions must be typed and include 5 to 8 unpublished poems. Reviews, interviews, and other prose, including how poems work, must be queried first. Pays $40/published page on publication. Guidelines and other information available on web site.

BC Studies: The British Columbian Quarterly
University of British Columbia, 1866 Main Mall, Buchanan E162,
    Vancouver, BC V6T 1Z1

Phone: (604) 822-3727 Fax: (604) 822-0606
E-mail: info@bcstudies.com
Web site: www.bcstudies.com
Contact: Carlyn Craig, managing editor
Circulation: 650

Established in 1968, *BC Studies* is a peer reviewed journal that explores British Columbia's cultural, economic, and political life, past and present. Each issue offers articles on a wide range of topics, in-depth reviews of current books, and a bibliography of recent publications. With a solid reputation for its authoritative and informative content, *BC Studies* is enjoyed by academics and general readers alike. Articles 7,000 to 8,000 words. Cannot pay for submissions and retains all rights to articles published. Guidelines available.

Brick, A Literary Journal
P.O. Box 537, Stn. Q, Toronto, ON M4T 2M5
E-mail: info@brickmag.com
Web site: www.brickmag.com
Contact: Rebecca Silver Slayter, managing editor
Circulation: 2,500
Published twice a year

Publishes literary non-fiction about books, writers, and literary pursuits. Pays $100 to $500 on publication for articles 250 to 7,500 words. Fees based on type of article and are paid on publication. "We do not read fiction or poetry. E-mail submissions of non-fiction are welcome. Please read the magazine to get an idea of what kind of work we publish." Guidelines available on web site.

Canadian Children's Literature
Centre for Research in Young People's Texts and Cultures,
   515 Portage Avenue, University of Winnipeg, Winnipeg, MB
   R3B 2E9
E-mail: ccl@uwinnipeg.ca
Web site: http://ccl.uwinnipeg.ca
Contact: Perry Nodelman, editor
Published quarterly

Presents in-depth criticism and reviews of Canadian literature for children and young adults. Directed toward teachers, librarians, academics, and parents. Scholarly articles (2,000 to 8,000 words), interviews, profiles, and reviews are supplemented by illustrations and photographs. Cannot pay but welcomes submissions. Guidelines available.

Canadian Ethnic Studies

Department of History, University of Calgary, 2500 University
   Drive N.W., Calgary, AB T2N 1N4
Phone: (403) 220-7257 Fax: (403) 210-8764
E-mail: ces@ucalgary.ca
Web site: www.ss.ucalgary.ca/ces
Contact: James S. Frideres, editor
Published 3 times a year
   An interdisciplinary journal devoted to the study of ethnicity, immigration, inter-group relations, and the history and cultural life of ethnic groups in Canada. Also carries book reviews, opinions, memoirs, creative writing, and poetry, and has an ethnic voice section. All material should address Canadian ethnicity. Charges a fee to evaluate work submitted – equivalent to an annual subscription   unless you are a member or already a subscriber. Research articles are from 20 to 30 double-spaced pages; book reviews from 750 to 850 words. Contributors of articles receive 2 copies of the journal and 25 complimentary reprints. Guidelines available. See web site for more information.

The Canadian Historical Review

UTP Journals, 5201 Dufferin Street, Toronto, ON M3H 5T8
Phone: (416) 667-7994 Fax: (416) 667-7881
E-mail: chr@utpress.utoronto.ca
Web site: www.utpjournals.com/chr
Contacts: Arthur J. Ray and Ken Cruikshank, co-editors
Published quarterly
   Publishes original research articles in all areas of Canadian history as well as research notes and book reviews. For academics and graduate students of Canadian history. Preferred length 5,000 to 10,000 words. Cannot pay but welcomes submission inquiries.

Canadian Journal of Film Studies

Editorial Office, Department of Art History and Communication
   Studies, McGill University, 853 Sherbrooke Street W., Arts
   Building W225, Montreal, QC H3A 2T6
Phone: (514) 398-4935   Fax: (514) 398-7247
E-mail: william.wees@mcgill.ca
Web site: www.filmstudies.ca
Contacts: William C. Wees, editor; Blaine Allan, managing editor
Published twice a year
   Distributed to members of the Film Association of Canada, to
Canadian and international libraries, and to individual subscribers.
Length of articles up to 6,000 words; shorter articles for "Ciné-
Documents" and "Ciné-Forum" up to 2,500 words. Rates vary
according to project.

Canadian Journal of History

Department of History, 9 Campus Drive, University of
   Saskatchewan, Saskatoon, SK S7N 5A5
Phone: (306) 966-5794   Fax: (306) 966-5852
E-mail: cjh@usask.ca
Web site: www.usask.ca/history/cjh
Contact: John McCannon, editor
Published 3 times a year
   Publishes general history of all countries in all periods. Articles to
be based on original research with primary sources. Usually assessed
by readers before publication. Detailed style guide on web site.

Canadian Literature

University of British Columbia, 1866 Main Mall, Buchanan E158,
   Vancouver, BC V6T 1Z1
Phone: (604) 822-2780   Fax: (604) 822-5504
E-mail: can.lit@ubc.ca
Web site: www.canlit.ca
Published quarterly
   Devoted to studying many aspects of Canadian literature and
offering a literary critique of Canadian writers. For academics,
researchers, libraries, schools, and universities. Contributors are
not paid. E-mail submission of articles is not accepted. Maximum

length of articles 6,500 words, including notes and works cited. Must be double-spaced and submitted in triplicate with author's name removed. A few poems by Canadian writers accepted for each issue; the maximum length is 2 pages/poem. Guidelines available.

Canadian Modern Language Review

UTP Journals, 5201 Dufferin Street, Toronto, ON M3H 5T8
Phone: (416) 667-7994 Fax: (416) 667-7881
E-mail: cmlr@utpress.utoronto.ca
Web site: www.utpjournals.com/cmlr
Contacts: Larry Vandergrift and Tracey Derwing, co-editors (new editors in fall 2007)
Circulation: 1,000
Published quarterly

Publishes applied, linguistic, second-language theory, and peda gogical articles, book reviews, current advertisements, and other material of interest to high-school and university language teachers and academics. A balance of theory and practice. All articles are voluntarily submitted rather than assigned and are refereed. Length to 6,500 words. Contributors are not paid, but submissions are welcome. Consult "Guide to Authors" in each issue and write to editors for further information.

Canadian Poetry: Studies, Documents, Reviews

Department of English, University of Western Ontario, London, ON N6A 3K7
Phone: (519) 661-3403 Fax: (519) 661-3776
E-mail: canadianpoetry@uwo.ca
Web site: www.canadianpoetry.ca
Contact: D. M. R. Bentley, editor
Published twice a year

A scholarly and critical refereed journal devoted to the study of poetry from all periods and regions of Canada. Prints articles, reviews, and documents – 500 to 5,000 words – directed toward university and college students and teachers. No original poetry. Cannot pay but welcomes submissions. Follow *MLA Style Manual*. Guidelines available.

Canadian Public Administration/Administration publique du Canada

1075 Bay Street, Suite 401, Toronto, ON M5S 2B1
Phone: (416) 924-8787 Fax: (416) 924-4992
E-mail: ntl@ipac.ca
Web site: www.ipac.ca
Contact: Barbara Wake Carroll, editor
Circulation: 3,500
Published quarterly

A refereed journal, written by public administrators and academics, that examines structures, processes, and outcomes of public policy and public management related to executive, legislative, judicial, and quasi-judicial functions in municipal, provincial, and federal spheres of government. "We are a high-quality, well-established journal that is distinctive in terms of its objectives and contents." Articles from 10 to 30 pages. Contributors are unpaid. Guidelines available on web site.

Canadian Social Work

383 Parkdale Avenue, Suite 402, Ottawa, ON K1Y 4R4
Phone: (613) 729-6668 Fax: (613) 729-9608
E-mail: casw@casw-acts.ca
Web site: www.casw-acts.ca
Contact: France Audet, administrative assistant
Circulation: 16,000
Published once a year

Publication of the Canadian Association of Social Workers. A bilingual forum for social-work professionals through which social workers and others share their knowledge, skills, research, and information with each other and with the general public. Peer reviewed. Articles from 2,500 to 5,000 words and shorter articles 250 to 1,000. Cannot pay but welcomes submission inquiries. First preference given to CASW members. Guidelines available.

Canadian Woman Studies

212 Founders College, York University, 4700 Keele Street, North York, ON M3J 1P3
Phone: (416) 736-5356 Fax: (416) 736-5765
E-mail: cwscf@yorku.ca

Contact: Luciana Ricciutelli, managing editor
Circulation: 5,000
Published quarterly

A bilingual, thematic journal featuring current scholarly writing and research on a wide variety of feminist topics. Welcomes creative writing, poetry, experiential articles, and essays of 750 to 3,000 words, as well as book reviews. Contributors are unpaid but receive a complimentary copy of the issue containing their work. Guidelines available.

The Capilano Review
2055 Purcell Way, North Vancouver, BC V7J 3H5
Phone: (604) 984-1712
E-mail: tcr@capcollege.bc.ca
Web site: www.thecapilanoreview.ca
Contact: Carol Hamshaw, managing editor
Circulation: 900
Published 3 times a year

A first-rate showcase of innovative literary and visual art, *The Capilano Review*'s production is notably fine, its editorial taste is intelligent and informed, its reputation is stellar. The journal is known for its fortitude in the avant-garde, and it solicits work that is fresh in form and aesthetics in the genres of visual art, poetry, drama, and fiction. *TCR* has earned 7 National Magazine Awards, 2 Western Magazine Awards, and a citation from the Canadian Studies Association. Has published Phyllis Webb, George Bowering, Daphne Marlatt, Sharon Thesen, Roy Kiyooka, bpNichol, and numerous other internationally acclaimed writers. Visual artists featured include Gathic Falk, Joey Morgan, Pierre Coupey, Lina Delano, and Melinda Mollineaux. Pays $50/page to a maximum of $200 on publication. Carries stories up to 8,000 words. Guidelines available.

Carousel
UC 274, University of Guelph, Guelph, ON N1G 2W1
E-mail: carouselbook@yahoo.ca
Web site: www.carouselmagazine.ca
Contact: Mark Laliberte, managing editor
Published twice a year

A hybrid literary and arts magazine, *Carousel* is interested in representing both new and established artists, with a specific focus on positioning Canadian talent within an international context. Imposes a small fee to non-subscribers to process poetry and fiction submissions sent by e-mail. Welcomes submissions of 3 to 7 poems and fiction less than 3,000 words. Pays an honorarium on publication of $10 for 2 to 4 pages of fiction, $20 for 5 and more pages of fiction, and $10/poem.

Challenger international

Phone: (250) 991-5567
E-mail: lukivdan@hotmail.com
Web site: http://challengerinternational.20m.com/index.html
Contact: Dan Lukiv, editor
Circulation: 60
Published once a year

This low-budget, high school–based literary journal publishes poetry and fiction by children through to seasoned authors. Distributed to Quesnel District high school students. Encourages young writers, especially teenagers, to submit poetry. Experimental work welcome if it makes sense. "We like poetry with vivid images and clear themes." Stories to 1,000 words. No profanity or pornography. Submissions by e-mail only. Include author details. Contributors paid in copies.

Contemporary Verse 2: The Canadian Journal of Poetry and Critical Writing

100 Arthur Street, Suite 207, Winnipeg, MB R3B 1H3
Phone: (204) 949-1365   Fax: (204) 942-5754
E-mail: cv2@mb.sympatico.ca
Web site: www.contemporaryverse2.ca
Contact: Clarise Foster, managing editor
Circulation: 700
Published quarterly

Established 1975 by Dorothy Livesay, *CV2* is Canada's oldest and best read poetry quarterly. Publishes critical writing (including interviews, articles, essays, and regular features on poetry) and original verse. Brings together established and emerging writers in a discussion of poetry that will appeal to a wide variety of readers, both the seasoned reader and the student of poetry. Each issue features interviews with experienced poets about their work, including popular trends, work habits, form, styles, and the importance of poetry. Preferred length of submission is 4 to 6 poems. For critical writing, please query first. Submission guidelines available on web site. Pays $30/poem; $20 to $40 for reviews (600 to 1,000 words); $50 to $75 for interviews and articles; $40 to $75 for essays. Please send a short bio and an SASE with your submission.

The Dalhousie Review
6209 University Avenue, Dalhousie University, Halifax, NS
    B3H 1X1
Phone: (902) 494-2541 Fax: (902) 494-3561
E-mail: Dalhousie.Review@Dal.ca
Web site: www.dal.ca/~dalrev/
Contact: Robert Martin, editor
Circulation: 500
Published 3 times a year
    Welcomes submissions of poetry, short fiction, and articles up to 5,000 words in such fields as history, literature, political science, sociology, and philosophy. Prefers poetry of fewer than 40 lines. Contributors to this distinguished quarterly, first published in 1921, are given 10 off-prints and 2 complimentary copies of the issue. "Please enclose an SASE for return of your manuscript." See web site for further guidelines.

dANDelion
Department of English, University of Calgary, 2500 University
    Drive N.W., Calgary, AB T2N 2B3
Phone: (403) 220-4679 Fax: (403) 289-1123
E-mail: editors@dandelionmagazine.ca
Web site: www.dandelionmagazine.ca
Contact: Jordan Nail, managing editor
Circulation: 500
Published twice a year
    Publishes experimental prose and poetry, including visual and concrete poetry. "We look for innovative form and content." Fiction is 2,500 to 3,500 words; postcard stories are 250 words

maximum. Pays $50 for submissions and 1 copy of the issue. Guidelines available.

The Danforth Review

P.O. Box 72056, 1562 Danforth Avenue, Toronto, ON M4J 5C1
E-mail: editor@danforthreview.com
Web site: www.danforthreview.com
Contact: Michael Bryson, editor
Circulation: 20,000 hits/month
Published quarterly

A web-based literary magazine with a special focus on the Canadian small-press scene and a soft spot for short fiction. "We publish fiction and poetry, plus book reviews, interviews, and feature articles on Canadian book issues. *TDR* is an online magazine only. Please visit the web site before submitting." Stories from 1,000 to 5,000 words. Fees vary and are paid upon publication.

Descant

P.O. Box 314, Stn. P, Toronto, ON M5S 2S8
Phone: (416) 593-2557　Fax: (416) 593-9362
E-mail: info@descant.on.ca
Web site: www.descant.ca
Contact: Mark Laliberte, managing editor
Circulation: 1,200
Published quarterly

A literary journal publishing short fiction, poetry, essays, drama, interviews, photography, and art. Pays an honorarium of $100 to all contributors on publication. "Each manuscript submission receives a critical reading and must be approved by three members of our editorial board before acceptance. This process can take up to 12 months. Only unpublished material will be considered, and we request first publication rights." Guidelines available.

The Devil's Artisan (DA)

c/o The Porcupine's Quill, 68 Main Street, Erin, ON N0B 1T0
Phone: (519) 833-9158　Fax: (519) 833-9845
E-mail: pql@sentex.net
Web site: www.sentex.net/~pql
Contact: Elke Inkster, general manager

Circulation: 500
Published twice a year
The *devil's artisan* was a medieval term for a practitioner of the art and mystery of printing. "In publishing this journal, our desire is to maintain that early sense of curiosity about the craft of printing and bookmaking. We also present information on bibliographic and historic matters, and on communicative, sociological, and technical subjects related to printing. Each issue contains a hand-printed keepsake." Pays $100 per article upon publication.

Echolocation

7 King's College Circle, Department of English, University of
Toronto, Toronto, ON M5S 3K1
E-mail: adam.hammond@echolocation.ca
Web site: www.echolocation.ca
Contact: Adam Hammond, editor
Published twice a year
Seeks submissions of poetry, short fiction, creative non-fiction, and interviews with authors. Maximum length for short fiction and creative non-fiction is 4,000 words. Do not send more than 5 poems per submission. Pays $10/page. Guidelines on web site.

Environments: A Journal of Interdisciplinary Studies

Geography and Environmental Studies, Wilfrid Laurier
University, 75 University Avenue W., Waterloo, ON N2L 3C5
Phone: (519) 884-0710, ext. 2781   Fax: (519) 725-1342
E-mail: sslocomb@wlu.ca
Web site: www.fes.uwaterloo.ca/research/environments/
Contact: D. Scott Slocombe, editor
Published 3 times a year
A refereed journal for scholars and practitioners. Promotes greater understanding of environmental, economic, and social change through papers (4,500 to 5,500 words) that assess the implications of change and provide information for improved decision-making. Reviews of individual publications should be 500 to 800 words. Overviews of several books or publications focusing on a topic should not exceed 2,500 words. Oriented to academics, students, professionals, and concerned citizens. Cannot pay but welcomes submission inquiries. Guidelines available on web site.

Event: The Douglas College Review

Douglas College, P.O. Box 2503, New Westminster, BC V3L 5B2
Phone: (604) 527-5293 Fax: (604) 527-5095
E-mail: event@douglas.bc.ca
Web site: http://event.douglas.bc.ca
Contact: Billeh Nickerson, editor
Circulation: 1,000
Published 3 times a year
  Features poetry, fiction, creative non-fiction, and reviews of Canadian books. Submit up to 2 short stories of 5,000 words each or 3 to 8 poems. Pays $22/page on publication to a maximum of $500. Include a brief cover letter and an SASE with Canadian postage or an International Reply Coupon. Guidelines available on web site.

Exile

134 Eastbourne Avenue, Toronto, ON M5P 2G6
E-mail: exq@exilequarterly.com
Web site: www.exilequarterly.com
Contact: Chris Doda
Published quarterly
  Aims to publish the best of both established and new writers. Does not accept multiple submissions or e-mail submissions (send by post only). For fiction and drama, submit about 10 to 20 pages; for poetry, submit up to 15 poems.

existere quarterly

027 Vanier College, 4700 Keele Street, York University, Toronto, ON M3J 1P3
E-mail: existere@yorku.ca
Web site: www.yorku.ca/existere
  The literary and arts quarterly of York University. Submissions must be accompanied by a brief letter of introduction. All genres and forms are welcome, including short plays, reviews, critical essays, etc. Prose submissions of no longer than 3,500 words; a maximum of 2 pieces of short fiction; 5 postcard stories; 5 poems; and/or 6 graphics will be considered from one submitter at one time. Mail queries must be accompanied by an SASE. Unable to pay. Guidelines available on web site.

The Fiddlehead
Campus House, 11 Garland Court, University of New Brunswick,
P.O. Box 4400, Fredericton, NB E3B 5A3
Phone: (506) 453-3501   Fax: (506) 453-5069
E-mail: fiddlehd@unb.ca
Web site: www.lib.unb.ca/texts/fiddlehead
Contact: Kathryn Taglia, managing editor
Circulation: 1,000
Published quarterly
A highly respected literary journal, established in 1945, publishing poetry, short fiction, and some book reviews. Focuses on freshness and vitality. While retaining an interest in writers of Atlantic Canada, it is open to outstanding work from all over the English-speaking world. Stories from 50 to 3,000 words, poetry up to 10 poems. Pays $20/published page on publication. "Find yourself an issue and read it to get an idea of what we're about. Do not fax or e-mail submissions, and include an SASE for replies." Guidelines available.

filling Station
P.O. Box 22135, Bankers Hall, Calgary, AB T2P 4J5
Phone: (403) 294-7492
E-mail: editor@fillingstation.ca
Web site: www.fillingstation.ca
Contact: Derek Beaulieu, managing editor
Published 3 times a year
Publishes poetry, fiction, one-act plays, essays, short film/video treatments, and scripts. Preferred length for prose 1,000 to 2,500 words. Submission deadlines March 15, July 15, and November 15. Pays with a 1-year subscription for accepted submissions. Guidelines available on web site.

Geist Magazine
341 Water Street, Suite 202, Vancouver, BC V6B 1B8
Phone: (604) 681-9161   Fax: (604) 669-8250
E-mail: geist@geist.com
Web site: www.geist.com
Contact: Mary Schendlinger, senior editor
Circulation: 9,000
Published quarterly

"Each issue of *Geist* is a meditation on the imaginary country we inhabit. Often that imaginary country has something to do with some part of Canada." Preferred length for creative non-fiction 200 to 1,000 words; for essays and short stories 2,000 to 5,000 words. Rates vary depending on project and are paid on publication. "We only accept submissions by snail mail. Please see our web site for guidelines and read the magazine."

Grain

P.O. Box 67, Saskatoon, SK S7K 3K1
Phone: (306) 244-2828 Fax: (306) 244-0255
E-mail: grain.mag@sasktel.net
Web site: www.grainmagazine.ca
Contact: Kent Bruyneel, editor
Circulation: 1,600
Published quarterly
A literary journal of national and international scope published by the Saskatchewan Writers Guild since 1973. Prints previously unpublished work by emerging and established writers that is fresh, startling, and imaginative. The work represents a range of mainstream poetry, prose, and occasionally creative non-fiction from writers in Canada and the world. Pays $50 to $225 on publication for fiction and poetry. Read back issues before submitting. Guidelines available.

International Journal

205 Richmond Street, Suite 302, Toronto, ON M5V 1V3
Phone: (416) 977-9000 or 1-800-668-2442 Fax: (416) 977-7521
E-mail: ij@ciia.org
Web site: www.ciia.org
Contact: Rima Berns-McGown, managing editor
Published quarterly
Established 1946. Recognized as Canada's preeminent scholarly publication on international relations. Writers are a mixture of scholars, practitioners, and policy-makers, Canadian and non-Canadian. Each issue has a specific theme. Length must not exceed 7,000 words. Articles assessed by at least 2 reviewers. Cannot pay contributors but welcomes submissions. Guidelines available on web site.

Journal of the Association for Research on Mothering

York University, 4700 Keele Street, 726 Atkinson, Toronto, ON
M3J 1P3
Phone: (416) 736-2100, ext. 60366   Fax: (416) 736-5766
E-mail: arm@yorku.ca
Web site: www.yorku.ca/crm
Contact: Renée Knapp, marketing and editorial co-ordinator
Circulation: 2,500
Published twice a year
Written for scholars, researchers, artists, activists, and feminist
mothers. Maximum length of articles 3,750 words. Cannot pay but
welcomes submission inquiries. Guidelines available.

Journal of Bahá'í Studies

34 Copernicus Street, Ottawa, ON K1N 7K4
Phone: (613) 233-1903   Fax: (613) 233-3644
E-mail: abs-na@bahai-studies.ca
Web site: www.bahai-studies.ca
Contact: Nilufar Gordon, administrative assistant
Circulation: 2,000
Published twice a year
Founded in 1975. The journal of the Association for Bahá'í
Studies aims to promote courses of study on the Bahá'í faith, to
foster relationships with various leaders of thought and persons of
capacity, to publish scholarly materials examining the Bahá'í faith,
especially on the application to the concerns and needs of human-
ity, and to demonstrate the value of this scholarly approach in rein-
forcing the endeavours of the Bahá'í community to reach the
diverse strata of society. Cannot pay but welcomes submissions.
Guidelines available.

lichen literary Journal

701 Rossland Road E., Suite 234, Whitby, ON L1N 9K3
E-mail: fiction@lichenjournal.ca or poetry@lichenjournal.ca
Web site: www.lichenjournal.ca
Contact: editorial board
Circulation: 400
Published twice a year

Publishes fiction, poetry, plays, essays, reviews, and black-and-white art and photography by local, Canadian, and international writers and artists. Presents a unique mix of city and country, of innovation and tradition. Stories 250 to 3,000 words. Contributors receive a copy of the issue and a 1-year subscription; sometimes an honorarium will also be paid. "Send us something more than unfocused anger, gratuitous sex, or chatty confession. If you can write beyond your own skin with a memorable voice, play freely with elements of the craft, and take risks, you have our attention." Guidelines available.

The Literary Review of Canada

581 Markham Street, Toronto, ON M6G 2L7
Phone: (416) 531-1483 Fax: (416) 531-1612
E-mail: editor@lrcreview.com
Web site: www.reviewcanada.ca
Contact: Bronwyn Drainie, editor-in-chief
Circulation: 5,000
Published 10 times a year
A tabloid in the style of *The New York Review of Books*, carrying substantive book reviews of Canadian non-fiction and fiction, although it also publishes poetry, occasional essays, and excerpts. Provides a forum for intellectual curiosity, critical thinking, and the vigorous examination of ideas. Intriguing, incisively written, and informative, it attracts a highly educated readership. Reviews are 2,000 to 3,500 words. Prefers e-mailed proposals and outlines over those faxed or mailed, but they are also acceptable. Accepts poetry submissions by e-mail from May 1 to October 1 each year. Payment is negotiable.

The Malahat Review

University of Victoria, P.O. Box 1700, Stn. CSC, Victoria, BC
    V8W 2Y2
Phone: (250) 721-8524 Fax: (250) 472-5051
E-mail: malahat@uvic.ca
Web site: www.malahatreview.ca
Contact: John Barton, editor
Circulation: 1,100
Published quarterly

Publishes Canadian and international poetry and short fiction, as well as reviews of Canadian literary titles. Submit 6 to 10 poems and stories of 2,000 to 6,000 words. Pays $30/page on acceptance. "Response time for poetry is 1–3 months; fiction 3–10 months. Submissions must be accompanied by an SASE with sufficient postage or an IRCS." Guidelines available.

Matrix Magazine

1400 de Maisonneuve W., Suite LB-502, Montreal, QC H3G 1M8
E-mail: matrix@alcor.concordia.ca
Web site: http://alcor.concordia.ca/~matrix
Contact: R. E. N. Allen, editor
Published quarterly
Publishes art, essays, fiction, poetry, and photography. Looking for book reviews (250 to 350 words), especially of titles published by small presses, and short articles – opinion, point of view, and essays on art and photography. Pays $25 to $40/poem or page of prose; $15/book review.

Mosaic, A Journal for the Interdisciplinary Study of Literature

208 Tier Building, University of Manitoba, Winnipeg, MB R3T 2N2
Phone: (204) 474-9763 Fax: (204) 474-7584
E-mail: mosaic_journal@umanitoba.ca
Web site: www.umanitoba.ca/mosaic
Contact: Jackie Pantel, business manager
Circulation: 900
Published quarterly
Explores the interaction between literary study and research in other disciplines. The journal features well-established scholars, as well as emerging researchers, all of whom contribute lively discussions about literature and literary issues from all periods and genres. Invites provocative, interdisciplinary submissions (7,000 to 7,500 words) that identify and engage key issues in a variety of areas, including memory, the archive, reconsidering the documentary, post-colonial literatures, the idea of community, travel writing, the interrelations of literature and film, cryptographic imagination, architecture and text, the poetics of space, and the literary

signature. Contributors are unpaid. Submission inquiries welcome. Guidelines available.

The Nashwaak Review

51 Deneen Drive, Fredericton, NB E3B 5G3
Phone: (506) 452-0614 Fax: (506) 452-9615
E-mail: tnr@stu.ca
Contacts: Margie Reed, managing editor; Stewart Donovan, editor
Circulation: 700
Published twice a year
A non-profit magazine for new and established artists. Funded solely by St. Thomas University. Stories 500 to 2,000 words. Cannot pay but welcomes submission inquiries. "We give free copies to contributors."

The New Quarterly: Canadian Writers & Writing

c/o St. Jerome's University, 290 University Avenue N., Waterloo, ON N2L 3G3
Phone: (519) 884-8111, ext. 28290 Fax: (519) 884-5759, attn: New Quarterly
E-mail: editor@tnq.ca
Web site: www.tnq.ca
Contact: Kim Jernigan, editor
Circulation: 1,000
Publishes short and long fiction, poetry, and essays on writing, with a focus on "new directions in Canadian writing." Prose can be anything from postcard fiction to novellas. "Reading us is the best way to get our measure. We don't have preconceived ideas about what we're looking for other than it must be by Canadian authors. We want something that is fresh, something that will repay a second reading, something in which the language soars." Pays $200 for fiction, $200 for essays, $30 for postcard fiction, and $30/poem, on publication. Tries to publish at least 1 or 2 new writers in each issue. "We are a volunteer-run magazine so writers must anticipate long waits on manuscripts – 3 to 6 months is typical. We do not publish reviews." Guidelines available.

Newfoundland & Labrador Studies
Faculty of Arts Publications, Memorial University, St. John's, NL
A1C 5S7
Phone: (709) 737-3453
E-mail: uls@mun.ca
Web site: www.mun.ca/nls
Contact: Irene Whitfield, managing editor
Circulation: 350
Published twice a year
A refereed academic journal containing articles, reviews, and documents. Published in English and French. Articles 12,000 words. Cannot pay but welcomes submission inquiries. Guidelines available.

Ontario History
34 Parkview Avenue, Willowdale, ON M2N 3Y2
Phone: (416) 226-9011   Fax: (416) 226-2740
E-mail: ohs@ontariohistoricalsociety.ca
Web site: www.ontariohistoricalsociety.ca
Contact: Thorold Tronrud, editor
Published twice a year
Specializes in the history of Ontario in any period: Native to newcomer to new millennium. Articles are scholarly yet accessible to all intelligent readers. Articles should be based on original research and be from 4,500 to 8,500 words. Cannot pay but welcomes submission inquiries. Guidelines on web site.

Optimum Online
263 Holmwood Avenue, Ottawa, ON K1S 2P8
Phone: (613) 688-0763   Fax: (613) 688-0767
E-mail: mcegalbreath@summitconnects.com
Web site: www.optimumonline.ca
Contact: McEvoy Galbreath, managing editor
Circulation: 10,000
Published quarterly
Optimum is an online, peer-reviewed journal on Canadian public sector management issues. Its readership are public servants and academics from around the world. Articles from 2,500 to 3,500

words. Cannot pay but welcomes submission inquiries. Guidelines available on web site.

Other Voices
P.O. Box 52059, 8210 – 109 Street, Edmonton, AB T6G 2T5
E-mail: info@othervoices.ca
Web site: www.othervoices.ca
Published twice a year
   A small literary journal seeking fiction, poetry, creative non-fiction, reviews, photographs, and artwork. Limit submissions to 5 poems or 4,000 words of prose. Please query on reviews. Payment for stories is a 1-year subscription. Welcomes established and new writers. Guidelines available.

Pacific Affairs
1855 West Mall, Suite 164, University of British Columbia,
   Vancouver, BC V6T 1Z2
Phone: (604) 822-6508, ext. 4534 Fax: (604) 822-9452
E-mail: enquiry@pacificaffairs.ubc.ca
Web site: www.pacificaffairs.ubc.ca
Contacts: Jacqueline Garnett, managing editor; Timothy Cheek,
   editor
Circulation: 1,600
Published quarterly
   A source of scholarly insight into the current social, cultural, political, and economic issues of Asia and the Pacific region, directed toward universities, institutions, governments, embassies, consulates, and increasingly, the business sector. Peer-reviewed articles and review articles are contributed by authors from around the world. Reviews about 50 books each issue (do not send unsolicited book reviews). Preferred length of articles is 6,000 words. Contributors are not paid. Academic referenced articles are welcome. Guidelines available on web site.

paperplates
19 Kenwood Avenue, Toronto, ON M6C 2R8
Phone: (416) 651-2551 Fax: (416) 651-2910
E-mail: magazine@paperplates.org
Web site: www.paperplates.org

Contact: Bernard Kelly, publisher/editor
Circulation: 2,000
Published quarterly
    An online publication that publishes poetry, fiction, plays, travel pieces, essays, interviews, and memoirs. Average length for "Homeplate" section is 2,500 words; prose averages 7,500 words; reviews are about 2,500 words. Cannot pay but welcomes submission inquiries. Guidelines available.

Prairie Fire
100 Arthur Street, Suite 423, Winnipeg, MB R3B 1H3
Phone: (204) 943-9066 Fax: (204) 942-1555
E-mail: prfire@mts.net
Web site: www.prairiefire.ca
Contact: Andris Taskans, editor
Circulation: 1,500
Published quarterly
    Publishes poetry, fiction, creative non-fiction, interviews, reviews, and occasionally literary criticism. Submissions may be from 200 to 5,000 words. Pays on publication: for fiction/poetry, $50 for first page, $45 for each additional page (maximum $500); for essays/articles/editorials, $45 for first page, $40 for each additional page (maximum $250); for interviews/profiles, $35 for first page, $30 for each additional page (maximum $200); and for reviews, 5¢/word. Guidelines and full payment schedule available. All submissions must be accompanied by an SASE.

Prairie Forum
Canadian Plains Research Centre, University of Regina, Regina, SK
    S4S 0A2
Phone: (306) 585-4758 Fax: (306) 585-4699
E-mail: brian.mlazgar@uregina.ca
Web site: www.cprc.uregina.ca
Contact: Patrick Douaud, editor
Circulation: 300
Published twice a year
    An interdisciplinary scholarly journal that publishes interdisciplinary scholarly research on the Canadian plains region. Market largely comprises university professors. Articles 3,500 to

10,000 words. Welcomes inquiries. No fees are paid. Guidelines available.

Prairie Journal

P.O. Box 61203, Brentwood P.O., Calgary, AB T2L 2K6
E-mail: prairiejournal@yahoo.com
Web site: www.geocities.com/prairiejournal
Contact: A. Burke, editor
Circulation: 600
Published twice a year

A literary journal featuring new and established Canadian writers of reviews, interviews, and creative and critical writing. Articles from 1,000 to 2,000 words. Any payment depends on grant. Query with samples before submitting reviews. No e-mail submissions accepted. "We acquire first North American rights only." Guidelines available on web site. "We also publish online (poems only). We welcome freelance submissions."

PRISM international

Creative Writing Program, University of British Columbia, 1866 Main Mall, Buch E462, Vancouver, BC V6T 1Z1
Phone: (604) 822-2514 Fax: (604) 822-3616
E-mail: prism@interchange.ubc.ca
Web site: www.prism.arts.ubc.ca
Contacts: Ben Hart, fiction editor; Bren Simmers, poetry editor
Published quarterly

Features innovative new fiction, poetry, drama, literary non-fiction, and translation from Canada and around the world. The oldest literary journal in Western Canada. Maximum submission length is 25 pages, double spaced; 1 piece of fiction, non-fiction, and drama; and a maximum of 5 poems. Pays on publication $40/published page for poetry, $20/published page for prose, plus a 1-year subscription. No multiple submissions. "We are looking for innovative, striking work in all areas. Show us originality of thought and close attention to language. No genre fiction, please." Guidelines available.

Public
358 Stong College, York University, 4700 Keele Street, Toronto, ON M3J 1P3
Phone: (416) 736-2100, ext. 70665
E-mail: public@yorku.ca
Web site: www.publicjournal.ca
Contact: Ari Berger, managing editor
Circulation: 700
Published twice a year
    An interdisciplinary journal combining scholarly and critical writing in cultural studies, focusing on the visual arts, performance, and literature. Dedicated to providing a forum in which artists, critics, and theorists exchange ideas on topics previously segregated by ideological boundaries of discipline. Articles 1,000 to 4,500 words. Has limited funds to pay for contributions but can pay up to $200 on publication. "Each issue is thematic. Please check web site for upcoming issues or e-mail *Public* before sending submission." Guidelines available.

Queen's Quarterly
Queen's University, 144 Barrie Street, Kingston, ON K7L 3N6
Phone: (613) 533-2667   Fax: (613) 533-6822
E-mail: qquarter@post.queensu.ca
Web site: www.queensu.ca/quarterly
Contact: Boris Castel, editor
Circulation: 3,000
    A distinctive and multidisciplinary university-based review with a Canadian focus and an international outlook. First published in 1893. Features scholarly articles (2,000 to 2,500 words) of general interest on politics, history, science, the humanities, and arts and letters, plus regular music and science columns, original poetry, fiction, and extensive book reviews. Fees, which are paid on publication, are negotiated. Guidelines available.

Resources for Feminist Research
OISE/UT, 252 Bloor Street W., Toronto, ON M5S 1V6
Phone: (416) 923-6641   Fax: (416) 926-4725
E-mail: rfrdrf@oise.utoronto.ca
Web site: www.oise.utoronto.ca/rfr

Contact: Philinda Masters, editor
Circulation: 2,000
Published quarterly

A journal of feminist scholarship containing research articles, abstracts, book reviews, and bibliographies. "*RFR* is an academic journal, so we accept research articles within a feminist perspective." Preferred length 7,000 to 10,000 words. Cannot pay but welcomes submissions. Guidelines are outlined on inside back cover of journal.

Rhubarb

100 Arthur Street, Suite 606, Winnipeg, MB R3B 1B3
Phone: (204) 956-0500
E-mail: rhubarb@mts.net
Circulation: 1,000
Published quarterly

Publishes new art and writing by people of Mennonite heritage for a general reading public. Poetry up to 30 lines; creative non-fiction and short fiction up to 2,500 words. Pays a small fee on publication.

RicePaper

P.O. Box 74174, Hillcrest RPO, Vancouver, BC V5V 5C8
Phone: (604) 677-1383   Fax: (604) 677-2147
E-mail: editor@ricepaperonline.com
Web site: www.ricepaperonline.com
Contact: Jessica Gin-Jade
Circulation: 2,000
Published quarterly

Focuses on Asian-Canadian art and culture. Publishes reviews, previews, interviews, profiles, essays, short fiction, poetry, visual artwork, scripts, and features on visual arts, music, dance, poetry, theatre, and culture. Notable missives (non-fiction narrative) are 200 to 1,500 words; work in progress is 400 to 3,500 words; excerpts from short stories, novels, poetry, and non-fiction are 300 to 1,500 words; long features and stories are 2,500 to 5,000 words. Pays an honorarium along with an issue of the magazine. Welcomes submission inquiries; query first.

Room of One's Own

P.O. Box 46160, Stn. D, Vancouver, BC V6J 5G5
E-mail: contactus@roommagazine.com
Web site: www.roommagazine.com
Contact: editorial collective
Published quarterly

Solicits fine writing and editing from women authors in Canada and other countries, both well-known and unknown. Features original poetry, fiction, reviews, artwork, and occasionally, creative non-fiction. Submit 4 to 5 poems at a time rather than a single poem. Stories 2,000 to 5,000 words. Pays a small honorarium on publication, plus 2 copies of the issue and a 1-year subscription. Guidelines are available on web site, but reading recent back issues will provide the best guidance.

Scrivener Creative Review

853 Sherbrooke Street W., Montreal, QC H3A 2T6
Phone: (514) 398-6588
E-mail. info@scrivenerreview.com
Web site: www.scrivenerreview.com
Contact: Lisa Guimond, co-ordinating editor
Circulation: 300
Published twice a year

Publishes poetry, fiction, and photography from new and established talent in Canada and abroad. Stories 200 to 9,000 words. Cannot pay but welcomes submissions of art, photography, poetry, and prose. Guidelines available.

Studies in Canadian Literature/Études en littérature canadienne

University of New Brunswick, English Department, P.O. Box
    4400, Fredericton, NB E3B 5A3
Phone: (506) 453-3501 Fax: (506) 453-5069
E-mail: scl@unb.ca
Web site: www.lib.unb.ca/Texts/Scl
Contact: Kathryn Taglia, managing ditor
Circulation: 450
Published twice a year

A bilingual, refereed journal of Canadian literary criticism of Canadian literature. Carries essays and author interviews of 6,000 to 8,000 words. Contributors receive a complimentary 1-year subscription. The market is scholarly libraries and professors of Canadian literature. Guidelines in journal. Use *MLA Handbook* for style. Papers are blind-vetted by 2 members of an advisory board, so author's name should be separate. Electronic submissions only.

sub-TERRAIN Magazine

P.O. Box 3008, MPO, Vancouver, BC V6B 3X5
Phone: (604) 876-8710 Fax: (604) 879-2667
E-mail: subter@portal.ca
Web site: www.subterrain.ca
Published 3 times a year

Publishes first-time and established writers from across North America. Interested in progressive writing – fiction, commentary, and poetry. No unsolicited poetry. Preferred length for fiction is a maximum of 3,000 words (2,000 is better); commentary and creative non-fiction should be 4,000 words maximum. Pays on publication $25/page for prose, $25/poem. Issues are theme-driven, so identify the theme issue for which you are writing (see the web site).

Taddle Creek

P.O. Box 611, Stn. P, Toronto, ON M5S 2Y4
Phone: (416) 324-9075
E-mail: editor@taddlecreekmag.com
Web site: www.taddlecreekmag.com
Contact: Conan Tobias, publisher/editor-in-chief
Circulation: 1,000
Published twice a year

Publishes urban fiction and poetry by Toronto authors. Only submissions of fiction and poetry are accepted; no preferred length. Authors must currently be residing in Toronto. Pays $25/page on publication. Guidelines available on web site. "Authors should not submit before reading guidelines."

Urban History Review

Becker Associates, P.O. Box 507, Stn. Q, Toronto, ON M4T 2M5

Phone: (416) 483-7282 Fax: (416) 489-1713
E-mail: editorial@urbanhistoryreview.ca
Web site: www.urbanhistoryreview.ca
Contact: Adam Becker, managing editor
Published twice a year

A bilingual interdisciplinary and refereed journal presenting lively articles covering such topics as architecture, heritage, urbanization, housing, and planning, all in a generously illustrated format. Regular features include in-depth articles, research notes, two annual bibliographies covering Canadian and international publications, comprehensive book reviews, and notes and comments on conferences, urban policy, and publications. Shorter papers should be from 1,000 to 3,000 words; articles should be 6,000 to 10,000 words. Contributors are unpaid.

West Coast Line

2027 East Annex, 8888 University Drive, Simon Fraser
   University, Burnaby, BC V5A 1S6
Phone: (604) 291-4287 Fax: (604) 291-4622
E-mail: wcl@sfu.ca
Web site: www.westcoastline.ca
Published 3 times a year

Publishes work by contemporary writers and artists who are experimenting with or expanding the boundaries of conventional forms and contexts. Interested in work that is engaged with problems of representation, race, culture, gender, sexuality, technology, media, urban/rural spaces, nature, and language. "We advise those considering submitting work to first familiarize themselves with the journal and with the work of our recent contributors." Fiction up to 5,000 words; poetry up to 400 lines. Pays $10/page to maximum of $200 after publication. Query first. Annual reading period is from June 1 to August 31. Guidelines available.

Windsor Review

Department of English Language, Literature, and Creative
   Writing, University of Windsor, Windsor, ON N9B 3P4
Phone: (519) 253-3000, ext. 2290 Fax: (519) 971-3676
E-mail: uwrevu@uwindsor.ca

Web site: www.windsorreview.com

Contacts: Alistair MacLeod, fiction editor; Susan Holbrook,
   poetry editor

Published twice a year

Published by the University of Windsor's Faculty of Arts and
Social Sciences. Features poetry, short fiction, and art. Fiction from
1,000 to 5,000 words. Contributors receive a small payment and
complimentary copies of the issue containing their work.

3

TRADE, BUSINESS, FARM, & PROFESSIONAL PUBLICATIONS

Trade publications are a potentially lucrative sector of the writer's market that is often overlooked. Although most pay no more than $500 for a full-length article, and usually less, the writing may require considerably fewer sources than are needed for consumer magazine features. An article can often be completed in a day or two, sometimes after research and interviews conducted solely by telephone. In terms of hours spent, therefore, the pay is generally relatively good. What's more, trade editors are often keen to find competent new writers.

The secret to making money from these publications is to work frequently for as many as possible, always bearing in mind that they may want a degree of technical detail that will inform readers already well acquainted with the specific fields they serve. If you have an area of specialist knowledge, you have a significant advantage. If not, you would do well to familiarize yourself with at least one trade or business area and the publications that serve it. Most trade periodicals, however, deliberately avoid becoming too technical, and aim to appeal to a wider readership. It bears repeating that before submitting, you must familiarize yourself with the magazine thoroughly by reading back issues.

Magazines in each of the following categories carry pieces about new products and developments, unusual marketing and promotion ideas, innovative management techniques, and prominent people and events specific to the industry, trade, or profession they serve. The regional business journals are highly recommended for freelance writers with business knowledge, since they often pay top dollar for timely and well-informed contributions. Those writers who have found markets through the main business section in Chapter 1 may profitably pursue this specialty further in the business listing below.

In many cases, staff writers produce the bulk of the feature writing and call on outside experts to provide specific material. But editors will often utilize freelancers when there is an editorial shortfall. Some cultivate long-term relationships with regular freelancers, who produce much of their copy. Often one editor is involved in several magazines, so making yourself and your work known to him or her can lead to further commissions, especially if you show yourself to be reliable and adaptable.

This chapter offers a broadly representative selection of trade publications across a wide range of industrial and professional areas, including many well-established, dependable employment sources, and provides a solid resource for the freelance writer looking to break into a new market. However, this is perhaps the most fluid sector in publishing: periodicals come and go and reappear under a new masthead; editors move from job to job relatively often in response to industry and structural changes. Chapter 11, Resources, lists some of the larger publishers of trade magazines in Canada, who can be contacted for a list of their publications.

For a monthly updated reference source, consult Rogers's *CARD* directory or refer to *Matthews Media Directory*, published four times a year, at your library. Check *CARD*, too, or the annual supplement *Publication Profiles* for upcoming editorial themes, media profiles, circulation figures, and other useful information.

Advertising, Marketing, & Sales

Blitz Magazine
1489 Marine Drive, Suite 544, West Vancouver, BC V7T 1B8
Phone: (604) 921-8735 or 1-866-632-5489 Fax: (604) 921-8738
E-mail: blitzmag@smartt.com
Contact: Louise Aird, publisher/editor-in-chief
Published bimonthly

Canadian Retailer
1255 Bay Street, Suite 800, Toronto, ON M5R 2A9
Phone: (416) 922-6678 Fax: (416) 922-8011
E-mail: general@dvtail.com
Contact: Theresa Rogers, editor-in-chief
Published bimonthly

Direct Marketing News
137 Main Street N., Suite 302, Markham, ON L3P 1Y2
Phone: (905) 201-6600 Fax: (416) 201-6601
Contact: Ron Glen, editor
Published monthly

Government Purchasing Guide
15 Wertheim Court, Suite 710, Richmond Hill, ON L4B 3H7
Phone: (905) 771-7333 Fax: (905) 771-7336
Contact: Blair Adams, editorial director
Published bimonthly

Marketing
1 Mount Pleasant Road, 7th Floor, Toronto, ON M4Y 2Y5
Phone: (416) 764-1570
Contact: Stan Sutter, associate publisher/editorial director
E-mail: stan.sutter@marketingmag.rogers.com
Published 41 times a year

Marketnews
701 Evans Avenue, Suite 102, Toronto, ON M9C 1A3
Phone: (416) 667-9945 Fax: (416) 667-0609
E-mail: mail@hereshow.ca
Contact: Robert Franner, editor
Published monthly

Pool & Spa Marketing
270 Esna Park Drive, Unit 12, Markham, ON L3R 1H3
Phone: (905) 513-0090 or 1-800-268-5503 Fax: (905) 513-1377
E-mail: david@poolspamarketing.com
Contact: David Barnsley, editor
Published 7 times a year

Sales Promotion
240 Edward Street, Aurora, ON L4G 3S9
Phone: (905) 727-0077 Fax: (905) 727-0017
E-mail: nmallett@clbmedia.ca
Contact: Nathan Mallett, editor
Published bimonthly

Strategy
366 Adelaide Street W., Suite 500, Toronto, ON M5V 1R9
Phone: (416) 408-2300 Fax: (416) 408-0870
E-mail: maddever@brunico.com
Contact: Mary Maddever, editorial director
Published monthly

Architecture, Building, Engineering, & Heavy Construction

Aggregates & Roadbuilding Magazine
4999 St. Catherine Street W., Suite 315, Montreal, QC H3Z 1T3
Phone: (514) 487-9868 Fax: (514) 487-9276
E-mail: rconsedine@rocktoroad.com
Contact: Robert L. Consedine, publisher/editor
Published bimonthly

Alberta Construction Magazine
5735 7th Street N.E., Suite 300, Calgary, AB T2E 8V3
Phone: (403) 265-3700 or 1-888-563-2946 Fax: (403) 265-3706
E-mail: dstonehouse@junewarren.com
Contact: Darrell Stonehouse, managing editor
Published bimonthly

Atlantic Construction & Transportation Journal
1888 Brunswick Street, Suite 609, Halifax, NS B3B 3J8
Phone: (902) 468-8027 Fax: (902) 468-2425
E-mail: kpartridge@hfxnews.ca
Contact: Ken Partridge, editor
Published quarterly

Award Magazine
4180 Lougheed Highway, 4th Floor, Burnaby, BC V5C 6A7
Phone: (604) 299-7311 Fax: (604) 299-9188
E-mail: wiseman@canadawide.com
Contact: Les Wiseman, editor
Published bimonthly

Building & Construction Trades Today
P.O. Box 186, 27 St. Clair Avenue E., Toronto, ON M4T 1L0
Phone: (416) 944-1217 Fax: (416) 944-0133
E-mail: hize@earthlink.net
Contact: Alan Heisey, publisher/editor
Published quarterly

Building Magazine
360 Dupont Street, Toronto, ON M5R 1V9
Phone: (416) 966-9944 Fax: (416) 966-9946
E-mail: albert@building.ca
Contact: Albert Warson, editor
Published bimonthly

Canadian Architect
12 Concorde Place, Suite 800, Toronto, ON M3C 4J2
Phone: (416) 442-5600 or 1-800-268-7742 Fax: (416) 510-5140
Contact: Ian Chodikoff, editor
Published monthly

Canadian Civil Engineer
4920 de Maisonneuve Boulevard W., Suite 201, Montreal, QC
    H3Z 1N1
Phone: (514) 933-2634 Fax: (514) 933-3504
E-mail: info@csce.ca
Contact: Louise Newman, editor
Published 5 times a year

Canadian Consulting Engineer
12 Concorde Place, Suite 800, Toronto, ON M3C 4J2
Phone: (416) 510-5111 Fax: (416) 510-5134
E-mail: bparsons@ccemag.com

Contact: Bronwen Parsons, editor
Published 7 times a year

Canadian Roofing Contractor
3 Kennett Drive, Whitby, ON L1P 1L5
Phone: (905) 430-7267 Fax: (905) 430-6418
Contact: Tanja Nowotny, editor
Published quarterly

Construction Alberta News
22 Rowland Crescent, Suite 50, St. Albert, AB T8N 5B3
Phone: (780) 460-8004 Fax: (780) 425-5886
E-mail: canews@telus.net
Contact: Grant Bush, editor
Published weekly

Construction Canada
15 Wertheim Court, Suite 710, Richmond Hill, ON L4B 3H7
Phone: (905) 771-7333 or 1-800-409-8688 Fax: (905) 771-7336
Contact: Blair Adams, editorial director
Published bimonthly

Contracting Canada
16987 Kelsey Court, Mississauga, ON L5L 3J8
Phone: (905) 569-2777 Fax: (905) 569-2444
E-mail: bonnie.toews@rogers.com
Contact: Bonnie Toews, managing editor
Published quarterly

Contractors Magazine
2323 Boundary Road, Suite 201, Vancouver, BC V5M 4V8
Phone: (604) 291-9900 Fax: (604) 291-1906
E-mail: kbarker@baumpub.com
Contact: Keith Barker, editor
Published bimonthly

Daily Commercial News
500 Hood Road, 4th Floor, Markham, ON L3R 9Z3
Phone: 1-800-465-6475 Fax: 1-800-570-5399

E-mail: patrick.mcconnell@reedbusiness.com
Contact: Patrick McConnell, national editor

Design Engineering
1 Mount Pleasant Road, 7th Floor, Toronto, ON M4Y 2Y5
Phone: (416) 764-1555 Fax: (416) 764-1686
E-mail: mike.mcleod@rci.rogers.com
Contact: Mike McLeod, editor
Published 9 times a year

Design Product News
240 Edward Street, Aurora, ON L4G 3S9
Phone: (905) 713-4389 Fax: (905) 727-0017
E-mail: medwards@clbmedia.ca
Contact: Michael Edwards, editor
Published bimonthly

Engineering Dimensions
25 Sheppard Avenue W., Suite 1000, Toronto, ON M2N 6S9
Phone: (416) 224-1100 or 1-800-339 3716 Fax: (416) 224-8168
Contact: Jennifer Coombes, managing editor
Published bimonthly

Equipment Journal
5160 Explorer Drive, Unit 6, Mississauga, ON L4W 4T7
Phone: (905) 629-7500 or 1-800-667-8541 Fax: (905) 629-7988
E-mail: office@equipmentjournal.com
Contact: Michael Anderson, editor
Published 17 times a year

Geomatica
1390 Prince of Wales Drive, Suite 400, Ottawa, ON K2C 3N6
Phone: (613) 224-9851 Fax: (613) 224-9577
E-mail: editgeo@magma.ca
Contact: Kelly Dean, editor
Published quarterly

Home Builder Magazine
4819 St. Charles Boulevard, Montreal, QC H9H 3C7
Phone: (514) 620-2200 Fax: (514) 620-6300
Contact: Nachmi Artzy, publisher
Published bimonthly

Home Improvement Retailing
245 Fairview Mall Drive, Suite 501, Toronto, ON M2J 4T1
Phone: (416) 494-1066 Fax: (416) 494-2536
E-mail: jhornyak@powershift.ca
Contact: Joe Hornyak, executive editor
Published bimonthly

Innovation
4010 Regent Street, Suite 200, Burnaby, BC V5C 6N2
Phone: (604) 929-6733 Fax: (604) 929-6753
Contact: Jennifer White, managing editor
Published bimonthly

Journal of Commerce
4299 Canada Way, Suite 101, Burnaby, BC V5G 1H3
Phone: (604) 433-8164 Fax: (604) 433-9549
Published twice a week

Ontario Home Builder
1074 Cooke Boulevard, Burlington, ON L7T 4A8
Phone: (905) 634-8003 Fax: (905) 634-7661
E-mail: steve@homesontario.com
Contact: Steve McNeil, editor
Published bimonthly

On-Site
1 Mount Pleasant Road, 7th Floor, Toronto, ON M4Y 2Y5
Phone: (416) 764-2000 Fax: (416) 764-3935
E-mail: jim.barnes@on-sitemag.rogers.com
Contact: Jim Barnes, editor
Published 7 times a year

The Pegg
10060 Jasper Avenue N.W., 1500 Scotia One, Edmonton, AB
T5J 4A2
Phone: (780) 426-3990 Fax: (780) 425-1722
E-mail: glee@apegga.org
Contact: George Lee, manager, editorial services
Published 10 times a year

Perspectives
P.O. Box 90510, 230 Markham Road, Scarborough, ON M1J 3N7
Phone: (416) 955-1550 Fax: (416) 955-1391
E-mail: info@capmagazines.ca
Contact: Gordon Grice, editor
Published quarterly

Toronto Construction News
500 Hood Road, 4th Floor, Markham, ON L3R 9Z3
Phone: 1-800-465-6475 Fax: (905) 752 5450
E-mail: patrick.mcconnell@reedbusiness.com
Contact: Patrick McConnell, national editor
Published 7 times a year

Woodworking
240 Edward Street, Aurora, ON L4G 3S9
Phone: (905) 727-0077 Fax: (905) 727-0017
E-mail: afreill@clbmedia.ca
Contact: Adam Freill, editor
Published 7 times a year

Yardstick
100 Sutherland Avenue, Winnipeg, MB R2W 3C7
Phone: (204) 975-0423 or 1-800-369-2456 Fax: 1-800-709-5551
E-mail: joneil@naylor.com
Contact: Jonah O'Neil, editor
Published bimonthly

Automotive (see also Transportation & Cargo)

Bodyshop
12 Concorde Place, Suite 800, Toronto, ON M3C 4J2
Phone: (416) 442-5600 or 1-800-268-7742 Fax: (416) 510-5140
E-mail: cmacdonald@businessinformationgroup.ca
Contact: Cindy MacDonald, editor
Published 8 times a year

Canadian Aftermarket Service Professional
2938 Terrasse Abenaquis, Suite 110, Longueuil, QC J4M 2B3
Phone: (450) 448-2220 Fax: (450) 448-1041
E-mail: remyrousseau@p-rousseau.com
Contact: Rémy L. Rousseau, publisher
Published 8 times a year

Canadian Auto World
447 Speers Road, Suite 4, Oakville, ON L6K 3S7
Phone: (905) 842-6591 Fax: (905) 842-4432
E-mail: crowe@wheels.ca
Contact: Philippe Crowe, managing editor
Published monthly

Canadian Automotive Fleet
447 Speers Road, Suite 4, Oakville, ON L6K 3S7
Phone: (416) 383-0302 Fax: (416) 383-0313
Contact: Fflon Llowyd-Jones, managing editor
Published bimonthly

Canadian Automotive Review
1 Mount Pleasant Road, 7th Floor, Toronto, ON M4Y 2Y5
Phone: (416) 764-1499 Fax: (416) 764-1740
E-mail: abrooks@rmpublishing.com
Contact: Andrew Brooks, editor
Published bimonthly

Car & Truck Digest
295 The West Mall, Suite 110, Toronto, ON M9C 4Z4
Phone: (416) 383-0302 Fax: (416) 383-0313
E-mail: digest@fleetbusiness.com
Contact: Ffion Llowyd-Jones, managing editor
Published quarterly

Collision Repair Magazine
86 John Street, Markham, ON L3T 1Y2
Phone: (905) 889-3544 Fax: (905) 889-4680
E-mail: collisionrepair@rogers.com
Contact: Darryl Simmons, publisher
Published bimonthly

4WD Magazine
1191 Hartman Road, Kelowna, BC V1P 1C1
Phone: (250) 765-8575 Fax: (250) 765-8585
E-mail: albert@can4x4.com
Contact: Albert Vandervelde, editor
Published 8 times a year

Jobber News
12 Concorde Place, Suite 800, Toronto, ON M3C 4J2
Phone: (416) 442-5600 or 1-800-268-7742 Fax: (416) 510-5140
E-mail: aross@jobbernews.com
Contact: Andrew Ross, publisher/editor
Published monthly

Octane
508 Lawrence Avenue W., Suite 201, Toronto, ON M6A 1A1
Phone: (416) 504-0504 Fax: (416) 256-3002
E-mail: jwiderman@fulcrum.ca
Contact: Jane Widerman, editor
Published quarterly

SSGM (Service Station & Garage Management)
12 Concorde Place, Suite 800, Toronto, ON M3C 4J2
Phone: (416) 442-5600 Fax: (416) 510-5140
E-mail: tvenetis@bizinfogroup.ca

Contact: Tom Venetis, editor
Published monthly

Taxi News
38 Fairmount Crescent, Toronto, ON M4L 2H4
Phone: (416) 466-2328 Fax: (416) 466-4220
E-mail: taxinews@the-wire.com
Contact: William McQuat, editor
Published monthly

Aviation & Aerospace

Airforce
P.O. Box 2460, Stn. D, Ottawa, ON K1P 5W6
Phone: (613) 232-6325 Fax: (613) 232-2156
E-mail: vjohnson@airforce.ca
Contact: Vic Johnson, editor
Published quarterly

Canadian Aviator
1080 Howe Street, Suite 900, Vancouver, BC V6Z 2T1
Phone: (604) 606-4644 Fax: (604) 687-1925
E-mail: myelic@oppublishing.com
Contact: Mark Yelic, publisher
Published bimonthly

Helicopters
P.O. Box 530, 105 Donly Drive S., Simcoe, ON N3Y 4N5
Phone: (519) 429-3966 or 1-888-599-2228 Fax: (519) 429-3094
E-mail: dmccarthy@annexweb.com
Contact: Drew McCarthy, editor
Published quarterly

ICAO Journal
999 University Street, Montreal, QC H3C 5H7
Phone: (514) 954-8222 Fax: (514) 954-6376
E-mail: emacburnie@icao.int

Contact: Eric MacBurnie, editor
Published bimonthly

Wings
P.O. Box 530, 105 Donly Drive S., Simcoe, ON N3Y 4N5
Phone: (519) 429-3966 or 1-888-599-2228 Fax: (519) 429-3094
E-mail: dmccarthy@annexweb.com
Contact: Drew McCarthy, editor
Published bimonthly

Business, Commerce, Banking, Law, Insurance, & Pensions

Alberta Venture
10350 – 124th Street, Suite 201, Edmonton, AB T5N 3V9
Phone: (780) 990-0839 Fax: (780) 425-4921
E-mail: rkelly@albertaventure.com
Contact: Ruth Kelly, publisher/editor-in-chief
Published 10 times a year

Benefits and Pensions Monitor
245 Fairview Mall Drive, Suite 501, Toronto, ON M2J 4T1
Phone: (416) 494-1066 Fax: (416) 494-2536
E-mail: jmclaine@powershift.ca
Contact: John L. McLaine, publisher/editorial director
Published 8 times a year

Benefits Canada
1 Mount Pleasant Road, 12th Floor, Toronto, ON M4Y 2Y5
Phone: (416) 764-3848 Fax: (416) 764-3938
E-mail: paulowilliams@rci.rogers.com
Contact: Paul O. Williams, publisher
Published monthly

Biz
1074 Cooke Boulevard, Burlington, ON L7T 4A8
Phone: (905) 634-8003 Fax: (905) 634-7661

E-mail: biz@townmedia.ca
Contact: Arend Kirsten, editor
Published quarterly

Biz X Magazine

P.O. Box 27035, 7720 Tecumseh Road E., Windsor, ON N8T 3N5
Phone: (519) 977-2199 Fax: (519) 979-4571
E-mail: deborah@bizxmagazine.com
Contact: Deborah Jones, publisher
Published 11 times a year

The Bottom Line

123 Commerce Valley Drive E., Suite 700, Markham, ON
    L3T 7W8
Phone: (905) 479-2665 or 1-800-668-6481 Fax: (905) 479-3758
E-mail: michael.lewis@lexisnexis.ca
Contact: Michael Lewis, editor
Published 16 times a year

Business Careers Canada

P.O. Box 90510, 230 Markham Road, Scarborough, ON M1J 3N7
Phone: (416) 955-1550 Fax: (416) 955-1391
E-mail: jeaton@capmagazines.ca
Contact: Jim Eaton, publisher
Published twice a year

Business Edge

525 – 11 Avenue S.W., Suite 500, Calgary, AB T2R 0C9
Phone: (866) 216-3343 Fax: (403) 264-4439
E-mail: inigo-jones@businessedge.ca
Contact: Terry Inigo-Jones, editor
Published biweekly

The Business Executive

466 Speers Road, Suite 220, Oakville, ON L6K 3W9
Phone: (905) 845-8300 Fax: (905) 845-9086
E-mail: wpeters@busexec.com
Contact: Wendy Peters, associate publisher/editor
Published monthly

Business in Calgary
101 – 6 Avenue S.W., Suite 1025, Calgary, AB T2P 3P4
Phone: (403) 264-3270 Fax: (403) 264-3276
E-mail: editorbic@shaw.ca
Contact: Camie Leard, editor
Published monthly

Business in Vancouver
1155 West Pender Street, Suite 500, Vancouver, BC V6E 2P4
Phone: (604) 688-2398 Fax: (604) 688-1963
Contact: Tim Renshaw, editor
Published weekly

Business Trends
1383 Confederation Street, Sarnia, ON N7S 5P1
Phone: (519) 336-1100 Fax: (519) 336-1833
E-mail: businesstrends@cogeco.net
Contact: Gord Bowes, editor
Published monthly

CA Magazine
277 Wellington Street W., Toronto, ON M5V 3H2
Phone: (416) 977-3222 Fax: (416) 977-8585
Contact: Louis D'Souza, associate publisher
Published 10 times a year

Canadian Insurance
111 Peter Street, Suite 500, Toronto, ON M5V 2H1
Phone: (416) 599-0772 Fax: (416) 599-0867
Contact: Barbara Aarsteinsen, editor
Published monthly

Canadian Investment Review
1 Mount Pleasant Road, 12th Floor, Toronto, ON M4Y 2Y5
Phone: (416) 301-5780 Fax: (416) 764-2864
E-mail: caroline.cakebread@rogers.com
Contact: Caroline Cakebread, editor
Published quarterly

The Canadian Manager
250 Consumers Road, Suite 301, Toronto, ON M2J 4V6
Phone: (416) 493-0155 or 1-800-387-5774 Fax: (416) 495-8723
E-mail: marketingandcommunications@cim.ca
Contact: Anna Victoria Wong, editor
Published quarterly

Canadian Underwriter
12 Concorde Place, Suite 800, Toronto, ON M3C 4J2
Phone: (416) 510-6781 or 1-800-268-7742 Fax: (416) 510-5140
E-mail: david@canadianunderwriter.com
Contact: David Gambrill, managing editor
Published monthly

Central Nova Business News
228 Main Street, Bible Hill, NS B2N 1H0
Phone: (902) 895-7948 Fax: (902) 893-1427
Contact: Jason Warren, editor-in-chief
Published monthly

CGA Magazine
1188 West Georgia Street, Suite 800, Vancouver, BC V6E 4A2
Phone: (604) 669-3555 Fax: (604) 689-5845
E-mail: cgamagazine@cga-canada.org
Contact: Peggy Homan, editor
Published bimonthly

Durham Business Times
138 Commercial Avenue, Ajax, ON L1S 2H5
Phone: (905) 426-4676 Fax: (905) 426-6598
E-mail: businesstimes@durhamregion.com
Contact: Joanne Burghardt, editor-in-chief
Published monthly

Edge
25 Sheppard Avenue W., Suite 100, Toronto, ON M2N 6S7
Phone: (416) 227-8312 or 1-800-387-5012 Fax: (416) 227-8324
Contact: Joe Tersigni, publisher
Published bimonthly

In Business Windsor
1775 Sprucewood, La Salle, ON N9J 1X7
Phone: (519) 250-2825 Fax: (519) 250-2881
E-mail: editor@inbusinesswindsor.com
Contact: Gary Baxter, publisher
Published monthly

Investment Executive
25 Sheppard Avenue W., Suite 100, Toronto, ON M2N 6S7
Phone: (416) 218-3588 Fax: (416) 218-3624
Contact: Tessa Wilmott, editor
Published 16 times a year

Investor's Digest of Canada
133 Richmond Street W., Suite 700, Toronto, ON M5II 3M0
Phone: (416) 869-1177 Fax: (416) 869-0456
Contact: Michael Popovich, editor
Published 24 times a year

Kootenay Business Magazine
100 – 7th Avenue S., Suite 100, Cranbrook, BC V1C 2J4
Phone: (250) 426-7253 or 1-800-663-8555 Fax: (250) 426-4125
E-mail: info@kpimedia.com
Contact: Jody Jacobs, editor
Published bimonthly

The Lawyers Weekly
1234 Commerce Valley Drive E., Suite 700, Markham, ON
   L3T 7W8
Phone: (905) 479-2665 or 1-800-668-6481 Fax: (905) 479-3758
Contact: Jean Cumming, managing editor
Published 48 times a year

Manitoba Business
294 Portage Avenue, Suite 508, Winnipeg, MB R3C 0B9
Phone: (204) 943-2931 Fax: (204) 943-2942
E-mail: rgage@mts.net
Contact: Ritchie Gage, publisher/editor
Published 10 times a year

Mississauga Business Times
3145 Wolfedale Road, Mississauga, ON L5C 3A9
Phone: (905) 273-8111 Fax: (905) 273-8118
E-mail: rdrennan@mississauga.net
Contact: Rick Drennan, editor
Published monthly

Montreal Business Magazine
204 St. Sacrement, Suite 201, Montreal, QC H2Y 1W8
Phone: (514) 286-8038 Fax: (514) 287-7346
E-mail: info@mbm-minc.com
Contact: Michael Carin, editor
Published quarterly

National
1 Mount Pleasant Road, 12th Floor, Toronto, ON M4Y 2Y5
Phone: (416) 764-3910 Fax: (416) 764-3933
Contact: Jordan Furlong, editor
Published 8 times a year

Northern Ontario Business
158 Elgin Street, Sudbury, ON P3E 3N5
Phone: (705) 673-5705 or 1-800-757-2766 Fax: (705) 673-9542
Contact: Craig Gilbert, managing editor
Published monthly

Northwest Business Magazine
3907 – 3A Street N.E., Bay 114, Calgary, AB T2E 6S7
Phone: (403) 250-1128 Fax: (403) 250-1194
Contact: Kathryn Engel, editor
Published 10 times a year

Okanagan Business Journal
2495 Enterprise Way, Kelowna, BC V1X 7K2
Phone: (250) 763-3212 or 1-800-787-3308 Fax: (250) 862-5275
E-mail: nlark@kelownacapnews.com
Contact: Nigel Lark, publisher
Published monthly

Ottawa Business Journal
5300 Canotek Road, Unit 30, Gloucester, ON K1J 8R7
Phone: (613) 744-4800 Fax: (613) 744-0866
Contact: Michael Curran, publisher
Published weekly

Sounding Board
999 Canada Place, Suite 400, Vancouver, BC V6C 3E1
Phone: (604) 681-2111 Fax: (604) 681-0437
E-mail: thadley@boardoftrade.com
Contact: Terry Hadley, editor
Published 10 times a year

Toronto Business Times
100 Tempo Avenue, Toronto, ON M2H 3S5
Phone: (416) 493-4400 Fax: (416) 493-4703
Contact: Deborah Bodine, editor-in-chief
Published monthly

Computers & Data Processing

CIO Canada
55 Town Centre Court, Suite 302, Toronto, ON M1P 4X4
Phone: (416) 290-0240 Fax: (416) 290-0238
E-mail: dccarey@itworldcanada.com
Contact: David Carey, editor
Published 11 times a year

Communications & Networking
25 Sheppard Avenue W., Suite 100, Toronto, ON M2N 6S7
Phone: (416) 733-7600 or 1-800-387-5012 Fax: (416) 227-8324
Contact: Joe Tersigni, publisher
Published monthly

Computer Dealer News
25 Sheppard Avenue W., Suite 100, Toronto, ON M2N 6S7
Phone: (416) 733-7600 or 1-800-387-5012 Fax: (416) 227-8324

Contact: Joe Tersigni, publisher
Published 18 times a year

Computerworld
55 Town Centre Court, Suite 302, Toronto, ON M1P 4X4
Phone: (416) 290-0240 Fax: (416) 290-0238
E-mail: genright@itworldcanada.com
Contact: Greg Enright, editor
Published 25 times a year

Computing Canada
25 Sheppard Avenue W., Suite 100, Toronto, ON M2N 6S7
Phone: (416) 733-7600 or 1-800-387-5012 Fax: (416) 227-8324
Contact: Joe Tersigni, publisher
Published 18 times a year

CRN Canada
1 Director Court, Suite 201, Woodbridge, ON L4L 4S5
Phone: (905) 851-8391 Fax: (905) 851-8482
E-mail: amckay@crncanada.ca
Contact: Andrew Mckay, editor
Published monthly

IT Focus
55 Town Centre Court, Suite 302, Toronto, ON M1P 4X4
Phone: (416) 290-0240 Fax: (416) 290-0238
E-mail: jpickett@itworldcanada.com
Contact: John Pickett, publisher
Published monthly

NetworkWorld Canada
55 Town Centre Court, Suite 302, Toronto, ON M1P 4X4
Phone: (416) 290-0240 Fax: (416) 290-0238
E-mail: mmartin@itworldcanada.com
Contact: Mike Martin, editor
Published 24 times a year

Technology in Government
25 Sheppard Avenue W., Suite 100, Toronto, ON M2N 6S7

Phone: (416) 733-7600 Fax: (416) 227-8324
E-mail: jtersigni@itbusiness.ca
Contact: Joe Tersigni, publisher
Published bimonthly

Education & School Management

Educational Digest
11966 Woodbine Avenue, Gormley, ON L0H 1G0
Phone: (905) 887-5048 Fax: (905) 887-0764
Contact: Janet Gardiner, publisher
Published quarterly

Professionally Speaking
121 Bloor Street E., 6th Floor, Toronto, ON M4W 3M5
Phone: (416) 961-8800 Fax: (416) 961-8822
Contact: Philip Carter, editor
Published quarterly

Quebec Home & School News
3285 Cavendish Boulevard, Suite 560, Montreal, QC H4B 2L9
Phone: (514) 481-5619 Fax: (514) 481-5610
Published quarterly

University Manager
2020 Portage Avenue, Suite 3C, Winnipeg, MB R3J 0K4
Phone: (204) 985-9780 Fax: (204) 985-9795
E-mail: kelman@videon.wave.ca
Contact: Craig Kelman, editor
Published quarterly

Electronics & Electrical

Canadian Electronics
240 Edward Street, Aurora, ON L4G 3S9
Phone: (905) 727-0077 Fax: (905) 727-0017
E-mail: tgouldson@clbmedia.ca

Contact: Tim Gouldson, editor
Published 7 times a year

Electrical Business
240 Edward Street, Aurora, ON L4G 3S9
Phone: (905) 727-0077 Fax: (905) 727-0017
E-mail: acapkun@clbmedia.ca
Contact: Anthony Capkun, editor
Published monthly

Electrical Line
3105 Benbow Road, West Vancouver, BC V7V 3E1
Phone: (604) 922-5516 Fax: (604) 922-5312
E-mail: kenb@electricalline.com
Contact: Ken Buhr, editor
Published bimonthly

Electricity Today
1885 Clements Road, Unit 215, Pickering, ON L1W 3V4
Phone: (905) 686-1040 Fax: (905) 686-1078
E-mail: hq@electricityforum.com
Contact: Don Home, editor
Published 9 times a year

EP & T (Electronic Products and Technology)
1200 Aerowood Drive, Unit 27, Mississauga, ON L4W 2S7
Phone: (905) 624-8100 Fax: (905) 624-1760
E-mail: info@ept.ca
Contact: Steven Law, editor
Published 8 times a year

Here's How
701 Evans Avenue, Suite 102, Toronto, ON M9C 1A3
Phone: (416) 667-9945 Fax: (416) 667-0609
E-mail: bgrierson@hereshow.ca
Contact: Bob Grierson, publisher
Published bimonthly

Energy, Mining, Forestry, Lumber, Pulp & Paper, & Fisheries

Atlantic Fisherman
130 Wright Avenue, Halifax, NS B3B 1R6
Phone: (902) 422-4990 Fax: (902) 422-4728
E-mail: ian@advocatemediainc.com
Contact: Ian Ross, editor
Published monthly

Canadian Forest Industries
90 Morgan Road, Unit 14, Baie d'Urfe, QC H9X 3A8
Phone: (514) 457-2211 Fax: (514) 457-2558
E-mail: sjamieson@forestcommunications.com
Contact: Scott Jamieson, editor
Published 8 times a year

Canadian Mining Journal
12 Concorde Place, Suite 800, Toronto, ON M3C 4J2
Phone: (416) 510-6891 Fax: (416) 510-5138
E-mail: jwerniuk@canadianminingjournal.com
Contact: M. Jane Werniuk, editor
Published 9 times a year

Canadian Wood Products
90 Morgan Road, Unit 14, Baie d'Urfe, QC H9X 3A8
Phone: (514) 457-2211 Fax: (514) 457-2558
E-mail: sjamieson@forestcommunications.com
Contact: Scott Jamieson, editor
Published 7 times a year

Energy Processing/Canada
900 – 6th Avenue S.W., Suite 500, Calgary, AB T2P 3K2
Phone: (403) 263-6881 or 1-800-526-4177 Fax: (403) 263-6886
E-mail: alister@northernstar.ab.ca
Contact: Alister Thomas, managing editor
Published bimonthly

The Fisherman
326 – 12th Street, 1st Floor, New Westminster, BC V3M 4H6
Phone: (604) 519-3638 Fax: (604) 524-6944
E-mail: fisherman@ufawu.org
Contact: Sean Griffin, editor
Published quarterly

The Forestry Chronicle
151 Slater Street, Suite 504, Ottawa, ON K1P 5H3
Phone: (613) 234-2242 Fax: (613) 234-6181
Contact: B. Haddon, editor
Published bimonthly

Hiballer Forest Magazine
P.O. Box 16052, Lynn Valley P.O., North Vancouver, BC V7J 2P0
Phone: (604) 984-2002 Fax: (604) 984-2820
E-mail: hiballer@shaw.ca
Contact: Paul Young, publisher/managing editor
Published bimonthly

Logging & Sawmilling Journal
P.O. Box 86670, 211 East 1st Street, North Vancouver, BC V7L 4L2
Phone: (604) 990-9970 or 1-866-405-6462 Fax: (604) 990-9971
Contact: Paul MacDonald, editor
Published 10 times a year

Mill Product News
2323 Boundary Road, Suite 203, Vancouver, BC V5M 4V8
Phone: (604) 298-3005 Fax: (604) 298-3966
E-mail: hbaum@bauminternational.com
Contact: Heri R. Baum, publisher
Published bimonthly

Northern Aquaculture
4623 William Head Road, Victoria, BC V9C 3Y7
Phone: (250) 478-3973 Fax: (250) 478-3979
E-mail: editor@northernaquaculture.com
Contact: Peter Chettleburgh, editor
Published monthly

Nickle's New Technology Magazine
999 – 8th Avenue S.W., Suite 300, Calgary, AB T2R 1N7
Phone: (403) 209-3500 Fax: (403) 245-8666
E-mail: msmith@nickles.com
Contact: Maurice Smith, editor
Published 8 times a year

The Northern Miner
12 Concorde Place, Suite 800, Toronto, ON M3C 4J2
Phone: (416) 510-6771 Fax: (416) 510-5138
E-mail: jcumming@northernminer.com
Contact: John Cumming, editor
Published weekly

Ocean Resources
162 Trider Crescent, Dartmouth, NS B3B 1R6
Phone: (902) 422-4990 Fax: (902) 422-4728
Contact: Joanne Elliott, editor
Published bimonthly

Oil & Gas Inquirer
6111 – 91st Street N.W., Edmonton, AB T6E 6V6
Phone: (780) 944-9333 Fax: (780) 944-9500
Contact: Darrell Stonehouse, managing editor
Published monthly

Oilweek
6111 – 91st Street N.W., Edmonton, AB T6E 6V6
Phone: (780) 944-9333 Fax: (780) 944-9500
Contact: Darrell Stonehouse, managing editor
Published monthly

Propane/Canada
900 – 6th Avenue S.W., Suite 500, Calgary, AB T2P 3K2
Phone: (403) 263-6881 or 1-800-526-4177 Fax: (403) 263-6886
E-mail: alister@northernstar.ab.ca
Contact: Alister Thomas, managing editor
Published bimonthly

Pulp & Paper Canada
1 Holiday Street, East Tower, Suite 705, Montreal, QC H9R 5N3
Phone: (514) 630-5955 or 1-800-363-1327 Fax: (514) 630-5980
Contact: Anya Orzechowska, managing editor
Published monthly

The Roughneck
900 – 6th Avenue S.W., Suite 500, Calgary, AB T2P 3K2
Phone: (403) 263-6881 Fax: (403) 263-6886
E-mail: alister@northernstar.ab.ca
Contact: Alister Thomas, managing editor
Published monthly

Truck Logger Magazine
4180 Lougheed Highway, 4th Floor, Burnaby, BC V5C 6A7
Phone: (604) 684-4291 Fax: (604) 684-7134
E-mail: trucklogger@canadawide.com
Contact: Sandra Bishop, editor
Published quarterly

Wood Industry
20 – 42nd Street, Markham, ON L3P 7K6
Phone: (416) 278-5250 Fax: (905) 477-5435
E-mail: kerry@woodindustry.ca
Contact: Kerry Knudsen, editor
Published bimonthly

Environmental Science & Management

Canadian Environmental Protection
2323 Boundary Road, Suite 201, Vancouver, BC V5M 4V8
Phone: (604) 291-9900 Fax: (604) 291-1906
E-mail: mzanotto@baumpub.com
Contact: Morena Zanotto, editor
Published 8 times a year

Environmental Science & Engineering
220 Industrial Parkway S., Unit 30, Aurora, ON L4G 3V6

Phone: (905) 727-4666 Fax: (905) 841-7271
Contact: Tom Davey, editor
Published bimonthly

HazMat Management
12 Concorde Place, Suite 800, Toronto, ON M3C 4J2
Phone: (416) 442-5600 Fax: (416) 510-5133
Contact: Connie Vitello, editor
Published bimonthly

Recycling Product News
2323 Boundary Road, Suite 201, Vancouver, BC V5M 4V8
Phone: (604) 291-9900 Fax: (604) 291-1906
E-mail: kbarker@baumpub.com
Contact: Keith Barker, editor
Published 9 times a year

Solid Waste & Recycling
1450 Don Mills Road, Toronto, ON M3B 2X7
Phone: (416) 442-5600 Fax: (416) 442-2204
Contact: Guy Crittenden, editor-in-chief
Published bimonthly

Farming

Better Farming
58 Teal Drive, Guelph, ON N1C 1G4
Phone: (613) 678-2232 Fax: (519) 763-4482
E-mail: rirwin@betterfarming.com
Contact: Robert Irwin, managing editor
Published 10 times a year

Canadian Cattlemen
P.O. Box 9800, 220 Portage Avenue, 15th Floor, Winnipeg, MB
    R3C 3K7
Phone: (204) 944-5760
Contact: G. Winslow, editor
Published 13 times a year

Canadian Hereford Digest
5160 Skyline Way N.E., Calgary, AB T2E 6V1
Phone: (403) 274-1734 Fax: (403) 275-4999
Contact: Kurt Gilmore, publisher/editor
Published 7 times a year

Canadian Jersey Breeder
350 Speedvale Avenue W., Unit 9, Guelph, ON N1H 7M7
Phone: (519) 821-9150 Fax: (519) 821-2723
E-mail: ryan@jerseycanada.com
Contact: Ryan Barrett, editor
Published 10 times a year

Canadian Poultry
P.O. Box 530, 105 Donly Drive S., Simcoe, ON N3Y 4N5
Phone: (519) 429-5193 Fax: (519) 429-3094
E-mail: jbauslaugh@annexweb.com
Contact: John Bauslaugh, publisher
Published monthly

Canola Guide
P.O. Box 9800, 220 Portage Avenue, 15th Floor, Winnipeg, MB
    R3C 3K7
Phone: (204) 944-5569 Fax: (204) 944-5562
E-mail: cory@fbcpublishing.com
Contact: Cory Bourheaud'Hui, editor
Published quarterly

Country Guide
P.O. Box 9800, 220 Portage Avenue, 15th Floor, Winnipeg, MB
    R3C 3K7
Phone: (204) 944-5569 Fax: (204) 944-5562
Contact: Jay Whetter, editor
Published 11 times a year

Country Life in B.C.
3917 Mildred Street, Victoria, BC V8Z 7A2
Phone: (250) 708-0085 Fax: (250) 708-0095
E-mail: countrylifeinbc@shaw.ca

Contact: Peter Wilding, publisher/editor
Published monthly

Dairy Update

P.O. Box 9800, 220 Portage Avenue, 15th Floor, Winnipeg, MB
R3C 3K7
Phone: (204) 944-5569 Fax: (204) 944-5562
Contact: G. Winslow, editor
Published 9 times a year

Farm Focus

1888 Brunswick Street, Suite 609, Halifax, NS B3J 3J8
Contact: Jeff Nearing, publisher
Published monthly

Farm Market

930 Richmond Street, Chatham, ON N7M 5J5
Phone: (519) 351-7331 Fax: (519) 351-2452
E-mail: farmmarketnews@bowesnet.com
Contact: Peter Epp, editor
Published 25 times a year

Farming for Tomorrow

2114 Robinson Street, Suite 203, Regina, SK S4T 2P7
E-mail: info@farmingfortomorrow.ca
Contact: Tom Bradley, publisher
Published twice a year

Fruit & Vegetable Magazine

P.O. Box 530, 105 Donly Drive S., Simcoe, ON N3Y 4N5
Phone: (519) 429-5193 Fax: (519) 429-3094
E-mail: editor@fruitandveggie.com
Contact: Margaret Land, editor
Published bimonthly

Germination

897 Corydon Avenue, Suite 203, Winnipeg, MB R3M 0W7
Phone: (204) 453-1965 Fax: (204) 475-5247
E-mail: issues@issuesink.com

Contact: Robynne Anderson, president
Published 5 times a year

Grainews

P.O. Box 9800, 220 Portage Avenue, 15th Floor, Winnipeg, MB
 R3C 3K7
Phone: (204) 944-5569 Fax: (204) 944-5562
Contact: Andy Sirski, editorial director
Published 18 times a year

The Grower

355 Elmira Road N., Unit 105, Guelph, ON N1K 1S5
Phone: (519) 763-8728 or 1-866-898-8488 Fax: (519) 763-6604
E-mail: editor@thegrower.org
Contact: Jamie Reaume, editor
Published monthly

Holstein Journal

30 East Beaver Creek Road, Suite 210, Richmond Hill, ON
 L4B 1J2
Phone: (905) 886-4222 Fax: (905) 886-0037
E-mail: peter@holsteinjournal.com
Contact: Peter English, publisher
Published monthly

Manitoba Co-Operator

P.O. Box 9800, 220 Portage Avenue, 15th Floor, Winnipeg, MB
 R3C 3K7
Phone: (204) 944-5569 Fax: (204) 944-5562
Contact: Andy Sirski, editorial director
Published weekly

The Milk Producer

6780 Campobello Road, Mississauga, ON L5N 2L8
Phone: (905) 821-8970 Fax: (905) 821-3160
E-mail: bdimmick@milk.org
Contact: Bill Dimmick, editor
Published monthly

Niagara Farmers' Monthly
P.O. Box 52, Smithville, ON L0R 2A0
Phone: (905) 957-3751 or 1-877-957-3751 Fax: (905) 957-0088
E-mail: editor@niagarafarmers.com
Contact: Steve Ecker, publisher/managing editor
Published 11 times a year

The Northern Horizon
901 – 100th Avenue, Dawson Creek, BC V1G 1W2
Phone: (250) 782-4888 Fax: (250) 782-6770
E-mail: publisher@prbn.ca
Contact: Brian Sims, publisher
Published bimonthly

Ontario Corn Producer
90 Woodlawn Road W., Guelph, ON N1H 1B2
Phone: (519) 837-1660 Fax: (519) 837-1674
Published 9 times a year

Ontario Dairy Farmer
P.O. Box 7400, London, ON N5Y 4X3
Phone: (519) 473-0010 Fax: (519) 473-2256
Contact: Paul Mahon, associate publisher/editor-in-chief
Published 8 times a year

Ontario Farmer
P.O. Box 7400, London, ON N5Y 4X3
Phone: (519) 473-0010 Fax: (519) 473-2256
Contact: Paul Mahon, associate publisher/editor-in-chief
Published weekly

Quebec Farmers' Advocate
P.O. Box 225, 555 Roland-Therrien Boulevard, Longueuil, QC
   J4H 4E7
Phone: (450) 679-0530 Fax: (450) 463-5291
Contact: Gib Drury, president
Published 11 times a year

Rural Roots
30 – 10th Street E., Prince Albert, SK S6V 0Y5
Fax: (306) 922-4237
E-mail: rural.roots@paherald.sk.ca
Contact: Ruth Griffiths, editor
Published weekly

Saskatchewan Farm Life
2206A Avenue C North, Saskatoon, SK S7L 6C3
Phone: 1-888-924-6397
Published biweekly

Top Crop Manager
145 Thames Road W., Exeter, ON N0M 1S3
Phone: (519) 235-2400 Fax: (519) 235-0798
E-mail: pdarbishire@annexweb.com
Contact: Peter Darbishire, editor
Published monthly

Voice of the Farmer
P.O. Box 490, Dresden, ON N0P 1M0
Phone: (519) 683-4485 Fax: (519) 683-4355
E-mail: sweditor@voiceofthefarmer.com
Contact: Mary Baxter, editor
Published biweekly

Western Dairy Farmer Magazine
4504 – 61 Avenue, Leduc, AB T9E 3Z1
Phone: (780) 986-2271 Fax: (780) 986-6397
Contact: Diana MacLeod, editorial
Published bimonthly

The Western Producer
P.O. Box 2500, 2310 Millar Avenue, Saskatoon, SK S7K 2C4
Phone: (306) 665-3544 Fax: (306) 934-2401
Contact: Barb Glen, editor
Published weekly

Food, Drink, Hostelry, & Hotel & Restaurant Supplies

Atlantic Restaurant News
2065 Dundas Street E., Suite 201, Mississauga, ON L4X 2W1
Phone: (905) 206-0150 or 1-800-201-8596 Fax: (905) 206-9972
E-mail: mcormack@can-restaurantnews.com
Contact: Mike Cormack, editor
Published bimonthly

Bakers Journal
P.O. Box 530, 105 Donly Drive S., Simcoe, ON N3Y 4N5
Phone: (519) 582-2513 or 1-888-599-2228 Fax: 1-888-404-1129
E-mail: editor@bakersjournal.com
Contact: Jane Ayer, editor
Published 10 times a year

Bar & Beverage Business Magazine
1740 Wellington Avenue, Winnipeg, MB R3H 0E8
Phone: (204) 954-2085 or 1-800-337-6372 Fax: (204) 954-2057
E-mail: jkgray@mts.net
Contact: Kelly Gray, editor
Published bimonthly

Canadian Grocer
1 Mount Pleasant Road, 7th Floor, Toronto, ON M4Y 2Y5
Phone: (416) 764-1679 Fax: (416) 764-1523
E-mail: jerry.tutunjian@canadiangrocer.rogers.com
Contact: Jerry Tutunjian, editor
Published 10 times a year

Canadian Pizza Magazine
P.O. Box 530, 105 Donly Drive S., Simcoe, ON N3Y 4N5
Phone: 1-800-265-2827 Fax: 1-888-404-1129
E-mail: cwood@annexweb.com
Contact: Cameron Wood, editor
Published 8 times a year

Food in Canada
1 Mount Pleasant Road, 7th Floor, Toronto, ON M4Y 2Y5
Phone: (416) 764-1502 Fax: (416) 764-1755
E-mail: carolyn.cooper@food.rogers.com
Web site: www.foodincanada.com
Contact: Carolyn Cooper, editor
Published 9 times a year

Foodservice and Hospitality
23 Lesmill Road, Suite 101, Toronto, ON M3B 3P6
Phone: (416) 447-0888 Fax: (416) 447-5333
E-mail: rcaira@foodservice.ca
Contact: Rosanna Caira, publisher/editor
Published monthly

Foodservice News
5255 Yonge Street, Suite 1000, Toronto, ON M2N 6P4
Phone: (416) 512-8186 Fax: (416) 512-8344
E-mail: info@cfsn.ca
Contact: Ellie Chesnutt, editor
Published 9 times a year

Grocer Today
4180 Lougheed Highway, 4th Floor, Burnaby, BC V5C 6A7
Phone: (604) 299-7311 Fax: (604) 299-9188
Contact: Les Wiseman, editor
Published bimonthly

Hotelier
23 Lesmill Road, Suite 101, Don Mills, ON M3B 3P6
Phone: (416) 447-0888 Fax: (416) 447-5333
E-mail: rcaira@foodservice.ca
Contact: Rosanna Caira, publisher/editor
Published 8 times a year

Ontario Restaurant News
2065 Dundas Street E., Suite 201, Mississauga, ON L4X 2W1
Phone: (905) 206-0150 or 1-800-201-8596 Fax: (905) 206-9972
E-mail: mdeibert@can-restaurantnews.com

Contact: Mike Deibert, editor
Published monthly

Vendor Magazine
4990 – 92 Avenue, Suite 107, Edmonton, AB T6B 2V4
Phone: (780) 415-5154 Fax: (780) 463-5280
Contact: Ellen Schnoek, editorial
Published quarterly

Western Grocer
1740 Wellington Avenue, Winnipeg, MB R3H 0E8
Phone: (204) 954-2085 or 1-800-337-6372 Fax: (204) 954-2057
E-mail: jkgray@mts.net
Contact: Kelly Gray, editor
Published bimonthly

Western Restaurant News
1740 Wellington Avenue, Winnipeg, MB R3H 0E8
Phone: (204) 954-2085 or 1-800-337-6372 Fax: (204) 954-2057
E-mail: jkgray@mts.net
Contact: Kelly Gray, editor
Published bimonthly

Your Convenience Manager
508 Lawrence Avenue W., Suite 201, Toronto, ON M6A 1A1
Phone: (416) 504-0504 Fax: (416) 256-3002
E-mail: jwiderman@fulcrum.ca
Contact: Jane Widerman, editor
Published bimonthly

Health, Dentistry, Medicine, Pharmacy, & Nursing

The Alberta Doctors' Digest
12230 – 106th Avenue N.W., Edmonton, AB T5N 3Z1
Phone: (780) 482-2626 Fax: (780) 482-5445
E-mail: amamail@albertadoctors.org
Contact: Dennis W. Jirsch, editor
Published bimonthly

British Columbia Medical Journal
1665 West Broadway, Suite 115, Vancouver, BC V6J 5A4
Phone: (604) 638-2814 Fax: (604) 638-2917
E-mail: jdraper@bcma.bc.ca
Contact: Jay Draper, managing editor
Published 10 times a year

Canadian Family Physician
2630 Skymark Avenue, Mississauga, ON L4W 5A4
Phone: (905) 629-0900 Fax: (905) 629-0893
E-mail: ma@cfpc.ca
Contact: Mairi Abbott, manuscript/circulation co-ordinator
Published monthly

Canadian Healthcare Manager
1 Mount Pleasant Road, 12th Floor, Toronto, ON M4Y 2Y5
Phone: (416) 764-3868 Fax: (416) 764-3942
E-mail: kim.laudrum@chm.rogers.com
Contact: Kim Laudrum, editor
Published 8 times a year

Canadian Healthcare Technology
1118 Centre Street, Suite 207, Thornhill, ON L4J 7R9
Phone: (905) 709-2330 Fax: (905) 709-2258
E-mail: info2@canhealth.com
Contact: Jerry Zeidenberg, publisher
Published 8 times a year

Canadian Journal of Continuing Medical Education
955 St. Jean Boulevard, Suite 306, Montreal, QC H9R 5K3
Phone: (514) 695-7623 Fax: (514) 695-8554
E-mail: paulb@sta.ca
Contact: Paul F. Brand, executive editor
Published monthly

The Canadian Journal of Hospital Pharmacy
30 Concourse Gate, Unit 3, Ottawa, ON K2E 7V7
Phone: (613) 736-9733 Fax: (613) 736-5660

Contact: Mary Ensom, editor
Published 7 times a year

Canadian Journal of Public Health
1565 Carling Avenue, Suite 400, Ottawa, ON K1Z 8R1
Phone: (613) 725-3769   Fax: (613) 725-9826
Contact: Elinor Wilson, managing editor
Published bimonthly

Canadian Medical Association Journal
1867 Alta Vista Drive, Ottawa, ON K1G 3Y6
Phone: (613) 731-8610 or 1-800-663-7336, ext. 2111   Fax: (613) 565-7488
Contact: David Hawkins, senior editor
Published biweekly

Canadian Nurse
50 Driveway, Ottawa, ON K2P 1E2
Phone. (613) 237-2133 or 1-800-361-8404 Fax: (613) 237-3520
E-mail: cnj@cna-aiic.ca
Contact: Muriel Hurst, editor-in-chief
Published 9 times a year

Canadian Pharmacists Journal (CPJ)
1785 Alta Vista Drive, Ottawa, ON K1G 3Y6
Phone: (613) 523-7877 or 1-800-917-9489 Fax: (613) 523-2332
E-mail: rdykeman@pharmacists.ca
Contact: Renée Dykeman, managing editor
Published 10 times a year

Dental Practice Management
12 Concorde Place, Suite 800, Toronto, ON M3C 4J2
Phone: (416) 510-6785 or 1-800-268-7742 Fax: (416) 510-5140
E-mail: cwilson@oralhealthjournal.com
Contact: Catherine Wilson, editorial director
Published quarterly

Doctor's Review
400 McGill Street, 3rd Floor, Montreal, QC H2Y 2G1
Phone: (514) 397-8833 Fax: (514) 397-0228
Contact: Annarosa Sabbadini, editor
Published monthly

Geriatrics & Aging
162 Cumberland Street, Suite 300, Toronto, ON M5R 3N5
Phone: (416) 480-9478 Fax: (416) 480-2740
E-mail: info@geriatricsandaging.ca
Contact: Barry Goldlist, editor-in-chief
Published 10 times a year

Healthbeat
9768 – 170 Street, Suite 319, Edmonton, AB T5T 5L4
Phone: (780) 413-9342 or 1-800-727-0782 Fax: (780) 413-9328
E-mail: info@mccronehealthbeat.com
Contact: Jay Sherwood, editor
Published monthly

Healthcare Management Forum
9 – 5th Avenue, Chateauguay, QC J6K 3L5
Phone: (450) 691-9515 Fax: (450) 699-8869
Contact: Patricia Brown, managing editor
Published quarterly

Hospital News
15 Apex Road, Toronto, ON M6A 2V6
Phone: (416) 781-5516 Fax: (416) 781-5499
E-mail: info@hospitalnews.com
Contact: Julie Abelsohn, editor
Published monthly

Journal of the Canadian Dental Association
1815 Alta Vista Drive, Ottawa, ON K1G 3Y6
Phone: (613) 523-1770 Fax: (613) 523-7736
E-mail: journal@cda-adc.ca
Contact: John O'Keefe, editor-in-chief
Published 10 times a year

Long Term Care
345 Renfrew Drive, Suite 102–202, Markham, ON L3R 9S9
Phone: (905) 470-8995 Fax: (905) 470-9595
Published quarterly

The Medical Post
1 Mount Pleasant Road, 12th Floor, Toronto, ON M4Y 2Y5
Phone: (416) 764-3902 Fax: (416) 764-1207
Published 40 times a year

Nursing BC
2855 Arbutus Street, Vancouver, BC V6J 3Y8
Phone: (604) 736-7331 Fax: (604) 738-2272
Contact: Bruce Wells, editor
Published 5 times a year

Ontario Dentist
4 New Street, Toronto, ON M5R 1P6
Phone: (416) 922-3900 Fax: (416) 922-9005
E-mail: jkuipers@oda.on.ca
Contact: Julia Kuipers, managing editor
Published 10 times a year

Ontario Medical Review
525 University Avenue, Suite 300, Toronto, ON M5G 2K7
Phone: (416) 599-2580 or 1-800-268-7215 Fax: (416) 340-2232
E-mail: media@oma.org
Contact: Elizabeth Petruccelli, managing editor
Published 11 times a year

Oral Health
12 Concorde Place, Suite 800, Toronto, ON M3C 4J2
Phone: (416) 510-6781 or 1-800-268-7742 Fax: (416) 510-5140
E-mail: cwilson@oralhealthjournal.com
Contact: Catherine Wilson, editorial director
Published monthly

Parkhurst Exchange
400 McGill Street, 3rd Floor, Montreal, QC H2Y 2G1

Phone: (514) 397-8833 Fax: (514) 397-0228
Contact: Milena Katz, managing editor
Published monthly

Patient Care
1 Mount Pleasant Road, 12th Floor, Toronto, ON M4Y 2Y5
Phone: (416) 764-3912 Fax: (416) 764-1207
Contact: Golda Goldman, editor
Published monthly

Pharmacy Practice
1 Mount Pleasant Road, 12th Floor, Toronto, ON M4Y 2Y5
Phone: (416) 764-3925
E-mail: rosalind.stefanac@pharmacygroup.rogers.com
Contact: Rosalind Stephanac, editor
Published monthly

The Standard
101 Davenport Road, Toronto, ON M5R 3P1
Phone: (416) 928-0900 or 1-800-387-5526 Fax: (416) 928-6507
E-mail: cno@cnomail.org
Contact: Deborah Jones, editor
Published quarterly

Stride Magazine
4981 Highway 7E, Suite 254, Markham, ON L3R 1N1
Phone: (905) 640-3048 Fax: (905) 640-7547
E-mail: editor@stridemagazine.com
Contact: John McKay, managing editor
Published quarterly

Industrial

Accident Prevention
5110 Creekbank Road, Suite 300, Mississauga, ON L4W 0A1
Phone: (705) 444-5402 or 1-800-669-4939 Fax: (416) 506-8880
E-mail: apmag@iapa.ca

Contact: Scott Williams, publisher/editor
Published 5 times a year

Advanced Manufacturing
240 Edward Street, Aurora, ON L4G 3S9
Phone: (905) 727-0077 Fax: (905) 727-0017
E-mail: tphillips@clbmedia.ca
Contact: Todd Phillips, associate publisher/editor
Published bimonthly

Canadian Chemical News
130 Slater Street, Suite 550, Ottawa, ON K1P 6E2
Phone: (613) 232-6252 Fax: (613) 232-5862
E-mail: editorial@accn.ca
Contact: Heather Dana Munroe, managing editor
Published 10 times a year

Canadian Industrial Equipment News
12 Concorde Place, Suite 800, Toronto, ON M3C 4J2
Phone: (416) 510-5113 Fax: (416) 442-2214
E-mail: omarkovich@cienmagazine.com
Contact: Olga Markovich, associate publisher/editor
Published 11 times a year

Canadian Industrial Machinery
5100 South Service Road, Burlington, ON L7L 6A5
Phone: (905) 637-2317 Fax: (905) 634-2776
E-mail: gord@cipmetalworking.com
Contact: Gordon Valley, publisher
Published monthly

Canadian Metalworking
1 Mount Pleasant Road, 7th Floor, Toronto, ON M4Y 2Y5
Phone: (416) 764-1508 Fax: (416) 764-1735
E-mail: dan.pelton@rci.rogers.com
Contact: Dan Pelton, editor
Published 7 times a year

Canadian Occupational Safety
240 Edward Street, Aurora, ON L4G 3S9
Phone: (905) 713-4387 Fax: (905) 727-0017
E-mail: jbrown@clbmedia.ca
Contact: Jennifer Brown, editor
Published bimonthly

Canadian Packaging
1 Mount Pleasant Road, 7th Floor, Toronto, ON M4Y 2Y5
Phone: (416) 764-1505
E-mail: george.guidoni@packaging.rogers.com
Contact: George Guidoni, editor
Published 11 times a year

Canadian Plastics
12 Concorde Place, Suite 800, Toronto, ON M3C 4J2
Phone: (416) 510-5112 Fax: (416) 442-2213
E-mail: rr@canplastics.com
Contact: Rebecca Reid, managing editor
Published monthly

Canadian Process Equipment & Control News
588 Edward Avenue, Suite 29, Richmond Hill, ON L4C 9Y6
Phone: (416) 481-6483 Fax: (416) 481-6436
E-mail: moverment@cpecn.com
Contact: Mike Overment, editor
Published bimonthly

Hardware Merchandising
1 Mount Pleasant Road, 7th Floor, Toronto, ON M4Y 2Y5
Phone: (416) 764-1662 Fax: (416) 764-1484
E-mail: frank.condron@rce.rogers.com
Contact: Frank Condron, editor
Published bimonthly

Heating–Plumbing–Air Conditioning
1 Mount Pleasant Road, 7th Floor, Toronto, ON M4Y 2Y5
Phone: (416) 764-1549 Fax: (416) 764-1746

E-mail: kerry.turner@hpacmag.rogers.com
Contact: Kerry Turner, editor
Published 7 times a year

Industrial Process Products & Technology
1011 Upper Middle Road E., Suite 1235, Oakville, ON L6H 5Z9
Phone: (905) 642-1215 Fax: (905) 642-1229
E-mail: gscholey@processwest.ca
Contact: Glen Scholey, editor
Published bimonthly

Laboratory Product News
12 Concorde Place, Suite 800, Toronto, ON M3C 4J2
Phone: (416) 510-6835 Fax: (416) 510-5140
E-mail: lburt@labcanada.com
Contact: Leslie Burt, publisher/editor
Published 7 times a year

Machinery & Equipment MRO
12 Concorde Place, Suite 800, Toronto, ON M3C 4J2
Phone: (416) 510-6749 Fax: (416) 442-2214
E-mail: brocbuck@mromagazine.com
Contact: Bill Roebuck, editor
Published bimonthly

Metalworking Production & Purchasing
240 Edward Street, Aurora, ON L4G 3S9
Phone: (905) 713-4388 Fax: (905) 727-0017
E-mail: jcook@clbmedia.ca
Contact: Jerry Cook, editor
Published bimonthly

OH & S Canada
12 Concorde Place, Suite 800, Toronto, ON M3C 4J2
Phone: (416) 510-5124 Fax: (416) 442-2200
E-mail: astelmakowich@ohscanada.com
Contact: Angela Stelmakowich, editor
Published 8 times a year

Ontario Industrial Magazine
1011 Upper Middle Road E., Suite 1159, Oakville, ON L6H 5Z9
Phone: (905) 446-1404 Fax: (905) 446-0502
Contact: Bill Bryson, associate editor
Published monthly

Plant, Canada's Industry Newspaper
1 Mount Pleasant Road, 7th Floor, Toronto, ON M4Y 2Y5
Phone: (416) 764-1546 Fax: (416) 764-1742
E-mail: joe.terrett@plant.rogers.com
Contact: Joe Terrett, editor
Published monthly

Plant Engineering & Maintenance
240 Edward Street, Aurora, ON L4G 3S9
Phone: (905) 727-0077 Fax: (905) 727-0017
E-mail: rrobertson@clbmedia.ca
Contact: Rob Robertson, editor
Published 7 times a year

Plastics in Canada Magazine
1 Mount Pleasant Road, 7th Floor, Toronto, ON M4Y 2Y5
Phone: (416) 764-1514 Fax: (416) 764-1740
E-mail: edward.mason@plastics.rogers.com
Contact: Edward Mason, editor
Published bimonthly

Report on Industry Magazine
282 Wellington Street, Sarnia, ON N7T 1H2
Phone: (519) 332-2255 Fax: (519) 332-6766
E-mail: jtost@roundtablecreative.com
Contact: James Tost, publisher/editor
Published quarterly

20/20 Magazine: Canada's Industry Association Magazine
1 Nicholas Street, Ottawa, ON K1N 7B7
Phone: (519) 332-2255 Fax: (519) 332-6766
E-mail: jeff.brownlee@cme-mec.ca

Contact: Jeff Brownlee, publisher
Published bimonthly

Landscaping & Horticulture

Canadian Florist
P.O. Box 530, 105 Donly Drive S., Simcoe, ON N3Y 4N5
Phone: 1-800-265-2827 Fax: 1-888-404-1129
E-mail: asonnenberg@annexweb.com
Contact: Anja Sonnenberg, editor
Published 8 times a year

Greenhouse Canada
P.O. Box 530, 105 Donly Drive S., Simcoe, ON N3Y 4N5
Phone: (519) 429-3966 Fax: (519) 429-3094
E-mail: greenhouse@annexweb.com
Contact: Dave Harrison, editor
Published monthly

Greenmaster
15 Wertheim Court, Suite 710, Richmond Hill, ON L4B 3H7
Phone: (905) 771-7333 or 1-800-409-8688 Fax: (905) 771-7336
Contact: Blair Adams, editorial director
Published bimonthly

Hortwest
5783 – 176A Street, Suite 102, Surrey, BC V3S 6S6
Phone: (604) 574-7772 Fax: (604) 574-7773
E-mail: rtriveri@telus.net
Contact: Renata Triveri, intern
Published 10 times a year

Landscape Trades
7856 Fifth Line S., R.R. #4, Milton, ON L9T 2X8
Phone: (905) 875-1805 Fax: (905) 875-0183
E-mail: sarahw@landscapeontario.com
Contact: Sarah Wills, editorial director
Published 9 times a year

Landscaping & Groundskeeping Journal
2323 Boundary Road, Suite 201, Vancouver, BC V5M 4V8
Phone: (604) 291-9900 Fax: (604) 291-1906
E-mail: lbuser@baumpub.com
Contact: Lawrence Buser, editorial director
Published bimonthly

Prairie Landscape Magazine
P.O. Box 85127, APPO, Calgary, AB T2A 7R7
Phone: (403) 273-6917 Fax: (403) 313-6917
E-mail: prairielandscape@shaw.ca
Contact: Jennett Jackson, publisher
Published bimonthly

Turf & Recreation
275 James Street, Delhi, ON N4B 2B2
Phone: (519) 582-8873 Fax: (519) 582-8877
Contact: Mike Jiggens, editor
Published 7 times a year

Media, Music, & Communications

Broadcast Dialogue
18 Turtle Path, Lagoon City, ON L0K 1B0
Phone: (705) 484-0752
E-mail: publisher@broadcastdialogue.com
Contact: Howard Christensen, publisher
Published 10 times a year

Broadcaster
12 Concorde Place, Suite 800, Toronto, ON M3C 4J2
Phone: (416) 510-6865 Fax: (416) 510-5134
E-mail: lrickwood@cablecastermagazine.com
Contact: Lee Rickwood, editor
Published 8 times a year

Canadian Music Trade
23 Hannover Drive, Unit 7, St. Catharines, ON L2W 1A3

Phone: (905) 641-3471   Fax: (905) 641-1648
E-mail: jmackay@nor.com
Contact: Jeff MacKay, editor
Published bimonthly

Media
1385 Woodroffe Avenue, Suite B224, Ottawa, ON K2G 1V8
Phone: (613) 526-8061   Fax: (613) 521-3904
E-mail: caj@igs.net
Contact: David McKie, editor/art director
Published 3 times a year

Network Cabling
240 Edward Street, Aurora, ON L4G 3S9
Phone: (905) 727-0077   Fax: (905) 727-0017
E-mail: fshoniker@clbmedia.ca
Contact: Frank Shoniker, publisher
Published bimonthly

News Canada
111 Peter Street, Suite 810, Toronto, ON M5V 2H1
Phone: (416) 599-9900   Fax: (416) 599-9700
Contact: Ruth Douglas, publisher
Published monthly

Playback
366 Adelaide Street W., Suite 500, Toronto, ON M5V 1R9
Phone: (416) 408-2300 or 1-888-988-7325   Fax: (416) 408-0870
E-mail: mwallace@brunico.com
Contact: Marcelle Wallace, publisher
Published 25 times a year

Press Review
P.O. Box 368, Stn. A, Toronto, ON M5W 1C2
Phone: (647) 287-7263   Fax: (416) 366-0104
E-mail: sbenitah@pressreview.ca
Contact: Sandie Benitah, editor
Published quarterly

Professional Sound
23 Hannover Drive, Unit 7, St. Catharines, ON L2W 1A3
Phone: (905) 641-3471 Fax: (905) 641-1648
E-mail: jmackay@nor.com
Contact: Jeff MacKay, editor
Published bimonthly

Sources
489 College Street, Suite 305, Toronto, ON M6G 1A5
Phone: (416) 964-7799 Fax: (416) 964-8763
E-mail: sources@sources.com
Contact: Ulli Diemer, publisher
Published twice a year

WholeNote
720 Bathurst Street, Suite 503, Toronto, ON M5S 2R4
Phone: (416) 603-3786 Fax: (416) 603-4791
E-mail: info@thewholenote.com
Contact: David Perlman, editorial
Published 10 times a year

Miscellaneous Trade & Professional

Blue Line Magazine
12A – 4981 Highway 7E, Suite 254, Markham, ON L3R 1N1
Phone: (905) 640-3048 Fax: (905) 640-7547
E-mail: blueline@blueline.ca
Contact: Mark Reesor, managing editor
Published 10 times a year

Boating Business
447 Speers Road, Suite 4, Oakville, ON L6K 3S7
Phone: (905) 842-6591 Fax: (905) 842-4432
E-mail: boating@formulapublications.com
Contact: Craig Ritchie, editor-in-chief
Published bimonthly

Canadian Apparel
124 O'Connor Street, Suite 504, Ottawa, ON K1P 5M9
Phone: (613) 231-3220 or 1-800-661-1187 Fax: (613) 231-2305
E-mail: editor@apparel.ca
Contact: Marsha Ross, managing editor
Published bimonthly

Canadian Defence Review
132 Adrian Crescent, Markham, ON L3P 7B3
Phone: (905) 472-2801 Fax: (905) 472-3091
E-mail: editor@canadiandefencereview.com
Contact: Peter A. Kitchen, editor-in-chief
Published bimonthly

Canadian Diamonds and Jewellery
4920 – 52nd Street, Suite 800, Yellowknife, NT X1A 3T1
Phone: (867) 766-6710 Fax: (867) 873-9876
E-mail: jake@uphere.ca
Contact: Jake Kennedy, editor
Published quarterly

Canadian Facility Management & Design
4195 Dundas Street W., Suite 338, Toronto, ON M8X 1Y4
Phone: (416) 236-5856 Fax: (416) 236-5219
E-mail: cfm@sympatico.ca
Contact: Tom Kelly, editor
Published 7 times a year

The Canadian Firefighter and EMS Quarterly
P.O. Box 530, 105 Donly Drive S., Simcoe, ON N3Y 4N5
Phone: 1-800-265-2827 Fax: 1-888-404-1129
E-mail: firefightcan@annexweb.com
Contact: Jim Haley, editor
Published quarterly

Canadian Footwear Journal
241 Senneville Road, Senneville, QC H9X 3X5
Phone: (514) 457-8787 Fax: (514) 457-5832

E-mail: bmcleish@footwearjournal.ca
Contact: Barbara McLeish, editor
Published 5 times a year

The Canadian Funeral Director Magazine
21 Hanlan Court, Whitby, ON L1N 9X4
Phone: (905) 686-7161 Fax: (905) 686-2159
E-mail: info@thefuneralmagazine.com
Contact: Scott Hillier, publisher/editor
Published monthly

Canadian Funeral News
101 – 6th Avenue S.W., Suite 1025, Calgary, AB T2P 3P4
Phone: (403) 264-3270 Fax: (403) 264-3276
E-mail: editorcnf@shaw.ca
Contact: Camie Leard, editor
Published monthly

Canadian Government Executive
10211 Yonge Street, Suite 202, Richmond Hill, ON L4C 3B3
Phone: (905) 508-1499 Fax: (905) 508-4899
E-mail: publisher@networkedgovernment.ca
Contact: John Jones, publisher
Published 10 times a year

Canadian Hairdresser Magazine
11 Spadina Road, Toronto, ON M5R 2S9
Phone: (416) 923-1111 Fax: (416) 968-1031
E-mail: joan@canhair.com
Contact: Joan Harrison, managing editor
Published 10 times a year

Canadian Home Style Magazine
146 Cavendish Court, Oakville, ON L6J 5S2
Phone: (905) 338-0799 Fax: (905) 338-5657
E-mail: laurie@homestylemag.ca
Contact: Laurie O'Halloran, publisher/editorial director
Published bimonthly

Canadian HR Reporter
1 Corporate Plaza, 2075 Kennedy Road, Toronto, ON M1T 3V4
Phone: (416) 298-5141 Fax: (416) 298-5031
E-mail: todd.humber@thomson.com
Contact: Todd Humber, managing editor
Published 22 times a year

Canadian Interiors
360 Dupont Street, Toronto, ON M5R 1V9
Phone: (416) 966-9944 Fax: (416) 966-9946
E-mail: kelly@canadianinteriors.com
Contact: Kelly Rude, editorial director
Published bimonthly

Canadian Jeweller
555 Richmond Street W., Suite 701, Toronto, ON M5V 3B1
Phone: (416) 203-6737 Fax: (416) 203-1057
E-mail: leslie@style.ca
Contact: Leslie Wu, editor
Published 7 times a year

Canadian Property Management
5255 Yonge Street, Suite 1000, Toronto, ON M2N 6P4
Phone: (416) 512-8186 Fax: (416) 512-8344
E-mail: barbc@mediaedge.ca
Contact: Barb Carrs, editor
Published 8 times a year

Canadian Rental Service
145 Thames Road W., Exeter, ON N0M 1S3
Phone: (519) 235-2400 Fax: (519) 235-0798
E-mail: pdarbishire@annexweb.com
Contact: Peter Darbishire, managing editor
Published 9 times a year

Canadian Retailer
1255 Bay Street, Suite 800, Toronto, ON M5R 2A9
Phone: (416) 922-6678 or 1-888-373-8245 Fax: (416) 922-8011
E-mail: general@dvtail.com

Contact: Theresa Rogers, editor-in-chief
Published bimonthly

Canadian Security
240 Edward Street, Aurora, ON L4G 3S9
Phone: (905) 727-0077 Fax: (905) 727-0017
Contact: Jennifer Brown editor
Published 9 times a year

The Canadian Veterinary Journal
339 Booth Street, Ottawa, ON K1R 7K1
Phone: (613) 236-1162 Fax: (613) 236-9681
E-mail: dhare@cvma-acmv.org
Contact: Doug Hare, editor
Published monthly

CM Condominium Manager
6835 Century Avenue, 2nd Floor, Mississauga, ON L5N 2L2
Phone: (905) 826-6890 Fax: (905) 826-4873
Contact: Susan Howard, executive editor
Published quarterly

Coatings
1 Mount Pleasant Road, 7th Floor, Toronto, ON M4Y 2Y5
Phone: (416) 764-1540 Fax: (416) 764-1740
E-mail: sandra.anderson@coatings.rogers.com
Contact: Sandy Anderson, editor
Published 7 times a year

Cosmetics
1 Mount Pleasant Road, 7th Floor, Toronto, ON M4Y 2Y5
Phone: (416) 764-1680
E-mail: dave.lackie@cosmetics.rogers.com
Contact: Dave Lackie, editor
Published bimonthly

Fabricare Canada
P.O. Box 968, Oakville, ON L6J 5E8
Phone: (905) 337-0516 Fax: (905) 337-0525

E-mail: marcia@fabricarecanada.com
Contact: Marcia Todd, publisher/editor-in-chief
Published bimonthly

Fire Fighting in Canada
P.O. Box 530, 105 Donly Drive S., Simcoe, ON N3Y 4N5
Phone: 1-800-265-2827 Fax: 1-888-404-1129
E-mail: firefightcan@annexweb.com
Contact: Jim Haley, editor
Published 8 times a year

Fitness Business Canada
30 Mill Pond Drive, Georgetown, ON L7G 4S6
Phone: (905) 873-0850 Fax: (905) 873-8611
E-mail: fbc@fitnet.ca
Contact: Don Longwell, editor
Published bimonthly

Gifts and Tablewares
12 Concorde Place, Suite 800, Toronto, ON M3C 4J2
Phone: (416) 510-6827 Fax: (416) 442-2213
E-mail: lsmith@gifts-and-tablewares.com
Contact: Lori Smith, editor
Published 7 times a year

Glass Canada
145 Thames Road W., Excter, ON N0M 1S3
Phone: (519) 235-2400 Fax: (519) 235-0798
E-mail: cskalkos@annexweb.com
Contact: Chris Skalkos, editor
Published bimonthly

The Hill Times
69 Sparks Street, Ottawa, ON K1P 5A5
Phone: (613) 232-5952 Fax: (613) 232-9055
E-mail: kmalloy@hilltimes.com
Contact: Kate Malloy, managing editor
Published weekly

Jewellery Business
15 Wertheim Court, Suite 710, Richmond Hill, ON L4B 3H7
Phone: (905) 771-7333 Fax: (905) 771-7336
Contact: Carol Besler, publisher/editor-in-chief
Published bimonthly

Luggage, Leathergoods & Accessories
96 Karma Road, Markham, ON L3R 4Y3
Phone: (905) 944-0265 Fax: (416) 296-0994
E-mail: la.vidabiz@sympatico.ca
Contact: Vida Jurisic, editor
Published quarterly

Municipal World
42860 Sparta Line, Union, ON N0L 2L0
Phone: (519) 633-0031 Fax: (519) 633-1001
E-mail: sgardner@municipalworld.com
Contact: Susan Gardner, executive editor
Published monthly

Optical Prism
250 The East Mall, Suite 1113, Toronto, ON M9B 6L3
Phone: (416) 699-4874 Fax: (416) 233-1746
Contact: Craig Saunders, editor
Published 10 times a year

Pet Biz
15 Wertheim Court, Suite 710, Richmond Hill, ON L4B 3H7
Phone: (905) 771-7333 Fax: (905) 771-7336
Contact: Blair Adams, editorial director
Published bimonthly

REM Canada's Magazine for Real Estate Professionals
808 Coxwell Avenue, Toronto, ON M4C 3E4
Phone: (416) 425-3504 Fax: (416) 425-0040
Contact: Jim Adair, editor
Published monthly

Salon Magazine
365 Bloor Street E., Suite 1902, Toronto, ON M4W 3L4
Phone: (416) 869-3131 or 1-800-720-6665 Fax: (416) 869-3008
E-mail: frontdesk@beautynet.com
Contact: Stephen Puddister, editor
Published 8 times a year

Spa Management
P.O. Box 365, Place d'Armes, Montreal, QC H2Y 3H1
Phone: (514) 274-0004 Fax: (514) 833-2444
E-mail: info@spamanagement.com
Contact: Bernard Urt, senior editor
Published 10 times a year

Style
555 Richmond Street W., Suite 701, Toronto, ON M5V 3B1
Phone: (416) 203-6737 or 1-800-720-6665 Fax: (416) 203-1057
E-mail: style@style.ca
Contact: Marilisa Racco, editor
Published monthly

Tour of Duty
180 Yorkland Boulevard, Toronto, ON M2J 1R5
Phone: (416) 491-4301 Fax: (416) 491-7421
E-mail: editor@tpassn.com
Published monthly

Toys & Games
61 Alness Road, Suite 216, Toronto, ON M3J 2H2
Phone: (416) 663-9229 Fax: (416) 663-2353
E-mail: cantoymag@look.ca
Contact: Lynn Winston, editor
Published bimonthly

Vision Magazine
495 St-Martin Boulevard W., Suite 202, Laval, QC H7M 1Y9
Phone: (450) 629-6005 Fax: (450) 629-6044
E-mail: breton@bretoncom.com
Published bimonthly

Woodworking
240 Edward Street, Aurora, ON L4G 3S9
Phone: (905) 727-0077 Fax: (905) 727-0017
E-mail: afreill@clbmedia.com
Contact: Adam Freill, editor
Published 7 times a year

Workplace News
240 Edward Street, Aurora, ON L4G 3S9
Phone: (905) 727-0077 Fax: (905) 727-0017
E-mail: nmallett@clbmedia.ca
Contact: Nathan Mallett, editor
Published monthly

Printing & Photography

Canadian Printer
1 Mount Pleasant Road, 7th Floor, Toronto, ON M4Y 2Y5
Phone: (416) 764-1530 Fax: (416) 764-1738
E-mail: doug.picklyk@printer.rogers.com
Contact: Doug Picklyk, editor
Published 8 times a year

Graphic Monthly
1606 Sedlescomb Drive, Unit 8, Mississauga, ON L4X 1M6
Phone: (905) 625-7070 Fax: (905) 625-4856
E-mail: ftamburri@graphicmonthly.ca
Contact: Filomena Tamburri, editor
Published bimonthly

PrintAction
4580 Dufferin Street, Suite 404, Toronto, ON M3H 5Y2
Phone: (416) 665-7333 Fax: (416) 655-7226
Contact: Jon Robinson, editor
Published monthly

Second Impressions
35 Mill Drive, St. Albert, AB T8N 1J5
Phone: (780) 458-9889 Fax: (780) 458-9839
E-mail: lpuckrin@secondimpressions.com
Contact: Loretta Puckrin, publisher
Published bimonthly

Science

Bio Business
30 East Beaver Creek Road, Suite 202, Richmond Hill, ON L4B 1J2
Phone: (905) 886-5040 or 1-800-613-6353 Fax: (905) 886-6615
E-mail: bjohnson@jesmar.com
Contact: Bernadette Johnson, editor
Published quarterly

Biotechnology Focus
10211 Yonge Street, Suite 202, Richmond Hill, ON L4C 3B3
Phone: (905) 508-3966 Fax: (905) 508-4866
E-mail: terrip@promotive.net
Contact: Terri Pavelic, publisher/editor-in-chief
Published monthly

Lab Business
30 East Beaver Creek Road, Suite 202, Richmond Hill, ON
    L4B 1J2
Phone: (905) 886-5040 or 1-800-613-6353 Fax: (905) 886-6615
E-mail: bjohnson@jesmar.com
Contact: Bernadette Johnson, editor
Published 5 times a year

Laboratory Product News
12 Concorde Place, Suite 800, Toronto, ON M3C 4J2
Phone: (416) 510-6835 Fax: (416) 510-5140
E-mail: lburt@labcanada.com
Contact: Leslie Burt, publisher/editor
Published quarterly

Microscopical Society of Canada Bulletin
1200 Main Street, Hamilton, ON L8N 3Z5
Phone: (905) 525-00
Contact: Michael Robertson, editor
Published quarterly

Physics in Canada
150 Louis Pasteur Pvt., Suite 112, McDonald Building, Ottawa,
    ON K1N 6N5
Phone: (613) 562-5614 Fax: (613) 562-5615
E-mail: cap@physics.uottawa.ca
Contact: Bela Joos, editor
Published bimonthly

Transportation & Cargo

Canadian Transportation & Logistics
12 Concorde Place, Suite 800, Toronto, ON M3C 4J2
Phone: (416) 510-6881 Fax: (416) 442-2214
E-mail: lou@transportationmedia.ca
Contact: Lou Smyrlis, editorial director
Published 11 times a year

Harbour & Shipping
1489 Marine Drive, Suite 510, West Vancouver, BC V7T 1B8
Phone: (604) 922-6717 Fax: (604) 922-1739
E-mail: harbour&shipping@telus.net
Contact: Allison Smith, editor
Published monthly

Highwaystar
451 Attwell Drive, Toronto, ON M9W 5C4
Phone: (416) 614-5811 Fax: (416) 614-8861
E-mail: jpark@newcom.ca
Contact: Jim Park, editor
Published monthly

Logistics Magazine
916 Ste-Adèle, Suite 115, Sainte-Adèle, QC J8B 2N2
Phone: (450) 229-7777 or 1-877-437-0888   Fax: (450) 229-3233
E-mail: info@vlogistics-mag.com
Contact: Michel Trudeau, editor
Published bimonthly

Motortruck
12 Concorde Place, Suite 800, Toronto, ON M3C 4J2
Phone: (416) 510-6881   Fax: (416) 510-51403
E-mail: lou@transportationmedia.ca
Contact: Lou Smyrlis, editorial director
Published bimonthly

Over the Road
18 Park Glen Drive, Ottawa, ON K2G 3G9
Phone: (613) 224-9947 or 1-800-416-8712   Fax: (613) 224-8825
E-mail: steve@otr.on.ca
Contact: Steve Jenkins, editor
Published monthly

Today's Trucking
451 Attwell Drive, Toronto, ON M9W 5C4
Phone: (416) 614-5828   Fax: (416) 614-8861
E-mail: pcarter@newcom.ca
Contact: Peter Carter, editor
Published 10 times a year

Truck News
12 Concorde Place, Suite 800, Toronto, ON M3C 4J2
Phone: (416) 510-5123   Fax: (416) 510-5143
E-mail: jmenzies@truckwestnews.com
Contact: James Menzies, executive editor
Published monthly

Truck West
12 Concorde Place, Suite 800, Toronto, ON M3C 4J2
Phone: (416) 510-5123   Fax: (416) 510-5143

E-mail: jmenzies@truckwestnews.com
Contact: James Menzies, executive editor
Published monthly

Travel

Canadian Travel Press
310 Dupont Street, Toronto, ON M5R 1V9
Phone: (416) 968-7252 Fax: (416) 968-2377
E-mail: ebaxter@baxter.net
Contact: Edith Baxter, editor-in-chief
Published weekly

Canadian Traveller
1104 Hornby Street, Suite 203, Vancouver, BC V6Z 1V8
Phone: (604) 669-9990 Fax: (604) 669-9993
E-mail: janices@canadiantraveller.net
Contact: Janice Strong, editor
Published monthly

GSA: The Travel Magazine for Western Canada
1104 Hornby Street, Suite 200, Vancouver, BC V6Z 1V8
Phone: (604) 689-2909 Fax: (604) 689-2989
E-mail: editor@gsapublishing.com
Contact: Lynda Cumming, editor
Published 24 times a year

Meetings & Incentive Travel
1 Mount Pleasant Road, 7th Floor, Toronto, ON M4Y 2Y5
Phone: (416) 764-1638 Fax: (416) 764-1419
E-mail: sandra.eagle@mtg.rogers.com
Contact: Sandra Eagle, director of content
Published bimonthly

The Road Explorer
100 Sutherland Avenue, Winnipeg, MB R2W 3C7
Phone: (204) 975-0423 or 1-800-369-2456 Fax: 1-800-709-5551
E-mail: jstrom@naylor.com

Contact: Janine Strom, managing editor
Published 3 times a year

Special Events & Travel

77 Nipissing Crescent, 2nd Floor, Brampton, ON L6S 4Z8
Phone: (905) 451-4199 Fax: (905) 451-2938
E-mail: specialevents@rogers.com
Contact: Nancy Larin, editor
Published quarterly

Travel Courier

310 Dupont Street, Toronto, ON M5R 1V9
Phone: (416) 968-7252 Fax: (416) 968-2377
E-mail: baginski@baxter.net
Contact. Mike Haginski, editor
Published weekly

Travelweek

282 Richmond Street E., Suite 100, Toronto, ON M5A 1P4
Phone: 1-800-727-1429
Contact: Patrick Dineen, editor
Published weekly

4

DAILY NEWSPAPERS

There are over a hundred English-language daily newspapers in Canada, making this a significant potential market for both experienced and less-seasoned freelance writers. Remember that many successful writing careers began in the pages of a local daily or small community newspaper.

Many of the larger city dailies pay as much as or more than the average consumer magazine for well-written, well-researched articles on important or intriguing subjects. And they settle faster: most pay at the end of the month, some even on acceptance.

Two keys to writing for newspapers are the accuracy of the story and delivering it on time. Because news loses its value as quickly as it changes, it is usually gathered hurriedly, on large and small papers, by staff reporters. Therefore, it is to your advantage to concentrate on background stories about ongoing issues or to write profiles of prominent, interesting, or unusual local citizens or institutions.

Editors look for feature articles with body and strength, as well as originality and freshness. Timing is important. Keep a calendar of dates for seasonal stories – Halloween, Thanksgiving, Christmas, Chinese New Year, Canada Day, and so on – and read behind the news for feature ideas.

The travel section of a paper typically buys the most freelance work, followed by the food section, but other categories where freelancers often contribute include hobbies, lifestyles, personal finance, business, and strong human-interest pieces, which are among the most popular in any newspaper. Most editors like to build up a resource of articles that do not have to be used immediately.

Your best preparation in tackling the newspaper market is to carefully read several issues of a specific paper. Note its editorial approach, style, story lengths, use of photographs, and the difference in content, construction, and tone between its news stories and feature articles. If you have never studied journalism, you might want to refer to *News Reporting and Writing*, by Melvin Mencher, a professor at Columbia University's Graduate School of Journalism (see Chapter 11, Resources).

You will, of course, need more experience to sell to large, well-staffed metropolitan dailies such as *The Toronto Star* or the *Winnipeg Free Press*. But even here, the outside contributor has a chance, provided he or she has some specialized knowledge, can handle human-interest material deftly, and can write full-bodied issue stories with conviction and authority.

When approaching a newspaper, the freelancer should not use the same procedures as for magazines. Speed is a primary factor here. If you are planning to write about a breaking news event, it is permissible to telephone the editor for his or her okay. Even for less time-sensitive articles, a query letter would take too long. Instead, send the completed piece to the editor along with an SASE and a cover letter. In the letter convince the editor that he or she should buy your article, include a short outline of your experience (with tearsheets of your published work and copies of any of your letters that that paper may have published), and note the availability of photographs.

To stretch the earning potential of your newspaper article, it is acceptable to sell it to more than one paper at a time, as long as the publications serve completely different regions and not one of the papers is a national.

Don't forget to also target the magazine-style weekly supplements put out by most newspapers. Here general-interest stories usually prevail, and opportunities exist for the freelance writer. Your first approach to the editor of a supplement should either be via a query letter or else by sending in the completed article.

If you are just beginning your writing career and need to gain confidence and assemble a file of tearsheets, consider weekly community newspapers as a good starting point. With small staffs, low budgets, and no wire services to rely on, their editors are often happy to accept outside contributions, particularly feature articles that cover the local scene. And since payment is modest, there is little competition from more experienced writers. Phone the editors directly, since they have neither the time nor the resources to respond to written queries.

In addition to writing for your city paper, look for opportunities to act as a correspondent, or stringer, for one published elsewhere. The full listing of English-language Canadian daily newspapers that follows will prove useful. For suburban weeklies, check the *CARD* directory. Canadian newspapers are also listed in *Matthews Media Directory* and annual publications such as the *Canadian Almanac & Directory* and *Scott's Canadian Sourcebook* (see Chapter 11, Resources).

Alberta

Calgary Herald
215 – 16th Street S.E., P.O. Box 2400, Stn. M, Calgary, AB
   T2P 0W8
Phone: (403) 235-7100 Fax: (403) 235-7379
E-mail: submit@theherald.canwest.ca
Web site: www.canada.com/calgaryherald

Calgary Sun
2615 – 12th Street N.E., Calgary, AB T2E 7W9
Phone: (403) 410-1010 Fax: (403) 250-4180
E-mail: callet@calgarysun.com
Web site: www.calgarysun.com

Daily Herald-Tribune
10604 – 100 Street, Bag 3000, Grande Prairie, AB T8V 6V4
Phone: (780) 532-1110 Fax: (780) 532-2120
E-mail: dht@bowesnet.com
Web site: www.dailyheraldtribune.com

Edmonton Journal
10006 – 101 Street, Edmonton, AB T5J 0S1
Phone: (780) 429-5100 Fax: (780) 429-5500
E-mail: city@thejournal.canwest.com
Web site: www.canada.com/edmontonjournal

Edmonton Sun
4990 – 92 Avenue, Suite 250, Edmonton, AB T6B 3A1
Phone: (780) 468-0100 Fax: (780) 468-0139
E-mail: citydesk@edmsun.com
Web site: www.edmontonsun.ca

Fort McMurray Today
8550 Franklin Avenue, Bag 4008, Fort McMurray, AB T9H 3G1
Phone: (780) 743-8186 Fax: (780) 715-3820
E-mail: today.editorial@fortmcmurraytoday.com
Web site: www.fortmcmurraytoday.com

Lethbridge Herald
504 – 7th Street S., P.O. Box 670, Lethbridge, AB T1J 3Z7
Phone: (403) 328-4411 Fax: (403) 329-9355
E-mail: dsugimoto@lethbridgeherald.com
Web site: www.lethbridgeherald.com

Medicine Hat News
3257 Dunmore Road S.E., P.O. Box 10, Medicine Hat, AB
   T1A 7E6
Phone: (403) 527-1101 Fax: (403) 527-1244
E-mail: apoirier@medicinehatnews.com
Web site: www.medicinehatnews.com

Red Deer Advocate
2950 Bremner Avenue, Red Deer, AB T4R 1M9
Phone: (403) 343-2400 Fax: (403) 341-6560
E-mail: editorial@reddeeradvocate.com
Web site: www.reddeeradvocate.com

British Columbia

Abbotsford News Daily
34375 Gladys Avenue, Abbotsford, BC V2S 2H5
Phone: (604) 853-1144　Fax: (604) 852-1641
E-mail: editor@abbynews.com
Web site: www.abbynews.com

Alaska Highway News
9916 – 98th Street, Fort St. John, BC V1J 3T8
Phone: (250) 785-5631　Fax: (250) 785-3522
E-mail: ahnews@awink.com
Web site: www.canada.com/cityguides/fortstjohn

The Alberni Valley Times
4918 Napier Street, Port Alberni, BC V9Y 3H5
Phone: (250) 723-8171　Fax: (250) 723-0586
E-mail: karenb-avtimes@shaw.ca
Web site: www.canada.com/vancouverisland/albernivalleytimes

Capital News Daily
2495 Enterprise Way, Kelowna, BC V1X 7K2
Phone: (250) 763-3212　Fax: (250) 862-5275
E-mail: edit@kelownacapnews.com
Web site: www.kelownacapnews.com

Cranbrook Daily Townsman
822 Cranbrook Street N., Cranbrook, BC V1C 3R9
Phone: (250) 426-5201　Fax: (250) 426-5003
E-mail: townsman@cyberlink.bc.ca
Web site: www.dailytownsman.com

The Daily Courier
550 Doyle Avenue, Kelowna, BC V1Y 7V1
Phone: (250) 762-4445　Fax: (250) 762-3866
E-mail: tom.wilson@ok.bc.ca
Web site: www.kelownadailycourier.ca

The Daily News
393 Seymour Street, Kamloops, BC V2C 6P6
Phone: (250) 371-6149 Fax: (250) 374-3884
E-mail: kamloopsnews@telus.net
Web site: www.kamloopsnews.ca

The Daily News
801 – 2nd Avenue W., Prince Rupert, BC V8J 1H6
Phone: (250) 624-6781 Fax: (250) 624-2851
E-mail: publisher@princerupertdailynews.ca
Web site: www.canada.com/princerupert

The Kimberley Daily Bulletin
335 Spokane Street, Kimberley, BC V1A 1Y9
Phone: (250) 427-5333 Fax: (250) 427-5336
E-mail: bulletin@cyberlink.bc.ca
Web site: www.dailytownsman.com

Maple Ridge/Pitt Meadows News Daily
22328 – 119th Avenue, Maple Ridge, BC V2X 2Z3
Phone: (604) 467-1122 Fax: (604) 463-4741
E-mail: editor@mapleridgenews.com
Web site: www.mapleridgenews.com

Metro
1190 Homer Street, Suite 250, Vancouver, BC V6B 2X6
Phone: (604) 602-1002 Fax: (604) 648-3222
E-mail: vancouverletters@metronews.ca
Web site: www.metronews.ca

The Morning Star Daily
4407 – 25th Avenue, Vernon, BC V1T 1P5
Phone: (250) 545-3322 Fax: (250) 558-3468
E-mail: letters@vernonmorningstar.com
Web site: www.vernonmorningstar

Nanaimo Daily News
2575 McCullough Road, Suite B-1, Nanaimo, BC V9S 5W5
Phone: (250) 729-4200 Fax: (250) 729-4288

E-mail: news@nanaimodailynews.com
Web site: www.canada.com/vancouverisland/nanaimo

Nelson Daily News
266 Baker Street, Nelson, BC V1L 4H3
Phone: (250) 352-3552 Fax: (250) 352-2418
E-mail: news@nelsondailynews.com
Web site: www.nelsondailynews.com

Peace River Block Daily News
901 – 100th Avenue, Dawson Creek, BC V1G 1W2
Phone: (250) 782-4888 Fax: (250) 782-6770
E-mail: news@prbn.ca
Web site: www.prbn.ca

Penticton Herald
186 Nanaimo Street W., Penticton, BC V2A 1N4
Phone: (250) 492-4002 Fax: (250) 492-2403
E-mail: editor@pentictonherald.ca
Web site: www.pentictonherald.ca

Prince George Citizen
150 Brunswick Street, P.O. Box 5700, Prince George, BC V2L 5K9
Phone: (250) 562-2441 Fax: (250) 562-7453
E-mail: news@princegeorgecitizen.com
Web site: www.princegeorgecitizen.com

The Province
200 Granville Street, Suite 1, Vancouver, BC V6C 3N3
Phone: (604) 605-2000 Fax: (604) 605-2720
E-mail: tabtips@png.canwest.com
Web site: www.canada.com/theprovince

Times Colonist
2621 Douglas Street, P.O. Box 300, Victoria, BC V8T 4M2
Phone: (250) 380-5211 Fax: (250) 380-5353
E-mail: localnews@tc.canwest.com
Web site: www.canada.com/victoriatimescolonist

Trail Daily Times
1163 Cedar Avenue, Trail, BC V1R 4B8
Phone: (250) 364-1242 Fax: (250) 368-8550
E-mail: editor@trailtimes.ca
Web site: www.canada.com/cityguides/trail

24 Hours
1070 S.E. Marine Drive, Vancouver, BC V5X 2V4
Phone: (604) 322-2340 Fax: (604) 322-3026
E-mail: news@24hrs.ca
Web site: www.24hrs.ca

The Vancouver Sun
200 Granville Street, Suite 1, Vancouver, BC V6C 3N3
Phone: (604) 605-2443 Fax: (604) 605-2323
E-mail: sunnewstips@png.canwest.com
Web site: www.canada.com/vancouversun

Manitoba

The Brandon Sun
501 Rosser Avenue, Brandon, MB R7A 0K4
Phone: (204) 727-2451 Fax: (204) 727-0385
E-mail: opinion@brandonsun.com
Web site: www.brandonsun.com

The Daily Graphic
1941 Saskatchewan Avenue W., P.O. Box 130, Portage La Prairie,
MB R1N 3B4
Phone: (204) 857-3427 Fax: (204) 239-1270
E-mail: news.dailygraphic@shawcable.com
Web site: www.portagedailygraphic.com

The Reminder
10 North Avenue, Flin Flon, MB R8A 0T2
Phone: (204) 687-3454 Fax: (204) 687-4473
E-mail: online@ffdailyreminder.com
Web site: www.ffdailyreminder.com

Winnipeg Free Press
1355 Mountain Avenue, Winnipeg, MB R2X 3B6
Phone: (204) 697-7000 Fax: (204) 697-7412
E-mail: city.desk@freepress.mb.ca
Web site: http://winnipegfreepress.com

Winnipeg Sun
1700 Church Avenue, Winnipeg, MB R2X 3A2
Phone: (204) 694-2022 Fax: (204) 697-0759
E-mail: citydesk@wpgsun.com
Web site: www.winnipegsun.com

New Brunswick

The Daily Gleaner
P.O. Box 3370, Fredericton, NB E3B 2T8
Phone: (506) 452-6671 Fax: (506) 452-7405
E-mail: news@dailygleaner.com
Web site: www.canadaeast.com

Telegraph-Journal
P.O. Box 2350, Saint John, NB E2L 3V8
Phone: (506) 633-5599 Fax: (506) 633-6758
E-mail: newsroom@nbpub.com
Web site: www.canadaeast.com

Times & Transcript
P.O. Box 1001, Moncton, NB E1C 5T8
Phone: (506) 859-4905 Fax: (506) 859-4904
E-mail: tteditor@timestranscript.com
Web site: www.canadaeast.com

Newfoundland & Labrador

The Telegram
1 Columbus Drive, P.O. Box 5970, St. John's, NL A1C 5X7
Phone: (709) 364-6300 Fax: (709) 364-3939

E-mail: telegram@thetelegram.com
Web site: www.thetelegram.com

The Western Star
106 West Street, P.O. Box 460, Corner Brook, NL A2H 6E7
Phone: (709) 637-4669 Fax: (709) 634-9824
E-mail: newsroom@thewesternstar.com
Web site: www.thewesternstar.com

Nova Scotia

Amherst Daily News
147 South Albion Street, Amherst, NS B4H 2X2
Phone: (902) 667-5102 Fax: (902) 667-0119
E-mail: bworks@amherstdaily.com
Web site: www.amherstdaily.com

Cape Breton Post
255 George Street, P.O. Box 1500, Sydney, NS B1P 6K6
Phone: (902) 563-3839 Fax: (902) 562-7077
E-mail: news@cbpost.com
Web site: www.capebretonpost.com

The Daily News
P.O. Box 8330, Stn. A, Halifax, NS B3K 5M1
Phone: (902) 444-4444 Fax: (902) 422-5667
E-mail: citydesk@hfxnews.ca
Web site: www.hfxnews.ca

The Mail-Star/The Chronicle-Herald/Sunday Herald
1650 Argyle Street, P.O. Box 610, Halifax, NS B3J 2T2
Phone: (902) 426-3088 Fax: (902) 426-1158
E-mail: newsroom@herald.ca
Web site: http://halifaxherald.com

The News
352 East River Road, P.O. Box 159, New Glasgow, NS B2H 5E2
Phone: (902) 752-3000 Fax: (902) 752-1945

E-mail: news@ngnews.ca
Web site: www.ngnews.ca

Truro Daily News
6 Louise Street, P.O. Box 220, Truro, NS B2N 5C3
Phone: (902) 893-9405 Fax: (902) 893-0518
E-mail: news@trurodaily.com
Web site: www.trurodaily.com

Ontario

The Barrie Examiner
571 Bayfield Street N., Barrie, ON L4M 4Z9
Phone: (705) 726-6537 Fax: (705) 726-5414
E-mail: news@thebarrieexaminer.com
Web site: www.thebarrieexaminer.com

The Beacon Herald
16 Packham Road, P.O. Box 430, Stratford, ON N5A 6T6
Phone: (519) 271-2220 Fax: (519) 271-1026
E-mail: lturnbull@bowesnet.com
Web site: www.stratfordbeaconherald.com

The Chatham Daily News
45 – 4th Street, Chatham, ON N7M 5M6
Phone: (519) 354-2000 Fax: (519) 354-9489
E-mail: news@chathamdailynews.ca
Web site: http://chathamdailynews.ca

The Chatham Sun
930 Richmond Street, Chatham, ON N7M 5J5
Phone: (519) 351-4397 Fax: (519) 351-7774
Web site: www.chathamsun.com

The Chronicle Journal
75 South Cumberland Street, Thunder Bay, ON P7B 1A3
Phone: (807) 343-6200 Fax: (807) 343-9409

E-mail: news@chroniclejournal.com
Web site: www.chroniclejournal.com

Cobourg Daily Star
99 King Street W., P.O. Box 400, Cobourg, ON K9A 4L1
Phone: (905) 372-0131 Fax: (905) 372-4966
E-mail: eargyris@northumberlandtoday.com
Web site: www.northumberlandtoday.com

The Daily Bulletin
116 First Street E., P.O. Box 339, Fort Frances, ON P9A 3M7
Phone: (807) 274-5373 Fax: (807) 274-7286
E-mail: news@fortfrancesonline.com
Web site: www.fftimes.com

The Daily Observer
186 Alexander Street, Pembroke, ON K8A 4T9
Phone: (613) 732-9830 Fax: (613) 732-2226
E-mail: editor@thedailyobserver.ca
Web site: www.thedailyobserver.ca

The Daily Post
15 William Street N., Lindsay, ON K9V 3Z8
Phone: (705) 324-2113 Fax: (705) 324-0174
E-mail: lineditorial@thepost.ca
Web site: www.thepost.ca

The Daily Press
187 Cedar Street S., Timmins, ON P4N 7G1
Phone: (705) 268-5050 Fax: (705) 268-7373
E-mail: editorial@thedailypress.ca
Web site: www.timminspress.com

The Expositor
53 Dalhousie Street, P.O. Box 965, Brantford, ON N3T 5S8
Phone: (519) 756-2020 Fax: (519) 756-4911
E-mail: expnews@theexpositor.com
Web site: www.brantfordexpositor.ca

The Globe and Mail
444 Front Street W., Toronto, ON M5V 2S9
Phone: (416) 585-5000 Fax: (416) 585-5085
E-mail: newsroom@globeandmail.com
Web site: www.globeandmail.com

The Guelph Mercury
14 Macdonell Street, Suite 8, Guelph, ON N1H 6P7
Phone: (519) 822-4310 Fax: (519) 767-1681
E-mail: editor@guelphmercury.com
Web site: www.guelphmercury.com

The Hamilton Spectator
44 Frid Street, P.O. Box 300, Hamilton, ON L8N 3G3
Phone: (905) 526-3333 Fax: (905) 526-1395
E-mail: letters@thespec.com
Web site: www.hamiltonspectator.com

The Intelligencer
45 Bridge Street E., Belleville, ON K8N 5C7
Phone: (613) 962-9171 Fax: (613) 962-9652
E-mail: newsroom@intelligencer.ca
Web site: www.intelligencer.ca

Kenora Daily Miner and News
33 Main Street S., P.O. Box 1620, Kenora, ON P9N 3X7
Phone: (807) 468-5555 Fax: (807) 468-4318
E-mail: minerandnews@norcomcable.ca
Web site: www.kenoradailyminerandnews.com

The Kingston Whig-Standard
6 Cataraqui Street, P.O. Box 2300, Kingston, ON K7L 4Z7
Phone: (613) 544-5000 Fax: (613) 530-4118
E-mail: cspencer@thewhig.com
Web site: www.thewhig.com

The London Free Press
369 York Street, P.O. Box 2280, London, ON N6A 4G1
Phone: (519) 679-6666 Fax: (519) 667-4528

E-mail: newsdesk@lfpress.com
Web site: www.lfpress.com

Metro
116 Albert Street, Suite 401, Ottawa, ON K1P 5G3
Phone: (613) 236-5058 Fax: (613) 253-2024
E-mail: ottawaletters@metronews.ca
Web site: www.metronews.ca

National Post
1450 Don Mills Road, Suite 300, Don Mills, ON M3B 3R5
Phone: (416) 383-2300 Fax: (416) 442-2209
E-mail: queries@nationalpost.com
Web site: www.nationalpost.com

The Niagara Falls Review
4801 Valley Way, Niagara Falls, ON L2E 6T6
Phone: (905) 358-5711 Fax: (905) 356-0785
E-mail: lwallace@nfreview.com
Web site: www.niagarafallsreview.ca

North Bay Nugget
259 Worthington Street W., North Bay, ON P1B 3B5
Phone: (705) 472-3200 Fax: (705) 472-1438
E-mail: news@nugget.ca
Web site: www.nugget.ca

Northern News
8 Duncan Avenue, Kirkland Lake, ON P2N 3L4
Phone: (705) 567-5321 Fax: (705) 567-6162
E-mail: news@northernnews.ca
Web site: www.northernnews.ca

The Observer
140 South Front Street, Sarnia, ON N7T 7M8
Phone: (519) 344-3641 Fax: (519) 332-2951
E-mail: editorial@theobserver.ca
Web site: www.thebserver.ca

Ottawa Citizen
1101 Baxter Road, P.O. Box 5020, Ottawa, ON K2C 3M4
Phone: (613) 829-9100 Fax: (613) 726-1198
E-mail: dshelly@thecitizen.canwest.com
Web site: www.canada.com/ottawacitizen

Ottawa Sun
P.O. Box 9729, Stn. T, Ottawa, ON K1G 5H7
Phone: (613) 739-7000 Fax: (613) 739-8041
E-mail: city@ott.sunpub.com
Web site: www.ottawasun.com

Packet & Times
31 Colborne Street E., Orillia, ON L3V 1T4
Phone: (705) 325-1355 Fax: (705) 329-5926
E-mail: newsroom@orilliapacket.com
Web site: www.orilliapacket.com

The Peterborough Examiner
730 The Kingsway, Peterborough, ON K9J 8L4
Phone: (705) 745-4641 Fax: (705) 743-4581
E-mail: newsroom@peterboroughexaminer.com
Web site: www.thepeterboroughexaminer.com

Port Hope Evening Guide
97 Walton Street S., P.O. Box 296, Port Hope, ON L1A 1N4
Phone: (905) 885-2471 Fax: (905) 885-7442
E-mail: eargyris@northumberlandtoday.com
Web site: www.northumberlandtoday.com

The Record
160 King Street E., Kitchener, ON N2G 4E5
Phone: (519) 894-2231 Fax: (519) 894-3829
E-mail: newsroom@therecord.com
Web site: www.therecord.com

The Recorder & Times
1600 California Avenue, Brockville, ON K6V 5T8
Phone: (613) 342-4441 Fax: (613) 342-4093

E-mail: wb.raison@recorder.ca
Web site: www.recorder.ca

St. Thomas Times-Journal
16 Hincks Street, St. Thomas, ON N5R 5Z2
Phone: (519) 631-2790 Fax: (519) 631-5653
E-mail: news@stthomastimesjournal.com
Web site: www.stthomastimesjournal.com

Sarnia Sun
1383 Confederation Street, Sarnia, ON N7S 5P1
Phone: (519) 336-1105 Fax: (519) 336-1833
E-mail: newsroom@sarniasun.com
Web site: www.sarniasun.com

The Sault Star
145 Old Garden River Road, Sault Ste. Marie, ON P6A 5M5
Phone: (705) 759-3030 Fax: (705) 759-0102
E-mail: ssmstar@saultstar.com
Web site: www.saultstar.com

Sentinel-Review
16 Brock Street, Woodstock, ON N4S 3B4
Phone: (519) 537-2341 Fax: (519) 537-3049
E-mail: sentinelreview@bowesnet.com
Web site: www.woodstocksentinelreview.com

Simcoe Reformer
50 Gilbertson Drive, Simcoe, ON N3Y 4L2
Phone: (519) 426-5710 Fax: (519) 426-9255
E-mail: refedit@bowesnet.com
Web site: www.simcoereformer.ca

The Standard
17 Queen Street, St. Catharines, ON L2R 5G5
Phone: (905) 684-7251 Fax: (905) 684-6032
E-mail: kreid@stcatharinesstandard.ca
Web site: www.stcatharinesstandard.ca

Standard Freeholder
44 Pitt Street, Cornwall, ON K6J 3P3
Phone: (613) 933-3160 Fax: (613) 933-3664
E-mail: news@standard-freeholder.com
Web site: www.standard-freeholder.com

The Sudbury Star
33 MacKenzie Street, Sudbury, ON P3C 4Y1
Phone: (705) 674-5271 Fax: (705) 674-6834
E-mail: editorial@thesudburystar.com
Web site: www.thesudburystar.com

The Sun Times
290 – 9th Street E., Owen Sound, ON N4K 5P2
Phone: (519) 376-2250 Fax: (519) 376-7190
E-mail: news@thesuntimes.ca
Web site: www.owensoundsuntimes.com

Today Daily News
1830 Ellesmere Road, Unit B, Scarborough, ON M1H 2V5
Phone: (416) 289-1234 Fax: (416) 289-8933
E-mail: today@todaydailynews.com
Web site: www.todaydailynews.com

Toronto Metro
1 Concorde Gate, Suite 703, Toronto, ON M3C 3N6
Phone: (416) 486-4900 Fax: (416) 482-8097
E-mail: newsdesk@metronews.ca
Web site: www.metronews.ca

The Toronto Star
1 Yonge Street, Toronto, ON M5E 1E6
Phone: (416) 367-2000 Fax: (416) 869-4328
E-mail: city@thestar.ca
Web site: www.thestar.com

Toronto Sun
333 King Street E., Toronto, ON M5A 3X5
Phone: (416) 947-2222 Fax: (416) 947-1664

E-mail: citydesk@tor.sunpub.com
Web site: www.torontosun.com

Toronto 24 Hours
333 King Street E., Toronto, ON M5A 3X5
Phone: (416) 350-6462 Fax: (416) 350-6524
E-mail: 24news@tor.sunpub.com
Web site: http://toronto.24hrs.ca

The Tribune
228 East Main Street, Welland, ON L3B 5P5
Phone: (905) 732-2411 Fax: (905) 732-3660
E-mail: tribune@wellandtribune.ca
Web site: www.wellandtribune.ca

The Windsor Star
167 Ferry Street, Windsor, ON N9A 4M5
Phone: (519) 255-5743 Fax: (519) 255-5515
E-mail: letters@thestar.canwest.com
Web site: www.canada.com/windsorstar

Prince Edward Island

The Guardian
165 Prince Street, Charlottetown, PE C1A 4R7
Phone: (902) 629-6000 Fax: (902) 566-3808
E-mail: newsroom@theguardian.pe.ca
Web site: www.theguardian.pe.ca

Journal Pioneer
316 Water Street, P.O. Box 2480, Summerside, PE C1N 4K5
Phone: (902) 436-2121 Fax: (902) 436-3027
E-mail: journal@journalpioneer.com
Web site: www.journalpioneer.com

Quebec

The Gazette
1010 Ste. Catherine Street W., Suite 200, Montreal, QC H3B 5L1
Phone: (514) 987-2222 Fax: (514) 987-2399
E-mail: letters@thegazette.canwest.com
Web site: www.montrealgazette.com

The Record
1195 Galt Street E., Sherbrooke, QC J1G 1Y7
Phone: (819) 569-6345 Fax: (819) 569-3945
E-mail: newsroom@sherbrookerecord.com
Web site: www.sherbrookerecord.com

Saskatchewan

Leader-Post
1964 Park Street, P.O. Box 2020, Regina, SK S4P 3G4
Phone: (306) 781-5300 Fax: (306) 565-2588
E-mail: feedback@canwest.com
Web site: www.canada.com/reginaleaderpost

Prince Albert Daily Herald
30 – 10th Street E., Prince Albert, SK S6V 0Y5
Phone: (306) 764-4276 Fax: (306) 763-3331
E-mail: editorial@paherald.sk.ca
Web site: www.paherald.sk.ca

The StarPhoenix
204 – 5th Avenue N., Saskatoon, SK S7K 2P1
Phone: (306) 657-6231 Fax: (306) 657-6437
E-mail: spnews@sp.canwest.com
Web site: www.canada.com/saskatoonstarphoenix

Times-Herald
44 Fairford Street W., Moose Jaw, SK S6H 1V1
Phone: (306) 692-6441 Fax: (306) 692-2101

E-mail: editorial@mjtimes.sk.ca
Web site: www.mjtimes.sk.ca

Yukon

Whitehorse Daily Star
2149 – 2nd Avenue, Whitehorse, YT Y1A 1C5
Phone: (867) 667-4481 Fax: (867) 668-7130
E-mail: star@whitehorsestar.com
Web site: www.whitehorsestar.com

5

BOOK PUBLISHERS

The first-time author should be under no illusions about the difficulties of breaking into book publishing – still less, of making a living from the often-slender proceeds, unless you are phenomenally talented or hit on that rare winning formula. Nonetheless, every year brings a new success story – another brilliant unknown author who takes the publishing world by storm. Every writer must be a realist, and an optimist.

Small presses are more likely to take an interest in an unpublished writer, and are generally more receptive to unsolicited manuscripts. They also may be more accessible, offer more personal attention to their authors, and be more willing to take a risk. Nino Ricci's prize-winning first novel, *Lives of the Saints*, was published by Cormorant Books, having been rejected by a raft of the larger players. But he had no difficulty placing his eagerly awaited second novel with McClelland & Stewart. Small presses almost always work with unagented writers. On the down side, small publishers offer small advances or none at all, their print runs tend to be low, and their distribution systems and marketing expertise cannot match those of the big houses.

Before you make any approaches to publishers, do some research. Use the following list to whittle down a selection of houses whose programs seem most compatible with your own work, then check out some of their books. Another approach is to browse through a bookstore compiling a list of publishers who are releasing books similar to yours. You can write to their publicity departments, including a large SASE, to request current catalogues, and visit their web sites to learn more about their publishing programs. Familiarity with the focus of several houses can help you develop an attractive proposal, as well as target the most appropriate potential publishers.

It is important to note the difference in selling fiction and non-fiction manuscripts to book publishers. Typically a manuscript of fiction must be fully finished before you approach an editor. For non-fiction, you must have done considerable research on your topic, but usually you are required to produce only a synopsis of your story, a chapter outline, and two or three sample chapters. Remember that whether your manuscript is fiction or non-fiction, it is imperative that it begin with a strong, attention-grabbing start. If you don't capture an editor's interest in the first few minutes, he or she is likely to set aside your work and move on to the next manuscript in the pile.

The Query Letter

If you are aiming to sell your manuscript directly to a book publisher without the benefit of a literary agent, your first approach should be through a query letter. This initial correspondence is extremely important. A poorly composed letter can nix your chances of getting published before an editor has even looked at your manuscript. A compelling query letter may get your manuscript onto someone's desk for a first read.

Your letter should be typed in a plain, readable font on unadorned, business-like stationery. Include your name, address, telephone and fax numbers, and your e-mail address. Refer to the editor (or other contact person) by name, and address him or her as Mr. or Ms.

In a letter of no more than two pages, plus enclosures, you must convince a publishing house to at least consider investing considerable money and effort in your manuscript. Spend time to craft it in your best writing style and seize the editor's attention with a gripping intro. Remember, an editor doesn't yet have your manuscript to read; his or her judgement will be based largely upon the strength of your query.

Tell the editor the working title of your book and describe what it is about; if it is fiction, outline the characters and provide a short plot synopsis. Next, mention any special qualifications you have to write this manuscript. These might include a background in the subject covered or special access to research sources. Indicate your publishing history, who published your previous books, how many copies were sold, and if any foreign rights were bought.

Tell the editor what competing books on a similar subject are in the marketplace, and confidently assert why yours will do equally well or be more successful. Also describe what makes your manuscript different from all the others; after all, publishers want something original. Inform the editor about any research you have done to determine the markets for your book and ideas you may have for promotion.

For non-fiction queries, include a one-page synopsis of your manuscript if it could not be adequately described in your letter. Also enclose a table of contents with a brief description of what each chapter is about and an indication of the research you will undertake in writing this book. You may send one or two sample chapters or wait for a request by the editor. For a fiction query, send along a one-page synopsis and three sample chapters (including the first chapter).

If you haven't received a reply after two months, you may wish to send the editor a note attached to a copy of your original query letter. But if after three months you still haven't heard, move on to another publisher. Due to long delays, which are typical in book publishing, it is permissible to send out multiple queries.

Sending the Manuscript

If you have received a positive reply from a query letter, or if you have targeted a publisher that will accept full manuscripts without an initial query, there is a certain protocol to follow when submitting your work.

Manuscripts should be prepared as indicated in the Introduction; that is, on 8-by-11-inch bond paper, typed on a computer in a readable font and double-spaced. Of course, you should never send the only copy of your work. Manuscripts should not be stapled, but fastened with elastic bands and held between two sheets of cardboard, front and back, or better still, placed in a box.

A covering letter should accompany your work. If this is an unsolicited manuscript, include a letter similar to the query letter (above), one that sells both you and your book to the prospective publisher. When an editor has asked to see your manuscript in response to a query, enclose a covering letter reminding him or her of your previous correspondence.

It may take three months or longer for a publishing company to reply to your submission, so it is advisable to include a self-addressed stamped postcard so they can acknowledge its receipt. Be sure to also send a postage-paid envelope large enough for your manuscript so an editor can return your work if it is not accepted, otherwise you may not receive it back.

While it is perfectly permissible to send out multiple submissions, there is a general protocol that you should follow. Indicate in your covering letter that you have sent the manuscript to other publishers; you do not need to specify which publishers these are. Also state a deadline for their decision – three months is standard – before which time you must not sign a contract from one publisher without allowing the others to make counter-offers.

Contracts

Receiving a contract from a book publisher is a dream come true. While your tendency may be to sign anything that will bring your manuscript into book form, it is a very important legal document, and you must proceed with caution.

First of all, you need to seek the advice of a professional who will explain the rights, obligations, and rewards being offered by such a document. You must understand the rights you are selling and agree that the compensation is fair, or negotiate to try to improve it. You should never sign away the copyright to your work.

Royalty rates vary, but average around 10 per cent for hardcover books and in the 8-per-cent range for paperbacks. Sometimes a sliding scale is offered whereby you receive a higher rate if your book sells more than a certain number of copies. For regular sales of your book (which doesn't include book-club sales or discount sales), you should receive the royalty as a percentage of the list price of the book, not the publisher's net.

An advance is a payment against the royalties your publisher expects the book will earn. It is typically paid in either two or three installments: when the contract is signed, when the manuscript is accepted, and sometimes when the book is published. While some small presses are unable to offer their authors advances, in the industry overall advances are rising, due to the increasing aggressiveness of Canadian publishers and agents, as well as international recognition of Canadian fiction. It is rare for a first-time novelist to receive over $15,000 as an advance; for business books, an average advance would range from $5,000 to $10,000.

As print-on-demand systems and e-books gain in popularity, new contractual issues arise. When a book is out of print for a certain period of time, the rights revert to the author. But now in the United States, those rights may not revert if the book exists in electronic form. In addition, if a book appears in an electronic medium, the writer has to ensure that he or she will receive adequate compensation.

For advice on publishing contracts, contact a lawyer who specializes in the publishing field, an experienced literary agent, or the Writers' Union of Canada.

Before outlining what we cover in the rest of this chapter, perhaps it's worth clarifying what we don't. Educational publishers are not listed unless they have a significant trade-publishing arm. Today more than ever, educational publishers are commissioning their books in close collaboration with schools and colleges to meet specific curricular needs. These texts are nearly always written by specialists in the field. Very few educational publishers consider unsolicited manuscripts or proposals, and fewer still are likely to look favourably upon them unless their author has a proven track record in the area. Neither, with a few exceptions, have we included publishers that specialize in poetry. For a comprehensive listing, consult *Poetry Markets for Canadians* (8th edition), published by the League of Canadian Poets, or *Poet's Market*, an annual publication by Writer's Digest Books.

The following list of publishers comprises English-language publishing houses only. It includes the major companies, as well as most of the mid-range and many of the smaller trade publishers currently operating in Canada. Some have large general-interest lists; others are more specialized, either in their subject areas or in their regional concerns.

Aardvark Enterprises

204 Millbank Drive S.W., Calgary, AB T2Y 2I19
Phone: (403) 256-4639
Contact: J. Alvin Speers, publisher/editor
Publishes how-to editions helpful to writers; otherwise concentrates on publishing works of J. Alvin Speers. Open to proposals nevertheless. Produced 6 books in 2006. Accepts written inquiries. "Be prepared to invest in your work – follow-up, communicate. As in any field of endeavour, there are 3 kinds of writers: those who make things happen, those who watch things happen, and some who wonder what happened."
Notable 2006 title: *The Drugstore Cowboys Short Story Collection*, J. Alvin Speers.

AB Collector Publishing

5835 Grant Street, Halifax, NS B3H 1C9
Phone: (902) 425-6935 Fax: (506) 385-1981
E-mail: darklady@nbnet.nb.ca
Web site: www.abcollectorpublishing.ca
Contact: Astrid Brunner, publisher/chief editor
Publishes biography, poetry, drama, short stories, anthology, and books about ceramics, photography, art, and history. "Your significant peripheral publisher since 1990. Each book is a thing of art, a dusting of poetry, a meaning of life." Has released 20 titles since 1990. First send an inquiry, then an outline, then sample chapters with a short bio. For more information, see web site.
Notable 2006 title: *A Quiet, Bashful Man: Remembering Malcolm*, authors and artists of the ABCP Malcolm Memorial Literary Competition.

Abbeyfield Publishers

1 Benvenuto Place, Suite 103, Toronto, ON M3V 2L1
Phone: (416) 925-6458 Fax: (416) 925-4165
E-mail: abbeyfld@istar.ca
Web site: www.abbeyfieldpublishers.com
Contact: Bill Belfontaine, publisher

Publishes non-fiction, biographies, memoirs, books about the Holocaust, corporate books, books on social issues, and custom books. No fiction, children's books, or art books. Produces 5 new titles a year. No unsolicited manuscripts. Inquire by telephone first. Author guidelines available.

Notable 2003 title: *Gabriel's Dragon*, Fr. Anthony Gabriel.

ABC Publishing
Anglican Book Centre, 80 Hayden Street, Toronto, ON M4Y 3G2
Phone: (416) 924-9192 Fax: (416) 968-7983
E-mail: abcpublishing@national.anglican.ca
Web site: www.abcpublishing.com
Contact: Robert Maclennan, publishing manager

Publishes books by Canadian authors on practical spirituality for everyday living and on church liturgy, ministry, mission, and education. Produced 10 new titles in 2006. No unsolicited manuscripts. Accepts inquiries. Author guidelines available.

Notable 2005 title: *Sacred Simplicities*, Lori Knutson.

Acorn Press
P.O. Box 22024, Charlottetown, PE C1A 1Y1
Phone: (902) 892-8151 or (902) 566-0956 Fax: (902) 566-0756
E-mail: brinklow@upei.ca
Web site: www.acornpresscanada.com
Contact: Laurie Brinklow, publisher

Publishes books about Prince Edward Island by Prince Edward Islanders. Releases about 4 new titles a year. Accepts unsolicited manuscripts about P.E.I. only, but send inquiry first. Guidelines available.

Notable 2006 title: *The Brow of Dawn: One Woman's Journey with MS*, Catherine Edward.

Thomas Allen Publishers
145 Front Street E., Suite 209, Toronto, ON M5A 1E3
Phone: (416) 361-0233 Fax: (416) 203-2773
Web site: www.thomas-allen.com
Contact: Patrick Crean, publisher

Publishes literary fiction and non-fiction. Non-fiction categories include history, memoirs, travel, nature, philosophy, and popular culture. No cookbooks, genre fiction, DIY, or financial books. Produces approximately 15 new titles annually. No unsolicited manuscripts; manuscript submissions must be agented or come by referral.

Notable 2006 title: *A Perfect Night to Go to China*, David Gilmour.

The Alternate Press

264 Queens Quay W., Suite 508, Toronto, ON M5J 1B5
Phone: (416) 260-0303
E-mail: editor@lifemedia.ca
Web site: www.lifemedia.ca/altpress
Contact: Wendy Priesnitz, editor-in-chief

Publishes adult non-fiction about ways families and individuals can live in a healthy, environmentally sound, self-reliant manner. Releases 1 new title a year. Accepts unsolicited manuscripts, but send an inquiry first. Guidelines available on web site.

Annick Press

15 Patricia Avenue, Toronto, ON M2M 1H9
Phone: (416) 221-4802 Fax: (416) 221-8400
E-mail: annickpress@annickpress.com
Web site: www.annickpress.com
Contact: Kathy Dearing, office manager

Established 1975. Publishes children's literature, including picture books, teen and middle-reader fiction, and non-fiction. "We seek out works that crackle with originality and become a passageway to new ideas. Our list is designed to excite, entertain, and promote self-awareness." Released 30 new titles in 2006. Accepts unsolicited manuscripts. "Please see our web site for full submission details."

Notable 2006 title: *Strange Times at Western High*, Emily Pohl-Weary.

Anvil Press

P.O. Box 3008, MPO, Vancouver, BC V6B 3X5
Phone: (604) 876-8710 Fax: (604) 879-2667
E-mail: info@anvilpress.com
Web site: www.anvilpress.com
Contact: Brian Kaufman, publisher

An independent literary press interested in work from new and established writers. Publishes contemporary work in all genres. Releases 8 to 10 books a year. Accepts unsolicited manuscripts. Send synopsis with sample chapter or two. Expect a wait of 4 to 6 months for reply. Send a #10 SASE for reply without manuscript. "Get our guidelines online, look at our books and catalogue to get a sense of the press, and submit if you feel your work is in line with our program."

Notable 2006 title: *Stolen*, Annette Lapointe.

Arbeiter Ring Publishing

121 Osborne Street, Suite 201E, Winnipeg, MB R3L 1Y4
Phone: (204) 942-7058 Fax: (204) 944-9198
E-mail: info@arbeiterring.com
Web site: www.arteiterring.com
Contact: Carolynn Smallwood, office manager

Publishes a combination of serious cultural work and non-fiction titles with an emphasis on progressive political analysis of social and cultural issues. Released 3 titles in 2006. Send an inquiry with an outline and sample chapters first. "Please consult our web site for submission guidelines and for further information on our publishing mandate/mission."

Notable 2006 title: *Another World Is Possible: Globalization and Anti-Capitalization* (2nd expanded and revised edition), David McNally.

Arsenal Pulp Press

341 Water Street, Suite 200, Vancouver, BC V6B 1G8
Phone: (604) 687-4233 Fax: (604) 687-4283
E-mail: info@arsenalpulp.com
Web site: www.arsenalpulp.com
Contact: Brian Lam, publisher

Established 1971. Genres include literary fiction, cultural studies, cooking, multicultural literature, gay and lesbian literature, and literary non-fiction. Releases about 20 titles a year. Accepts unsolicited manuscripts, but send an outline and sample chapters first. "No guaranteed response without an SASE (or e-mail address). Does not accept submissions by fax." Guidelines available on web site.

Banff Centre Press

P.O. Box 1020, 107 Tunnel Mountain Drive, Banff, AB T1L 1H5
Phone: (403) 762-6410 Fax: (403) 762-6699
E-mail: press@banffcentre.ca
Web site: www.banffcentre.ca/press
Contact: Sarah Bernath

The Banff Centre Press specializes in publications on contemporary art, culture, and literature. It seeks to explore, disseminate, and garner support for the arts. Releases 4 to 6 new titles annually. Does not accept unsolicited manuscripts; submit an outline, sample chapters, and author bio first.

Notable 2006 title: *Reflections in a Dancing Eye: Investigating the Artist's Role in Canadian Society*, edited by Carol Anderson and Joysanne Sidimus.

The Battered Silicon Dispatch Box

P.O. Box 204, Shelburne, ON L0N 1S0
Fax: (519) 925-3482
E-mail: gav@bmts.com
Web site: www.batteredbox.com
Contact: George A. Vanderburgh, publisher

A small press specializing in detective fiction from the golden age. "A Sherlockian publisher of first and last resort." Publishes about 40 books a year. Does not accept unsolicited manuscripts.

Notable 2006 title: *Uptown Downtown*, Raymond Souster.

Between the Lines

720 Bathurst Street, Suite 404, Toronto, ON M5S 2R4
Phone: (416) 535-9914 Fax: (416) 535-1484
E-mail: btlbooks@wcb.ca
Web site: http://btlbooks.com
Contact: Paul Eprile, editorial co-ordinator

Established 1977. Publishes critical, accessible non-fiction, primarily on Canadian history, economics, culture, and social issues. Accepts unsolicited manuscripts, but prefers to receive an inquiry first with an outline, sample chapters, and author bio.

Notable 2006 title: *Gatekeepers: Reshaping Immigrant Lives in Cold War Canada*, Franca Iacovetta.

Black Moss Press

2450 Byng Road, Windsor, ON N8W 3E8
Fax: (519) 253-7809
Web site: www.blackmosspress.com
Contact: Marty Gervais, editor

Seeking new poetry, fiction, and non-fiction. Publishes two theme anthologies each year. "Looking for new and innovative writing with an edge." Accepts unsolicited manuscripts, but send an inquiry first. Submission details on web site.

Notable 2007 title: *Left Hand Horses*, John B. Lee.

BookLand Press

6021 Yonge Street, Suite 1010, Toronto, ON M2M 3W2
Phone: (416) 607-6176　Fax: (416) 352-1993
E-mail: books@booklandpress.com
Web site: www.booklandpress.com
Contact: Robert Morgan, general manager

BookLand Press is an independent publisher of quality literature. Interests range from important contemporary poetry to beautifully written fiction and non-fiction. Strives to present books with topics that are relative to the needs of today's society. Releases about 10 books a year. Does not accept unsolicited manuscripts. Send an outline first. Guidelines available.

Notable 2006 title: *Alexandra Orlando: In Pursuit of Victory*, Martin Avery and Alexandra Orlando.

Borealis Press

110 Bloomingdale Street, Ottawa, ON K2C 4A4
Phone: (613) 829-0150　Fax: (613) 829-7783
E-mail: drt@borealispress.com
Web site: www.borealispress.com

Established 1972. A general publisher, but specializes in Canadiana, including the Tecumseh Press subsidary reserved for Canadian material. "We do not consider multiple submissions or unsolicited full manuscripts. Query first, including synopsis and a sample chapter or equivalent, together with return postage or international postal coupons and adequate-sized envelope." Guidelines available on web site.

Notable 2006 title: *You Through Your Dreams*, Paul Edward Napora.

The Boston Mills Press
132 Main Street, Erin, ON N0B 1T0
Phone: (519) 833-2407 Fax: (519) 833-2195
E-mail: books@bostonmillspress.com
Web site: www.bostonmillspress.com
Contact: Noel Hudson, managing editor
    Established 1974. "We're looking for more North American–oriented projects. Interested in history, transportation, travel, and architecture." Released 16 new titles in 2006. Accepts unsolicited manuscripts, but first send an inquiry. Guidelines available on web site.
    Notable 2006 title: *Great Lakes Lighthouses Encyclopedia*, Larry Wright and Patricia Wright.

Boulder Publications
11 Boulder Lane, Portugal Cove, NL A1M 2K1
Phone: (709) 895-6483 Fax: (709) 895-0133
E-mail: boulder@nl.rogers.com
Web site: www.boulderpublications.ca
Contact: Gavin Will, president
    Publisher of Canadian non-fiction, with an emphasis on Newfoundland and Labrador. Released 3 new titles in 2006. Accepts unsolicited manuscripts but send an outline first. Guidelines available.
    Notable 2006 title: *Wildflowers of Newfoundland and Labrador*, Peter J. Scott and Dorothy Black.

Breakwater Books
P.O. Box 2188, 100 Water Street, St. John's, NL A1C 6E6
Phone: (709) 722-6680 Fax: (709) 753-0708
E-mail: info@breakwater.nf.net
Contact: Kim O'Keefe, CEO
    Publishes fiction, non-fiction, and educational titles, especially those related to the culture and history of Newfoundland and Labrador. Releases about 15 new titles a year. Does not accept

unsolicited manuscripts. Send an inquiry with outline and sample chapters.

Notable 2006 title: *Fisheries of Newfoundland: An Ecological History*, George Rose.

Brick Books

431 Boler Road, P.O. Box 20081, London, ON N6K 4G6
Phone: (519) 657-8579
E-mail: brick.books@sympatico.ca
Web site: www.brickbooks.ca
Contact: Kitty Lewis, general manager
Established 1975. Publishes Canadian poetry by Canadian authors only. Reads manuscripts January 1 through April 30 every year. Releases 7 new titles annually. Accepts unsolicited manuscripts, but first send an inquiry. Guidelines available.
Notable 2006 title: *When Earth Leaps Up*, Anne Szumigalski.

Brindle & Glass Publishing

11339 – 91st Street, Edmonton, AB T5B 4A4
Phone: (780) 438-7173 Fax: (780) 479-7801
E-mail: info@brindleandglass.com
Web sites: www.brindleandglass.com; www.bluecouchbooks.com
Contact: Ruth Linka, publisher
A literary publisher of fiction, drama, and non-fiction. The Blue Couch Books imprint publishes regional guide books and food-related books. Publishes 12 to 15 new titles annually. Accepts unsolicited manuscripts, but inquire first. "Please see our web site for more information."
Notable 2006 title: *Looking Good*, Keith Maillard.

Broadview Press

5 Douglas Street, Suite 101, Guelph, ON N1H 2S8
Phone: (519) 837-1403 Fax: (519) 767-1643
E-mail: customerservice@broadviewpress.com
Web site: www.broadviewpress.com
Contact: Brandee Faulds, sales and marketing assistant
Established 1985. Specializes in the arts and social sciences, incorporating a variety of viewpoints: liberal, conservative, libertarian,

feminist, and Marxist. Subject areas include anthropology, politics, history, philosophy, sociology, English literature, and medieval studies. Most titles are relevant for undergraduate course use. Publishes about 60 new titles a year. Very rarely accepts unsolicited manuscripts. Send an inquiry with an outline. Guidelines available on web site.

Notable 2006 title: *The Broadview Anthology of British Literature*, volumes 1–6.

Broken Jaw Press

P.O. Box 596, Stn. A, Fredericton, NB E3B 5A6
Phone: (506) 454-5127   Fax: (506) 454-5127
E-mail: editors@brokenjaw.com
Web site: www.brokenjaw.com
Contact: Joe Blades, publisher

An independent literary arts publisher with Canadian-authored poetry, fiction, and creative non-fiction. Publishes some works in translation (especially from Spanish) with poetry often in bilingual editions. Released 6 new titles in 2006. Does not accept unsolicited manuscripts. Guidelines available at www.brokenjaw.com/submissions.htm.

Notable 2006 title: *Aubade*, Rob McLennan.

The Brucedale Press

P.O. Box 2259, Port Elgin, ON N0H 2C0
Phone: (519) 832-6025
E-mail: brucedale@bmts.com
Web site: www.bmts.com/~brucedale
Contact: Anne Duke Judd, publisher

Presents books of literary, historical, and pictorial merit focusing on the Queen's Bush and Bruce Peninsula areas of Ontario. Also publishes *The Leaf*, a twice-yearly journal with the same regional focus. Averages 3 new titles a year. Considers unsolicited manuscripts. Send an inquiry with an outline and sample chapters for fiction, the full manuscript for children's or YA books. "The reading period begins in November. Please follow guidelines carefully."

Notable 2006 title: *Yet More Tales of the Unusual*, Diane Madden.

The Caitlin Press

P.O. Box 219, Madeira Park, BC V0N 2H0
Phone: (604) 883-2730 Fax: (604) 883-9451
E-mail: info@harbourpublishing.com
Web site: www.harbourpublishing.com
Contact: editor

Established 1977. A regional publisher specializing in trade books by B.C. Interior authors. Some literary titles by B.C. authors. Publishes 2 titles a year. "We are interested primarily in Canada's North, and more particularly northern British Columbia." Accepts unsolicited manuscripts that meet these criteria. Send outline and sample chapters. Guidelines available on web site. "Please follow those guidelines."

Notable 2006 title: *Sternwheelers and Canyon Cats*, Jack Boudreau.

Callawind Publications

3551 St. Charles Boulevard, Suite 179, Kirkland, QC H9H 3C4
Phone: (514) 685-9109 Fax: (514) 685-7952
E-mail: info@callawind.com
Web site: www.callawind.com
Contact: Marcy Claman, project manager

Provides complete publishing development (editing, design, layout, and printing) and consultation for cookbook and children's book authors. Releases 4 new titles annually. Does not accept unsolicited manuscripts. Send an inquiry.

Notable 2006 title: *The Inn Chef: Creative Ingredients, Sensational Flavors*, Michael Smith.

Canadian Circumpolar Institute (CCI) Press

University of Alberta, 8625 – 112 Street, Suite 308, Campus
    Tower, Edmonton, AB T6E 0H1
Phone: (780) 492-4512 Fax: (780) 492-1153
E-mail: ccinst@gpu.srv.ualberta.ca
Web site: www.ualberta.ca/polar
Contact: Elaine L. Maloney, managing editor

Publishes peer-reviewed scholarly works, educational volumes, and trade titles on northern polar and circumpolar subjects. Thematic series include Studies in Whaling, Northern Hunter-Gatherer Research, Solstice (Community Voices), the Northern

Reference Series, and the Circumpolar Research Series. Publishes 3 to 5 titles a year. Accepts unsolicited manuscripts, but first send an inquiry, outline, and sample chapters. Guidelines available.

Canadian Museum of Civilization
100 Laurier Street, P.O. Box 3100, Stn. B, Gatineau, QC J8X 4H2
Phone: (819) 776-8394 Fax: (819) 776-8393
E-mail: pam.coulas@civilization.ca
Web site: www.civilization.ca
Contact: Pam Coulas, promotional co-ordinator
Publishes research and disseminates information on the disciplines of Canadian history, ethnography, archaeology, and folk culture. Publishes 15 titles a year. Does not accept unsolicited manuscripts.
Notable 2006 title: *A World Inside. A 150-Year History of the Canadian Museum of Civilization*, C. Vodden and L. Dyck.

Canadian Scholars' Press Inc.
180 Bloor Street W., Suite 801, Toronto, ON M5S 2V6
Phone: (416) 929-2774 Fax: (416) 929-1926
Web sites: www.cspi.org; www.womenspress.ca
Contact: publishing manager
CSPI is a publisher of scholarly books and textbooks. The company also has two imprints: Women's Press (for feminist writing, both trade and academic) and Kellom Books (trade only). Publishes 25 new books annually. First send a proposal. Guidelines available on web site.
Notable 2006 title: *Canada's Economic Apartheid: The Social Exclusion of Racialized Groups in the New Century*, Grace-Edward Galabuzi.

Cape Breton University Press
P.O. Box 5300, Sydney, NS B1P 6L2
Phone: (902) 563-1955 Fax: (902) 563-1177
E-mail: cbu_press@cbu.ca
Web site: www.cbupress.ca
Contact: Mike Hunter, editor-in-chief
Serves as a link between Cape Breton University and its broader communities, publishing literature of significance to Cape Breton

Island that enhances knowledge about the island, its history, and cultural preservation. A leading publisher of works related to community development (CED), which are read by scholars and activists around the world. Released 8 new titles in 2006. Accepts unsolicited manuscripts, but first send an inquiry and outline. Guidelines available.

Notable 2007 title: *North of Smokey*, David Doucette.

Captus Press

1600 Steeles Avenue W., Units 14 & 15, Concord, ON L4K 4M2
Phone: (416) 736-5537 Fax: (416) 736-5793
E-mail: info@captus.com
Web site: www.captus.com

As well as textbooks and professional books, Captus Press publishes non-fiction trade. Accepts unsolicited manuscripts. Guidelines available. "We assist authors in development of their books, with emphasis on those designed to enhance post-secondary education and furnish information to practising professionals. To determine the feasibility of your project, submit an author/editor questionnaire at www.captus.com/information/manuscript-contents.htm. We will contact you with our initial assessment and offer publishing suggestions. We may also wish to review sample chapters as soon as they are available, which would assist us to confirm the acceptance of your project for publication."

Notable 2006 title: *The Stranger, the Native and the Land: Perspectives on Indigenous Tourism*, Claudia Notzke.

CHA Press

17 York Street, Ottawa, ON K1N 9J6
Phone: (613) 241-8005, ext. 264 Fax: (613) 241-5055
E-mail: chapresss@cha.ca
Web site: www.cha.ca/publishing
Contact: Eleanor Sawyer, director, publishing

CHA Press, the publisher for the Canadian Healthcare Association, is a direct-mail, specialty publisher whose mission is to support Canadian authors writing about issues concerning the delivery of healthcare across the system. "Our target audience are the senior/middle managers of health facilities/agencies in Canada's health delivery system, including its governors." Prefers shorter,

35- to 50-page manuscripts on key issues in healthcare management for both smaller print runs and for e-publishing. Publishes 4 titles a year. Send an inquiry with an outline and sample chapters. Guidelines available.

Notable 2006 title: *Change and Continuity in Canada's Health Care System*, Aleck Ostry.

Chestnut Publishing Group

4005 Bayview Avenue, Suite 610, Toronto, ON M2M 3Z9
Phone: (416) 224-5824 Fax: (416) 486-4752
E-mail: hgoldhar@sympatico.ca or sharkstark@sympatico.ca
Web site: www.chestnutpublishing.com
Contacts: Harry Goldhar, vice-president, editorial; Stanley Starkman, president

Publishes children's literature, general trade titles, education books for school and college, books for reluctant readers, and books on English as a second language. Produces about 8 new titles annually. Accepts unsolicited manuscripts; send an outline and sample chapters first.

Notable 2006 title: *Survive Any Emergency*, Betty-Anne Lawlor.

Coach House Books

401 Huron Street (rear – on bpNichol Lane), Toronto, ON M5S 2G5
Phone: (416) 979-2217 Fax: (416) 977-1158
E-mail: mail@chbooks.com
Web site: www.chbooks.com
Contacts: Alana Wilcox, senior editor; Christina Pallassio, managing editor; Evan Munday, publicist

Publishes innovative poetry, fiction, and drama by Canadian writers. Releases approximately 15 new titles annually. Does not accept unsolicited manuscripts. Send an inquiry. Guidelines available on web site.

Notable 2007 title: *The Girls Who Saw Everything*, Sean Dixon.

Colombo & Company

42 Dell Park Avenue, Toronto, ON M6B 2T6
Phone: (416) 782-6853 Fax: (416) 782-0285
E-mail: jrc@ca.inter.net

Web site: www.colombo.ca

Contact: John Robert Colombo

Publishes about 6 new titles annually; 101 in print. Does not accept unsolicited manuscripts. "Demonstrate that you have read at least 5 of our publications before sending an inquiry."

Commoners' Publishing

631 Tubman Crescent, Ottawa, ON K1V 8L5

Phone: (613) 523-2444 Fax: (613) 260-0401

E-mail: commoners@rogers.com

Web site: www.commonerspublishing.com

Contact: Glenn Cheriton, editor

Established 1973. Publishes Canadian fiction and educational titles with a particular specialty in books on men's culture, history, and issues. Releases about 5 new books a year. Accepts unsolicited manuscripts with an SASE: for fiction, full manuscripts are preferred with author bio; for non-fiction, writers should send an outline with sample chapter. Writer guidelines are available with an SASE.

Notable 2007 title: *The Incessant Knock of Opportunity*, Cliff Livingstone.

Conundrum Press

P.O. Box 55003, CSP Fairmount, Montreal, QC H2T 3E2

Web site: www.conundrumpress.com

Contact: Andy Brown, publisher

Publishes an eclectic mix of books of art, graphic novels, and fiction. No poetry. Has been called "one of the most innovative publishers in Canada." Released 7 new titles in 2006. Does not accept unsolicited manuscripts.

Notable 2007 title: *Missing the Arc*, Catherine Kidd.

Cordillera Books

8415 Granville Street, P.O. Box 46, Vancouver, BC V6P 4Z9

Phone: (604) 261-1695 Fax: (604) 266-4469

E-mail: richbook@shaw.ca

Contact: S. C. Heal, president

Specializes in maritime history, shipping, tug and barge transportation, and fishing industry books. Published 3 new titles in 2006. Does not accept unsolicited manuscripts; send an inquiry first. "We have a full publishing program for 2007. Not considering any fresh works at this time."

Notable 2006 titles: *Inbound to Vancouver* and *Outbound from Vancouver.*

Cormorant Books
215 Spadina Avenue, Studio 230, Toronto, ON M5T 2C7
Phone: (416) 929-4957
E-mail: cormorantbooksinc@bellnet.ca
Web site: www.cormorantbooks.com
Contact: Marc Côté, publisher
Publishes superior literary fiction and non-fiction. Released 16 new titles in 2006. Does not accept unsolicited manuscripts.
Notable 2006 title: *Home Schooling,* Carol Windley.

Coteau Books
2517 Victoria Avenue, Regina, SK S4P 0T2
Phone: (306) 777-0170   Fax: (306) 522-5152
E-mail: coteau@coteaubooks.com
Web site: www.coteaubooks.com
Contact: N. L. L. Burton, managing editor
Established 1975. Aims to publish and present to the world market Canadian literary writing, with an emphasis on prairie and Saskatchewan writers, and to develop and publish works of juvenile fiction that demonstrate literary excellence as well as an understanding between people and the value of community. Published 18 new titles in 2006. Accepts unsolicited manuscripts but not multiple submissions. Guidelines on web site.
Notable 2006 title: *The Hour of Bad Decisions,* Russell Wangersky.

Crabtree Publishing Co.
612 Welland Avenue, St. Catharines, ON L2M 5V6
Phone: (905) 682-5221   Fax: 1-800-682-7166
E-mail: editor@crabtreebooks.com
Web site: www.crabtreebooks.com
Established 1978. Publishes children's illustrated non-fiction series written at a specific reading level to meet educational demands for the children's library market. Main subjects are social studies and science. Does not accept unsolicited manuscripts.

Notable 2006 title: *Refugee Child: My Memories of the 1956 Hungarian Revolution*, Bobbie Kalman.

Creative Book Publishing

P.O. Box 1815, Stn. C, 367 Water Street, St. John's, NL A1C 5P9
Phone: (709) 579-1312 Fax: (709) 579-6511
E-mail: nl.books@transcontinental.ca
Web site: www.creativebookpublishing.ca
Contact: Donna Francis, sales/marketing coordinator
Established 1983. Publishes under 3 imprints, each having a distinctive focus. Titles released under its Creative Publishers imprint include primarily histories, biographies, pictorials, cookbooks, books of humour, and travel/guide books. Under its Killick Press imprint, the company publishes poetry, fiction, drama, creative non-fiction, belles lettres, essays, feminist literature, and fine art reproduction. The Tuckamore Books imprint is devoted to children's books and young-adult literature. Publishes 12 to 15 new titles a year. Send a cover letter describing the genre of the manuscript and the intended audience, an author résumé, a manuscript summary, the full manuscript, and an SASE. Guidelines on web site.
Notable 2006 title: *What If Your Mom Made Raisin Buns?*, Catherine Hogan Safer (Tuckamore Books).

Creative Bound International

P.O. Box 424, Carp, ON K0A 1L0
Phone: (613) 831-3641 Fax: (613) 831-3643
E-mail: resources@creativebound.com
Web site: www.creativebound.com
Contact: Gail Baird, managing editor
Publishes resources for personal growth and enhanced performance in business. "We help experts get their messages out." Released 10 new titles in 2006. Does not accept unsolicited manuscripts. Send an inquiry with an outline first. "Please visit our web site. We specialize in non-fiction; please no inquiries regarding fiction, poetry, or the children's market."
Notable 2007 title: *Six Degrees of Dignity: Disability in an Age of Freedom*, David W. Shannon.

Creekstone Press

7456 Driftwood Road, Smithers, BC V0J 2N7
Phone: (250) 847-3663 Fax: (250) 847-3663
E-mail: info@creekstonepress.com
Web site: www.creekstonepress.com
Contact: Lynn Shervill, editor
    Provides a vehicle for creative writers and artists in northern British Columbia. "Diversity of expression, accuracy, originality, craftsmanship, and regional relevance govern selection. Creekstone Press applies exacting design and production standards, which compliment and enhance selected works." Publishes 1 new title a year. No unsolicited manuscripts. Send an inquiry. Guidelines available.
    Notable 2007 title: *In the Hand of the Red Goat*, Bob Henderson.

Cumulus Press

P.O. Box 5205, Stn. B, Montreal, QC H3B 4B5
Phone: (514) 523-1975
E-mail: info@cumuluspress.com
Web site: www.cumuluspress.com
Contact: David Widgington, publisher
    Established 1998. "Cumulus Press takes the stairs instead of the escalator. Gravity is an ally. Poetry, fiction, social justice, and the open road fill the space between the cracks. All of our titles are well crafted, one by one. We bring publishing to the surface, where spoken and written words pull down fences and lift paving stones, helping raise the stakes for independent, creative expression. Our Tendril Anthology Series reserves apprenticed space on the literary surface for talented young writers to cast shadows of themselves." Publishes 4 books a year. Does not accept unsolicited manuscripts. Send an outline first. A founding organizer of Expozine, Montreal's annual small press, comic, and zine fair.

DC Books

P.O. Box 666, St. Laurent Stn., Montreal, QC H4L 4V9
Phone: (514) 843-8130 Fax: (514) 939-0569
E-mail: dcbooks@videotron.ca
Contact: Steve Luxton, editor-in-chief

A literary publisher specializing in fiction, poetry, drama, and books about railroads. Published 8 books in 2007. Accepts unsolicited manuscripts but prefers inquiries.

Notable 2007 title: *Suddenly the Minotaur*, Marie Hélène Poitras.

Detselig Enterprises

1220 Kensington Road N.W., Unit 210, Calgary, AB T2N 3P5
Phone: (403) 283-0900 Fax: (403) 283-6947
E-mail: temeron@telusplanet.net
Web site: www.temerondetselig.com
Contact: T. E. Giles, president

Established 1975. Publishes academic (education, social science, and the humanities) and general trade books. Averages 14 new books each year. Accepts unsolicited manuscripts, but first send inquiry letter with outline and sample chapters.

Notable 2006 title: *History of the 31st Canadian Infantry Battalion*, Darrell Knight.

Doubleday Canada

1 Toronto Street, Suite 300, Toronto, ON M5C 2V6
Phone: (416) 364-4449 Fax: (416) 957-1587
Web site: www.randomhouse.ca
Contact: acquisitions editor

Publishes quality trade fiction and non-fiction by leading and award-winning authors. Does not accept unsolicited manuscripts. An inquiry should be accompanied by an outline and sample chapters.

Notable 2006 title: *The Judgment of Paris*, Ross King.

Douglas & McIntyre

2323 Quebec Street, Suite 201, Vancouver, BC V5Y 2A8
Phone: (604) 254-7191 Fax: (604) 254-9099
E-mail: dm@douglas-mcintyre.com
Web site: www.douglas-mcintyre.com
Contact: Chris Labonte, assistant to the publisher

Established 1964. Publishes general trade books in 2 publishing units: Douglas & McIntyre and Greystone Books. Douglas & McIntyre specializes in Canadian art and culture, military and maritime history, northwest coast First Nations and Inuit studies, and literary fiction. Greystone Books specializes in natural history, ecology and the environment, popular science, health, and travel and outdoor guidebooks. Produces 50 new titles annually. Submit an outline with 2 or 3 sample chapters. "Research our web site first." Notable 2006 titles: *Dead Man in Paradise*, J. B. McKinnon (Douglas & McIntyre), and *David Suzuki: The Autobiography*, David Suzuki (Greystone).

DreamCatcher Publishing

55 Canterbury Street, Suite 8, Saint John, NB E2L 2C6
Phone: (506) 632-4008 Fax: (506) 632-4009
E-mail: info@dreamcatcherpublishing.ca
Web site: www.dreamcatcherpublishing.ca
Contact: Elizabeth Margaris, publisher

Publishes good mainstream fiction, with first consideration to Atlantic Canadian writers. "Especially interested in 'green' theme fiction and 'hope and inspiration' non-fiction (including autobiographies) with a humorous twist." Produces 4 to 6 new titles annually. No unsolicited manuscripts. Send an inquiry first. "Make your query letter businesslike. Include a synopsis and short bio."
Notable 2007 title: *Harper's New Clothes*, Walter J. Belisto.

The Dundurn Group

3 Church Street, Suite 500, Toronto, ON M5E 1M2
Phone: (416) 214-5544 Fax: (416) 214-5556
E-mail: info@dundurn.com
Web site: www.dundurn.com
Contact: Kirk Howard, publisher

Established 1973. Publishes Canadian history (notably of Ontario), biography, art, and literary criticism. Encompasses Dundurn (serious non-fiction), Hounslow (popular non-fiction), Simon & Pierre (literary), the Castle Street Mysteries, and Boardwalk (young adult) imprints. Submission should include a synopsis, an outline of previous publishing experience, and either the full manuscript or sample chapters.
Notable 2006 title: *Pearson's Prize: Canada and the Suez Crisis*, John Melady.

ECW Press

2120 Queen Street E., Suite 200, Toronto, ON M4E 1E2

Phone: (416) 694-3348 Fax: (416) 698-9906
E-mail: info@ecwpress.com
Web site: www.ecwpress.com
Contact: Jack David, publisher
  Established 1974. Publishes books on entertainment, culture, and writing. Released 37 titles in 2006. Does not accept unsolicited manuscripts. Send an outline for non-fiction and samples for fiction and poetry. Guidelines available. "Authors should include an SASE if they wish their material returned."
  Notable 2006 title: *The Biker Trials*, Paul Cherry.

EDGE Science Fiction & Fantasy Publishing
P.O. Box 1714, Calgary, AB T2P 2L7
Phone: (403) 254-0160 Fax: (403) 254-0456
Web site: www.edgewebsite.com
Contact: Kimberly Gammon, editorial manager
  "We are dedicated to producing thought-provoking, intelligent, and well-written novel-length science fiction and fantasy works between 75,000 and 100,000 words in length." Publishes 6 to 8 new titles annually. Accepts unsolicited manuscripts, but first send outline, sample chapters, and an SASE. Web site has complete submission information. No electronic submissions.
  Notable 2006 title: *Stealing Magic*, Tanya Huff.

Ekstasis Editions
P.O. Box 8474, Main Postal Outlet, Victoria, BC V8W 3S1
Phone: (250) 361-9941 Fax: (250) 385-3378
E-mail: ekstasis@islandnet.com
Web site: http://ekstasiseditions.com
Contact: Richard Olafson, publisher
  A literary press dedicated to publishing poetry, fiction, belle lettres, and translation. Averages 15 new titles annually. Accepts unsolicited manuscripts, but send sample chapters first. "Always send an SASE for a reply or return of materials." Guidelines available.
  Notable 2006 title: *Beyond the Pale*, Elizabeth Rhett Woods.

Fernwood Publishing
32 Ocean Vista Lane, Site 2A, Box 5, Black Point, NS B0J 1B0
Phone: (902) 857-1388 Fax: (902) 857-1328

E-mail: info@fernwoodpublishing.ca
Web site: www.fernwoodpublishing.ca
Contact: Errol Sharpe, publisher

Publishes critical non-fiction that provides in-depth analysis and challenges existing norms, focusing on the social sciences and humanities. Releases 20 to 25 new titles a year; has published over 250 titles in 15 years of publishing. Send an inquiry, outline, and sample chapters. Guidelines available.

Notable 2006 title: *Butterbox Babies: Baby Sales, Baby Deaths*, Bette Cahill.

Fifth House Publishers
1800 – 4th Street S.W., Suite 1511, Calgary, AB T2S 2S5
Phone: (403) 571 5232 Fax: (403) 571-5235
E-mail: charlene@fifthhousepublishers.ca
Web site: www.fitzhenry.ca
Contact: Charlene Dobmeier, publisher

Established 1982. Publishes general trade non-fiction, specializing in Western Canadiana, emphasizing history, biography, gardening, nature, and First Nations titles. Releases from 18 to 20 books a year. Accepts unsolicited manuscripts, but send an inquiry with an outline and sample chapters first. "No phone calls, please." Guidelines available on request.

Notable 2006 title: *Portraits of Canada: Photographic Treasures of the CPR*, Jonathan Hanna.

Firefly Books
66 Leek Crescent, Richmond Hill, ON L4B 1H1
Phone: (416) 499-8412 Fax: (416) 499-8313
E-mail: service@fireflybooks.com
Web site: www.fireflybooks.com

Publishes practical how-to and illustrated books, with a special interest in gardening, cooking, astronomy, health, natural history, pictorial books, reference books (especially for children), and sports. No unsolicited manuscripts, but accepts proposals for illustrated non-fiction.

Notable 2006 title: *The World of the Polar Bear*, Norbert Rosing.

Folklore Publishing
10116 – 80 Avenue, Suite 212, Edmonton, AB T6E 6V7
Phone: (780) 910-6216
E-mail: fboer@folklorepublishing.com
Web site: www.folklorepublishing.com
Publishes popular history books and biographies of important Canadian figures. Releases 5 to 10 new titles annually. Accepts unsolicited manuscripts, but first send an inquiry with an outline and sample chapters. Guidelines available.
Notable 2006 title: *Canada in Space*, Chris Gainor.

Formac Publishing Company
5502 Atlantic Street, Halifax, NS B3H 1G4
Phone: (902) 421-7022 Fax: (902) 425-0166
E-mail: editassist@formac.ca
Web site: www.formac.ca
Contact: Erinna Gilkison
Publishes trade guides for Canadian destinations, children's books (series), and a wide range of illustrated and text-only books for the regional market. Releases 15 new titles a year. Accepts unsolicited manuscripts, but send an outline first. "For children's books, note that we publish in only 2 genres: series and regional interest. E-mail petitions are welcome." Guidelines available on web site.
Notable 2006 title: *Heritage Houses of Prince Edward Island*, James MacNutt.

Frontenac House
1138 Frontenac Avenue S.W., Calgary, AB T2T 1B6
Phone: (403) 245-2491 Fax: (403) 245-2380
E-mail: editor@frontenachouse.com
Web site: www.frontenachouse.com
Contact: Rose Scollard, publisher
Primarily a poetry press. "Frontenac's mandate is to publish as wide a range of poetic expression from as varied and diverse a group of poets as we can find." Released 8 new titles in 2006. Accepts unsolicited manuscripts, but send an outline and samples first. "Please follow the instructions on our web site regarding submission dates and format."

Notable 2006 title: *The Lightness Which Is Our World Seen from Afar*, Ven Begamudré.

Garamond Press

63 Mahogany Court, Aurora, ON L4G 6M8
Phone: (905) 841-1460 Fax: (905) 841-3031
E-mail: garamond@web.ca
Web site: www.garamond.ca
Contact: Peter Saunders, publisher
Established 1981. Publishes academic monographs and university texts offering a critical perspective. Subject areas include women's studies, cultural and labour studies, education, the Third World, and ethnicity. Releases about 6 new titles a year. No unsolicited manuscripts. Written inquiries only. Specific submission guidelines available on web site.

Gaspereau Press

47 Church Avenue, Kentville, NS B4N 2M7
Phone: (902) 678-6002
E-mail: info@gaspereau.com
Web site: www.gaspereau.com
Contact: Kate Kennedy, editor
Publishes poetry, fiction, and creative non-fiction titles in quality first-edition paperbacks aimed at the Canadian and U.S. markets. Releases 10 new titles a year. Accepts unsolicited manuscripts and sample chapters. Guidelines available. "Please include a cover letter with all submissions. Samples and full manuscripts accepted. Please include a detailed synopsis of the work in full. No e-mail submissions."

General Store Publishing House

499 O'Brien Road, P.O. Box 415, Renfrew, ON K7V 4A6
Phone: (613) 432-7697 or 1-800-465-6072 Fax: (613) 432-7184
E-mail: publisher@gsph.com
Web site: www.gsph.com
Contact: Tim Gordon, publisher
Established 1980. Publishes history, military, cookbooks, regional titles pertaining to the Ottawa Valley, and sports books. Releases 20

to 25 titles a year. Accepts unsolicited manuscripts, but phone first. Guidelines available.

Notable 2006 title: *In the Line of Duty II: From Fort Macleod to Mayerthorpe*, Robert Knuckle.

Goose Lane Editions

500 Beaverbrook Court, Suite 330, Fredericton, NB E3B 5X4
Phone: (506) 450-4251 Fax: (506) 459-4991
E-mail: gooselane@gooselane.com
Web site: www.gooselane.com
Contact: Susanne Alexander, publisher

Established 1954. Publishes Canadian adult literary fiction, non-fiction, and poetry. Publishes 18 to 20 print titles and 10 audio titles annually. Considers unsolicited manuscripts, but first send outline or synopsis and a 30- to 50-page sample for novels. No electronic queries or submissions. Please send a query first for poetry, story collections, and non-fiction. Guidelines available with an SASE.

Notable 2006 title: *The Famished Lover*, Alan Cumyn.

Granville Island Publishing

1656 Duranleau, Suite 212, Vancouver, BC V6H 3S4
Phone: (604) 688-0320 or 1-877-688-0320 Fax: (604) 688-0132
E-mail: info@granvilleislandpublishing.com
Web site: www.granvilleislandpublishing.com
Contact: Jo Blackmore, publisher

Publishes books that are financed by the author. The publisher provides publicity and marketing, and distributes the books in Canada and the U.S. Does not accept unsolicited manuscripts; send a query first. Guidelines available.

Notable 2007 title: *Hockey Play-by-Play: Around the NHL with Jim Robson*, Jason Farris.

Great Plains Publications

70 Arthur Street, Suite 420, Winnipeg, MB R3B 1G7
Phone: (204) 475-6799 Fax: (204) 475-0138
E-mail: info@greatplains.mb.ca
Web site: www.greatplains.mb.ca
Contact: Gregg Shilliday, publisher

An independent regional publisher specializing in prairie history and fiction. Publishes 8 to 10 titles a year. Accepts unsolicited manuscripts; send an outline and sample chapters first. Guidelines available.

Notable 2007 title: *Encyclopedia of Manitoba*.

Groundwood Books

110 Spadina Avenue, Suite 801, Toronto, ON M5V 2K4
Phone: (416) 363-4343 Fax: (416) 363-1017
E-mail: genmail@groundwoodbooks.com
Web site: www.groundwoodbooks.com
Contact: Nan Froman, managing editor

Publishes high-quality Canadian picture books, both fiction and non-fiction, plus a line of Spanish-language titles, Libros Tigrillo, aimed at the U.S. Latino market and the export market in Mexico and Central America. Released 27 new titles in 2006. Accepts unsolicited manuscripts; send a synopsis and sample chapters first. No e-mail submissions. Guidelines available on web site.

Notable 2007 title: *Pure Spring*, Brian Doyle.

Guernica Editions

P.O. Box 117, Stn. P, Toronto, ON M5S 2S6
Phone: (416) 658-9888 Fax: (416) 657-8885
E-mail: guernicaeditions@cs.com
Web site: www.guernicaeditions.com
Contact: Antonio D'Alfonso, editor

Established 1978. Specializes in fiction, non-fiction, plays, poetry, and translations. Also translates Québécois authors. Publishes about 23 new titles a year. No unsolicited manuscripts. Inquiries welcome. "A publisher is not just an outlet. It is the home for minds with similar ideas on what literature is about."

Notable 2006 title: *Touch Earth*, M. Travis Lane.

Hancock House Publishers Ltd.

19313 Zero Avenue, Surrey, BC V3S 9R9
Phone: (604) 538-1114 or 1-800-938-1114 Fax: (604) 538-2262
   or 1-800-983-2262
E-mail: promo@hancockhouse.com

Web site: www.hancockhouse.com
Contact: Theresa Laviolette, editor
    Established 1970. Specializes in Pacific Northwest history and biography, Native culture, nature guides, natural history, aviculture, and cryptozoology. Does not publish novels. Publishes about 20 titles a year. Accepts unsolicited manuscripts. "E-mail queries with author bio, book outline, table of contents, and sample chapters recommended. Do not send hard copy manuscripts or original photos or illustrations." Guidelines available on web site.
    Notable 2007 title: *Vancouver's Bravest: 120 Years of Firefighting History*, Alex Matches.

Harbour Publishing
P.O. Box 219, Madeira Park, BC V0N 2H0
Phone: (604) 883-2730 Fax: (604) 883-9451
E-mail: info@harbourpublishing.com
Web site: www.harbourpublishing.com
Contact: Shyla Seller, assistant to the publisher
    Primarily focuses on regional non-fiction titles, but publishes in all genres, mainly on topics concerning the West Coast of B.C. Publishes about 20 titles a year. Accepts unsolicited manuscripts, but first send an inquiry with an outline, author bio, publication credits, and sample chapters. Guidelines available on web site.
    Notable 2006 title: *Encyclopedia of British Columbia*, edited by Daniel Francis.

Harlequin Enterprises
225 Duncan Mill Road, Don Mills, ON M3B 3K9
Phone: (416) 445-5860 Fax: (416) 448-7191
Web sites: www.eharlequin.com (also www.mirabooks.com;
    www.reddressink.com; www.luna-books.com;
    www.steeplehill.com)
Contact: Loriana Sacilotto, executive vice-president, global publishing and strategy
    Established 1949. Each year Harlequin publishes more than 1,100 new titles in all formats (mass-market, trade, and hardcover), including series romance (Harlequin and Silhouette imprints), single-title women's fiction (MIRA Books, Red Dress Ink, and HQN imprints), inspirational fiction (Steeple Hill imprint), fantasy (Luna

imprint), and mystery and action adventure (Gold Eagle and Worldwide Library imprints). Accepts query letters. Tip sheets available. Check web site for updated information, especially the Learn to Write channel. New authors are contracted only on full manuscript.

HarperCollins Publishers
2 Bloor Street E., 20th Floor, Toronto, ON M4W 1A8
Phone: (416) 975-9334 Fax: (416) 975-9884
Web site: www.harpercollins.ca
Contact: editorial department
Publishes a wide range of fiction, non-fiction, business, reference, young-adult, and children's books. Produces over 90 new titles each year. No unsolicited manuscripts or proposals.

The Frederick Harris Music Co.
5865 McLaughlin Road, Unit 1, Mississauga, ON L5R 1B8
Phone: (905) 501-1595 Fax: (905) 501-0929
E-mail: fhmc@frederickharrismusic.com
Web site: www.frederickharrismusic.com
Established 1904. A not-for-profit publisher of music education materials, particularly curriculum material for the Royal Conservatory of Music. Interested in manuscripts in 6 main categories: piano, violin, guitar, voice, theory, and musicianship. Send a sample chapter and table of contents. Guidelines available.

Hedgerow Press
P.O. Box 2471, Sidney, BC V8L 3Y3
Phone: (250) 656-9320 Fax: (250) 656-9320
E-mail: hedgep@telus.net
Web site: www.hedgerowpress.com
Contact: Joan Caldwell, publisher
Publishes high quality paperbacks of literary and visual beauty, limiting annual production so as to give greater attention to each book. Preference given to Canadian authors and artists. Does not publish novels, academic works, or illustrated children's books. Releases 1 new title a year. Accepts unsolicited manuscripts, but first send an inquiry with an outline and sample chapters.
Notable 2006 title: *Decked and Dancing: Poems*, Christine Smart.

Heritage House Publishing Co. Ltd.

17665 – 66A Avenue, Suite 108, Surrey, BC V3S 2A7
Phone: (250) 468-5328 Fax: (250) 468-5318
E-mail: editorial@heritagehouse.ca
Web site: www.heritagehouse.ca
Contact: Rodger Touchie, publisher
  Publishes Canadian non-fiction with a focus on subjects of regional interest in British Columbia and Alberta. Releases about 20 titles annually. Accepts unsolicited manuscripts, but send an outline and sample chapter first, noting why you think your book would sell and who would buy it. Guidelines available on web site.
  Notable 2006 title: *Robert Service: Under the Spell of the Yukon*, Enid Mallory.

House of Anansi Press

110 Spadina Avenue, Suite 801, Toronto, ON M5V 2K4
Phone: (416) 363-4343 Fax: (416) 363-1017
E-mail: info@anansi.ca
Web site: www.anansi.ca
Contact: editorial department
  Publishes literary fiction, non-fiction, and poetry. Releases 20 to 25 new titles a year. Accepts unsolicited manuscripts, but first send an outline and sample chapters. "We regret that we are unable to respond to queries regarding our submission guidelines. For complete guidelines, please visit our web site."
  Notable 2006 title: *De Niro's Game*, Rawi Hage.

Insomniac Press

192 Spadina Avenue, Suite 403, Toronto, ON M5T 2C2
Phone: (416) 504-6270 Fax: (416) 504-9313
E-mail: mike@insomniacpress.com
Web site: www.insomniacpress.com
Contact: Mike O'Connor, publisher
  Established 1992. Publishes fiction, non-fiction in a wide variety of areas, and poetry. Releases about 20 new titles annually. Accepts unsolicited manuscripts, but first send sample chapters by mail only. Guidelines available on web site. "Please visit our web site for an idea of the books we have published recently."
  Notable 2006 title: *Why I Didn't Say Anything*, Sheldon Kennedy.

ISER Books, Faculty of Arts Publications (Institute of Social and Economic Research)

Memorial University of Newfoundland, St. John's, NL A1C 5S7
Phone: (709) 737-7474 Fax: (709) 737-7560
E-mail: iser-books@mun.ca
Web site: www.mun.ca/iser
Contact: Al Potter, manager

Publishes research relevant to Newfoundland and Labrador, and the North Atlantic Rim, especially research pertaining to social and economic development in Newfoundland and Labrador. Specializes in anthropology, sociology, folklore, women's studies, geography, history, and economics. Periodic collections on Native peoples and the nation-state, social-science advocacy, and the fishing crisis. Publishes 3 or 4 titles each year. Does not accept unsolicited manuscripts. Send an inquiry with an outline and sample chapters. Guidelines available.

Notable 2005 title: *Global Game, Local Arena: Restructuring in Corner Brook, Newfoundland*, Glen Norcliffe.

Island Studies Press

Institute of Island Studies, University of Prince Edward Island, Charlottetown, PE C1A 4P3
Phone: (902) 566-1386 Fax: (902) 566-0756
E-mail: inovaczek@upei.ca
Web site: www.islandstudies.com
Contact: Irene Novaczek

Releases 1 to 2 new titles a year. Accepts unsolicited manuscripts about P.E.I. and other islands, mostly with a scholarly focus, but send inquiry first.

Notable 2006 title: *Chinese Islanders: Making a Home in the New World*, Hung-Min Chiang.

Jesperson Publishing

100 Water Street, 3rd Floor, P.O. Box 2188, St. John's, NL A1C 6E6
Phone: (709) 757-2216 Fax: (709) 753-0708
E-mail: info@jespersonpublishing.nf.net
Web site: www.jespersonpublishing.ca
Contact: Annamarie Beckel, editor

Publishes fiction and non-fiction, especially related to the culture of Newfoundland and Labrador and to Canada. Released 6 new titles in 2006. Accepts unsolicited manuscripts, but send a query with an outline and sample chapters first. Guidelines available. Notable 2006 title: *Half Moon*, K. L. Vidal.

Kegedonce Press

Cape Croker First Nation, R.R. #5, Wiarton, ON N0H 2T0
Phone: (519) 371-1434 Fax: (519) 371-5011
E-mail: info@kegedonce.com
Web site: www.kegedonce.com
Contact: R. K. Abram, publishing co-ordinator
Committed to the development, promotion, and publication of the work of indigenous writers. Releases 2 new titles on average per year. Accepts unsolicited manuscripts, but first send an inquiry and sample chapters. "Prior publishing credits (magazines, etc.) are required for serious consideration. Aboriginal/indigenous authors only." Guidelines available on web site.
Notable 2005 title: *Kynship*, Daniel Heath Justice.

Key Porter Books

6 Adelaide Street E., 10th Floor, Toronto, ON M5C 1H6
Phone: (416) 862-7777 Fax: (416) 862-2304
E-mail: info@keyporter.com
Web site: www.keyporter.com
Contact: editorial department
Established 1980. Specializes in high-profile non-fiction books on politics, history, biography, celebrities, cooking, natural history, and the environment. Also publishes literary fiction, short-story collections, and children's fiction and non-fiction. "We do not publish poetry, novellas, speculative fiction, or mysteries." Publishes approximately 75 new titles a year. No unsolicited manuscripts. Accepts outlines and sample chapters. See web site for guidelines.
Notable 2006 title: *Full Circle: Death and Resurrection in Canadian Conservative Politics*, Bob Plamondon.

Kids Can Press

29 Birch Avenue, Toronto, ON M4V 1E2
Phone: (416) 925-5437 Fax: (416) 960-5437

E-mail: info@kidscan.com
Web site: www.kidscanpress.com
Contact: Karen Boersma, vice-president/publisher
Established 1973. Publishes quality books for children of all ages, including picture books, poetry, non-fiction, fiction, crafts, and activity books. Released 70 new titles in 2006. Accepts unsolicited manuscripts. Send outline and sample chapters for longer fiction. "Please familiarize yourself with our list before sending a manuscript. Request a catalogue if you're having trouble getting a good sense of the entire publishing program." Guidelines available on web site.

Notable 2006 title: *Scaredy Squirrel*, Mélanie Watt.

Alfred A. Knopf Canada

1 Toronto Street, Suite 300, Toronto, ON M5C 2V6
Phone: (416) 364-4449   Fax: (416) 364-6863
Web site: www.randomhouse.ca
Contact: Angelika Glover, associate editor
"Knopf Canada publishes exceptional literary fiction and nonfiction from Canada and around the world." Releases approximately 40 new titles a year. Does not accept unsolicited manuscripts.

Notable 2006 title: *The Other Side of the Bridge*, Mary Lawson.

Lobster Press

1600 Sherbrooke Street, Suites C & D, Montreal, QC H3H 1C9
Phone: (514) 904-1100   Fax: (514) 904-1101
E-mail: editorial@lobsterpress.com
Web site: www.lobsterpress.com
Contact: Meghan Nolan, editor
Publishes high quality books – fiction and non-fiction – for children, tweens, and teens. Published 15 new titles in 2006. Does not accept unsolicited manuscripts. Send an inquiry with outline and sample chapters first. Guidelines available on web site.

Notable 2006 title: *Our Game: The History of Hockey in Canada*, Dave Stubbs.

Lone Pine Publishing

10145 – 81st Avenue, Edmonton, AB T6E 1W9
Phone: (780) 433-9333   Fax: (780) 433-9646

E-mail: info@lonepinepublishing.com
Web site: www.lonepinepublishing.com
Established 1980. Specializes in regional books on natural history, outdoor recreation, gardening, and popular history. Offices in Edmonton and Washington State. Publishes about 35 new titles each year. Accepts unsolicited manuscripts, but first send an inquiry by mail (after familiarizing yourself with Lone Pine's current titles). Guidelines available.

James Lorimer & Company
317 Adelaide Street W., Suite 1002, Toronto, ON M5V 1P9
Phone: (416) 362-4762 Fax: (416) 362-3939
E-mail: production@lorimer.ca
Web site: www.lorimer.ca
Contact: Catherine MacIntosh, production editor
Seeking manuscripts on the following Canadian topics that fit into our current series: biography, history, cookbooks (with a Canadian or regional focus), education, public issues, and children's fiction. Published 32 new titles in 2006. Does not accept unsolicited manuscripts. Send an inquiry with an outline and sample chapters. Submission guidelines available on web site.
Notable 2006 title: *Ignatieff's World: A Liberal Leader for the 21st Century?*, Denis Smith.

McClelland & Stewart Ltd.
75 Sherbourne Street, 5th Floor, Toronto, ON M5A 2P9
Phone: (416) 598-1114 Fax: (416) 598-7764
E-mail: editorial@mcclelland.com
Web site: www.mcclelland.com
Contact: editorial department
Established 1906. Publishes fine fiction by authors such as Margaret Atwood, Alistair MacLeod, Rohinton Mistry, Alice Munro, Madeleine Thien, and Trevor Cole; a wide selection of non-fiction books on biography, history, natural history, politics, Native issues, religion, and sports; and poetry by writers such as Lorna Crozier and Don McKay. No unsolicited manuscripts; send a query for fiction, an outline for non-fiction.
Notable 2006 title: *Moral Disorder*, Margaret Atwood.

McGill-Queen's University Press

Montreal office: McGill University, 3430 McTavish Street,
Montreal, QC H3A 1X9
Phone: (514) 398-3750 Fax: (514) 398-4333
E-mail: mqup@mqup.mcgill.ca
Web site: www.mcgill.ca/mqup
Contact: Philip Cercone, editor-in-chief
Kingston office: Queen's University, Kingston, ON K7L 3N6
Phone: (613) 533-2155 Fax: (613) 533-6822
E-mail: mqup@post.queensu.ca
Contact: D. H. Akenson, senior editor
Established 1969. A non-profit joint venture of McGill and
Queen's Universities. Its mission is to serve the Canadian and inter-
national scholarly communities as a vehicle for the publication of
scholarly works of the highest quality. Publishes scholarly books on
northern studies and history, political science, Canadian literature,
anthropology, architecture, philosophy, and religion. Does not
publish works of fiction. Averages 130 new titles a year, a third of
which are destined for the trade market. Submit a proposal before
sending a manuscript. Guidelines available on web site.
Notable 2006 title: *Satanic Purses*, R. T. Naylor.

Maple Tree Press

51 Front Street E., Suite 200, Toronto, ON M5E 1B3
Phone: (416) 304-0702 Fax: (416) 304-0525
E-mail: info@mapletreepress.com
Web site: www.mapletreepress.com
Contact: submissions editor
Publishes high-quality, innovative information books, activity
books, and picture books with an emphasis on science, nature,
animals, and children's activities such as crafts. Averages 10 to 12
new titles a year. Accepts unsolicited manuscripts, but first send
query and outline for longer non-fiction works; the full manuscript
for picture books. "Before submitting, spend some time familiarizing yourself with Maple Tree Press books in the library or on our
web site. An SASE is required for any response. Maple Tree Press
does not accept electronic submissions and does not publish
novels." Guidelines available.

Notable 2006 title: *I Found a Dead Bird: The Kids' Guide to the Cycle of Life and Death*, Jan Thornhill.

Micromedia ProQuest
20 Victoria Street, Toronto, ON M5C 2N8
Phone: (416) 362-5211 or 1-800-387-2689 Fax: (416) 362-6161
E-mail: info@micromedia.ca
Web site: www.micromedia.ca
Contact: Mike Baida, director of sales

Canada's largest developer, publisher, and distributor of value-added reference information for the academic, library, K–12, government, and corporate markets. Founded in 1972, it has a longstanding and established industry presence. Publishes electronically and on microform; no printed material. Releases 6 new titles annually. No unsolicited manuscripts. First send a query.

MOD Publishing
4 Fairview Boulevard, Toronto, ON M4K 1L9
Phone: (416) 466-9275 Fax: (416) 466-7493
E-mail: jean.weihs@rogers.com
Web site: www.modpublishing.com
Contact: Jean Weihs, joint owner

Publishes materials for teachers and students – resource materials and study guides. Released 5 new titles in 2006. Does not accept unsolicited manuscripts.

Notable 2006 title: *Study Guide to La Salle & the Rise of New France*, Jean Weihs.

Moose Enterprise Book and Theatre Play Publishing
684 Walls Road, Sault Ste. Marie, ON P6A 5K6
Phone: (705) 779-3331 Fax: (705) 779-3331
E-mail: mooseenterprises@on.aibn.com
Web site: www.moosehidebooks.com
Contact: Richard Mousseau, editor

"We assist new and up-and-coming writers, those needing help developing their work. We accept submissions from unpublished and published authors." Imprint is Moose Hide Books. Released 6 titles in 2006. Accepts unsolicited manuscripts, but first send a

query. "We accept only works of moral content. Be original."
Guidelines available.
Notable 2006 title: *Rusty Butt: Treasure of the Ocean Mist*, Robin E. Forester.

Morgaine House
3 Kamouraska, Pointe Claire, QC H9S 5V2
E-mail: kamouraska3@sympatico.ca
Contact: Mary Gurekas, editor
Established 1994. A small literary press interested in well-crafted manuscripts of poetry and short fiction. Publishes 2 to 5 new titles annually. No unsolicited manuscripts. Queries only; send by e-mail.
Notable 2006 title: *To Pause and Flutterby*, G. Robert Morrison.

Mosaic Press
1252 Speers Road, Units 1 & 2, Oakville, ON L6L 5N9
Phone: (905) 825-2130 Fax: (905) 825-2130
E-mail: info@mosaic-press.com
Web site: www.mosaic-press.com
Contact: Keith Daniel, managing director
Focuses on literature, including fiction, short fiction, and poetry; the arts, including theatre, art, architecture, and music; social studies; and international studies. Publishes 20 new titles annually. Accepts unsolicited manuscripts, but send sample chapters, résumé, and outline/prospectus first.

Napoleon Publishing/Rendez Vous Press
178 Willowdale Avenue, Suite 201, Toronto, ON M2N 4Y8
Phone: (416) 730-9052 Fax: (416) 730-8096
E-mail: admin@transmedia95.com
Web site: www.napoleonpublishing.com
Contact: Allister Thompson, editor
Publishers of children's books of all kinds. Adult imprint focuses on fiction. Released 12 new titles in 2006. "We may accept unsolicited manuscripts if they are in line with our focus." Send inquiries by e-mail. "Check web site under 'Contact' to see what we are accepting."
Notable 2007 title: *Honour Among Men*, Barbara Fradkin.

Natural Heritage Books

P.O. Box 95, Stn. O, Toronto, ON M4A 2M8
Phone: (416) 694-7907 Fax: (416) 690-0819
E-mail: submissions@naturalheritagebooks.com
Web site: www.naturalheritagebooks.com
Contact: Barry L. Penhale, publisher

Primarily a non-fiction press specializing in history, heritage, out-of-doors, natural history, the environment, African-Canadian history, and genealogy/immigration. Committed to quality Canadian non-fiction. Averages 12 titles a year. Accepts unsolicited manuscripts, but first send an inquiry with outline and sample chapters to see if the subject matter is of interest. Guidelines available on web site.

Notable 2006 title: *Legends in Their Time: Young Heroes and Victims of Canada*, George Sherwood.

New Star Books

3477 Commercial Drive, Suite 107, Vancouver, BC V5N 4E8
Phone: (604) 738-9429 Fax: (604) 738-9332
E-mail: info@newstarbooks.com
Web site: http://newstarbooks.com
Contact: Carellin Brooks, managing editor

Publishes progressive books on social issues, politics, British Columbia, and the West, along with literary novels and short fiction. Does not accept unsolicited poetry. For non-fiction, send either the full manuscript with a query letter or an outline and sample chapters with a query letter. For fiction, send the full manuscript with a query letter. No fax or e-mail submissions, and no telephone queries. Guidelines available on web site.

Notable 2006 title: *Backup to Babylon*, Maxine Gadd.

NeWest Press

8540 – 109th Street, Suite 201, Edmonton, AB T6G 1E6
Phone: (780) 432-9427 Fax: (780) 433-3179
E-mail: info@newestpress.com
Web site: www.newestpress.com
Contact: Linda Huffman, general manager

A literary publisher that focuses on Western Canadian authors of fiction, poetry, drama, literary criticism, and regional non-fiction.

Releases approximately 15 new books a year. Accepts unsolicited manuscripts. "Manuscripts are reviewed by an editorial board, and it can take up to 9 months to receive a response." Guidelines available on web site.

Notable 2006 title: *Ride the Rising Wind*, Barbara Kingscote.

Nightwood Editions
Web site: www.nightwoodeditions.com
Contacts: Silas White, managing editor; Carleton Wilson, poetry editor

Has provided 40 years of Canadian literature. Released 9 new titles in 2006. "We do not accept unsolicited manuscripts."

Notable 2006 title: *By the Length of One Life*, Philip Kevin Paul.

Nimbus Publishing
3731 Mackintosh Street, P.O. Box 9166, Halifax, NS B3K 5M8
Phone: (902) 455-5956 Fax: (902) 455-5440
E-mail: smcintyre@nimbus.ns.ca
Web site: www.nimbus.ns.ca
Contact: Sandra McIntyre, managing editor

Established 1978. The largest trade publisher in Atlantic Canada. Publishes and distributes books on all aspects of Atlantic Canada. Non-fiction topics include natural history, political and social issues, and history. Also publishes guidebooks, cookbooks, books of photography, and children's literature; and under the Vagrant Press imprint, fiction. Does not publish poetry or genre fiction. Releases about 32 new titles each year. Does not accept unsolicited manuscripts. Send an inquiry or an outline with sample chapters. "Notice of receipt will be given but only those whose submissions are being considered will be contacted. Do not send original materials." Guidelines available. "We've redesigned our web site. Visit us at our web site."

Notable 2006 title: *The View from a Kite*, Maureen Hull (Vagrant Press).

Novalis
Saint Paul University, 223 Main Street, Ottawa, ON K1S 1C4
Phone: (613) 236-1393, ext. 2200 Fax: (613) 751-4020
E-mail: kburns@ustpaul.ca

Web site: www.novalis.ca

Contact: Kevin Burns, director of publishing (English)

Established 1936. Publishes resources that help people explore the dynamics of their faith, to pray, and to foster their spiritual growth. Founded by a Roman Catholic yet dedicated to ecumenical and interfaith dialogue and understanding. Releases about 30 new books each year in English and a similar number in French. Also publishes a number of periodicals, including *Living with Christ* and *Celebrate!* Accepts unsolicited manuscripts, but first send an inquiry with sample chapters and author résumé. Guidelines available.

"Developing a book is a long, slow creative process. Think of your book as the book you'd most like to read if you hadn't written it yourself. Approach us early with your idea. Since we publish both periodicals and books, we let our periodicals address short-term and topical subjects. By comparison, we like to choose books that will have a longer than usual shelf life. We look for subject matter and literary approaches that will not fade with yesterday's headlines. We are interested in reaching people who are searching for meaning, while at the same time we support those with a clear faith commitment."

Notable 2006 title: *Religion and Alienation*, Gregory Baum.

Oberon Press

145 Spruce Street, Suite 205, Ottawa, ON K1R 6P1

Phone: (613) 238-3275 Fax: (613) 238-3275

E-mail: oberon@sympatico.ca

Web site: www.oberonpress.ca

Contact: Nicholas Macklem, publisher

Established 1966. Publishes Canadian literary fiction, poetry, and non-fiction (biographies, memoirs, literary criticism, and essays). No genre fiction. Averages 8 new books a year. Accepts unsolicited manuscripts, but first send outline and sample chapters. Multiple submissions not considered. Guidelines available on web site.

Notable 2007 title: *07: Best Canadian Stories*, edited by John Metcalf.

Optimum Publishing International

P.O. Box 524, 10 Highland Drive, Naxville, ON K0C 1T0

Phone: (613) 527-2222 Fax: (613) 527-3333

E-mail: info@optimumbooks.com

Web site: www.optimumbooks.com

Contacts: Michael Baxendale, publisher; Craig MacLaine, editor

Publishes non-fiction, including biographies of notable people, true crime, cooking, child care, politics, current affairs, war, how-to reference, sports, and gardening. Released 6 new titles in 2006. Send an inquiry with outline and sample chapters.

Notable 2006 title: *Northern Connection: Inside Canada's Deadliest Mafia Family*, Peter Edwards.

Oolichan Books

P.O. Box 10, Lantzville, BC V0R 2H0

Phone: (250) 390-4839 Fax: (866) 299-0026

E-mail: oolichanbooks@telus.net

Web site: www.oolichan.com

Contact: Hiro Boga, managing editor

Since 1974 Oolichan has published quality Canadian literary fiction, poetry, and literary non-fiction. Also publishes selected children's books. No genre fiction. Releases 8 new titles a year. Considers unsolicited submissions, but send initial letter of inquiry and sample. "Please check our web site for submission guidelines before submitting."

Notable 2006 title: *The Blue Sky*, Galsan Tschinag.

Orca Book Publishers

P.O. Box 5626, Stn. B, Victoria, BC V8R 6S4

Phone: (250) 380-1229 Fax: (250) 380-1892

E-mail: orca@orcabook.com

Web site: www.orcabook.com

Contacts: Bob Tyrrell or Andrew Wooldridge for teen fiction; Andrew Wooldridge for juvenile fiction and Soundings; Maggie de Vries for early readers and picture books

Established 1984. Publishes award-winning books for young readers by Canadian authors, including picture books, first readers, and juvenile and teen fiction. Only occasionally publishes non-fiction. Releases approximately 60 new titles a year. Unsolicited manuscripts accepted for picture books (send an SASE); for novels, send query, outline, and sample chapters (send an SASE). See submission guidelines on web site before submitting. No submissions via e-mail.

Notable 2006 title: *Safe House*, James Heneghan.

Oxford University Press

70 Wynford Drive, Don Mills, ON M3C 1J9
Phone: (416) 441-2941 Fax: (416) 444-0427
Web site: www.oup.com/ca
Contact: Phyllis Wilson, managing editor

Established in Canada 1904. The Canadian trade publishing program is small and focuses mainly on history and reference. It includes only books intended for a general audience, and everything on this list either has a Canadian subject or examines a topic from a distinctly Canadian point of view. No novels, short stories by one author, how-to or self-help books, cookbooks, coffee-table books, books of poetry, or books for children or young adults. Accepts unsolicited manuscripts, but first send a query with a brief synopsis. Guidelines available on web site.

Pathfinder Books

2238 Dundas Street W., Suite 201, Toronto, ON M6R 2C9
Fax: (416) 535-9036
E-mail: pathfinderbooks@bellnet.ca
Web site: www.pathfinderpress.com
Contact: John Steele, business manager

"Pathfinder publishes materials produced in the heat of political battle. We let revolutionists speak for themselves, in their own words. Revolutionary-minded workers and farmers, and youth attracted toward them, don't primarily need interpreters for intermediaries. They need the words themselves, presented accurately and completely, translated honestly and clearly, plus the glossaries, maps, and other materials useful to a reader today who lives in a different time and place." Released 2 new titles in 2006. Does not accept unsolicited manuscripts.

Notable 2006 title: *Our History Is Still Being Written: The Story of Three Chinese-Cuban Generals in the Cuban Revolution*, Armando Choy, Gustavo Chui, Moisés Sío Wong, and Mary-Alice Waters.

Pedlar Press

P.O. Box 26, Stn. P, Toronto, ON M5S 2S6
Phone: (416) 534-2011
E-mail: feralgrl@interlog.com

Web site: www.pedlarpress.com
Contact: Beth Follett, publisher/editor
Publishes Canadian fiction, poetry, and art books. Sees its role as an innovator; produces beautiful books. Released 6 new titles in 2006. Accepts unsolicited manuscripts, but first send an inquiry, outline, and sample chapters. Guidelines available. "Canada's most important small-press publisher from a literary standpoint." – George Fetherling
Notable 2006 title: *The Book of Skeletons*, Rachel Vigier.

Pemmican Publications Inc.
150 Henry Avenue, Winnipeg, MB R3B 0J7
Phone: (204) 589-6346 Fax: (204) 589-2063
E-mail: pemmican@pemmican.mb.ca
Web site: www.pemmican.mb.ca
Contact: Audreen Hourie, managing editor
Established 1980 by the Manitoba Métis Federation as a creative and vocational venue for the Métis people of Manitoba. Publishes adult fiction and non-fiction, with an emphasis on social history and biography reflecting Métis experience, and children's and YA titles. Accepts unsolicited manuscripts, but first send author bio and synopsis. E-mail and fax submissions will not be accepted. Guidelines available on web site.

Penguin Group (Canada)
90 Eglinton Avenue E., Suite 700, Toronto, ON M4P 2Y3
Phone: (416) 925-2249 Fax: (416) 925-0068
Web site: www.penguin.ca
Contact: Elizabeth McKay, editorial assistant
Established in Canada in 1974. Mainstream publisher that features fiction, fantasy fiction, non-fiction, and young-adult titles for 8- to 12-year-olds. Notable authors include Margaret MacMillan, Michael Ignatieff, John Ralston Saul, Stuart McLean, Mark Kingwell, Guy Gavriel Kay, Jack Whyte, Adrienne Clarkson, and Joan Clark. Released 131 new titles in 2006. No unsolicited manuscripts.
Notable 2006 title: *Nixon in China*, Margaret MacMillan.

Penumbra Press
1225 Potter Drive, Manotick, ON K4M 1C9
Phone: (613) 692-5590 Fax: (613) 692-5589
E-mail: john@penumbrapress.com
Web site: www.penumbrapress.com
Contact: John Flood, president
   Publishes northern, eastern Ontario, and Native literature and art; archives of Canadian art; children's books; poetry books; diplomatic memoirs; and books on Canadian-Russian relations. Releases about 10 new titles a year. Accepts unsolicited manuscripts, but first send an inquiry with outline and sample chapters.

Playwrights Canada Press
215 Spadina Avenue, Suite 230, Toronto, ON M5T 2C7
Phone: (416) 703-0013 Fax: (416) 408-3402
Web site: www.playwrightscanada.com
Contact: Angela Rebeiro, publisher
   Established 1972. Publishes drama only, and only plays that have had professional theatre production. Accepts unsolicited manuscripts. Guidelines available.
   Notable 2006 title: *I Still Love You: Five Plays*, Daniel MacIvor.

The Porcupine's Quill
68 Main Street, Erin, ON N0B 1T0
Phone: (519) 833-9158 Fax: (519) 833-9845
E-mail: pql@sentex.net
Web site: www.sentex.net/~pql
Contact: Tim Inkster, publisher
   Established 1974. Specializes in Canadian literary fiction. Published 9 new titles in 2006. Does not accept unsolicited manuscripts.
   Notable 2006 title: *Hand Luggage*, P. K. Page.

Portage & Main Press
318 McDermot Avenue, Suite 100, Winnipeg, MB R3A 0A2
Phone: 1-800-667-9673 Fax: (866) 734-8477
E-mail: books@portageandmainpress.com
Web site: www.portageandmainpress.com
Contact: Catherine Gerbasi, director

A publisher of educational resources for teachers of grades K to 8 in all subjects. Publishes about 20 new titles a year. Does not accept unsolicited manuscripts. Send a query. Guidelines available. Notable 2006 title: *The World Today: Its People and Places*, William Norton, Michelle Visser-Wikkerink, and Linda Connor.

Pottersfield Press
83 Leslie Road, East Lawrencetown, NS B2Z 1P8
Web site: www.pottersfieldpress.com
Contact: Lesley Choyce, editor
Established 1979. Publishes general non-fiction, novels, and books of interest to Atlantic Canada. Particularly interested in biography proposals. Averages 6 new titles a year. Accepts proposals and/or full manuscripts. No phone calls, please.

Prairie House Books
P.O. Box 84007, Market Mall, Calgary, AB T3A 5C4
Phone: (403) 202-5438 Fax: (403) 202-5437
E-mail: phbooks@telusplanet.net
Web site: http://english-idioms.net/wm
Contact: Wayne Magnuson, publisher/editor
A self-publishing company providing services from editing to proofreading to shipping of printed, bound books. Publishes 2 books annually. Does not accept unsolicited manuscripts. First send an e-mail inquiry. "A book worth reading bares the soul of its author." – Ken Lewis.
Notable 2006 title: *English Idioms, Sayings & Slang*, Wayne Magnuson.

Productive Publications
P.O. Box 7200, Stn. A, Toronto, ON M5W 1X8
Phone: (416) 483-0634 Fax: (416) 322-7434
Web site: www.productivepublications.ca
Contact: Iain Williamson, publisher
Publishes softcover books on small business, entrepreneurship, business management, computers, and the Internet – non-fiction books to help people succeed. Published about 6 new titles in 2006 (19 revised titles). Accepts unsolicited manuscripts, but send an

inquiry first. "We are looking for books of 100 to 200 pages that are well written by people who know their subject well."

Notable 2006 title: *E-Business for Beginners.*

Purich Publishing
P.O. Box 23032, Market Mall P.O., Saskatoon, SK S7J 5H3
Phone: (306) 373-5311   Fax: (306) 373-5315
E-mail: purich@sasktel.net
Web site: www.purichpublishing.com
Contacts: Don Purch; Karen Bolstad

Specializes in books on Aboriginal issues, law, and Western history for the academic and reference market. Released 3 new titles in 2006. Accepts unsolicited manuscripts, but first send a query and outline. Guidelines available.

Notable 2006 title: *Justice for Young Offenders: Their Needs, Our Responses*, Mary E. Vandergoot.

Raincoast Books
9050 Shaughnessy Street, Vancouver, BC V6P 6E5
Phone: (604) 323-7100   Fax: (604) 323-2600
E-mail: info@raincoast.com
Web site: www.raincoast.com
Contact: editorial department

Publishes adult non-fiction in the areas of natural history, the environment, history, current affairs, biography and memoir, popular culture, sports, and travel; publishes fiction for young adult and teen readers; publishes picture books and illustrated stories for children aged 3 and older; and publishes non-fiction for older children. "We do not accept adult fiction or adult poetry." Releases about 25 new titles a year. See submission guidelines posted on web site. Query by mail with SASE and allow 9 months for a reply. Queries without SASE will not be answered nor will queries by e-mail. No unsolicited manuscripts or phone calls.

Notable 2006 title: *Walking after Midnight*, Katy Hutchinson.

Random House Canada
1 Toronto Street, Suite 300, Toronto, ON M5C 2V6
Phone: (416) 364-4449   Fax: (416) 364-6863
Web site: www.randomhouse.ca

A general trade publisher of quality fiction and non-fiction, primarily general interest, literary, and culinary titles. Only accepts manuscripts submitted by an agent.

Notable 2006 title: *JPod*, Douglas Coupland.

Red Deer Press
1800 4th Street S.W., Suite 1512, Calgary, AB T2S 2S5
Phone: (403) 509-0802 Fax: (403) 228-6503
E-mail: rdp@reddeerpress.com
Web site: www.reddeerpress.com
Contacts: Dennis Johnson, publisher; Peter Carver, children's and YA editor
Established 1975. Publishes literary fiction and non-fiction for adults and children, illustrated children's books, young-adult and teen fiction, poetry, and drama. Produced 15 books in 2006. Accepts unsolicited manuscripts. Send a synopsis and 3 sample chapters first. Canadian authors only. "Children's list is usually booked 2 to 3 years in advance. Reports in 4 to 6 months." Guidelines available on web site.

Notable 2006 title: *On Thin Ice*, Jamie Bastedo.

Rocky Mountain Books
406 – 13 Avenue N.E., Calgary, AB T2E 1C2
Phone: (403) 249-9490 Fax: (403) 249-2968
E-mail: tonyd@rmbooks.com
Web site: www.rmbooks.com
Contact: Tony Daffern, publisher
Established 1976. Specializes in outdoor recreational guides to the Canadian Rockies and Western Canada, and books on mountain culture, mountaineering, mountain people, and local history in mountain areas. Does not accept unsolicited manuscripts. Send a query letter with an outline and sample chapter. Phone queries are also welcome.

Notable 2006 title: *My Mountain Album*, Glen Boles.

Ronsdale Press
3350 West 21st Avenue, Vancouver, BC V6S 1G7
Phone: (604) 738-4688 Fax: (604) 731-4548
E-mail: ronsdale@shaw.ca

Web site: www.ronsdalepress.com
Contact: Ronald B. Hatch, director
   Established 1988. A literary press specializing in fiction, poetry, biography, regional literature, and books of ideas. Also publishes children's literature, but not picture books. Interested in quality and experimental literature. Released 11 new titles in 2006. Accepts unsolicited manuscripts. "We expect our authors to read widely in contemporary and past literature. Poets must have some publishing credits. With children's literature, we are interested in Canadian historical fiction." Guidelines available on web site.
   Notable 2006 title: *Half in the Sun: Anthology of Mennonite Writing*, edited by Elsie K. Neufeld.

Royal BC Museum Publishing
675 Belleville Street, Victoria, BC V8W 9W2
Phone: (250) 387-2478 Fax: (250) 387-0102
E-mail: gtruscott@royalbcmuseum.bc.ca
Web site: www.royalbcmuseum.bc.ca
Contact: Gerry Truscott, publisher
   Established 1891. Publishes scholarly and popular non-fiction concerning the human and natural history of British Columbia, and about the collections and activities of the provincial museum and archives. Produces about 4 new titles a year. No unsolicited manuscripts. Send an inquiry. Guidelines available.
   Notable 2006 title: *Wild Flowers*, Emily Carr.

Saxon House Canada
P.O. Box 6947, Stn. A, Toronto, ON M5W 1X6
Phone: (416) 488-7171 Fax: (416) 488-2989
Contact: W. H. Wallace, general manager
   Seeking works of history, philosophy, and fiction with literary integrity, historical accuracy, and fresh narrative skills. No longer publishes poetry. Averages 4 titles a year. Send an inquiry and outline.
   Notable 2006 title: *The Strategy*, David Mills.

Scholastic Canada Ltd.
175 Hillmount Road, Markham, ON L4C 1Z7
Phone: (905) 887-7323 Fax: (905) 887-3643

Web site: http://scholastic.ca

Contact: editor

Publishes books for children and young people up to age 14 with a focus on Canadian authors and illustrators. No unsolicited manuscripts at the present time. For up-to-date information on the submissions policy, phone (905) 887-7323, extension 4308, or visit the web site.

Second Story Press

20 Maud Street, Suite 401, Toronto, ON M5V 2M5

Phone: (416) 831-0602 Fax: (416) 537-7850

E-mail: info@secondstorypress.ca

Web site: www.secondstorypress.ca

Contact: Margie Wolfe, publisher

An award-winning publisher of progressive books for children and adults. At the core of the list are books with anti-sexist, anti-racist, socially conscious themes, mostly by women. Released 14 titles in 2006. Accepts unsolicited manuscripts. "Please ensure that your manuscript is a good fit for our list by perusing our web site and reviewing our titles and submission guidelines prior to contact."

Notable 2006 title: *Hiding Edith: A True Story*, Kathy Kacer.

Self-Counsel Press

1481 Charlotte Road, North Vancouver, BC V7J 1H1

Phone: (604) 986-3366 Fax: (604) 986-3947

E-mail: editor@self-counsel.com

Web site: www.self-counsel.com

Contact: Richard Day, acquisitions editor

Established 1971. Publishes non-fiction in 3 categories: legal series for lay readers, business series for small-business operators, and how to start and run a specific type of business. Also publishes how-to books on topics such as buying a house and understanding accounting. Produces at least 24 new titles each year. Accepts unsolicited manuscripts, but first send an outline, sample chapter, a résumé of your credentials, and the reasons this book is needed. "We seek fact-rich books written by experts in their field. Most manuscripts accepted are 70,000 to 80,000 words. We publish for the Canadian and U.S. markets." Guidelines available on web site.

J. Gordon Shillingford Publishing
P.O. Box 86, RPO, Winnipeg, MB R3M 3S3
Phone: (204) 779-6967 Fax: (204) 779-6970
E-mail: jgshill@allstream.net
Contact: Gordon Shillingford, president
Publishes Canadian drama, poetry, and non-fiction (social history, biography, native issues, and politics). Produces about 12 new titles a year. No unsolicited manuscripts. Send an inquiry. "We do not publish fiction or children's books."
Notable 2006 title: *Into the Hurricane: Attacking Socialism and the CCF*, John Boyko.

Shoreline
23 Ste-Anne, Ste-Anne-de-Bellevue, QC H9X 1L1
Phone: (514) 457-5733 Fax: (514) 457-5733
E-mail: shoreline@sympatico.ca
Web site: www.shorelinepress.ca
Contact: Judy Isherwood, editor
Aims to give first-time authors a chance in the marketplace, but it must be quality work. Publishes non-fiction (biographies, history, and social and church stories) and some poetry. Released 7 new titles in 2006. No unsolicited manuscripts. Send a query with an outline and sample chapters. Author guidelines available.
Notable 2006 title: *Bauxite, Sugar and Mud: Memoirs of Living in Colonial Guyana, 1928–1944*, Wendy Dothan.

Signature Editions
P.O. Box 206, RPO Corydon, Winnipeg, MB R3M 3S7
Phone: (204) 779-7803 Fax: (204) 779-6970
E-mail: signature@allstream.net
Web site: www.signature-editions.com
Contact: Karen Haughian, publisher
Publishes literary works by Canadians in the genres of fiction, non-fiction, poetry, and drama. Releases 6 to 7 new titles a year. Accepts unsolicited manuscripts or a sample with a covering letter, a synopsis, and a C.V. specifying previous published works. Include an SASE for a reply. Does not usually publish novice writers. Guidelines available on web site.
Notable 2006 title: *Two Hands Clapping*, Kit Brennan.

Sumach Press

1415 Bathurst Street, Suite 202, Toronto, ON M5R 3H8
Phone: (416) 531-6250 Fax: (416) 531-3892
E-mail: info@sumachpress.com
Web site: www.sumachpress.com
Contact: Lois Pike, marketing co-ordinator

Sumach Press is dedicated to publishing feminist writing, both non-fiction and fiction, for adult as well as young adult readers. Supports work that challenges the conventions of contemporary life, particularly concerning issues that touch the lives of Canadian women. Aims to publish writing that explores grassroots activism and informed critiques on subjects as widespread as health, politics, history, and sexuality. Sumach Press is committed to promoting a diversity of voices and opinions through a variety of genres from serious studies to literary works. Publishes about 10 new titles annually. Accepts unsolicited manuscripts, but please include an SASE if you want your manuscript returned. Guidelines available on web site.

Notable 2006 title: *The Book of Mary: A Novel*, Gail Sidonie Sobat

Talonbooks

P.O. Box 2076, Vancouver, BC V6B 3S3
Phone: (604) 444-4889 Fax: (604) 444-4119
E-mail: info@talonbooks.com
Web site: www.talonbooks.com
Contact: Karl Siegler, publisher

Established 1967. Specializes in drama, literary fiction, poetry, Québécois translation, women's literature, social issues, First Nation literature, and ethnography. Published 19 new titles in 2006. Accepts unsolicited manuscripts, but send an inquiry first. "We consider for publication only playscripts that have been professionally produced. We do not accept poetry manuscripts or publish historical, romance, adventure, science fiction, children's literature, or cookbooks." Guidelines available.

Notable 2006 title: *Vermeer's Light: Poems 1996–2006*, George Bowering.

Theytus Books

Lot 45, Green Mountain Road, R.R. #2, Site 50 Comp. 8,
Penticton, BC V2A 6J7

Phone: (250) 493-7181 Fax: (250) 493-5302
E-mail: info@theytusbooks.ca
Web site: www.theytusbooks.ca

An Aboriginal-owned and -run publishing house that publishes Aboriginal authors only. *Theytus* is a Salishan word that means "preserving for the sake of handing down." "We strive to produce appropriate reading material and information about Aboriginal peoples through the promotion of Aboriginal authors." Publishes literary fiction, non-fiction in social history and policy as it relates to Aboriginal issues, Aboriginal critical literary pieces, non-fiction (creative and humorous), and children's and YA titles. Send synopsis with sample chapters by mail only; no e-mail or fax submissions. Guidelines available on web site.

Notable 2006 title: *Behind Closed Doors*, edited by Agnes Jack.

Thistledown Press
633 Main Street, Saskatoon, SK S7H 0J8
Phone: (306) 244-1722 Fax: (306) 244-1762
E-mail: tdpress@thistledownpress.com
Web site: www.thistledownpress.com
Contact: Jackie Forrie, publications co-ordinator

Established 1975. Aims to publish Canadian literature of the highest quality, representing the wealth of the nation's culture and heritage. Specializes in Canadian fiction, poetry, and young adult fiction. Publishes about 14 new titles a year. The New Leaf Editions series is devoted to books of 64 pages by previously unpublished writers from Saskatchewan. Does not accept unsolicited manuscripts. Query first. Guidelines available on web site.

Notable 2006 title: *Compensation*, Devin Krukoff.

Timeless Books
3 MacDonell Avenue, Toronto, ON M6R 2A3
Phone: (416) 645-6747 Fax: (416) 588-3490
E-mail: contact@timeless.org
Web site: www.timeless.org
Contact: Clea McDougall, editor

For over 25 years, Timeless Books has been printing quality work that broadens the concept of what it means to do yoga in the West. Seeks to expand minds and help transform lives. Publishes 4 new titles a year. Accepts unsolicited manuscripts, but send a query first. Guidelines available on request.

Notable 2006 title: *Hatha Yoga: The Hidden Language*, Swami Sivananda Radha.

Touchwood Editions

356 Simcoe Street, Suite 6, Victoria, BC V8V 1L1
Phone: (250) 360-0829 Fax: (250) 385-0829
E-mail: editorial@heritagehouse.ca
Web site: www.touchwoodeditions.com

Publishes mostly non-fiction, with a focus on history, biography, nautical subjects, and architecture/design. Looks for a creative approach to history and has expanded its line to include historical fiction. Accepts unsolicited manuscripts, but first send a synopsis, table of contents, the first 2 or 3 chapters, and a total word count. Guidelines on web site.

Tradewind Books

1807 Maritime Mews, Suite 202, Vancouver, BC V6H 3W7
Phone: (604) 662-4405 Fax: (604) 730-0154
E-mail: tradewindbooks@telus.net
Web site: www.tradewindbooks.com
Contact: Michael Katz, publisher

Publishes high-quality literature for children and young adults. Released 5 new titles in 2006. Accepts unsolicited manuscripts, but send a sample chapter first. "We ask that writers read at least 3 of our titles before submitting a manuscript."

Notable 2006 title: *If I Had a Million Onions*, Sheree Fitch.

Tundra Books

75 Sherbourne Street, 5th Floor, Toronto, ON M5A 2P9
Phone: (416) 598-4786 Fax: (416) 598-0247
E-mail: lbailey@mcclelland.com
Web site: www.tundrabooks.com
Contact: Lauren Bailey, editorial assistant

Established 1967. Specializes in children's publishing: picture books, YA non-fiction, YA fiction, and historical fiction. Released 37 new titles in 2006. Accepts unsolicited manuscripts. "Please visit our web site."

Turnstone Press
100 Arthur Street, Suite 018, Winnipeg, MB R3B 1H3
Phone: (204) 947-1555 Fax: (204) 942-1555
E-mail: info@turnstonepress.com
Web site: www.turnstonepress.com
Contact: Todd Besant, managing editor
Established 1976. A literary press publishing fiction, poetry, non-fiction, and literary criticism. Through its imprint Ravenstone, it publishes non-formula genre fiction. Releases 12 new titles a year. Accepts unsolicited manuscripts. Send sample chapters first. Guidelines available on web site.
Notable 2006 title: *Houdini's Shadow*, Brent Robillard.

UBC Press
2029 West Mall, Vancouver, BC V6T 1Z2
Phone: (604) 822-4161 Fax: (604) 822-6083
E-mail: info@ubcpress.ca
Web site: www.ubcpress.ca
Contact: Jean Wilson, associate director, editorial
Established 1971. Publishes non-fiction for scholarly, educational, and general audiences in the social sciences and natural sciences. Subject areas include history, political science, Native studies, Asian studies, law and society, natural resources, planning, and health and sexuality studies. Releases approximately 60 new titles each year. No unsolicited manuscripts. Send an inquiry first. Guidelines available. "Check the web site for a fuller description of the press's publications and procedures."
Notable 2006 title: *Unsettling Encounters: First Nations Imagery in the Art of Emily Carr*, Gerta Moray.

Ulysses Travel Guides
4176 St-Denis Street, Montreal, QC H2W 2M5
Phone: (514) 843-9882 Fax: (514) 843-9448
E-mail: info@ulysses.ca
Web site: www.ulyssesguides.com
Contact: Daniel Desjardins, president
Publishes travel guides and outdoor activity guides for Canadians. Releases 2 new titles a year. Accepts unsolicited manuscripts, but

first send an outline and sample chapters. Guidelines available. Notable 2007 title: *Ulysses Travel Guide Ontario*, Pascale Couture.

United Church Publishing House

3250 Bloor Street W., Suite 300, Toronto, ON M8X 2Y4
Phone: (416) 231-5931   Fax: (416) 231-3103
Web site: www.united-church.ca/ucph
Contact: Rebekah Chevalier, senior editor
Established in 1829 as Ryerson Press. Aims to meet the spiritual needs of both its church members and others. Committed to publishing books that help people engage in Christian ministry, attracting readers, regardless of denomination or faith, to consider the spiritual aspects of their lives. Not accepting unsolicited manuscripts.

Notable 2006 title: *Seismic Shifts: Leading in Times of Change,* Christopher White.

University of Alberta Press

Ring House 2, University of Alberta, Edmonton, AB T6G 2E1
Phone: (780) 492-3662   Fax: (780) 492-0719
Web site: www.uap.ualberta.ca
Contact: Linda Cameron, director
Established 1969. The UAP publishes in the areas of biography, history, literature, natural history, regional interest, travel narratives, and reference books. Special series include Alberta Reflections (Alberta 2005 Centennial History series); the University of Alberta Centennial Series; Mountain Cairns, a series on the history and culture of the Canadian Rocky Mountains; and cuRRents, a Canadian literature series. Publishes 25 to 28 new titles a year. Accepts unsolicited scholarly manuscripts, but does not accept unsolicited poetry or fiction. First send a query with an outline and/or sample chapters. Guidelines available on request and on web site.

Notable 2006 title: *Reading Writers Reading: Canadian Authors' Reflections*, Danielle Schaub.

University of Calgary Press

2500 University Drive N.W., Calgary, AB T2N 1N4
Phone: (403) 220-7578   Fax: (403) 282-0085

E-mail: ucpress@ucalgary.ca
Web site: www.uofcpress.com
Contact: John King, senior editor
Established 1981. Publishes books and journals primarily for the scholarly market, although many titles have a broader appeal within the educated general public. Manuscripts must be considered either original contributions to knowledge or works of significant literary or other merit.

The press has a strong emphasis on history (e.g. archaeology, biography, folklore, heritage, military, northern, ranching, and social) and culture (e.g. communications, economics, film, Jewish and Holocaust studies, literature and criticism, media, museology, Native studies, parks and heritage, post-colonialism, and women's studies). It is also interested in anthropology, Canadian studies, education, environmental studies, geography, health, natural history, philosophy, politics, public policy, religious studies, and sociology, as well as architecture, art, music, technology, theatre, and urban planning. Whereas many recent titles have focused on the Canadian and American West (including the mountains and the Great Plains), the press has also established series in Latin American, African, and Arctic studies.

Released 35 new titles in 2006. Accepts unsolicited manuscripts. First send an inquiry with an outline and sample chapters. Author guidelines available on web site.

Notable 2006 title: *Mind Technologies: Humanities Computing and the Canadian Academic Community*, edited by Raymond Siemens and David Moorman.

University of Manitoba Press
301 St. John's College, Winnipeg, MB R3T 2M5
Phone: (204) 474-9495 Fax: (204) 474-7566
E-mail: carr@cc.umanitoba.ca
Web site: www.umanitoba.ca/publications/uofmpress
Contact: David Carr, director
Established 1967. Publishes non-fiction for trade and academic markets in Native and Canadian history, Native studies, and Canadian literary studies. Averages 5 to 8 new titles each year. Accepts either an electronic proposal or a paper manuscript, along with an author bio and assessment of the market. Manuscripts

under consideration are peer reviewed. Complete guidelines available on web site.

Notable 2006 title: *A Great Restlessness: The Life and Politics of Dorise Nielson*, Faith Johnston.

University of Ottawa Press

542 King Edward Avenue, Ottawa, ON K1N 6N5
Phone: (613) 562-5246 Fax: (613) 562-5247
E-mail: press@uottawa.ca
Web site: www.uopress.uottawa.ca
Contact: Jessica Dallaire, office coordinator

Reflecting the major interests of its parent institute, the UOP publishes scholarly works, textbooks, and general interest books. Areas of interest include Canadian studies, Canadian literature, history, governance, criminology, women's studies, religion, and translation. The UOP is also venturing into the realm of serious fiction. Releases about 24 new titles annually. Accepts unsolicited manuscripts, but please enquire first. Author guidelines available on web site.

Notable 2007 title: *Calling for Change: Women, Law, and the Legal Profession*, Elizabeth Sheehy and Sheila McIntyre, eds.

University of Toronto Press

10 St. Mary Street, Suite 700, Toronto, ON M4Y 2W8
Phone: (416) 978-2239 Fax: (416) 978-4738
E-mail: publishing@utpress.utoronto.ca
Web site: www.utppublishing.com

Established 1901. A large university press publishing scholarly and general works, and many academic journals. Editorial program includes classical, medieval, Renaissance, and Victorian studies, modern languages, English and Canadian literature, literary theory and criticism, women's studies, social sciences, Native studies, philosophy, law, religion, music, education, modern history, geography, and political science. Accepts unsolicited manuscripts, but first send query letter with outline, partial bibliography, sample chapters, and a C.V. Use *Chicago* or *MLA* for style, though internal consistency is most important.

Notable 2007 title: *The Filled Pen: Selected Non-Fiction of P. K. Page*, edited by Zailig Pollock.

Véhicule Press
P.O. Box 125, Place du Parc, Montreal, QC H2X 4A3
Phone: (514) 844-6073   Fax: (514) 844-7543
E-mail: vp@vehiculepress.com
Web site: www.vehiculepress.com
Contact: Vicki Marcok, general manager
Established 1973. Publishes literature in the context of social history – fiction, poetry, and non-fiction, as well as guidebooks. Authors are mostly Canadian. Releases approximately 15 new titles annually. Accepts unsolicited manuscripts, but send sample chapters first. "Send an SASE with submissions or we do not respond." Guidelines available.
Notable 2006 title: *The Rent Collector*, B. Glen Rokhin.

West Coast Paradise Publishing
P.O. Box 2093, Sardis Stn. Main, Sardis, BC V2R 1A5
Phone: (604) 824-9528   Fax: (604) 824-9541
E-mail: rga@shaw.ca
Web site: http://rg.anstey.ca
Contact: Robert G. Anstey, president
Publishes poetry, biography, and non-fiction literary books. Releases 10 books annually. Does not accept unsolicited manuscripts. First send an inquiry. Guidelines available.
Notable 2006 title: *Love Like a Left Hook*, Robert G. Anstey.

White Knight Books
1 Benvenuto Place, Suite 103, Toronto, ON M4V 2L1
Phone: (416) 925-6458   Fax: (416) 925-4165
E-mail: whitekn@istar.ca
Web site: www.whiteknightbooks.ca
Contact: Bill Belfontaine, publisher
Publishes non-fiction books on social issues, self-help, inspiration, advocacy, and education by Canadian authors. No unsolicited manuscripts. First inquire by e-mail or telephone. Guidelines available. "Will consider non-published, first-time authors with credible backgrounds in their topics."
Notable 2006 title: *From Student to Citizen*, Peter H. Hennessy.

Whitecap Books

351 Lynn Avenue, North Vancouver, BC V7J 2C4
Phone: (604) 980-9852 Fax: (604) 980-8197
E-mail: whitecap@whitecap.ca
Web site: www.whitecap.ca
Contact: Robert McCullough, publisher
Established 1977. Publishes books on cookery, children's fiction, and scenic colour books on U.S. and Canadian topics. Releases 30 books a year. Accepts unsolicited manuscripts; please send an outline and sample chapters first. Guidelines available on web site.
Notable 2006 title: *More Recipes from Ace Bakery*, Linda Haynes.

Wilfrid Laurier University Press

75 University Avenue W., Waterloo, ON N2L 3C5
Phone: (519) 884-0710, ext. 6124 Fax: (519) 725-1399
E-mail: press@wlu.ca
Web site: www.press.wlu.ca or www.wlupress.wlu.ca
Contact: Lisa M. Quinn, acquisitions editor
Established 1974. Publishes scholarly books (and academic journals) in the humanities and social sciences, and literary non-fiction. Subject areas include film, literature, literary criticism, literature in translation, cultural studies, native studies, religious studies, Canadian studies, life writing, philosophy, history, and women's studies. Produces 20 to 30 new books a year. Accepts unsolicited manuscripts, but first send C.V., outline, and sample chapter. Guidelines available on web site.

Wolsak and Wynn

69 Hughson Street N., Suite 102, Hamilton, ON L8R 1G5
Phone: (905) 972-9885
E-mail: info@wolsakandwynn.ca
Web site: www.wolsakandwynn.ca
Contact: Noelle Allen, publisher
A small literary press specializing in poetry and non-fiction. Published 8 new titles in 2006. Accepts unsolicited manuscripts; send an inquiry first. "Poetry submissions are accepted only during the first quarter of the year." Guidelines available.
Notable 2007 title: *Portraits: Selected Poetry*, Ron Charach.

XYZ Publishing
1781 Saint-Hubert Street, Montreal, QC H2L 3Z1
Phone: (514) 525-2170 Fax: (514) 525-7537
E-mail: xyzed@shaw.ca
Web site: www.xyzedit.qc.ca
Contact: Rhonda Bailey, editorial director
   A bilingual literary press, publishing in English as XYZ Publishing, and in French as XYZ éditeur. Founded in 1985, the company has 400 titles in print (7 new English titles in 2006). Since 1999, the English-language imprint has produced the Quest Library series of Canadian biographies (29 titles in print), as well as novels and non-fiction. "Our current fiction project is to bring the Jalna series by Mazo de la Roche back into print in a new trade paperback format." Does not accept unsolicited manuscripts. Send an inquiry first. "Please visit our web site for information on manuscript submissions. Manuscripts for the Quest Library series are commissioned by the editorial director in consultation with the editorial board."
   Notable 2006 title: *Jalna* (new edition), Mazo de la Roche.

6

LITERARY AGENTS

Acquiring a literary agent can sometimes be more challenging than finding a publisher. So why bother? Why pay a percentage of your hard-earned royalties to someone who didn't share those long hours writing at your computer, agonizing over every word, tormented with insecurity and overwork?

If you focus your writing on periodicals, you probably will not require an agent, but if your aspiration is to have a book published, an agent is someone you should seriously consider. Canadian book publishers are increasingly reluctant to deal with unagented manuscripts, or if they do accept them, it is often without the same serious scrutiny that is given to work submitted by an agent. Publishers respect the professionalism of agents, and realize that if an agent considers a manuscript to be worth their while, it must be a saleable commodity.

Good agents have extensive contacts in the publishing industry, affording them valuable insight as to which publishers and editors to approach with your project. They are experienced in negotiating the most favourable contracts for their clients, obtaining the best royalty rate and highest advance, and typically do business with the larger publishers, those who have the most money to spend. Agents will attempt to retain as many rights to their clients' work as possible, then pursue the sale of subsidiary rights, which may include foreign and film rights. They will follow up on contracts to ensure that all obligations are fulfilled, examining royalty statements and collecting all monies due. An agent's expertise is in the business side of publishing, an area in which most writers have neither the time nor inclination to become proficient.

In addition, agents can provide writers with professional career guidance and be an invaluable sounding-board for ideas, since they are acutely familiar with the marketplace. They will critique your work so that changes can be made before a publisher has the opportunity to turn it down.

Finding an agent to represent you can be a difficult task, especially if you are an unpublished author. Typically, agencies work overtime to represent the clients they already have and are often reluctant to invest their time and money in an unproven entity. That is why some of them charge a reading fee. A referral from an interested publisher or from one of their clients could help pique some interest, but getting your foot in an agent's door is not an easy process.

Although this chapter lists most of the active literary agencies in Canada, you will notice that many of them will not accept unsolicited manuscripts. In such cases, a query letter will be your first entry into an agent's office. Resist the urge to send out a mass mailing to every agent in the country. First, examine their subject interests and specialties, as indicated below, noting only the agencies that represent the type of work you are writing, then target those. Contacting agencies who do not handle your area of interest is a waste of everyone's time.

A query letter to an agent should contain a brief outline of the work you want him or her to sell and a description of your writing experience. If you have previously had a book in print, a prospective agent will want to know who published it, as well as how many copies and which foreign rights were sold. In other words, a busy agency must be convinced that your work has earning power. If you have no publishing history, your query letter needs to persuade an agent that your project will appeal to a lucrative market. Enclose an SASE for his or her reply.

Before agreeing to be represented by an agency, you should check its track record and ask for a client list. You may wish to obtain specialized legal advice before signing a contract with it or, alternatively, contact the Writers' Union of Canada or your regional branch of the Canadian Authors Association to assist you with any questions you may have.

Agents in Canada usually charge 15 per cent of the value of all rights sold, which may increase to 20 per cent for foreign sales. Some agencies also tack on fees for reading, evaluation, and editorial services, as well as charging the author for such office costs as photocopying, postage, couriers, and long-distance telephone and fax expenses. Be certain that all such obligations are disclosed and agreed to before you become that agency's client, and insist on an accounting of fees and expenses, as well as an upper limit to such charges.

Acacia House Publishing Services Ltd.

62 Chestnut Avenue, Brantford, ON N3T 4C2
Phone: (519) 752-8349 Fax: (519) 752-8349
E-mail: fhanna.acacia@rogers.com
Contacts: Frances Hanna and Bill Hanna

Subject interests: Fiction with international potential. No horror, occult, science fiction, or adult fantasy. For non-fiction, no self-help, fitness, true crime, or business books. Special non-fiction interest in history and military subjects.

Comments: Accepts unsolicited queries only, with writing sample (up to 50 double-spaced pages). Reads unpublished writers. Does not charge evaluation, editorial, or other handling fees. All queries and submissions must be accompanied by an SASE.

Aurora Artists

19 Wroxeter Avenue, Toronto, ON M4K 1J5
Phone: (416) 463-4634 Fax: (416) 463-4889
Contact: Janine Cheeseman

Subject interests: Primarily a film and television literary agency with cross-over management of rights for publication, etc.

Comments: Accepts unsolicited queries only. Does not read unpublished writers.

Author Author Literary Agency Ltd.

P.O. Box 56534, Lougheed Town Centre, Burnaby, BC V3J 7W2
Phone: (604) 415-0056
E-mail: joan@authorauthorliteraryagency.com

Web site: www.authorauthorliteraryagency.com
Contact: Joan Rickard
Subject interests: Book-length adult/juvenile fiction and non-fiction.

Comments: Welcomes unpublished writers. No evaluation fees for authors with a book already published in the same genre as current endeavours (excluding electronic, print-on-demand, and self-published books). Otherwise, there is a refundable entry evaluation fee of $75 U.S. per proposal (certified cheques or bank money orders; international bank money order if outside Canada). Evaluation fees are deducted from agency's commission on authors' properties sold to publishers. Submit hard copy only (no faxed or disk submissions). Reports in about 8 weeks from receipt of submission.

"Study thoroughly your chosen genre to learn writing techniques and what publishers are buying. Ensure manuscripts are properly formatted: double-spaced with 1-inch borders. Provide an SASE, International Reply Coupon, certified cheque, or adequate funds for response to inquiries and/or return of manuscripts. For writers' guidance, we offer a 22-page booklet, 'Crash Course for Proposals to Book and Magazine Publishers: Business Letters, Basic Punctuation/Information Guidelines and Manuscript Formatting,' for $8.95 U.S., including S/H. We make every attempt to provide writers with constructive evaluation and editorial feedback that will enhance their creative and technical skills."

Authors Marketing Services Ltd.
P.O. Box 84668, 2336 Bloor Street W., Toronto, ON M6S 4Z7
Phone: (416) 763-8797 Fax: (416) 763-1504
E-mail: authorslhoffman@cs.com
Contact: Larry Hoffman
Subject interests: Adult fiction and non-fiction.

Comments: Accepts unsolicited queries, but no unsolicited manuscripts. Unpublished writers are charged evaluation/handling fees.

Johanna M. Bates Literary Consultants Inc.
171 Somme Avenue S.W., Calgary, AB T2T 5J8
Phone: (403) 282-7370
E-mail: query@telusplanet.net

Web site: www.batesliterary.com
Contact: Johanna M. Bates
Subject interests: Literary fiction, children's books, and thriller/
suspense novels.
Comments: Accepts queries from unpublished writers. No unso-
licited manuscripts. An evaluation fee is charged.

Rick Broadhead & Associates Literary Agency

47 St. Clair Avenue W., Suite 501, Toronto, ON M4V 3A5
Phone: (416) 929-0516 Fax: (416) 927-8732
E-mail: rickb@rbaliterary.com
Web site: www.rbaliterary.com
Contact: Rick Broadhead, president/CEO
Subject interests: Seeks books in a variety of non-fiction cate-
gories, especially history, politics, current affairs, investigative
journalism, food narratives, business, sports/hockey, self-help,
health and medicine, parenting, science, true crime, memoir, mili-
tary history, and quirky/offbeat reference. Sales include *Life in the
Balance* by Dr. Marla Shapiro (HarperCollins Canada), *The Secret
Life of Meat* by Susan Bourette (Penguin Canada and Putnam/
Penguin USA), *Bad Bridesmaid: Bachelorette Brawls and Taffeta
Tantrums* by Siri Agrell (HarperCollins Canada and Henry Holt
USA), *When the Lights Went Out: How One Brawl Ended Hockey's Cold
War and Changed the Game* by Gare Joyce (Doubleday Canada/
Random House Canada), *Why Mexicans Don't Drink Molson*
(Douglas and McIntyre), *Ten Years Thinner: The Ultimate Lifestyle
Program for Winding Back Your Physiological Clock – and Your
Bathroom Scale* (Penguin Canada/DaCapo Press USA), *Why Do
Dogs . . . ?* and *Why Do Cats . . . ?* by Dr. Justine Lee (Three Rivers
Press/Random House USA), *Full Circle: Death and Resurrection in
Canadian Conservative Politics* (Key Porter Books), and *The Trouble
with Africa: Why Foreign Aid Isn't Working* by Robert Calderisi
(Palgrave/St. Martin's Press/Yale University Press U.K.).
Comments: In addition to its Canadian clientele, the agency has
an extensive roster of U.S. clients and has excellent relationships
with U.S. and foreign publishers. The agency is especially interested
in working with high-profile experts who have excellent credentials
and media visibility. The agency was founded in 2002 by bestselling

author and entrepreneur Rick Broadhead, who has the rare distinction of having authored and co-authored 34 books.

E-mail queries are preferred, and you are welcome to contact the agency via e-mail with a brief description of the book you are writing and a brief overview of your background and credentials. A polished, compelling book proposal will help in the evaluation of your project. Please do not send attachments unless requested.

The Bukowski Agency
14 Prince Arthur Avenue, Suite 202, Toronto, ON M5R 1A9
Phone: (416) 928-6728 Fax: (416) 963-9978
E-mail: assistant@thebukowskiagency.com
Web site: www.thebukowskiagency.com
Contact: Denise Bukowski
Subject interests: General adult trade books. Prefers literary fiction and non-fiction. No genre fiction (science fiction, romance, westerns); no children's books; no scriptwriters or playwrights. Specializes in projects with international potential and suitability for other media.
Comments: No unsolicited manuscripts or unpublished writers. Does not charge evaluation or other handling fees. Query first, by mail only, with writing samples and credentials. "What future projects do you have planned? Before making an investment in a little-known writer, I need to be convinced that you are not only talented but ambitious and driven as a writer." No phone or e-mail queries, please.

Canadian Speakers' & Writers' Service Limited
44 Douglas Crescent, Toronto, ON M4W 2E7
Phone: (416) 921-4443 Fax: (416) 922-9691
E-mail: pmmj@idirect.com
Contacts: Matie Molinaro, Paul Molinaro, and Julius Molinaro
Subject interests: Non-fiction, children's subjects, and dramatic works.
Comments: Sometimes reads unpublished writers. "If an unpublished writer presents an interesting project, we do charge an evaluation fee, as working on manuscripts and promoting new writers is becoming more and more costly." No unsolicited manuscripts.

The Cooke Agency
278 Bloor Street E., Suite 305, Toronto, ON M4W 3M4
Phone: (416) 406-3390 Fax: (416) 406-3389
E-mail: agents@cookeagency.ca
Contact: Dean Cooke
  Subject interests: Non-fiction and literary fiction.
  Comments: Accepts inquiries from unpublished writers, but no unsolicited manuscripts. No evaluation or other handling fees are charged. Requires an SASE or e-mail address for response.

The Core Group Talent Agency Inc.
89 Bloor Street W., Suite 300, Toronto, ON M5S 1M1
Phone: (416) 955-0819 Fax: (416) 955-0861
E-mail: literary@coregroupta.com
Contact: Charles Northcote
  Subject interests: Writing for film, theatre, and television. Deals primarily with scripts and producing and publishing them. Does not handle novels, short stories, poetry, etc.
  Comments: Accepts queries from unpublished writers. No unsolicited manuscripts. No evaluation fee.

Credentials
55 Livingston Road, PH 2, Toronto, ON M1G 1K9
Phone: (416) 926-1507 Fax: (416) 926-0372
E-mail: credent@rogers.com
Contact: Lynn Kinney
  Subject interests: Published or unpublished material suitable for film and television.
  Comments: No unsolicited manuscripts; send a query letter first with a 23-page synopsis. No evaluation fee.

Arnold Gosewich, Literary Agent and Consultant
40 Oaklands Avenue, Suite 207, Toronto, ON M4V 2E5
Phone: (416) 927-7836
E-mail: jackee@sympatico.com
Contact: Arnold Gosewich
  Subject interests: Non-fiction.
  Comments: No unsolicited manuscripts; send a query first. Reads unpublished writers. No evaluation fee.

Great North Artists Management, Inc.

350 Dupont Street, Toronto, ON M5R 1V9
Phone: (416) 925-2051 Fax: (416) 925-3904
E-mail: info@gnaminc.com
Contacts: Ralph Zimmerman, Rena Zimmerman, and Abigail
Algar
Subject interests: Film and television properties.
Comments: No evaluation or other handling fees. Queries by
mail or e-mail only. No unsolicited manuscripts. Prefer referral
from industry professional.

Great Titles Inc.

18 Greenfield Drive, Etobicoke, ON M9B 1G9
Phone: (416) 231-6686 Fax: (416) 231-7913
E-mail: atsallas@allstream.net
Contact: Tina Tsallas
Subject interests: Women's fiction and mainstream fiction with
strong characters. Also interested in mysteries and science fiction.
Children's material must be for the YA market. Non-fiction must
have broad audience appeal.
Comments: Accepts queries from unpublished and published
writers. Submit query with first 3 chapters and a detailed synopsis
(or complete manuscript with detailed synopsis). "Know the
market for which you are writing." No reading fee. No submissions
by e-mail. Always send an SASE.

Green Light Artist Management, Inc.

1240 Bay Street, Suite 804, Toronto, ON M5R 2A7
Phone: (416) 920-5110 Fax: (416) 920-4113
E-mail: info@glam.on.ca
Web site: www.glam.on.ca
Contact: Lara Bryant
Subject interests: Film and television writers only in the areas of
animation, comedy, and drama.
Comments: Does not accept unsolicited queries or manuscripts.
Will not consider unpublished writers. No reading fee. Does not
represent novelists or poets.

The Harding Agency
P.O. Box 76003, Vancouver, BC V6E 4T2
Phone: (604) 331-9330 Fax: (604) 331-9328
E-mail: reception@thehardingagency.com
Web site: www.thehardingagency.com
Contact: Sally Harding
   Subject interests: Commercial and literary fiction, and narrative non-fiction.
   Comments: Accepts unsolicited queries but no unsolicited manuscripts. Reads work from unpublished writers and does not charge an evaluation fee. Please go to our web site for more information about the agency and for submission guidelines.

Robert Lecker Agency, Inc.
4055 Melrose Avenue, Montreal, QC H4A 2S5
Phone: (514) 830-4818 Fax: (514) 483-1644
E-mail: leckerlink@aol.com
Web site: www.leckeragency.com
Contact: Robert Lecker
   Subject interests: Non-fiction sports, food, travel, popular science, and academic books with trade potential.
   Comments: Accepts queries from unpublished writers. No unsolicited manuscripts. No evaluation or handling fee.

Lucas Talent Inc.
100 West Pender Street, 7th Floor, Vancouver, BC V6B 1R8
Phone: (604) 685-0345 Fax: (604) 685-0341
E-mail: doreen.holmes@lucastalent.com;
   anna.archer@lucastalent.com
Web site: www.lucastalent.com
Contacts: Doreen Holmes and Anna Archer
   Subject interests: Writing for film and television only.
   Comments: Accepts inquiries from western Canadian writers only. No unsolicited manuscripts. Occasionally considers unpublished writers. No evaluation or other handling fees are charged.

Anne McDermid and Associates Ltd.
83 Willcocks Street, Toronto, ON M5S 1C9
Phone: (416) 324-8845 Fax: (416) 324-8870

E-mail: info@mcdermidagency.com
Web site: www.mcdermidagency.com
Contact: Anne McDermid
Subject interests: Literary and commercial fiction and narrative non-fiction. Associate Lise Henderson also accepts children's and young adult literature. No self-help or how-to.
Comments: Accepts mailed queries with synopsis, C.V., and a short sample, but no unsolicited manuscripts. No telephone or e-mail queries, please. Check web site for details.

Mensour Agency Ltd.

41 Springfield Road, Ottawa, ON K1M 1C8
Phone: (613) 241-1677   Fax: (613) 241-4360
E-mail: kate@mensour.ca
Web site: www.mensour.ca
Contact: Catherine Mensour
Subject interests: Theatre, animation, television, and film.
Comments: Does not accept unsolicited queries or manuscripts, but will sometimes read unpublished writers. No evaluation or other handling fees are charged.

Pamela Paul Agency Inc.

12 Westrose Avenue, Toronto, ON M8X 2A1
Phone: (416) 410-5395   Fax: (416) 410-4949
E-mail: agency@interlog.com
Contact: James Gordon
Subject interests: Literary fiction, children's fiction, film, theatre, television, and radio.
Comments: Will review new writers' material only with a referral.

Bella Pomer Agency Inc.

355 St. Clair Avenue West, Suite 801, Toronto, ON M5P 1N5
Phone: (416) 920-4949
Web site: www.bellapomeragency.com
Contact: Bella Pomer
Subject interests: Quality fiction, quality mystery, and general-interest non-fiction.
Comments: No queries or unsolicited manuscripts. "Not taking on new clients. List is closed."

The Saint Agency
18 Gloucester Lane, Suite 200, Toronto, ON M4Y 1L5
Phone: (416) 944-8200 Fax: (416) 944-3700
E-mail: mala@thesaintagency.com
Contact: Mala Khosla
Subject interests: Screenplays for television and film.
Comments: "Please call or write to enquire before sending scripts." Accepts inquiries, but no unsolicited scripts. Reads unpublished writers. No evaluation fee.

Seventh Avenue Literary Agency
1663 West 7th Avenue, Vancouver, BC V6J 1S4
Phone: (604) 734-3663 Fax: (604) 734-8906
Web site: www.seventhavenuelit.com
Contact: Robert Mackwood
Subject interests: Primarily non-fiction in the following areas: business, popular culture, technology/science, travel, house and home, sports, food, and memoir.
Comments: Accepts unsolicited queries; see web site for submission guidelines. No unsolicited manuscripts. Will occasionally read work from unpublished writers if the subject area is of interest. No evaluation fee. "Our client list includes writers from Canada, the U.S., the U.K., and other parts of the world. We have been successful selling translation rights through an expanding team of sub-agents."

Beverley Slopen Literary Agency
131 Bloor Street W., Suite 711, Toronto, ON M5S 1S3
Phone: (416) 964-9598 Fax: (416) 921-7726
E-mail: beverley@slopenagency.ca
Web site: www.slopenagency.ca
Contact: Beverley Slopen
Subject interests: Narrative non-fiction and commercial fiction.
Comments: No unsolicited manuscripts. Only occasionally reads unpublished writers if referred. Does not charge evaluation/handling fees.

P. Stathonikos Agency

146 Springbluff Heights S.W., Calgary, AB T3H 5E5
Phone: (403) 245-2087 Fax: (403) 245-2087
E-mail: pastath@telus.net
Contact: Penny Stathonikos
 Subject interests: Juvenile, young adult, and Canadiana. No academic material, science fiction, or plays.
 Comments: Accepts queries and unsolicited manuscripts from unpublished writers. Charges a handling fee of $100.

Carolyn Swayze Literary Agency Ltd.

P.O. Box 39588, White Rock, BC V4B 5L6
Phone: (604) 538-3478 Fax: (604) 531-3022
E-mail: carolyn@swayzeagency.com
Web site: www.swayzeagency.com
Contact: Carolyn Swayze
 Subject interests: Literary fiction, teen fiction, limited commercial fiction, military history, humour, strong, well-written narrative non-fiction, science, and social history.
 Comments: Accepts queries and unsolicited manuscripts of non-fiction works. For fiction, send first 50 pages. Reads work by unpublished writers. No evaluation or handling fees. "No science fiction, romance, fantasy, or screenplays, please. Representing Mark Zuehlke, W. P. Kinsella, Will Ferguson, Genni Gunn, Aislinn Hunter, Miriam Toews, Karen Rivers, Bill Gaston, John Lekich, Andrew Gray, Taras Grescoe, and Mark Frutkin."

Transatlantic Literary Agency, Inc.

1603 Italy Cross Road, Petite Riviere, NS B0J 2P0
Phone: (902) 693-2026 Fax: (902) 693-2026
E-mail: wordbyword@eastlink.ca
Web site: www.tla1.com
Contact: Don Sedgwick
 Subject interests: Adult, young adult, and children's fiction and non-fiction.
 Comments: Accepts queries but no unsolicited manuscripts. Usually not interested in unpublished writers. Also has offices in the United States and the Netherlands, and has more than 20 sub-agents worldwide. "The company currently represents 200 authors

and illustrators across Canada and around the world. Review the web site for further guidelines and submission information."

Westwood Creative Artists
94 Harbord Street, Toronto, ON M5S 1G6
Phone: (416) 964-3302   Fax: (416) 975-9209
E-mail: wca_office@wcaltd.com
Contact: Chris Casuccio
    Subject interests: Literary fiction and non-fiction, some YA. No poetry or screenplays.
    Comments: Will consider unpublished writers. Please query before sending an unsolicited manuscript. No evaluation or handling fees. "We do not accept e-mail queries or submissions."

Woolf & Lapin
777 rue de Bellechasse, Suite 203, Montreal, QC H2S 3M9
Phone: (514) 271-2440   Fax: (514) 271-6291
E mail: sdubreuil@wolfelapin.com
Web site: www.wolfelapin.com
Contact: Stephan Dubreuil
    Subject interests: English and French adult and children's fiction, historical and graphic novels, biography, and screenplays of all genres.
    Comments: Send queries by e-mail only. No unsolicited manuscripts. Will consider unpublished writers. No evaluation or handling fees. "Your query letter should include a brief synopsis. We represent talent for the book publishing, motion picture, television, and new media industries."

7

WRITING AWARDS & COMPETITIONS

This chapter surveys a broad range of the literary prizes and competitions open to Canadian writers. Most of the prizes and competitions may be applied for directly. Among a number of high-profile exceptions are the Charles Taylor Prize, conferred each year for an exemplary work of non-fiction, and the Journey Prize, sponsored by the Writers' Trust of Canada and McClelland & Stewart, for the best short fiction from Canada's literary journals. In some cases, the judges prefer to receive submissions from publishers, but usually, as long as the application criteria are met, individual applications are also accepted.

Please note that application deadlines and details are subject to change, and that the following entries do not include full eligibility criteria or entry conditions. Many awards, for instance, require the provision of several copies of the work so that it can be circulated among the nominating jury. Applicants should always obtain full guidelines before making a submission.

Canadian writers are also eligible for a range of overseas awards, and you'll find many of these listed in standard international reference books such as *Literary Market Place*. New Canadian awards are usually advertised in *Quill & Quire* and in some literary journals.

Acorn-Plantos Award
Jeff Seffinga, 36 Sunset Avenue, Hamilton, ON L8R 1V6
Phone: (905) 521-9196

E-mail: jeffseff@allstream.net

Deadline: June 30

A $500 prize and the People's Poet medal is awarded annually to a poet based on the best volume in the People's Poetry tradition published during the previous calendar year. Entry fee $25. May be entered by the poet or the publisher. Authors must be Canadian citizens or landed immigrants. No posthumous awards.

Acrostic Story Contest

The Brucedale Press, P.O. Box 2259, Port Elgin, ON N0H 2C0

Phone: (519) 832-6025

E-mail: brucedale@bmts.com

Web site: www.bmts.com/~brucedale

Deadline: January 31

Alphabetically arranged, 26 sentences must tell a complete story. The opening phrase is set by the contest administrators and changes each year. Following sentences must begin with words in the sequence of the English alphabet. Any subject or theme is acceptable, and the stories should be original and unpublished. First prize 25% of entry fees, second prize 15% of entry fees, third prize 10% of entry fees. There may be up to 3 honourable mentions. Winning stories will be published in *The Leaf.* Entry fee $5/story. Annual.

John Alexander Media Awards

Marketing and Communications Department, Multiple Sclerosis Society of Canada, 175 Bloor Street E., Suite 700, North Tower, Toronto, ON M4W 3R8

Phone: (416) 922-6065

E-mail: info@mssociety.ca

Web site: www.mssociety.ca

Deadline: December 31

A $500 award is given annually to the author of the best English or French newspaper or magazine article (and another $500 to the creator of the best television or radio broadcast) about some aspect of multiple sclerosis.

The Antigonish Review Writing Contests

P.O. Box 5000, St. Francis Xavier University, Antigonish, NS B2G 2W5

Phone: (902) 867-3962
E-mail: tar@stfx.ca
Web site: www.antigonishreview.com

Sheldon Currie Fiction Prize
Deadline: May 31
A first prize of $600, second prize of $400, and third prize of $200 are awarded for the best stories on any subject. Prizes also include publication in *The Antigonish Review.* Total entry not to exceed 20 pages (double-spaced). Entry fee $25 ($35 if outside North America), which includes a 1-year subscription. Send only original, unpublished material. Annual.

Great Blue Heron Poetry Contest
Deadline: June 30
A first prize of $600, second prize of $400, and third prize of $200 are awarded to the best poems on any subject matter. Prizes also include publication in *The Antigonish Review.* Total entry not to exceed 4 pages (maximum 150 lines), which may include 1 long poem or several shorter ones. Entry fee $25 ($35 if outside North America), which includes a 1-year subscription. Send only original, unpublished material. Annual.

Arc Poetry Contests and Prizes
P.O. Box 7219, Ottawa, ON K1L 8E4
Phone: (613) 729-3550
E-mail: arc.poetry@cyberus.ca

Arc Poem of the Year Contest
Deadline: June 30
Prizes of $1,000, $750, and $500 are awarded for the best unpublished poetry not to exceed 100 lines. Entry fee $20 for up to 4 poems, which includes a 1-year subscription to *Arc.* Annual.

Diana Brebner Prize
Deadline: September 15
A $500 award for Ottawa poets who have not been published in book form. Length of poem not to exceed 30 lines. Entry fee $12 for up to 2 poems, which includes a 1-year subscription to *Arc.* Annual.

Confederation Poets Prize

Honouring Archibald Lampman, William Wilfred Campbell, and Duncan Campbell-Scott. A cash prize of $100 is awarded for the best poem published in *Arc* in the previous calendar year. All poems published in *Arc* are automatically entered. Annual.

Critic's Desk Award

Honours excellence in reviewing books of poetry. A prize of $100 is given annually for both a feature review and a brief review that has been published in *Arc* in the previous calendar year. Reviews are automatically entered for this award.

Archibald Lampman Award

Deadline: January 31

Named after the 19th-century Confederation poet Archibald Lampman, the $500 award recognizes an outstanding book of English-language poetry by an author living in the Ottawa area. Books must have been published between January and December of the previous year and have no fewer than 48 pages.

Ascent Aspirations Magazine Anthology Contests

David Fraser, Ascent Aspirations Publishing, 1560 Arbutus Drive, Nanoose Bay, BC V9P 9C8

Phone: (250) 468-7313

E-mail: ascentaspirations@shaw.ca

Web site: http://ascentaspirations.ca

Ascent Aspirations publishes anthologies comprising the best submissions to their contests. One anthology consists of poetry only with the following awards: first prize $100, second prize $75, third prize $50, fourth prize $25, and each prize winner receives 2 copies of the anthology. In addition, 5 honourable mentions receive $10 each and 1 copy of the anthology. The other anthology consists of poetry and flash fiction: first prize for poetry and fiction $100, second prize $50, third prize $25, and each prize winner receives 1 copy of the anthology. In addition, 5 honourable mentions receive $10 each and 1 copy of the anthology.

Poems and flash fiction may have been published elsewhere. Maximum length for poems is 60 lines. Entry fees $5 for 1 poem or $10 for 3 poems. Maximum length for flash fiction is 800 words.

Entry fee $10/story. See web site for submissions details and deadlines.

Atlantic Journalism Awards

Bill Skerret, Co-ordinator, 6175 Almon Street, Halifax, NS
  B3K 5N2
Phone: (902) 425-2727 Fax: (902) 462-1892
E-mail: office@ajas.ca
Web site: www.ajas.ca
Deadline: end of January
  Framed certificates are awarded to the winners in 23 categories. Only print and broadcast journalists working in the Atlantic region are eligible. Entry fee $50. Annual.

Atlantic Poetry Prize. *See* Writers' Federation of Nova Scotia Awards.

Atlantic Writing Competition for Unpublished Manuscripts. *See* Writers' Federation of Nova Scotia Awards.

Aurora Awards

Dennis Mullin, The Canadian Science Fiction and Fantasy
  Association, 88 Bruce Street, Suite 501, Kitchener, ON N2B 1Y8
E-mail: dmullin@sentex.net
Web site: www.sentex.net/~dmullin/aurora
Deadline: dates vary (check web site)
  A hand-crafted trophy by Alberta artist Frank Johnson is awarded for the best work in 3 categories of writing in English. Annual.

Best Long-Form Work in English

Awarded for the best science-fiction or fantasy novel or fiction collection by a Canadian writer released in Canada in the previous calendar year.

Best Short-Form Work in English

Awarded for the best science-fiction or fantasy novella, novelette, short story, or poem by a Canadian writer released in Canada in the previous calendar year.

Best Work in English – Other

Awarded for the best piece of science-fiction or fantasy writing by a Canadian not encompassed by the previous 2 categories; for example, critical writing, media presentations, anthologies, magazines, or translation into English.

The Alfred G. Bailey Prize. *See* **Writers' Federation of New Brunswick Literary Competition.**

Marilyn Baillie Picture Book Award. *See* **Canadian Children's Book Centre Awards.**

Bancroft Award. *See* **the Royal Society of Canada Awards.**

Banff Mountain Book Competition

P.O. Box 1020, 107 Tunnel Mountain Drive, Banff, AB T1L 1H5

Phone: (403) 762-6347   Fax: (403) 762-6277

E-mail: banffmountainbooks@banffcentre.ca

Web site: www.banffmountainfestivals.ca

Deadline: June 30

Over $5,000 will be awarded to books in the following categories: mountain literature, mountain exposition, mountain image, and adventure travel. Presented in conjunction with the Banff Mountain Book Festival. Annual.

B.C. Book Prizes

Bryan Pike, Executive Director, 207 West Hastings Street, Suite 902, Vancouver, BC V6B 1H7

Phone: (604) 687-2405   Fax: (604) 687-2435

E-mail: info@bcbookprizes.ca

Web site: www.bcbookprizes.ca

Deadline: December 1

BC Booksellers' Choice Award in Honour of Bill Duthie

A $2,000 prize is awarded annually to the originating publisher and author of the best book in terms of public appeal, initiative, design, production, and content. The publisher must have its head office in B.C. or the Yukon, and the creative control in terms of editing, design, and production must have been within B.C. or the

Yukon. The membership of the B.C. Booksellers' Association determines the winner by ballot.

Sheila A. Egoff Children's Prize

A $2,000 prize is awarded annually to the author of the best novel for juveniles and young adults, and the best non-fiction book for children (including biography) that has not been highly illustrated. The author must be a B.C. or Yukon resident or have lived in B.C. or the Yukon for 3 of the past 5 years. The book may have been published anywhere.

Hubert Evans Non-Fiction Prize

A $2,000 prize is awarded annually to the author of the best original non-fiction literary work (philosophy, belles lettres, biography, history, etc.). Quality of research and writing, insight, and originality are major considerations in the judging of this prize. The author must be a B.C. or Yukon resident or have lived in B.C. or the Yukon for 3 of the past 5 years. The book may have been published anywhere.

Roderick Haig-Brown Regional Prize

A $2,000 prize is awarded annually to the author of the book that contributes most to the enjoyment and understanding of B.C. The book may deal with any aspect of the province (people, history, geography, oceanography, etc.) and must be original. Reprints, revised editions, guide books, and how-to books are not considered. The book may have been published anywhere, and the author may reside outside B.C.

Christie Harris Prize for Illustrated Children's Books

An annual $2,000 prize is shared by the author and illustrator of the best children's picture book, picture storybook, or illustrated non-fiction book. The author and/or illustrator must be a B.C. or Yukon resident or have lived in B.C. or the Yukon for 3 of the past 5 years. The book may have been published anywhere.

Lieutenant Governor's Literary Lifetime Achievement Award

A $5,000 prize is awarded annually to honour late-career authors for their entire body of work. There will also be a province-wide author tour of shortlisted writers during B.C. Book and Magazine Week.

The Dorothy Livesay Poetry Prize

A $2,000 prize is awarded annually to the author of the best work of poetry. The author must be a B.C. or Yukon resident or have lived in B.C. or the Yukon for 3 of the past 5 years. No anthologies or "best of" collections. The book may have been published anywhere.

The Ethel Wilson Fiction Prize

A $2,000 prize is awarded annually to the author of the best work of fiction. The author must be a B.C. or Yukon resident or have lived in B.C. or the Yukon for 3 of the past 5 years. No anthologies.

The B.C. Lieutenant-Governor's Award for Historical Writing

Barb Hynek, Chair/Judge of the BCHF Book Competition, B.C. Historical Federation, 2477 – 140th Street, Surrey, BC V4P 2C5
Phone: (604) 535-9090
E-mail: bhynek@telus.net
Deadline: December 31

Awarded to the writer whose book contributes most significantly to the recorded history of British Columbia. Any new book presenting any facet of B.C. history is eligible. Judges look for appropriate illustrations, careful proofreading, and an adequate index, table of contents, and bibliography. The prizes are $600, $400, and $200, plus an invitation to the awards banquet. Books must be submitted in their year of publication. Annual.

BC Booksellers' Choice Award in Honour of Bill Duthie.
See B.C. Book Prizes.

The Pierre Berton Award

Canada's Natural History Society, 167 Lombard Avenue, Suite 478, Winnipeg, MB R3B 0T6
Phone: 1-800-816-6777 Fax: (204) 988-9309
E-mail: info@historysociety.ca
Web site: www.historysociety.ca
Deadline: April 27

Celebrates those who have brought Canadian history to a wider audience. Canada's National History Society established this award in 1994 for distinguished achievement in presenting Canadian history in an informative and engaging manner. Canadian writer and popular historian Pierre Berton was the first recipient and agreed to lend his name to future awards. The award continues to honour those who, like the award's namesake, have introduced Canadian characters and events of the past to the national and international public. Eligible nominees are individuals or organizations that have helped popularize Canadian history with the written word through such means as publications, film, radio, television, theatre, or the web. The recipient(s) will receive a medal and a $5,000 cash prize. Annual.

Geoffrey Bilson Award for Historical Fiction for Young People. *See* **Canadian Children's Book Centre Awards.**

Earle Birney Prize for Poetry. *See* **PRISM international Writing Prizes.**

CAA Carol Bolt Award. *See* **Canadian Authors Association Awards.**

Joseph Brant Award. *See* **Ontario Historical Society Awards for Authors.**

Diana Brebner Prize. *See* **Arc Poetry Contests and Prizes.**

Ann Connor Brimer Award
Heather MacKenzie, Halifax Public Libraries, 60 Alderney Drive, Dartmouth, NS B2Y 4P8
Phone: (902) 490-5991 Fax: (902) 490-5889
E-mail: mackenh@halifaxpubliclibraries.ca
Web site: http://nsla.ns.ca/aboutnsla/brimeraward.html
Deadline: October 30
A framed certificate and $1,000 prize is awarded annually to the author of a children's book published in the 12 months preceding the deadline. Books must be intended for youth up to age 15, and the prize is awarded for text, not illustration. Authors must be

resident in Atlantic Canada. Co-sponsored by the Nova Scotia Library Association and the Writer's Federation of Nova Scotia, the award is presented at the Atlantic Book Awards ceremony in the spring of each year.

John Bullen Prize. *See* **Canadian Historical Association Awards.**

Burnaby Writers' Society Competition

Eileen Kernaghan, Burnaby Writers' Society, 6584 Deer Lake
    Avenue, Burnaby, BC V5G 3T7
Phone: (604) 522-1811
E-mail: info@bws.bc.ca
Web site: www.bws.bc.ca
Deadline: May 31
    Annual cash prizes of $200, $100, and $50 are given to the top 3 entries in the competition. Categories and themes change from year to year. Open to B.C. residents only. Entry fee $5. Write for guidelines.

Canada-Japan Literary Awards

Janet Riedel Pigott, Acting Director, Endowments and Prizes,
    Canada Council for the Arts, P.O. Box 1047, 350 Albert Street,
    Ottawa, ON K1P 5V8
Phone: (613) 566-4414 or 1-800-263-5588, ext. 5041   Fax: (613)
    566-4430
E-mail: janet.riedel@canadacouncil.ca
Web site: www.canadacouncil.ca
Deadline: Spring 2008
    Two cash prizes of $10,000 are usually awarded every 2 years for outstanding books of fiction, non-fiction, drama, or poetry about Japan or on Japanese themes by Canadian authors or for translations of Japanese books into French or English. Only publishers of eligible books may nominate titles for this award.

Canadian Authors Association Awards

Alec McEachern, P.O. Box 419, 320 South Shores Road,
    Campbellford, ON K0L 1L0
Phone: (705) 653-0323 or 1-866-216-6222   Fax: (705) 653-0593

E-mail: admin@canauthors.org
Web site: www.canauthors.org/awards/awards.html

CAA – BookTelevision Award

Deadline: March 31

A prize of $500, a silver medal, and travel to and from the CAA Conference is awarded for the Canadian or landed immigrant under age 30 deemed to show the most promise in the field of literary creation. This award is made possible by BookTelevision. No entry fee. Annual.

CAA Carol Bolt Award

Deadline: December 15

Winners receive $1,000 and a silver medal for the best English-language play for adults by a Canadian author or landed immigrant. All entries must have been published or performed in the previous year. Made possible by the Playwrights Guild of Canada and Playwrights Canada Press. Entry fee $35/title. Annual.

CAA Lela Common Award for Canadian History

Deadline: December 15

A prize of $2,500 for the best work of historical non-fiction on a Canadian topic written in English by a Canadian author. Entry fee $35. Annual.

CAA MOSAID Technologies Inc. Award for Fiction

Deadline: December 15

A prize of $2,500 and a sterling-silver medal is awarded in recognition of the year's outstanding full-length novel by a Canadian writer. Entries should manifest "literary excellence without sacrifice of popular appeal." Nominations from the author, publisher, an individual, or group are eligible. Entry fee $35. Annual.

CanWrite Conference Story Contest

Evan Kenney, 32 Green Meadow Crescent, Welland, ON L3C 6X3
Phone: (905) 734-7180
E-mail: tweed@allstream.net
Deadline: February 28

The top 10 winners of this short-fiction contest will have their work published in an anthology and the top 3 winners will receive $500, $200, and $100. Stories to be no longer than 1,500 words. Open to all Canadian and U.S. residents. Entry fee $15. Annual.

CAA Poetry Award
Deadline: December 15
   A prize of $1,000 and a sterling-silver medal is awarded in recognition of the year's outstanding book of poetry by a Canadian writer. Entries should manifest "literary excellence without sacrifice of popular appeal." Nominations from author, publisher, individual, or group are eligible. Entry fee $35. Annual.

Canadian Booksellers Association Libris Awards
789 Don Mills Road, Suite 700, Toronto, ON M3C 1T5
Phone: (416) 467-7883 Fax: (416) 467-7886
E-mail: esinkins@cbabook.org
Web site: www.cbabook.org
Contact: Emily Sinkins, general manager

Author of the Year Award
Deadline: June 1
   A trophy is awarded to the Canadian author of an outstanding literary work that contributes to Canadian culture and combines readability with strong sales. A call for nominations is sent to members of the book community. The shortlist comprises the 3 candidates with the most nominations.

Children's Author of the Year Award
Deadline: June 1
   A trophy is awarded to the Canadian author of an outstanding literary work for children that combines readability with strong sales and demonstrates a strong connection with his or her reading audience. The shortlist comprises the 3 candidates with the most nominations.

Fiction Book of the Year Award
Deadline: June 1
   A trophy is awarded for a Canadian work of fiction that had an outstanding impact on the Canadian bookselling industry, created

wide media attention, brought people into bookstores, and had strong sales. A call for nominations is sent to members of the book community. The shortlist comprises the 3 candidates with the most nominations.

Non-Fiction Book of the Year Award
Deadline: June 1

A trophy is awarded for a Canadian work of non-fiction that had an outstanding impact on the Canadian bookselling industry, created wide media attention, brought people into bookstores, and had strong sales. A call for nominations is sent to members of the book community. The shortlist comprises the 3 candidates with the most nominations.

Canadian Children's Book Centre Awards
40 Orchard View Boulevard, Suite 101, Toronto, ON M4R 1B9
Phone: (416) 975-0010 Fax: (416) 975-8970
E-mail: info@bookcentre.ca
Web site: www.bookcentre.ca

Marilyn Baillie Picture Book Award
Contact: Charlotte Teeple
E-mail: charlotte@bookcentre.ca
Deadline: April 30

A $10,000 prize is awarded to an outstanding picture book in which the author and the illustrator achieve artistic and literary unity. Should be aimed at children ages 3 to 6. To be eligible, it must be an original work in English, written and illustrated by Canadians, and first published in Canada. Genres include fiction, non-fiction, and poetry. Annual.

Geoffrey Bilson Award for Historical Fiction for Young People
Contact: Naseem Hrab
E-mail: naseem@bookcentre.ca
Deadline: January 15

An annual prize of $1,000 is awarded to the author of an outstanding work of historical fiction for young people. The author must be Canadian. The winner is chosen by a jury appointed by the CCBC. Annual.

The Norma Fleck Award for a Canadian Children's Non-Fiction Book
Contact: Charlotte Teeple
E-mail: charlotte@bookcentre.ca
Deadline: March 30
   A $10,000 prize is awarded to the author of the best children's non-fiction book. The text must be of exceptional quality and present the subject matter in a way that both informs and excites interest. Visuals, also of exceptional quality, should clarify, extend, and complement the text. Only books written and illustrated by Canadian citizens or landed immigrants will be considered. Annual.

TD Canadian Children's Literature Award
Contact: Charlotte Teeple
E-mail: charlotte@bookcentre.ca
Deadline: March 15
   A grand prize of $20,000 is awarded for the most distinguished book written in English and for the most distinguished book written in French. In addition, there is a total of $20,000 for honour book winners, with a maximum of 4 books on the honour list in each language category. All books in any genre written by a Canadian for children ages 1 through 13 will be eligible. In the case of a picture book, both the author and illustrator must be Canadian. Only books first published in Canada will be considered. Annual.

Canadian Ethnic Media Association Awards
Ben Viccari, President, 22 Walmer Road, Suite 801, Toronto, ON
   M5R 2W5
Phone: (416) 944-8175   Fax: (416) 260-3586
E-mail: canscene@rogers.com
Web site: www.canadianethnicmedia.com
Deadline: March 31
   Annual prizes of a plaque and free tickets to the awards event are presented for the best working journalists in ethnic print, radio, television, and Internet or a mainstream journalist writing on subjects concerning Canada's diversity. Awards are given for the best news or feature story and for the best editorial or opinion piece in 4 categories: print, radio, television, and Internet magazine. Annual.

Canadian Farm Writer's Federation Annual Writers Award
Jeannie Bryson, Awards Administrator, Quanglo, P.O. Box 250,
   Ormstown, QC J0S 1G0
Phone: (450) 829-2224
E-mail: jeannie@quanglo.ca
Web site: www.cfwf.ca
Deadline: early summer (check web site for details)
   Annual award for stories from general periodicals, news releases, technical features, press features, editorials, columns, and daily, weekly, and monthly press reports. Writing must be about production agriculture. First prize $300, second $200, and third $100. Announced at annual CFWF meeting in early October.

Canadian Historical Association Awards
Joanne Mineault, 395 Wellington Street, Ottawa, ON K1A 0N4
Phone: (613) 233-7885 Fax: (613) 567-3110
E-mail: cha-shc@archives.ca
Web site: www.cha-shc.ca

John Bullen Prize
Deadline: November 30
   A prize of $500 is awarded for the best doctoral historical dissertation written by a Canadian citizen or landed immigrant.

The Clio Awards
Deadline: December 31
   Annual awards given for meritorious publications or for exceptional contributions by individuals or organizations to regional history.

The Wallace K. Ferguson Prize
Deadline: December 2
   A $1,000 prize is awarded annually to a Canadian citizen or landed immigrant who has published an outstanding scholarly book in a field of history other than Canadian history.

The Eugene A. Forsey Prize
Deadline: June 1
   Prizes are awarded annually for the best undergraduate essay, or

the equivalent, and the best graduate thesis completed in the past 3 years on Canadian labour and working-class history.

Sir John A. Macdonald Prize
Deadline: December 2
A prize of $1,000 is awarded in recognition of the non-fiction work of Canadian history judged to have made the most significant contribution to an understanding of Canada's past. Annual.

The Hilda Neatby Prize in Women's History
Deadline: February 1
Awarded for an academic article (one in English and the other in French), published in a Canadian journal or book during the previous year, deemed to have made an original and scholarly contribution to the field of women's history and gender history as it relates to women. Annual.

Prize for Best Article on the History of Sexuality in Canada
Canadian Committee on the History of Sexuality, c/o Steven Maynard, Department of History, Queen's University, Kingston, ON K7L 3N6
Deadline: February 1
An award designed to recognize excellence in, and encourage the growth of, scholarly work in the history of sexuality in Canada. The winning article will be one that makes an original contribution in this field. Articles must be previously published and written in either English or French. Awarded every 2 years.

Canadian Library Association Book Awards
Valerie Delrue, CLA Membership Services, 328 Frank Street, Ottawa, ON K2P 0X8
Phone: (613) 232-9625, ext. 301 Fax: (613) 563-9895
Web site: www.cla.ca

Book of the Year for Children Award
Presented annually to the author of an outstanding book suitable for children up to the age of 12 published in Canada during the previous calendar year. Any creative work (fiction, poetry, anthologies, etc.) will be deemed eligible. Author must be a Canadian

citizen or permanent resident. Nominations invited from CLA members and publishers.

Young Adult Canadian Book Award

This award recognizes the author of an outstanding English-language book written in the preceding calendar year that appeals to young adults between the ages of 13 and 18. The book must be a work of fiction published in Canada, and the author a Canadian citizen or landed immigrant. Annual.

Canadian Political Science Association Prizes

260 Dalhousie Street, Suite 204, Ottawa, ON K1N 7E4
Phone: (613) 562-1202 Fax: (613) 241-0019
E-mail: cpsa@csse.ca
Web site: www.cpsa-acsp.ca

C. B. Macpherson Prize
Deadline: December 2007

A biennial award of $750 is presented to the author of the best book published in English or French in the field of political theory. No textbooks, edited texts, collections of essays, or multiple-authored works will be considered. The 2008 prize is for books published in 2006 and 2007. The author must be a Canadian citizen or permanent resident.

Donald Smiley Prize
Deadline: December 2008

An annual award of $1,000 will be given to the author of the best book, published in English or French, in a field relating to the study of government and politics in Canada. The 2009 prize is for books published in 2008. The author must be a Canadian citizen or permanent resident.

Canadian Writer's Journal Semi-Annual Short Fiction Contest

P.O. Box 1178, New Liskeard, ON P0J 1P0
Phone: (705) 647-5424 Fax: (705) 647-8366
E-mail: cwj@cwj.ca

Web site: www.cwj.ca

Deadlines: March 31 and September 30

The writers of the best short fiction receive awards of $100, $50, and $25, a 1-year subscription to the *Canadian Writer's Journal*, and publication in a chapbook entitled *Choice Works*. Entries must be original, unpublished stories in any genre to a maximum length of 1,200 words. Entry fee $5/story.

CanWrite Conference Story Contest. *See* **Canadian Authors Association Awards.**

Bliss Carman Poetry Award. *See* **Prairie Fire Writing Contests.**

CBC Literary Awards

Sophie Cazenave, Awards Administrator, 1400 René Lévesque E., Montreal, QC H4V 1Z6

Phone: 1-877-888-6788

E-mail: literary_awards@cbc.ca

Web site: www.cbc.ca/literaryawards

Deadline: November 1

An annual writing competition, in partnership with the Canada Council for the Arts, that offers $10,000 in prizes in each of 3 categories, in English and French, for a total of $60,000. First- and second-place texts are published in *enRoute* magazine and are also produced for broadcast on CBC Radio One. The categories are short stories, travel literature, and poetry. Entry fee $20/submission. Entry forms available on web site. You may also request an information brochure by e-mail or phone.

The Lina Chartrand Poetry Award. *See* **Contemporary Verse 2 Literary Contests.**

Chocolate Lily Book Awards

Karen Ehrenholz, P.O. Box 18135, 1215C – 56th Street, Delta, BC V4L 2B0

Phone: (604) 943-3051

E-mail: chocolily@uniserve.com

Web site: www.chocolatelilyawards.com
Deadline: January 31

Through an annual non-profit program, students in British Columbia read books nominated for the Chocolate Lily Book Awards – the best fiction by B.C. authors and illustrators – and vote for the winners. Nominated books are selected by a panel of teachers, librarians, and authors. There are 2 categories: best picture book (for students in kindergarten–grade 3) and best chapter book/novel (for readers in grades 4–8). Authors must reside part- or full-time in British Columbia and the books must have been published in the previous year.

The City of Calgary W. O. Mitchell Book Prize. *See* **Writers Guild of Alberta Awards.**

The City of Edmonton Book Prize. *See* **Writers Guild of Alberta Awards.**

City of Toronto Book Award

Bev Kurmey, Toronto Protocol Office, 10th Floor, West Tower,
    City Hall, Toronto, ON M5H 2N2
Phone: (416) 392-8191
Deadline: end of February

Each year prize money totalling $15,000 is apportioned in recognition of works of literary merit in all genres that are evocative of Toronto. Fiction and non-fiction published in English for adults and/or children are eligible. Each shortlisted author (usually 4 to 6) receives $1,000, the balance going to the winner. No residency requirements. Reprints, textbooks, and manuscripts are not eligible.

City of Vancouver Book Award

Marnie Rice, Office of Cultural Affairs, City of Vancouver,
    453 West 12th Avenue, Vancouver, BC V5Y 1V4
Phone: (604) 871-6634 Fax: (604) 871-6005
E-mail: marnie.rice@vancouver.ca
Web site: www.vancouver.ca/bookaward
Deadline: mid-May

An annual $2,000 cash prize is awarded in October to recognize books for their excellence and their contribution to an appreciation and understanding of Vancouver, its history, and the achievements of its residents. Entered books must be primarily set in or about Vancouver, though the author's place of residence is not restricted, and the book may have been written/published anywhere in the world. Books may be fiction, non-fiction, poetry, or drama, written for children or adults, and may deal with any aspect of the city, including its history, geography, current affairs, or the arts. Apply for guidelines.

City of Victoria Butler Book Prize

Bess Jillings, Chair, Victoria Book Prize Society, 1464 Fort Street, Suite 1, Victoria, BC V8S 1Z5
Phone: (250) 592-1464
E-mail: info@victoriabutlerbookprize.ca
Web site: www.victoriabutlerbookprize.ca
Deadline: May 15

Honours Victoria's literary community with its renowned writers and passionate readers. It is a partnership between the City of Victoria, which funds the $5,000 prize; Brian H. Butler of Butler Brothers Supplies, which funds the administrative costs; and the Victoria Book Prize Society, which sets the policy, appoints the jury, and administers the process. It is also sponsored by the Greater Victoria Public Library, the Union Club, and the Magnolia Hotel and Spa.

Writers must have been resident in Greater Victoria for the previous 2 years and must be either a Canadian citizen or permanent resident. Fiction, literary non-fiction, poetry, and children's literature are all eligible; bibliographies, cookbooks, travel guides, exhibition catalogues, instruction manuals, self-help books, scholarly books, textbooks, reference books, chapbooks, and self-published books are not. Annual.

Claremont Review Annual Writing Contests

4980 Wesley Road, Victoria, BC V8Y 1Y9
Phone: (250) 658-5221 Fax: (250) 658-5387
Web site: www.theclaremontreview.com

Fiction Contest
Deadline: March 15

First prize $500, second prize $300, and third prize $200 for the best work of fiction by a writer aged 13 to 19. Entry fee $18 for 1 category and $20 for both. Each entrant receives a 1-year subscription to *The Claremont Review*.

Poetry Contest
Deadline: March 15
First prize $500, second prize $300, and third prize $200 for the best poem by a writer aged 13 to 19. Entry fee $18 for 1 category and $20 for both. Each entrant receives a 1-year subscription to *The Claremont Review*.

The Clio Awards. *See* **Canadian Historical Association Awards.**

Matt Cohen Award: In Celebration of a Writing Life. *See* **the Writers' Trust of Canada Awards.**

Shaughnessy Cohen Prize for Political Writing. *See* **the Writers' Trust of Canada Awards.**

The Winston Collins/Descant Prize for the Best Canadian Poem
Mark Laliberte, Managing Editor, Descant, P.O. Box 314, Stn. P, Toronto, ON M5S 2S8
Phone: (416) 593-2557 Fax: (416) 593-9632
E-mail: info@descant.ca
Web site: www.descant.ca/contest.html
Deadline: October 10, 2007
Awarded in memory of Winston Collins, writer and enthusiastic teacher of literature at the universities of Cincinnati, Princeton, and Toronto. The prize perpetuates his remarkable talent for encouraging self-expression through writing. First prize is $1,000 plus payment for publication in *Descant*. Two honourable mentions will also be awarded. Applicants must be Canadian citizens or landed immigrants. Maximum length of poems is 100 lines. Previously published material is not accepted. Entry fee $29, which includes a 1-year subscription to *Descant*. Annual.

CAA Lela Common Award for Canadian History. *See* **Canadian Authors Association Awards.**

Confederation Poets Prize. *See* **Arc Poetry Contests and Prizes.**

Contemporary Verse 2 Literary Contests
Clarise Foster, 100 Arthur Street, Suite 207, Winnipeg, MB
R3B 1H3
Phone: (204) 949-1365 Fax: (204) 942-5754
E-mail: cv2@mts.net
Web site: www.contemporaryverse2.ca
CV2 sponsors the 2-Day Poem Contest in the spring. Awards are $300 for first prize, $150 for second, and $75 for third. Each winner also receives a 1-year subscription to the magazine, and the first- and second-prize winners are published as part of the award. Guidelines and themes are available on the web site.

The Lina Chartrand Poetry Award
A cash prize (which varies) recognizes a distinguished contribution by an emerging female poet published by *CV2* in the previous year. Her work must reflect the dedication and values represented by Lina Chartrand, rights activist, writer, poet, publisher, dramaturge, and screenwriter. Annual.

Donald Grant Creighton Award. *See* **Ontario Historical Society Awards for Authors.**

Critic's Desk Award. *See* **Arc Poetry Contests and Prizes.**

Sheldon Currie Fiction Prize. *See* **the Antigonish Review Writing Contests.**

Dafoe Book Prize
James Fergusson, Honorary Secretary, J. W. Dafoe Foundation,
359 University College, University of Manitoba, Winnipeg, MB
R3T 2M8
Phone: (204) 474-6606 Fax: (204) 474-7645

E-mail: ferguss@cc.umanitoba.ca

Deadline: early December

A $10,000 prize is awarded annually for distinguished writing by a Canadian or resident of Canada that contributes to the understanding of Canada and/or its place in the world.

Dartmouth Book Awards

Heather MacKenzie, Halifax Public Libraries, 60 Alderney Drive,
   Dartmouth, NS B2Y 4P8

Phone: (902) 490-5991 Fax: (902) 490-5889

E-mail: mackenh@halifaxpubliclibraries.ca

Web site: www.halifax.ca/bookawards

Deadline: December 3

Two prizes of $1,500 each are awarded to honour the adult fiction and non-fiction books that have contributed most to the enjoyment and understanding of the cultural heritage of Nova Scotia. The winning titles best celebrate the spirit of Nova Scotia and its people. Open to any Canadian citizen or landed immigrant. Submission fee $10. The awards are presented at the Atlantic Writing Awards ceremony in the spring of each year. Annual.

The Margaret and John Savage First Book Award

Deadline: December 3

A prize of $1,500 is awarded annually to the best first published book (adult fiction or non-fiction) by an Atlantic Canadian author.

The Donner Prize

Prize Manager, The Donner Prize, c/o Meisner Publicity and
   Promotion, 394A King Street E., Toronto, ON M5A 1K9

Phone: (416) 368-8253 Fax: (416) 363-1448

E-mail: meisnerpublicity@sympatico.ca

Deadline: November 30

An annual award of $30,000 is awarded for the best book on Canadian public policy, with prizes of $5,000 each to the 5 finalists. The jury is looking for provocative, readable, and inspiring books on Canadian public policy that cover a broad spectrum of issues, including healthcare, social issues, educational reform, public finance, environment, regulatory and legal reform, urban affairs, youth issues, and social policy. The author must be Canadian, and the publisher of the book must be either Canadian or American.

Sheila A. Egoff Children's Prize. *See* **B.C. Book Prizes.**

Arthur Ellis Awards

Cheryl Freedman, Executive Director, Crime Writers of Canada, P.O. Box 113, 3007 Kingston Road, Scarborough, ON M1M 1P1
Phone: (416) 597-9938
E-mail: info@crimewriterscanada.com
Web site: www.crimewriterscanada.com
Deadline: January 15, 2008

Established 1984 and named after the *nom de travail* of Canada's official hangman. Prizes are awarded annually for works published for the first time in the preceding year in the following crime genre categories: best crime novel, best non-fiction, best first crime novel, best crime short story, best juvenile/young adult crime book, and best crime publication in French. Cash prizes awarded depending on availability. Open to any writer resident in Canada or any Canadian living abroad. Setting and imprint immaterial. Rules posted on web site in early December. No entry fee.

Arthur Ellis Award for Best Unpublished First Crime Novel
Open to any writer resident in Canada or a Canadian living abroad who has never had a novel published commercially. Winner receives a cash prize plus the opportunity of having the manuscript published.

Marian Engel Award. *See* **the Writers' Trust of Canada Awards.**

Norma Epstein Award for Creative Writing

Eleanor Dennison, University College, 15 King's College Circle, Room A102, Toronto, ON M5S 3H7
Phone: (416) 978-8083   Fax: (416) 971-2806
E-mail: eleanor.dennison@utoronto.ca
Deadline: May 15

Open to any student regularly enrolled in an undergraduate or graduate degree course at a Canadian university. A prize of $1,000 is available every other year for substantial work in each of these categories: fiction, drama, and verse.

Hubert Evans Non-Fiction Prize. *See* **B.C. Book Prizes.**

Event Creative Non-Fiction Contest
P.O. Box 2503, New Westminster, BC V3L 5B2
Phone: (604) 527-5293 Fax: (604) 527-5095
E-mail: event@douglas.bc.ca
Web site: http://event.douglas.bc.ca
Deadline: April 16
Event magazine's annual contest invites good writing that explores the creative non-fiction forms of personal narrative, essay, biography, documentary, and life and travel writing. Three winners each receive $500 plus payment for publication in *Event*. Accepts previously unpublished submissions up to 5,000 words. Entry fee $29.95/submission, which includes a 1-year subscription to *Event*.

The Wallace K. Ferguson Prize. *See* **Canadian Historical Association Awards.**

The Fiddlehead Contests
Kathryn Taglia, Managing Editor, The Fiddlehead, Campus
    House, 11 Garland Court, Fredericton, NB E3B 5A3
Phone: (506) 453-3501 Fax: (506) 453-5069
E-mail: fiddlhd@unb.ca
Web site: www.lib.unb.ca/Texts/Fiddlehead
Deadline: December 15

Fiction Prize for Best Story
A prize of $1,000 is awarded, plus publication, for first place, and $500 each for 2 runners-up. Submissions to be no more than 25 pages. No previously published stories are accepted. Entry fee $30, which includes a 1-year subscription to *The Fiddlehead*. Annual.

Ralph Gustafson Prize for Best Poem
A prize of $1,000 is awarded, plus publication, for first place, and $500 each for 2 runners-up. Submissions to be no more than 5 poems, a maximum of 100 lines/poem. No previously published

poems are accepted. Entry fee $30, which includes a 1-year subscription to *The Fiddlehead*. Annual.

Finding the Right Words Flash Fiction Contest
Betty Dobson, 163 Main Avenue, Halifax, NS B3M 1B3
Phone: (902) 444-1691 Fax: (902) 482-3403
E-mail: contests@inkspotter.com
Web site: http://inkspotter.com/contests.htm
Deadline: July 21
A first prize of $60 and second prize of $30, plus publication in *InkSpotter News*, is awarded for fiction of 500 words or less on a new theme each year (check web site). Entry fee $1.50. Annual.

Timothy Findley Award. *See* **the Writers' Trust of Canada Awards.**

The Sheree Fitch Prize. *See* **Writers' Federation of New Brunswick Literary Competition.**

The Norma Fleck Award for a Canadian Children's Non-Fiction Book. *See* **Canadian Children's Book Centre Awards.**

The Eugene A. Forsey Prize. *See* **the Canadian Historical Association Awards.**

Yves Fortier Earth Science Journalism Award. *See* **Science in Society Journalism Awards.**

Freefall's Fiction and Poetry Contests
Lynn C. Fraser, Managing Editor, Freefall, 922 – 9th Avenue
S.E., Calgary, AB T2G 0S4
Phone: (403) 264-4730
E-mail: awcs@telusplanet.net or freefallmagazine@yahoo.ca
Web site: www.alexandrawriters.org
Deadline: December 31
Prizes of $200 for first place and $100 for second place are awarded for the fiction and poetry categories. Open to anyone. Maximum length for fiction is 3,000 words. May submit up to 5 poems,

not to exceed 6 pages each. Entry fee for members of the Alexandra Writers' Centre Society is $10; non-members $20; additional entries $5. Annual.

Fresh Fish Award for Emerging Writers. *See* **Writers' Alliance of Newfoundland and Labrador Literary Awards.**

Mavis Gallant Prize for Non-Fiction. *See* **Quebec Writers' Federation Book Awards.**

The Lionel Gelber Prize
Prize Manager, Munk Centre for International Studies, University of Toronto, 1 Devonshire Place, Toronto, ON M5S 3K7
Phone: (416) 946-8901 Fax: (416) 946-8915
E-mail: gelberprize.munk@utoronto.ca
Web site: www.utoronto.ca/mcis/gelber
Deadline: October 31
   A $15,000 prize is awarded to the best non-fiction book on international affairs written in English or translated into English. Each submission should deal with significant issues in foreign relations. Priority is given to books that provide information to the general audience through new perspectives and analysis. Biographies, autobiographies, and historical works are appropriate. Presented by the Lionel Gelber Foundation in partnership with the Munk Centre for International Studies at the University of Toronto and the Washington-based *Foreign Policy Magazine*. Annual.

The Giller Prize. *See* **the Scotiabank Giller Prize.**

John Glassco Translation Prize
Micheline Sainte-Marie, 2230 Étienne Brûlé Avenue, Montreal, QC H2B 1Y9
Phone: (514) 384-1198
E-mail: tap1@videotron.ca
Web site: www.attlc-ltac.org/glasscoe.htm
Deadline: June 30
   A $1,000 prize is awarded by the Literary Translators' Association of Canada for a translator's first book-length literary translation

into English or French published in Canada during the previous year. Eligible genres include fiction, non-fiction, poetry, and children's literature. Entrants must be Canadian citizens or landed immigrants. Annual.

Danuta Gleed Literary Award. *See* **the Writers' Union of Canada Awards and Competitions.**

Government of Newfoundland and Labrador Arts and Letters Awards

P.O. Box 1854, St. John's, NL A1C 5P9
Phone: (709) 729-5253
Web site: www.gov.nf.ca/artsandletters
Deadline: mid-February

Percy Janes First Novel Award
One prize of $1,500 is awarded for the best unpublished manuscript of at least 30,000 words. Entrants must be unpublished novelists who reside in Newfoundland and Labrador. One entry permitted per person.

Literary Arts Section Awards – Junior Division
Four prizes of $250 are awarded every year for ages 12 to 14 in 2 categories: poetry and prose. Six prizes of $250 are also awarded for ages 15 to 18 in the same categories. Entrants must be residents of Newfoundland and Labrador.

Literary Arts Section Awards – Senior Division
Prizes of $1,000 are awarded every year in recognition of outstanding original work in each of the following categories: 6 awards for poetry, 5 awards for short fiction (maximum 5,000 words), 3 awards for non-fiction prose (maximum 5,000 words), and 2 awards for dramatic script. Entrants must be residents of Newfoundland and Labrador. The awards are open to amateurs and professionals.

Governor General's Literary Awards

Robyn Pollex, Writing and Publishing Section, Canada Council for the Arts, P.O. Box 1047, 350 Albert Street, Ottawa, ON K1P 5V8

Phone: (613) 566-4414, ext. 5576, or 1-800-263-5588 Fax:
(613) 566-4410
E-mail: robyn.pollex@canadacouncil.ca
Web site: www.canadacouncil.ca
Deadlines: March 15, June 1, and August 7
Seven annual awards of $15,000 are conferred in recognition of
the best books of the year in English and in French in the following
categories: fiction, literary non-fiction, poetry, drama, children's literature (text), children's literature (illustration), and translation
(from French to English). In addition, the publishers of the winning
titles receive a $3,000 grant for the promotion of the prize-winning
books. Non-winning finalists each receive $1,000. Books must be
first edition trade books and be written, translated, or illustrated by
Canadian citizens or permanent residents. For translations, the
original work, written in French, must also be written by a Canadian.
Administered by the Canada Council for the Arts. Write for eligibility criteria and other guidelines or consult the web site.

Great Blue Heron Poetry Contest. *See* **the Antigonish
Review Writing Contests.**

The Great Canadian Literary Hunt. *See* **THIS Magazine
Writing Awards.**

The Griffin Poetry Prize
Ruth Smith, Manager, The Griffin Trust for Excellence in Poetry,
6610 Edwards Boulevard, Mississauga, ON L5T 2V6
Phone: (905) 565-5993 Fax: (905) 564-3645
E-mail: info@griffinpoetryprize.com
Web site: www.griffinpoetryprize.com
Deadline: December 31
Two prizes of $50,000 are awarded annually in the categories of
international and Canadian poetry. In each category, the prize will
be for the best collection of poetry in English published during the
preceding year. Entries must be worldwide first editions and may
only be submitted by publishers.

Ralph Gustafson Prize for Best Poem. *See* **the Fiddlehead
Contests.**

Hackmatack Children's Choice Book Award

Norene Smiley, 3770 Kempt Road, Halifax, NS B3K 4X8
Phone: (902) 424-3774 Fax: (902) 424-0633
E-mail: hackmatack@hackmatack.ca
Web site: www.hackmatack.ca
Deadline: October 31

A plaque is awarded annually for the best book in each of three categories – English fiction, English non-fiction, and French – written by a Canadian author for readers in grades 4 to 6. Books are chosen for their literary, cultural, and enjoyment factors, with an emphasis on Atlantic-authored materials. Children in reading groups vote for the nominees, who tour the region, giving readings to hundreds of children.

Roderick Haig-Brown Regional Prize. *See* B.C. Book Prizes.

Jason A. Hannah Medal. *See* the Royal Society of Canada Awards.

Christie Harris Prize for Illustrated Children's Books. *See* B.C. Book Prizes.

Hibernating with Words. *See* Pandora's Collective Poetry Contests.

Hidden Brook Press Poetry Awards

109 Bayshore Road, R.R. #4, Brighton, ON K0K 1H0
Phone: (613) 475-2368
E-mail: writers@hiddenbrookpress.com
Web site: www.hiddenbrookpress.com

The Open Window Poetry Anthology Contest
Deadline: November 1

Ten cash prizes from $10 to $100 plus 10 honourable mentions are awarded annually. Submit 5 poems, previously unpublished, of any style, theme, or length. Up to 300 poems will be published. Entry fee of $15 includes purchase of the resulting book.

Seeds International Poetry Chapbook Anthology Contest
Deadlines: April 1 and October 1
Cash prizes and honourable mentions are awarded twice a year. Submit 3 poems of any style, theme, or length. Up to 300 poems will be published. Entry fee of $12 includes purchase of the resulting book.

Ray Burrell Poetry Award. *See* **the Valley Writers' Guild Awards.**

The John Hirsch Award for Most Promising Manitoba Writer. *See* **Manitoba Writing and Publishing Awards.**

K. M. Hunter Artists Awards
Awards Office, Ontario Arts Council, 151 Bloor Street W., 5th
   Floor, Toronto, ON M5S 1T6
Phone: (416) 969-7422 or 1-800-387-0058, ext. 7422 Fax: (416)
   961-7796
E-mail: mwarren@arts.on.ca
Web site: www.arts.on.ca
Supports projects that advance an individual's career. Five awards of $8,000 each are given in the disciplines of visual arts, dance, literature, theatre, interdisciplinary arts, and music. Recipients are chosen from a selection of grant applications recommended by the Ontario Arts Council juries; in the case of writers, the shortlist comes from the OAC's Works in Progress program. Annual.

Innis-Gérin Medal. *See* **the Royal Society of Canada Awards.**

International 3-Day Novel Contest
341 Water Street, Suite 200, Vancouver, BC V6B 1B8
E-mail: info@3daynovel.com
Web site: www.3daynovel.com
Deadline: Friday before Labour Day
Writers must pre-register, then write a novel over the 3-day Labour Day weekend. Research and brief outlines are permitted before the contest. The winner is published by 3-Day Books (with distribution by Arsenal Pulp Press). Cash and other prizes are offered to the runner-up and shortlist. Entry fee $50. Annual.

IODE Violet Downey Book Award

40 Orchard View Boulevard, Suite 254, Toronto, ON M4R 1B9
Phone: (416) 487-4416
Web site: www.iode.ca
Deadline: December 31

Awarded for the author of the best English-language book in any category, suitable for children ages 13 and under. The author must be Canadian and the book must have been published in Canada during the previous year. Books are submitted by the publisher. Annual.

Alexander Kennedy Isbister Award for Non-Fiction. *See* **Manitoba Writing and Publishing Awards.**

Percy Janes First Novel Award. *See* **Government of Newfoundland and Labrador Arts and Letters Awards.**

The Joker Is Wild Awards for Humour. *See* **Valley Writers' Guild Awards.**

Kisses and Popsicles Spring Poetry Contest. *See* **Pandora's Collective Poetry Contests.**

A. M. Klein Prize for Poetry. *See* **Quebec Writers' Federation Book Awards.**

The Kobzar Literary Award

Ukrainian Canadian Foundation of Taras Shevchenko, 952 Main Street, Suite 202, Winnipeg, MB R2W 3P4
Phone: (204) 944-9128 or 1-866-524-5314 Fax: (204) 944-9135
E-mail: lesia@shevchenkofoundation.ca
Web site: www.shevchenkofoundation.ca
Deadline: May 15

A $25,000 award ($20,000 to the author, $5,000 to the publisher) to recognize an outstanding contribution to Canadian literature with a Ukrainian-Canadian theme. Accepts literary non-fiction, fiction, children's literature, poetry, and drama in English, French, or Ukrainian. Awarded every 2 years.

Gerald Lampert Memorial Award. *See* **League of Canadian Poets Awards.**

Herb Lampert Student Writing Award. *See* **Science in Society Journalism Awards.**

Archibald Lampman Award. *See* **Arc Poetry Contests and Prizes.**

Fred Landon Award. *See* **Ontario Historical Society Awards for Authors.**

Lydia Langstaff Memorial Prize

Diane Walton, Managing Editor, *On Spec* Magazine, P.O. Box 4727, Edmonton, AB T6E 5G8
Phone: (780) 413-0215 Fax: (780) 413-1538
E-mail: onspec@onspec.ca
Web site: www.onspec.ca
Deadline: January 31

A prize of $100 and a certificate are awarded to an emerging Canadian writer under the age of 30 whose work has been published in *On Spec* during the preceding calendar year. The winner is selected by the editors of the magazine.

Margaret Laurence Award for Fiction. *See* **Manitoba Writing and Publishing Awards.**

Lawrence House Short Story Competition

Lawrence House Centre for the Arts, 127 Christina Street S., Sarnia, ON N7T 2M8
Phone: (519) 337-0507 Fax: (519) 337-0482
E-mail: lhcarts@hotmail.com
Web site: www.lawrencehouse.ca
Deadline: September 30

A first prize of $250, second prize of $150, and third prize of $100 are awarded for the best short story. Stories must be unpublished, 2,500 words or less, and in English. Entry fee $20. Open to all Canadian citizens and landed immigrants. Annual.

Stephen Leacock Memorial Medal for Humour
Judith Rapson, Chair, Awards Committee, Stephen Leacock
  Association, R.R. #2, Coldwater, ON L0K 1E0
Phone: (705) 835-3218 Fax: (705) 835-5171
E-mail: drapson@encode.com or wayne@rural-roots.com
Web site: www.leacock.ca
Deadline: December 31
  A sterling-silver medal and a cash award of $10,000 is awarded
for the year's best book of humour written by a Canadian in prose,
verse, or as drama. Send 10 copies of the book, a $100 entry fee,
plus author bio and photo. Annual.

League of Canadian Poets Awards
920 Yonge Street, Suite 608, Toronto, ON M4W 3C7
Phone: (416) 504-1657 Fax: (416) 504-0096
E-mail: marketing@poets.ca
Web sites: www.poets.ca or www.youngpoets.ca

Gerald Lampert Memorial Award
Deadline: November 1
  This $1,000 annual award recognizes the best first book of poetry
published by a Canadian in the preceding year. Entry fee $15.

Pat Lowther Memorial Award
Deadline: November 1
  A $1,000 annual prize for the best book of poetry by a Canadian
woman published in the preceding year. Entry fee $15.

The Poetic Licence Contest for Canadian Youth
Deadline: see www.youngpoets.ca
  The contest's categories consist of junior and senior age groups.
Winning poets in each group are awarded a cash prize of $200 (first
place), $150 (second place), and $100 (third place). The winning
poems and those that receive an honourable mention will be featured in the April issue of the LCP e-zine, *Re:verse*. No entry fee.

**Lieutenant Governor's Literary Lifetime Achievement
  Award.** *See* **B.C. Book Prizes.**

The Dorothy Livesay Poetry Prize. *See* **B.C. Book Prizes.**

Pat Lowther Memorial Award. *See* **League of Canadian Poets Awards.**

Lush Triumphant

sub-Terrain Magazine, P.O. Box 3008, MPO, Vancouver, BC
    V6B 3X5
Phone: (604) 876-8710   Fax: (604) 879-2667
E-mail: subter@portal.ca
Web site: www.subterrain.ca
Deadline: May 15

The winning entries in 3 categories – fiction, poetry, and creative non-fiction – will receive a $500 cash prize and be published in the fall issue of *sub-Terrain*. The first runner-up in each category will be published in a future issue of the magazine. Fee is $20/entry. Entrants may submit as many entries in as many categories as they wish. All work must be previously unpublished. All entrants will receive a complimentary 1-year subscription to *sub-Terrain*. Annual.

Abbyann D. Lynch Medal in Bioethics. *See* **the Royal Society of Canada Awards.**

Sir John A. Macdonald Prize. *See* **Canadian Historical Association Awards.**

The Grant MacEwan Author's Award

Alberta Community Development, 10708 – 105 Avenue,
    Edmonton, AB T5H 0A1
Phone: (780) 427-6315
Deadline: December 31

Dr. MacEwan wrote more than 50 books on nature, folklore, agriculture, politics, the environment, literature, history, and the people of Alberta. This new award of $25,000 is presented annually to the Alberta author whose book (published the previous calendar year) best reflects Alberta and/or Dr. MacEwan's interests. Books must be original or translated works, written in either English or French.

C. B. Macpherson Prize. *See* **Canadian Political Science Association Prizes.**

The Malahat Review Prizes

John Barton, *The Malahat Review*, University of Victoria, P.O. Box 1700, Stn. CSC, Victoria, BC V8W 2Y2
Phone: (250) 721-8524
E-mail: malahat@uvic.ca
Web site: www.malahatreview.ca

Long Poem Prize
Deadline: February 1
   Two prizes of $400, plus payment for publication, are awarded biennially for the best original, unpublished long poems or cycles of poems of no more than 20 pages. Entry fee of $35 covers a subscription to *The Malahat Review*.

Novella Prize
Deadline: February 1, 2008
   A prize of $500, plus payment for publication, is awarded biennially for the best original, unpublished prose work no longer than 30,000 words. Entry fee $35 covers a subscription to *The Malahat Review*.

Manitoba Writing and Publishing Awards

Robyn Maharaj or Jamis Paulson, Manitoba Writers' Guild,
   100 Arthur Street, Suite 206, Winnipeg, MB R3B 1H3
Phone: (204) 942-6134 or 1-888-637-5802   Fax: (204) 942-5754
E-mail: info@mbwriter.mb.ca
Web site: www.mbwriter.mb.ca

The John Hirsch Award for Most Promising Manitoba Writer
Deadline: January
   A cash prize of $2,500, donated by the estate of the late John Hirsch, co-founder of the Manitoba Theatre Centre, is awarded annually to the most promising Manitoba writer. Authors of poetry, fiction, creative non-fiction, and drama are eligible.

Alexander Kennedy Isbister Award for Non-Fiction
Deadline: December

A cash prize of $3,500 is presented to the Manitoba writer whose book is judged the best book of adult non-fiction (excluding encyclopedias, textbooks, and dictionaries) written in English during the previous year. Entry fee $25. Annual.

Margaret Laurence Award for Fiction
Deadline: December

An annual cash prize of $3,500 is presented to the Manitoba writer whose book is judged the best book of adult fiction written in English and published during the previous year. Entry fee $25.

The McNally Robinson Book for Young People Awards
Deadline: December

Two annual cash prizes of $2,500, donated by McNally Robinson Booksellers, are awarded for the best young person's books written by a Manitoba author, one in the category of young adult and the other for children. Books of fiction, poetry, non-fiction, and drama are eligible. Entry fee $25.

The McNally Robinson Book of the Year Award
Deadline: December

An annual cash prize of $5,000, donated by McNally Robinson Booksellers, is awarded for an outstanding book in any genre (except YA or children's books) written by a Manitoba resident. The title must be non-academic and written in English. Books of fiction, poetry, creative non-fiction, non-fiction, and drama are eligible. Entry fee $25.

Eileen McTavish Sykes Award for Best First Book
Deadline: December

Presented annually to the author whose first professionally published book is judged the best written. The author receives a cash prize of $1,500, donated by Manitoba children's author Eileen McTavish Sykes through the Winnipeg Foundation. Each entry must be a non-academic title written in English. Books of fiction, poetry, non-fiction, children's and young adult literature, and drama will be considered. Entry fee $25/title.

The Mary Scorer Award for Best Book by a Manitoba Publisher
Deadline: December
   Presented annually for the best book published by a Manitoba publisher written for the trade, educational, academic, or scholarly market. The author receives a cash prize of $1,000, donated by Friesens Corporation. Books are judged on innovation of content, quality of editing and writing, and excellence in design and illustrations. Promotional activity and market acceptance will be considered. Entry fee $25.

The Carol Shields Winnipeg Book Award
Deadline: December
   A juried annual prize of $5,000 honouring books that evoke the special character of Winnipeg, or contribute to the appreciation or understanding of the city. All genres are eligible and entries may be written in English or French. Entry fee $25.

McAuslan First Book Award. *See* **Quebec Writers' Federation Book Awards.**

The McNally Robinson Book for Young People Awards. *See* **Manitoba Writing and Publishing Awards.**

The McNally Robinson Book of the Year Award. *See* **Manitoba Writing and Publishing Awards.**

Margaret McWilliams Competition
Manitoba Historical Society, 250 McDermot Street, Suite 304,
   Winnipeg, MB R3B 0S5
Phone: (204) 947-0559 Fax: (204) 943-1093
E-mail: info@mhs.mb.ca
Web site: www.mhs.mb.ca
Deadline: December 14
   Margaret McWilliams Medals are offered in the following categories: scholarly book, popular book, university essay/thesis, special projects and displays, local history, audio/visual, historical fiction, and organizations/associations/institutions. The purpose of the award is to encourage the study and preservation of the history of all parts of Manitoba and of the records and memories of the

pioneers who made Manitoba what it is. Awards are granted for meritorious work only and therefore are not necessarily awarded in every category each year. Annual.

Vicky Metcalf Award for Children's Literature. *See* the Writers' Trust of Canada Awards.

W. O. Mitchell Literary Prize. *See* the Writers' Trust of Canada Awards.

CAA MOSAID Technologies Inc. Award for Fiction. *See* Canadian Authors Association Awards.

National Business Book Awards
Mary Ann Freedman, Freedman & Associates, 121 Richmond
    Street W., Suite 604, Toronto, ON M5H 2K1
Phone: (416) 868-1500
E-mail: mafreedman@freedmanandassociates.com
Web site: www.pwc.com/ca/nbba
Deadline: December 15
    An annual award of $10,000 recognizes excellence in business writing for books published in Canada during the previous year. PricewaterhouseCoopers and the BMO Financial Group are co-sponsors of this award. The media sponsor is the *Globe and Mail*.

National Magazine Awards
425 Adelaide Street W., Suite 700, Toronto, ON M5V 3C1
Phone: (416) 422-1358 Fax: (416) 504-0437
E-mail: staff@magazine-awards.com
Web site: www.magazine-awards.com
Deadline: January 10
    The written categories are as follows: humour; business; science, technology and the environment; health and medicine; politics and public interest; society; investigative reporting; fiction; arts and entertainment; sports and recreation; columns; travel; service – health and family; service – personal finance and business; service – lifestyle; how-to; essays; personal journalism; profiles; poetry; editorial package; one-of-kind; words and pictures; best new writer; and best student writer. Category definitions are on the

web site. Most entries are $85 each and must be entered online at www.magazine-awards.com and followed by tearsheets couriered to the office.

In order to ensure that the contest truly acknowledges the best work in the Canadian magazine industry, the National Magazine Awards Foundation offers a co-financing plan to help smaller magazines participate. Details on the web site.

Canadian staff or freelance contributors are eligible. Magazine publishers, editors, or freelancers may submit. Gold awards, Best New Writer, and Best New Writer awards are $1,000 and a certificate; silver awards are $500 and a certificate. Editors are encouraged to make submissions on behalf of new writers. Annual.

The Hilda Neatby Prize in Women's History. *See* **Canadian Historical Association Awards.**

Nereus Writers' Trust Non-Fiction Prize. *See* **the Writers' Trust of Canada Awards.**

Newfoundland and Labrador Book Awards. *See* **Writers' Alliance of Newfoundland and Labrador Literary Awards.**

The bpNichol Chapbook Award
The Phoenix Community Works Foundation, 344 Bloor Street W., Suite 505, Toronto, ON M5S 3A7
Phone: (416) 964-3380 Fax: (416) 964-8516
E-mail: info@pcwf.ca
Web site: www.pcwf.ca
Deadline: March 30
A prize of $1,000 is offered each year for the best poetry chapbook published in English in Canada. Entry made by publisher or author. The chapbook should be between 10 and 48 pages long. Send 3 copies (not returnable) and a short C.V.

The Alden Nowlan Award for Excellence in English-Language Literary Arts
Pauline Bourque, Executive Director, New Brunswick Arts Board, 634 Queen Street, Suite 300, Fredericton, NB E3B 1C2

Phone: (506) 444-4444 Fax: (506) 444-5543
E-mail: rbryar@artsnb.ca
Web site: www.artsnb.ca
Deadline: October 1

Designed to recognize outstanding achievement and contribution to the English-language literary arts of New Brunswick, this award includes a cash prize of $5,000 and is presented by the lieutenant governor during an annual ceremony. Nominees must have been born in New Brunswick or have lived there for at least 5 years. An application can be downloaded from the web site. Annual.

Ontario Historical Society Awards for Authors
34 Parkview Avenue, Willowdale, ON M2N 3Y2
Phone: (416) 226-9011 Fax: (416) 226-2740
E-mail: ohs@ontariohistoricalsociety.ca
Web site: www.ontariohistoricalsociety.ca
Deadlines: end of October

An annual program that honours individuals who have contributed significantly to the preservation and promotion of Ontario's heritage. All award recipients receive recognition in publicity and a framed certificate accompanied by a copy of the citation acknowledging their contribution. Self-nominations are accepted. A book may be nominated in one award category only.

Joseph Brant Award

Honours the best book on multicultural history in Ontario. Must have been published within the past 3 years. Entry fee $10/title with 3 copies of each book.

Donald Grant Creighton Award

Honours the best book of biography or autobiography highlighting life in Ontario, past or present, published within the past 3 years. Entry fee $10/title with 3 copies of each book.

Fred Landon Award

Honours the best book on regional history in Ontario. Must have been published within the past 3 years. Entry fee $10/title with 3 copies of each book.

Alison Prentice Award

Honours the best book on women's history. Must have been published within the past 3 years. Entry fee $10/title with 3 copies of each book.

Riddell Award

Honours the best article on Ontario's history. Must have been published within the award year.

The Open Window Poetry Anthology Contest. *See* **Hidden Brook Press Poetry Awards.**

Ottawa Book Awards
Faith Seltzer, Office of Cultural Affairs, 110 Laurier Avenue W.
(01-49), Ottawa, ON K1P 1J1
Phone: (613) 580-2424, ext. 27412 Fax: (613) 580-2632
E-mail: faith.seltzer@ottawa.ca
Web site: www.ottawa.ca/arts
Deadline: January 9
A $5,000 award is presented each year to the author of a book of literary merit in each of 4 categories: English fiction, English non-fiction, French fiction, and French non-fiction. The author must reside in the city of Ottawa.

Pandora's Collective Poetry Contests
P.O. Box 29118, Delamont P.O., 1950 West Broadway, Vancouver, BC V6J 5C2
Phone: (604) 321-4039
E-mail: blnish_pandoras@yahoo.ca
Web site: www.pandorascollective.com
Pandora's Collective offers 4 contests each year: 3 are traditional "blind submission" contests, and the other is part of the annual Summer Dream Reading Festival.

Hibernating with Words
Deadline: January 15
Accepts poems on any theme and up to 40 lines. No previously published poems. Blind submission. Awards for adults: first prize $100 and publication, second prize $50 and publication, third prize

is publication. Awards for teens (ages 14–19): first prize $70 and publication, second prize $35 and publication, third prize is publication. Awards for children (13 and under): first prize $40 and publication, second prize $20 and publication, third prize is publication. Entry fees $5/poem for adults; $4/poem for teens; $3/poem for children. Annual.

Kisses and Popsicles Spring Poetry Contest
Deadline: May 15

Accepts poems on any theme and up to 40 lines. No previously published poems. Blind submission. Awards for adults: first prize $100 and publication, second prize $50 and publication, third prize is publication. Awards for teens (ages 14–19): first prize $70 and publication, second prize $35 and publication, third prize is publication. Awards for children (13 and under): first .prize $40 and publication, second prize $20 and publication, third prize is publication. Entry fees $5/poem for adults; $4/poem for teens; $3/poem for children. Annual.

The Summer Dream Poetry Contest
Deadline: September 15

Accepts poems on any theme and up to 40 lines. No previously published poems. Blind submission. Awards for adults: first prize $100 and publication, second prize $50 and publication, third prize is publication. Awards for teens (ages 14–19): first prize $70 and publication, second prize $35 and publication, third prize is publication. Awards for children (13 and under): first prize $40 and publication, second prize $20 and publication, third prize is publication. Entry fees $5/poem for adults; $4/poem for teens; $3/poem for children. Annual.

Words on Robson Poetry Contest
Deadline: January 15

Part of the annual Summer Dream Reading Festival. Accepts poems on any theme or form; may be previously written or composed at the festival. No previously published poems. Half of the contest money generated is awarded to the top 5 winners, and the winning poems will be published on the Pandora's Collective web site. Entry fee $5/poem. Annual.

Paragraphe Hugh MacLennan Prize for Fiction. *See* **Quebec Writers' Federation Book Awards.**

Lorne Pierce Medal. *See* **the Royal Society of Canada Awards.**

The Poetic Licence Contest for Canadian Youth. *See* **League of Canadian Poets Awards.**

Poets' Corner Award

BS Poetry Society, P.O. Box 596, Stn. A, Fredericton, NB E3B 5A6

Phone: (506) 454-5127

Web site: www.brokenjaw.com/poetscorner.htm

Deadline: September 1

This award is given by the BS Poetry Society to the author of the best poetry manuscript. Winner receives $500, and the winning manuscript will be published by Broken Jaw Press. Individual poems may have been previously published in periodicals, anthologies, and chapbooks. Entry fee $20. Annual.

Prairie Fire Writing Contests

100 Arthur Street, Suite 423, Winnipeg, MB R3B 1H3

Phone: (204) 943-9066

E-mail: prfire@mts.net

Web site: www.prairiefire.ca

Deadline: November 30

Offers 3 writing contests, each with a first prize of $1,250, second prize of $500, and third prize of $250, plus publication in *Prairie Fire*. Each submission must be unpublished. Entry fee $27/category, which includes a 1-year subscription to *Prairie Fire*. Annual.

Bliss Carman Poetry Award

First prize is in part donated by the Banff Centre for the Arts, which will also award a jeweller-cast replica of Carman's silver-and-turquoise ring to the first-prize winner. Submit 1–3 poems, with a maximum of 150 lines/poem.

Short Fiction Contest

Submit a maximum of 15,000 words; 1 story/submission.

Creative Non-Fiction Contest
Submit a maximum of 5,000 words; 1 story/submission.

The E. J. Pratt Medal and Prize in Poetry

Rosemary Cameron, Awards Manager, Admissions and Awards,
  University of Toronto, 315 Bloor Street W., Toronto, ON
  M5S 1A3
Phone: (416) 978-2190
E-mail: ask@adm.utoronto.ca
Web site: www.adm.utoronto.ca/awd/schp_index.htm
Deadline: April 2

The E. J. Pratt Medal plus a $100 prize are awarded as a stimulus to poetic composition in the belief that good poetry is the best assurance of a vital language and a healthy culture. The competition is open to any student proceeding toward a first or a post-graduate degree at the University of Toronto. Entries should be approximately 100 lines long. No previously published compositions will be considered, except for work in campus student publications. The award will be offered annually; however, if the selection committee determines that no submission is of sufficient excellence, the award will not be given.

Alison Prentice Award. *See* Ontario Historical Society Awards for Authors.

PRISM international Writing Prizes

Creative Writing Program, University of British Columbia, Buch
  E462, 1866 Main Mall, Vancouver, BC V6T 1Z1
Phone: (604) 822-2514 Fax: (604) 822-3616
E-mail: prism@interchange.ubc.ca
Web site: www.prism.arts.ubc.ca

Earle Birney Prize for Poetry
Deadline: not applicable

One award of $500 will be won by a poet whose work has appeared in *PRISM international* during the previous year. Poets need not apply; their work is automatically considered upon publication. Annual.

PRISM international Literary Non-Fiction Contest
Deadline: September 30

A $1,500 first prize is awarded annually to the author of an out-standing piece of literary non-fiction (up to 25 double-spaced pages). The winning entry will be published in *PRISM international*, will earn an additional payment of $20/page for publication, and receive a 1-year subscription. Works of translation are eligible. Entry fee $25 for 1 story, plus $7 for each additional piece. Anyone who has taken a UBC creative writing course within the previous 2 years is ineligible.

PRISM international Annual Short Fiction Contest
Deadline: January 31

A $2,000 prize is awarded for the best original, unpublished short story (up to 25 double-spaced pages). Five runner-up prizes of $200 are also conferred. All winners receive publication payment for inclusion in *PRISM international*'s Fiction Contest issue. Works of translation are eligible. Entry fee $25 for one story, plus $7 for each additional story.

Quebec Writers' Federation Book Awards
Lori Schubert, Executive Director, Quebec Writers' Federation,
      1200 Atwater Avenue, Montreal, QC H3Z 1X4
Phone: (514) 933-0878 Fax: (514) 933-0878
E-mail: admin@qwf.org
Web site: www.qwf.org
Deadlines: May 31 and August 15 (for books published between
      October 1 and September 30)
All entry fees $20. Write for criteria and entry forms. Books may be submitted by publishers or authors.

Mavis Gallant Prize for Non-Fiction
An annual cash prize of $2,000 is awarded for the best book of literary non-fiction written in English by a writer who has lived in Quebec for at least 3 of the past 5 years.

A. M. Klein Prize for Poetry
An annual cash prize of $2,000 is awarded for the best work of poetry written in English by a writer who has lived in Quebec for at least 3 of the past 5 years.

McAuslan First Book Award

An annual cash prize of $2,000 is awarded for the best first book written in English by a writer who has lived in Quebec for at least 3 of the past 5 years.

Paragraphe Hugh MacLennan Prize for Fiction

An annual cash prize of $2,000 is awarded for the best work of fiction written in English by a writer who has lived in Quebec for at least 3 of the past 5 years.

Translation Prize

An annual cash prize of $2,000 is awarded for the best translation. The prize alternates on an annual basis between a book translated from English to French and a book translated from French to English, with a 2-year eligibility span for each. The two subcategories have very different eligibility criteria.

Thomas Head Raddall Atlantic Fiction Award. *See* **Writers' Federation of Nova Scotia Awards.**

Red Cedar Book Awards
E-mail: info@redcedaraward.ca
Web site: www.redcedaraward.ca
Deadline: October 15

Awarded to the author and/or illustrator of the best book of fiction and non-fiction for children. No monetary value, but the prize-winners receive engraved red cedar plaques. These are children's choice awards, voted on by children throughout B.C. during the program year. The authors/illustrators must be Canadian citizens or landed immigrants who have lived in Canada for at least 2 years. The books must have been published by a recognized publisher and be recognized as being of general interest to students in grades 4 to 7. Annual.

Regina Book Award. *See* **Saskatchewan Book Awards.**

The Richards Prize. *See* **Writers' Federation of New Brunswick Literary Competition.**

Evelyn Richardson Non-Fiction Award. *See* **Writers' Federation of Nova Scotia Awards.**

Riddell Award. *See* **Ontario Historical Society Awards for Authors.**

Rocky Mountain Book Award
Michelle Dimnik or Ruth McMahon, Co-Chairs, P.O. Box 42, Lethbridge, AB T1J 3Y4
Phone: (403) 381-7164 (Michelle Dimnik) or (403) 327-4953 (Ruth McMahon) Fax: (403) 320-9124
E-mail: rockymountainbookaward@shaw.ca
Web site: http://rmba.lethsd.ab.ca
Deadline: January 15
   Alberta students and educators participate in this readers' choice program, which is designed to stimulate the reading interests of students in grades 4–7 by introducing them to exemplary Canadian literature. The winner is chosen from 10 fiction books, including 1 picture book and 10 non-fiction books. Books must be copyrighted in the previous 3 years. The value of the award is a gold medal and an expense-paid trip to Alberta to visit 4 or 5 schools and possibly take part in some other activities such as conferences and writing workshops. Annual.

Rogers Writers' Trust Fiction Prize. *See* **the Writers' Trust of Canada Awards.**

The Royal Society of Canada Awards
170 Waller Street, Ottawa ON K1N 9B9
Phone: (613) 991-6990 Fax: (613) 991-6996
E-mail: theacademies@rsc.ca
Web site: www.rsc.ca

Bancroft Award
Deadline: December 1, 2007
   A presentation scroll and a prize of $2,500 is offered every 2 years if there is a suitable candidate. The award is given for publication, instruction, and research in the earth sciences that have conspicuously contributed to public understanding and appreciation of

the subject. Nominations must be put forward by 3 persons, 1 of whom must be a fellow of the Royal Society of Canada.

Jason A. Hannah Medal
Deadline: March 1

A bronze medal and a prize of $1,500 is offered annually, if there is a suitable candidate, for an important Canadian publication in the history of medicine. The work must have been published in the 2 years preceding its nomination. It must be Canadian either through the citizenship or residence of the author, or through content that is clearly relevant to Canadian medicine and healthcare.

Innis-Gérin Medal
Deadline: December 1, 2008

A bronze medal is awarded every 2 years, if there is a suitable candidate, for a distinguished and sustained contribution to the literature of the social sciences, including human geography and social psychology. Nominations must be put forward by 3 persons, 1 of whom must be a fellow of the Royal Society of Canada.

Abbyann D. Lynch Medal in Bioethics
Deadline: December 1

A bronze medal and a cash award of $2,000 is offered every year, if there is a suitable nomination, for a major contribution in bio-ethics by a Canadian. The contribution may be a book, a report, a scholarly article, a monograph, or a series of articles that have been published in the 2 years preceding the nomination. Nominations must be put forward by 3 organizations and/or persons, 1 of whom must be a fellow of the Royal Society of Canada.

Lorne Pierce Medal
Deadline: December 1, 2007

A gold plated silver medal is awarded every 2 years, if there is a suitable candidate, for an achievement of special significance and conspicuous merit in imaginative or critical literature written in either English or French. Critical literature dealing with Canadian subjects has priority. Nominations must be put forward by 3 persons, 1 of whom must be a fellow of the Royal Society of Canada.

Sanofi Pasteur Medal for Excellence in Health Research Journalism

Julieta Bach, Canadians for Health Research, P.O. Box 126,
Westmount, QC H3Z 2T1

Phone: (514) 398-7478 Fax: (514) 398-8361

E-mail: info@chrcrm.org

Web site: www.chrcrm.org

Deadline: March 12

This annual national award recognizes the role of journalists in raising public awareness of the importance of health research in Canada. The award consists of a medal and a $2,500 bursary. The winning article must have been published in a Canadian newspaper or magazine during the previous calendar year.

Saskatchewan Book Awards

Glenda James, Saskatchewan Book Awards, 2314 – 11th Avenue, Suite 205B, Regina, SK S4P 0K1

Phone: (306) 569-1585 Fax: (306) 569-4187

E-mail: director@bookawards.sk.ca

Deadlines: July 31 (for books published between September 15 and July 31) and September 15 (for books published between August 1 and September 15)

Children's Literature Award

An award of $2,000 will be given to a Saskatchewan author for the best published book of children's or young adult literature. Entry fee $20/title. Annual.

Fiction Award

An award of $2,000 will be given to a Saskatchewan author for the best published work of fiction (novel or short fiction). Entry fee $20/title. Annual.

First Book Award Honouring Brenda MacDonald Riches

An award of $2,000 will be given to a Saskatchewan author for the best published first book in the following categories: children's, drama (published plays), fiction (short fiction, novellas, novels), non-fiction (not including cookbooks, how-to books, directories, or bibliographies of minimal critical content), and poetry. Entry fee $20/title. Annual.

Non-Fiction Award

An award of $2,000 will be given to a Saskatchewan author for the best published work of non-fiction. Entry fee $20/title. Annual.

Poetry Award Honouring Anne Szumigalski

An award of $2,000 will be given to a Saskatchewan author for the best published book of poetry. Entry fee $20/title. Annual.

Regina Book Award

In recognition of the vitality of the literary community of Regina, this $2,000 award is presented to a Regina writer for the best book in the following categories: children's, drama (published plays), fiction (short fiction, novellas, novels), non-fiction (not including cookbooks, how-to books, directories, or bibliographies of minimal critical content), and poetry. Entry fee $20/title. Annual.

Saskatchewan Book of the Year Award

An award of $3,000 will be given to a Saskatchewan author for the best published book in the following categories: children's, drama (published plays), fiction (short fiction, novellas, novels), non-fiction (not including cookbooks, how-to books, directories, or bibliographies of minimal critical content), and poetry. Entry fee $20/title. Annual.

Saskatoon Book Award

In recognition of the vitality of the literary community of Saskatoon, this $2,000 award is presented to a Saskatoon writer for the best book in the following categories: children's, drama (published plays), fiction (short fiction, novellas, novels), non-fiction (not including cookbooks, how-to books, directories, or bibliographies of minimal critical content), and poetry. Entry fee $20/title. Annual.

Scholarly Writing Award

An award of $2,000 will be given to a Saskatchewan author for the published work that is judged to contribute most to scholarship. His or her work must recognize or draw on specific theoretical work within a community of scholars, and participate in the creation and transmission of knowledge. The work must show potential readability by a wider audience and be accessible to those outside an academic milieu. Works in the following categories will be considered: refereed publications, reference works, and/or those published by an academic press. Entry fee $20/title. Annual.

Saskatoon Book Award. *See* **Saskatchewan Book Awards.**

Margaret and John Savage First Book Award. *See* **Dartmouth Book Awards.**

The Ruth and Sylvia Schwartz Children's Book Award
Ontario Arts Council, 151 Bloor Street W., 5th Floor, Toronto, ON
  M5S 1T6
Phone: (416) 969-7438 or 1-800-387-0058, ext. 7438 Fax: (416)
  961-7796
E-mail: lhilyer@arts.on.ca
Web site: www.arts.on.ca
   A panel of children's booksellers from across Canada selects 2 shortlists of 5 young adult and 5 picture books in February; 2 juries of children then select a winner in each category. There is no application process; all Canadian authored/illustrated children's trade books published in the previous year are eligible. The annual awards are $5,000 for the picture book category, shared between author and illustrator; $5,000 for the YA category.

Science in Society Journalism Awards
c/o Canadian Science Writers' Association, P.O. Box 75, Stn. A,
  Toronto, ON M5W 1A2
Phone: 1-800-796-8595
E-mail: awards@sciencewriters.ca
Web site: www.sciencewriters.ca

Yves Fortier Earth Science Journalism Award
Deadline: January 14
   An annual cash prize of $1,000 and a certificate is awarded for the writer of an outstanding article on earth science topics, varying from earth to ocean to atmosphere.

Herb Lampert Student Writing Award
Deadline: March 15

An annual cash prize of $1,000 is awarded to the student science writer of the best original material in either print or TV and radio categories. Any student writer who has a science article published in a student or other newspaper or magazine or aired on a radio or TV station in Canada is eligible.

SIS Book Awards
Deadline: December 15

Three $1,000 cash prizes are awarded annually to the authors of books that made outstanding contributions to science writing for the general public, for youth, and for children. Entries may address aspects of basic or applied science or technology, historical or current, in any area including health, science, environmental issues, regulatory trends, etc. Books are judged on literary excellence and scientific content. The writer must be a Canadian citizen or resident.

The Mary Scorer Award for Best Book by a Manitoba Publisher. *See* **Manitoba Writing and Publishing Awards.**

The Scotiabank Giller Prize
Elana Rabinovitch, 576 Davenport Road, Toronto, ON M5R 1K9
Phone: (416) 934-0755 Fax: (416) 934-0971
E-mail: elanar@sympatico.ca
Web site: www.scotiabankgillerprize.ca
Deadline: staggered throughout May, June, and August, with final deadline usually mid-August

Each year the Scotiabank Giller Prize awards $40,000 to the author of the best Canadian full-length novel or collection of short stories published in English, either originally or in translation, as judged by a jury panel of 3. Each finalist is awarded $2,500. The author must be a Canadian citizen or permanent resident, and the book must have been published by a Canadian publisher.

Seeds International Poetry Chapbook Anthology Contest. *See* **Hidden Brook Press Poetry Awards.**

The Carol Shields Winnipeg Book Award. *See* **Manitoba Writing and Publishing Awards.**

Dorothy Shoemaker Literary Awards Contest
Michele McBride-Roach, Events Planner, Kitchener Public
Library, 85 Queen Street N., Kitchener, ON N2N 2H1
Phone: (519) 743-0271, ext. 254 Fax: (519) 579-2382
E-mail: literarycontest@kpl.org
Web site: www.kpl.org
Deadline: contest runs between June 1 and July 31
Named in honour of Dorothy Shoemaker, former chief librarian and ardent supporter of writers, and funded by her generous endowment. First-, second-, and third-prize winners in both prose and poetry categories receive cash awards of $150, $100, and $75. Winning entries are published in the anthology *The Changing Image.* Open to residents of Ontario in 3 age categories: junior (under 12 years), intermediate (12 to 17 years), and senior (18 years and older). Submissions accepted by e-mail only for unpublished work. Commercially published writers are not eligible. No entry fee, but a limited number of submissions permitted. See web site for complete guidelines.

Short Grain Writing Contest
Grain Magazine, P.O. Box 67, Saskatoon, SK S7K 3K1
Phone: (306) 244-2828 Fax: (306) 244-0255
E-mail: grainmag@sasktel.net
Web site: www.grainmagazine.ca
Deadline: February 28
Offered annually for unpublished dramatic monologues, postcard stories (narrative fiction), and prose (lyric) poetry – all no more than 500 words long – and non-fiction creative prose – no longer than 5,000 words. Three prizes of $500 are offered in each category, plus publication in *Grain.* Open to any writer. No fax or e-mail submissions. Entry fee $30 for 2 entries in any 1 or 2 categories; $8 for up to 3 more entries in any categories. Entry fee includes a 1-year subscription.

Donald Smiley Prize. *See* **Canadian Political Science Association Prizes.**

Edna Staebler Award for Creative Non-Fiction

Kathryn Wardropper, Administrator, Wilfrid Laurier University,
75 University Avenue W., Waterloo, ON N2L 3C5
Phone: (519) 884-0710, ext. 3999   Fax: (519) 884-8202
E-mail: kwardrop@wlu.ca
Web site: www.library.wlu.ca/internet/prizes/staebler.html
Deadline: April 30

A $3,000 prize is awarded annually for an outstanding work of creative non-fiction, which must have been written by a Canadian and have a Canadian location and significance. To be eligible, an entry must be the writer's first or second published book. Established to give recognition and encouragement to new writers. Administered by Wilfrid Laurier University.

Stellar Book Awards

E-mail: info@stellaraward.ca
Web site: www.stellaraward.ca
Deadline: October 15

B.C.'s Teen Readers' Choice Award, voted on by teens, is administered by a steering committee of teens and adults as part of the Young Readers' Choice Awards Society of B.C. Books must be recognized as being of interest to teens, been written by Canadian citizens or landed immigrants who have lived in Canada for at least 2 years, and been published by a recognized publisher in the 2 years prior to the deadline. Prize-winners receive an etched glass plaque. Annual.

The Annual Dan Sullivan Memorial Poetry Contest. *See* Writers' Circle of Durham Region Contests.

The Summer Dream Poetry Contest. *See* Pandora's Collective Poetry Contests.

The Sunburst Award for Canadian Literature of the Fantastic

Rebecca Simkin, Secretary, 2 Farm Greenway, Toronto, ON
M3A 3M2
Phone: (416) 869-4881

Web site: www.sunburstaward.org
Deadline: January 31
   Presented to a Canadian writer who has published a speculative
fiction novel or book-length collection of speculative fiction any
time during the previous calendar year. Named after the first novel
by Phyllis Gotlieb, one of the first published authors of contemporary Canadian science fiction. The award consists of $1,000 and a
medallion with the Sunburst logo. The work may include science
fiction, fantasy, horror, magic realism, or surrealism. Annual.

Sunday Star Short Story Contest
1 Yonge Street, Toronto, ON M5E 1E6
Phone: (416) 869-4881
Web site: www.thestar.com
Deadline: December 31
   A first prize of $5,000 (plus tuition for a 30-week course from
the Humber School for Writers Creative Writing Correspondence
Program), a second of $2,000, and a third of $1,000 are awarded
for the best original, unpublished short stories up to 2,500 words.
They will be published in *The Star*. Rules available on StarPhone at
(416) 865-3641 and on the web site.

Eileen McTavish Sykes Award for Best First Book. *See*
Manitoba Writing and Publishing Awards.

The Charles Taylor Prize for Literary Non-Fiction
June Dickenson, 18 Blackberry Place, Carlisle, ON L0R 1H2
Phone: (905) 689-0388 Fax: (905) 689-2944
E-mail: junedickenson@cogeco.ca
Web site: www.thecharlestaylorprize.ca
   Commemorates Charles Taylor's pursuit of excellence in the field
of literary non-fiction. Awarded to the author whose book best combines a superb command of the English language, elegance of style,
and a subtlety of thought and perception. The winner receives
$25,000, and the finalists each receive $2,000 as well as promotional
support so that all shortlisted books stand out in the national media,
bookstores, and libraries. Entries must be submitted by the publisher of the work. Only Canadian authors are considered. Annual.

TD Canadian Children's Literature Award. *See* **Canadian Children's Book Centre Awards.**

Terasen Lifetime Achievement Award for an Outstanding Literary Career in British Columbia
c/o B.C. BookWorld, 3516 West 13th Avenue (rear), Vancouver, BC V6R 2S3
Phone: (604) 736-4011
A $5,000 prize is awarded annually for the exemplary literary career of a British Columbia resident. Administered by *B.C. BookWorld*.

THIS Magazine Writing Awards
401 Richmond Street W., Suite 396, Toronto, ON M5V 3A8
Phone: (416) 979-8400   Fax: (416) 979-1143
E-mail: info@thismagazine.ca
Web site: www.thismagazine.ca

The Great Canadian Literary Hunt
Deadline: July 1
"On the trail of Canada's brightest new creative writers." Annual prizes are awarded in two categories: poems up to 100 lines and short stories up to 5,000 words. First prize wins $750 and publication in *THIS Magazine*'s annual literacy issue; second and third place wins a prize pack plus publication in *THIS Magazine*'s annual literacy issue. All entries must be unpublished. Entry fees are $20 for one piece of fiction and $20 for two poems; subsequent submissions are $5 each. Entry fee includes a 1-year subscription to *THIS*. For regular updates on the Great Canadian Literary Hunt, send an e-mail to contests@thismagazine.ca or visit the web site.

Tracking a Serial Poet Contest
lichen literary Journal, 701 Rossland Road E., Suite 234, Whitby, ON L1N 9K3
E-mail: info@lichenjournal.ca
Web site: www.lichenjournal.ca
Deadline: December 31
An annual award with a prize of $500 and publication in the

lichen literary Journal. Submit 3 poems for a maximum of 75 lines total. Poems should be subtly linked or share a common thread, be unpublished, and be written in English. Entry fee $20, which includes a 1-year subscription; each additional entry $5. Open to Canadian and international entries.

Larry Turner Award. *See* **the Valley Writers' Guild Awards.**

Valley Writers' Guild Awards
Peter de Lepper, Co-ordinator, P.O. Box 534, Merrickville, ON
    K0G 1N0
Phone: (613) 269-4700
E-mail: joyhm@ripnet.com

Ray Burroll Poetry Award
Deadline: November 30
    An annual award for poetry in any style that is up to 60 lines and unpublished. Entry fee $5/poem. Winners receive a percentage of the entry fees.

The Joker Is Wild Awards for Humour
    Awarded for the best unpublished, humorous prose, fiction, or non-fiction up to 1,000 words. Three prizes are given annually in either prose or verse (alternates each year). The writer must live within commuting distance of Ottawa.

Larry Turner Award
Deadline: March 15
    An annual award for literary or personal essays, articles, memoirs, travel pieces, etc., that are up to 2,500 words and unpublished. Grand prize–winner receives a percentage of the entry fees, and the top 3 winners will be published in *The Grist Mill*.

The Bronwen Wallace Memorial Award. *See* **the Writers' Trust of Canada Awards.**

Willow Awards
Claire Isaac, President, Saskatchewan Young Readers' Choice Awards, 2270 Argyle Street, Regina, SK S4T 3T1

Phone: (306) 565-3106
E-mail: willowawards@sasktel.net
Web site: www.willowawards.ca
Deadline: October 31

A glass sculpture created by Saskatchewan artist Jacqueline Berting is awarded to the winners of the 3 Willow Awards, determined by the voting of students in the province. Books must be written by Canadian citizens or permanent residents, be fiction or non-fiction, be published in Canada, and have been copyrighted in the previous 2 years.

The Shining Willow Award
For books written for children in kindergarten to grade 3.

The Diamond Willow Award
For books written for children in grades 4–6.

The Snow Willow Award
For books written for children in grades 7–9.

Portia White Prize
Lois Ward, Program Officer, Nova Scotia Department of Tourism, Culture and Heritage, 1800 Argyle Street, Suite 601, P.O. Box 456, Halifax, NS B3J 2R5
Phone: (902) 424-6392 Fax: (902) 424-0710
E-mail: wardlm@gov.ns.ca
Web site: www.gov.ns.ca/dtc

Awarded annually by the Province of Nova Scotia to recognize artistic excellence and achievement by a Nova Scotia artist. The prize consists of an award of $18,000 to the recipient and $7,000 to the recipient's protegé, which may be an individual artist or a Nova Scotia arts organization.

Jon Whyte Memorial Essay Prize. *See* **Writers Guild of Alberta Awards.**

The Ethel Wilson Fiction Prize. *See* **B.C. Book Prizes.**

The Kenneth R. Wilson Awards

Alison Wood, KRW Co-ordinator, 4195 Dundas Street W.,
Suite 346, Toronto, ON M8X 1Y4
Phone: (416) 239-1022 Fax: (416) 239-1076
E-mail: krwawards@cbp.ca
Web site: www.cbp.ca
Deadline: February

Recognizing excellence in writing and graphic design in specialty business, professional, and farm publications and their web sites. Open to editorial or design staff, freelancers, and other contributors to such publications. Twenty categories cover editorial, marketing, retail, technology, industrial, profiles, features, news, graphic design, photography, illustration, web design, and more. Winners of gold and silver awards receive cash prizes of $1,000 and $500 respectively. Annual.

Winterset Award

Ken Murphy, Program Manager, Newfoundland and Labrador
Arts Council, P.O. Box 98, Stn. C, St. John's, NL A1C 5H5
Phone: (709) 726-2212 or 1-866-726-2212 Fax: (709) 726-0619
E-mail: nlacmail.nf.ca
Web site: www.nlac.nf.ca
Deadline: December 31

The Winterset Award will be awarded to an outstanding literary work in any writing genre (fiction, non-fiction, poetry, published drama), regardless of the subject matter. The overriding consideration will be excellence in writing by Newfoundlanders and Labradorians as determined by the jury. Sponsored by the Sandra Fraser Gwyn Foundation, and administered by the Newfoundland and Labrador Arts Council. One prize of $5,000 and 2 prizes of $1,000 will be awarded. Annual.

Published literary works, written either by a native-born Newfoundlander and Labradorian or by a resident of the province (residency is defined as having lived in Newfoundland and Labrador for 12 months at the time of submission of the work) are eligible for consideration. Works must have been published in the calendar year for which the award is being considered. Both emerging or established writers may be considered. Submissions must be made by the publisher.

Words on Robson Poetry Contest. *See* **Pandora's Collective Poetry Contests.**

Writers' Alliance of Newfoundland and Labrador Literary Awards

Libby Creelman, Executive Director, P.O. Box 2681, St. John's, NL A1C 6K1
Phone: (709) 739-5215
E-mail: wanl@nf.aibn.com
Web site: www.writersalliance.nf.ca

Newfoundland and Labrador Book Awards

Deadline: January 13

Award categories alternate from poetry and non-fiction in one year (2007) to fiction and children's literature in the following year (2008). The prize is $1,500 for the winner in each category, and 2 runners-up in each category receive $500. Contests are open to residents of Newfoundland and Labrador only. Books must have been published in the previous 2 years.

Fresh Fish Award for Emerging Writers

Deadline: June

Sponsored by Newfoundland-born author Brian O'Dea and intended to serve as an incentive for emerging writers in Newfoundland and Labrador by providing them with financial support, recognition, and professional editing services for a book-length manuscript in any genre. The winning author will receive $4,000, the editing services of an editor valued at up to $1,000, and a miniature sculpture in the style of *Man Nailed to a Fish* by sculptor Jim Maunder, plus his or her name will be inscribed on a brass plaque. Writers must be a member of the Writers' Alliance of Newfoundland and Labrador and be a resident of the province. Writers with a published book in any genre are not eligible.

Writers' Circle of Durham Region Contests

P.O. Box 323, Ajax, ON L1S 3C5
Phone: (905) 259-6520
E-mail: info@wcdr.org
Web site: www.wcdr.org

Short Fiction Contest
Submission: shortstory@wcdr.org
Deadline: June 1 by e-mail; ground mail postmarked June 1

Entries must be original, unpublished, not submitted or accepted elsewhere for publication or broadcast, and not entered simultaneously in any other competition, including different versions of the same story. Stories may be of any subject matter, type, or style, and must not exceed 1,200 words. The prizes are proportionately funded by contest entry fees and by the Writers' Circle of Durham Region. No limit to the number of entries, but each must be submitted separately with appropriate entry fee. Entries will be judged on their originality and the sense of craft in the work. Winners will be published in *The Word Weaver*, the bimonthly magazine of the Writers' Circle of Durham Region and on its web site. Winners may be invited to read their story at future WCDR events. Annual.

The Annual Dan Sullivan Memorial Poetry Contest
Deadline: February 15

Open to writers from all countries (English poems only). Length of each entry must not exceed 30 lines total, which may be 1 poem or up to 3 short poems. Prizes awarded in 3 categories – children (under 12), youth (under 18), and adults – for the best poetry on any subject matter and of any type or style. Check web site for listing of cash prizes. Entry fee $15/submission for adults and free for children and youth.

WCDR Online 24-Hour Non-Fiction Contest
Submission: www.wcdr.org/nonfictioncontest.html
Deadline: see web site for dates

Style can be humorous, touching, dramatic, stream-of-consciousness, etc. Pre-registration is mandatory and limited to the first 400 registrants. Writers have 24 hours from the announcement of the topic and word count to submit their entry electronically. Cash prizes awarded for the best personal essays on the topic provided; check web site for amounts. Winners will be published online at the WCDR web site and in *The Word Weaver*, the WCDR's newsletter.

Writers' Federation of New Brunswick Literary Competition

Mary Hutchman, Writers' Federation of New Brunswick, 404
　Queen Street, P.O. Box 37, Stn. A, Fredericton, NB E3B 4Y2
Phone: (506) 459-7228　Fax: (506) 459-7228
E-mail: wfnb@nb.aibn.com
Deadline: November 11

Cash prizes (first $150, second $75, third $50) are awarded annually in the following categories: poetry, fiction, non-fiction, and writing for children. Manuscripts may be on any subject and should not exceed 15 pages (4,000 words) for prose, 100 lines maximum for poetry, and a maximum of 20,000 words for the children's category. All awards open to Canadian residents.

The Alfred G. Bailey Prize

An annual cash prize of $400 is awarded for an outstanding unpublished poetry manuscript of at least 48 pages. Some individual poems may have been previously published or accepted for publication.

The Sheree Fitch Prize

A first prize of $150, second of $75, and third of $50 are offered to young writers, aged 14 to 18 as of January 1 in the year of the contest, which alternates yearly between poetry and prose – 2007 is for poetry entries; 2008 for prose. Maximum length for poetry is 100 lines; for prose, up to 4,000 words. Work must be original and unpublished.

The Richards Prize

An annual award of $400 goes to the author of a collection of short stories, a short novel, or a substantial portion (up to 30,000 words) of a longer novel. Work must be unpublished, although some individual stories may have been published.

Writers' Federation of Nova Scotia Awards

Jane Buss, 1113 Marginal Road, Halifax, NS B3H 4P7
Phone: (902) 423-8116　Fax: (902) 422-0881
E-mail: talk@writers.ns.ca
Web site: www.writers.ns.ca

Atlantic Poetry Prize
Deadline: first Friday in December
A $2,000 prize is awarded annually for an outstanding full-length book of poetry by a native or resident of Atlantic Canada. No entry fee.

Atlantic Writing Competition for Unpublished Manuscripts
Deadline: first Friday in December
There are 6 categories for unpublished manuscripts – novel, short story, poetry, writing for children, writing for juvenile/YA audiences, and essay/magazine article. Winners receive small cash prizes of between $50 and $200 for first, second, and third places. All entries receive a brief evaluation. Open to Atlantic Canada residents only. Annual.

Thomas Head Raddall Atlantic Fiction Award
Deadline: first Friday in December
A $10,000 prize is awarded each year for an outstanding novel or collection of short stories, in English, by a native or resident of Atlantic Canada. No entry fee.

Evelyn Richardson Non-Fiction Award
Deadline: first Friday in December
A $2,000 prize is awarded annually for an outstanding work of non-fiction by a native or resident of Nova Scotia. No entry fee.

Writers Guild of Alberta Awards
Percy Page Centre, 11759 Groat Road N.W., Edmonton, AB
T5M 3K6
Phone: (780) 422-8174 Fax: (780) 422-2663
E-mail: mail@writersguild.ab.ca
Web site: www.writersguild.ab.ca
Deadline: December 29
A $1,000 prize is awarded annually for excellent achievement by an Alberta writer in each of the following categories: children's literature, drama, non-fiction, novel, poetry, and short fiction. Eligible books may have been published anywhere in the world. Authors must have resided in Alberta for at least 12 of the 18 months prior to December 31.

The City of Edmonton Book Prize
Deadline: December 29

A $2,000 award to honour the books that contribute to the appreciation and understanding of the City of Edmonton by emphasizing its special character and/or the achievements of its residents. Subjects may include history, geography, current affairs, Edmonton's arts, or its people, or be written by an Edmonton author. Entries may be fiction, non-fiction, poetry, or drama written for adults or children in published form. Entry fee $25.

The City of Calgary W. O. Mitchell Book Prize
Deadline: December 29

Awarded in honour of acclaimed Calgary writer W. O. Mitchell and recognizes achievement by Calgary authors. The $2,000 prize is awarded annually for an outstanding book (fiction, poetry, non-fiction, children's literature, or drama) published in the previous year. The author must be a Calgary resident on December 31 of the event year and for a minimum of 2 years prior. Entry fee $25.

Jon Whyte Memorial Essay Prize
Deadline: December 29

Awarded in recognition of the best essay (no longer than 2,800 words and not previously published) submitted to this province-wide competition. First prize is $1,000, and 2 runners-up receive $500 each. Open to residents aged 18 years and older who have resided in Alberta for 12 of the past 18 months. Both beginning and established writers may apply. Entry fee $10.

The Writers' Trust of Canada Awards
90 Richmond Street E., Suite 200, Toronto, ON M5C 1P1
Phone: (416) 504-8222 Fax: (416) 504-9090
E-mail: info@writerstrust.com
Web site: www.writerstrust.com

Matt Cohen Award: In Celebration of a Writing Life

An award of $20,000 is conferred on a Canadian writer whose life has been dedicated to writing as a primary pursuit to honour his or her body of distinguished work of poetry or prose in English or in French.

Shaughnessy Cohen Prize for Political Writing

A $15,000 prize is awarded annually to a Canadian author of a work of non-fiction, written in English, that enlarges our understanding of contemporary Canadian political and social issues and in the opinion of the judges shows the highest literary merit. Up to 4 runner-up prizes of $2,000 each will also be awarded.

Marian Engel Award

An annual award of $15,000 is conferred on a Canadian female writer in mid-career, recognizing her body of work and the promise of her future contribution to Canadian literature. Canada's premier literary award for women.

Timothy Findley Award

An annual award of $15,000 is conferred on a Canadian male writer in mid-career, recognizing his body of work and the promise of his future contribution to Canadian literature.

Vicky Metcalf Award for Children's Literature

An annual award of $15,000 is conferred on a Canadian writer of children's literature in recognition of his or her body of work that in the opinion of the judges shows the highest literary standards.

W. O. Mitchell Literary Prize

A $15,000 prize is awarded annually to a Canadian writer who has produced an outstanding body of work, has acted during his/her career as a "caring mentor" for writers, and has published a work of fiction or had a new stage play produced during the 3-year period specified for each competition.

Nereus Writers' Trust Non-Fiction Prize

Deadlines: June 30 or November 1, depending on publishing date

A $15,000 prize is awarded annually to the Canadian author of the work of non-fiction, written in English, that in the opinion of the judges shows the highest literary merit. Up to 4 runner-up prizes of $2,000 each will be awarded to the shortlisted authors.

Rogers Writers' Trust Fiction Prize
Deadlines: June 30 or November 1, depending on publishing date
    A $15,000 prize is awarded to the author of the year's outstanding novel or short story collection, written in English, by a Canadian citizen or landed immigrant. Up to 4 runner-up prizes of $2,000 each will be awarded to the shortlisted authors.

The Bronwen Wallace Memorial Award
    An award of $1,000 is presented, in alternate years, to a Canadian poet or a Canadian short-fiction writer under the age of 35 who is unpublished in book form but whose work has appeared in at least 1 independently edited magazine or anthology. Applicants should submit 5 to 10 pages of unpublished poetry or up to 2,500 words of unpublished prose fiction.

The Writers' Trust of Canada/McClelland & Stewart Journey Prize
McClelland & Stewart Ltd., 75 Sherbourne Street, 5th Floor, Toronto, ON M5A 2P9
Phone: (416) 598-1114 Fax: (416) 598-7764
E-mail: journeyprize@mcclelland.com
Web site: www.mcclelland.com/jps
Deadline: January 15
    The $10,000 Journey Prize is awarded annually to a new and developing writer of distinction for a short story published in a Canadian literary journal. Established in 1988, it is the most significant monetary award given in Canada to a writer at the beginning of his or her career for a short story or excerpt from a fiction work in progress. In recognition of the vital role journals play in discovering new writers, an additional $2,000 is awarded to the literary journal that originally published the winning story. The longlisted stories are selected from literary journal submissions and published annually by McClelland & Stewart as *The Journey Prize Stories*. Only submissions from literary journals/magazines are accepted.

The Writers' Union of Canada Awards and Competitions
90 Richmond Street E., Suite 200, Toronto, ON M5C 1P1
Phone: (416) 703-8982, ext. 223 Fax: (416) 504-9090

E-mail: projects@writersunion.ca
Web site: www.writersunion.ca

Danuta Gleed Literary Award
Deadline: January 31
Awarded for the best first collection of short stories in the English
language, written by a Canadian citizen or landed immigrant and
published in the previous calendar year. First prize $10,000; two
runners-up receive $500 each. Annual.

Short Prose Competition for Developing Writers
Deadline: November 3
An annual award to discover developing writers of fiction and
non-fiction. A $2,500 prize is awarded for the best piece of unpub-
lished prose up to 2,500 words by a Canadian citizen or landed
immigrant who has not previously been published in book format
and does not have a contract with a publisher. The winner agrees to
permit possible publication of the winning entry in a Canadian literary magazine. Entry fee $25. Full entry conditions available on
the web site.

Postcard Story Competition
Deadline: February 14
Open to all writers. A prize of $500 will be given for any text
(fiction, non-fiction, prose, poetry, verse, dialogue, etc.) up to 250
words in length. Entry fee $5/submission. Annual.

Writing for Children Competition
Deadline: April 24
A prize of $1,500 is awarded annually for the best fiction or non-
fiction (up to 1,500 words) written for children. Open to Canadian
citizens and landed immigrants whose work has not previously
been published in book format and who do not have a contract with
a publisher. The winner's and finalists' entries will be submitted to
3 publishers of children's literature. Entry fee $5/submission.

8

PROVINCIAL & FEDERAL
WRITER SUPPORT PROGRAMS

Outlined below are the main sources of provincial and federal funding for Canadian writers. Arts council and other government grants are designed to buy the writer time to devote to his or her work for a specified period in order to support a work in progress or the completion of a particular creative project through meeting a varying combination of living, research, travel, or professional-development costs. Such financial support is most often given to the successful published author, but gifted inexperienced writers are sometimes also eligible. Several provincial initiatives are open to new as well as established writers.

All these programs require applicants to develop detailed project proposals and budgets and to provide writing samples and other support materials.

Alberta Foundation for the Arts
10708 – 105 Avenue, Edmonton, AB T5H 0A1
Phone: (780) 427-6315 Fax: (780) 422-1162
Web site: www.affta.ab.ca
Contact: Arts Development Branch

Writers who have been previously published, produced, or aired may apply to the Alberta Foundation for the Arts for the following projects:

1) Art production includes the creation of a new manuscript or

work in progress that has not been published, produced, or aired. Eligible genres include fiction, drama, non-fiction, translation, adaptations, and anthologies.

2) Training and/or career development include a workshop, master class, retreat, mentorship program, and course of study in creative writing, editing, or translation. All writers regardless of experience may apply under this category.

3) Travel and/or marketing may include attending a book launch, non-academic conferences by invitation, literary festivals by invitation, acceptance of an award by invitation, promotional tours, and computer software purchase.

4) Research includes activities that support or result in the development of a writing project.

Writers who have not been published may apply for training projects only. Usually the maximum project grant under this program will not exceed $10,000 and may include up to $2,000/month subsistence allowance. Application deadlines are February 15 and September 1.

Alberta Community Development also offers the Grant MacEwan Young Writer's Scholarships. Scholarships of $2,500 each are awarded annually to 4 young Alberta writers who create a literary work between 1,000 and 5,000 words that reflects Alberta and/or Dr. MacEwan's interests. Applicants must be Alberta residents between the ages of 16 and 25. Deadline is December 31.

British Columbia Arts Council

Box 9819, Stn. Prov. Govt., Victoria, BC V8W 9W3
Phone: (250) 356-1728 Fax: (250) 387-4099
E-mail: walter.quan@gov.bc.ca
Web site: www.bcartscouncil.ca
Contact: Walter K. Quan, co-ordinator, Arts Awards Programs

Project Assistance for Creative Writers is available to B.C. professional writers with at least the equivalent of 1 book previously published professionally. Awards of up to $5,000 ($10,000 for writers with 3 or more books published professionally) may be used for specific creative projects. Eligible genres include fiction, drama, non-fiction, poetry, and juvenile. One juried competition is held annually. Application deadline September 15.

The Canada Council for the Arts

350 Albert Street, P.O. Box 1047, Ottawa, ON K1P 5V8
Phone: (613) 566-4414, ext. 5537 locally or after hours, or
1-800-263-5588 Fax: (613) 566-4410
E-mail: firstname.lastname@canadacouncil.ca
Web site: www.canadacouncil.ca

The Canada Council offers Canadian writers substantial financial support through a variety of programs, most notably Grants for Professional Writers – Creative Writing and Travel Grants, Literary Readings, Literary Festivals, and Author Residencies. It should be noted, however, that these grants are not available to unpublished writers. Applicants must have had at least 1 book published by a professional house or 4 major texts (short stories, excerpts from a novel, etc.) published on 2 separate occasions in recognized literary periodicals or anthologies.

Creative Writing Grants help authors working on new projects in fiction, poetry, children's literature, graphic novel, or literary non-fiction. (Literature creation projects based on the spoken word or technology may be submitted to the Spoken Word and Storytelling Program.) Grants range from $1,000 to $20,000. (Contact Peter Schneider, ext. 5537, or Paul Seesequasis, ext. 5482.)

Travel Grants help writers with career-related travel expenses (e.g., being a keynote speaker at an international conference or festival). Grants are $500, $750, $1,000, $1,500, $2,000, and $2,500. (Contact Marcel Hull, ext. 4571.)

The Literary Readings and Literary Festivals program provides opportunities for writers to read from their works and discuss them with the public. (Contact Mona Kiame, ext. 4016.)

Author Residencies provide financial assistance to organizations such as universities, libraries, and writers' associations to retain the services of a writer-in-residence, thus encouraging exchanges between the author and the community as well as enabling the author to work on a writing project. (Contact Mona Kiame, ext. 4016.)

The Spoken Word and Storytelling Program supports innovative literary projects not based upon conventional book or printed magazine formats through grants to creation, production, public performance, broadcast, or dissemination. This includes dub and rap poetry, poetry performance, and storytelling. Priority is given to projects that extend the boundaries of literary expression and are not just representing existing literature in a new format. (Contact Paul Seesequasis, ext. 5482.)

The Grants to Aboriginal Writers, Storytellers, and Publishers Program offers grants to Aboriginal writers and storytellers as well as Aboriginal-controlled publishers, periodicals, and collectives. (Contact Paul Seesequasis, ext. 5482.)

Please note that these programs are subject to change. Write for eligibility conditions and guidelines.

Conseil des arts et des lettres du Québec

79 René-Lévesque Boulevard E., 3rd Floor, Quebec, QC G1R 5N5
Phone: (418) 643-1707 or 1-800-897-1707 Fax: (418) 643-4558
500 Place d'Armes, 15th Floor, Montreal, QC H2Y 2W2
Phone: (514) 864-3350 or 1-800-608-3350 Fax: (514) 864-4160

Grants are offered for Quebec's professional writers and story-tellers (in English or French) in the following categories: artistic research and creation, literary or storytelling performances, development, and travel. The program fosters research and creation by making available to professional writers and storytellers the resources necessary for creating works and carrying out activities related to their artistic development throughout their careers. Type A grants of $25,000 maximum for a writer or storyteller with at least 10 years' experience; type B grants of $20,000 maximum for a writer or storyteller with 2–10 years' experience; career grants of $60,000 are awarded every 2 years to a writer or storyteller whose career spans at least 20 years.

Manitoba Arts Council

93 Lombard Avenue, Suite 525, Winnipeg, MB R3D 3B1
Phone: (204) 945-0422 or 1-866-994-2787 (toll-free in MB)
   Fax: (204) 945-5925
E-mail: jthomas@artscouncil.mb.ca
Web site: www.artscouncil.mb.ca
Contact: Joan Thomas, program consultant (literary)

Offers several potential sources of funding for writers: The Writers A Grant, worth up to $10,000, is designed to support concentrated work on a major writing project by professional Manitoba writers who have published 2 books and who show a high standard of work and exceptional promise. The Writers B Grant, for

Manitoba writers with 1 published book, is worth up to $5,000. The Writers C Grant, worth up to $2,000, for emerging writers with a modest publication background, is available to support a variety of developmental writing projects. Writers A, B, and C grants have 2 deadlines a year.

The Major Arts Grant supports personal creative projects of 6 to 10 months' duration by writers who have made a nationally or internationally recognized contribution to their discipline. Covering living and travel expenses and project costs, this grant is worth up to $25,000. Finally, published Manitoba writers can apply for a Travel and Professional Development Grant, to a maximum of $1,500, to support significant career opportunities. Guidelines for all programs are available on the web site. Please note that these programs are open to Manitoba residents only.

New Brunswick Arts Board
634 Queen Street, Suite 300, Fredericton, NB E3B 1C2
Phone: (506) 444-4444 Fax: (506) 444-5543
E-mail: rbryar@artsnb.ca
Web site: www.artsnb.ca
Contacts: R. Bryar, programs officer; L.M. Dugas, assistant
    programs officer
Several potential sources of funding exist for both professional artists and students pursuing a career in the arts as well as full-time or short-term studies in the arts. Permanent residency in New Brunswick is required. Deadlines for applications vary by program. Consult the web site for available programs. Application forms can be downloaded from web site.

Newfoundland and Labrador Arts Council
P.O. Box 98, Stn. C, St. John's, NL A1C 5H5
Phone: (709) 726-2212 or 1-866-726-2212 Fax: (709) 726-0619
E-mail: nlacmail@nfld.net
Web site: www.nlac.nf.ca
Newfoundland and Labrador writers can apply to the NLAC for funding support under the Project Grant Program for the March 15 and September 15 annual deadlines. Project grants are intended to help support artists as they carry out work in their discipline.

Grants may be used for living expenses and materials, study, and travel costs. They generally range from $1,000 to $5,000. The amount of funding to be awarded changes at each deadline based on the total request for funding in the writing discipline.

Northwest Territories Arts Council

Department of Education, Culture and Employment,
  Government of the N.W.T., P.O. Box 1320, Yellowknife, NT
  X1A 2L9
Phone: (867) 920-6370 Fax: (867) 873-0205
E-mail: boris_atamanenko@gov.nt.ca
Web site: www.pwnhc.ca/artscouncil
Contact: Boris Atamanenko, manager, community programs

The mandate of the N.W.T. Arts Council is to promote the visual, literary, and performing arts in the territories. Contributions of up to $14,000 (10% of the total funding budget) may be applied for. Deadline is January 31 each year. For applications and guidelines, call or write to the community programs manager.

Nova Scotia Department of Tourism, Culture and Heritage

1800 Argyle Street, Suite 402, P.O. Box 456, Halifax, NS B3J 2R5
Phone: (902) 424-3422 Fax: (902) 424-0710
E-mail: kirbypc@gov.ns.ca
Web site: www.gov.ns.ca/dtc
Contact: Peter Kirby, program officer

The Arts Section of the Culture Division of the Department of Tourism, Culture and Heritage is directed to support the creation of new work by professional artists (both established and emerging) in all disciplines, including literary, media arts (experimental film, video, and electronic art), performing arts (music, theatre, and dance), visual arts and craft, and multidisciplinary work. Applicants must be Canadian citizens or landed immigrants who have lived in Nova Scotia for at least 12 months prior to the application deadline.

Professional Development Grants offer assistance up to $3,000 for formal study programs or to participate in other professional development programs such as mentoring, apprenticeships, conferences, etc. Deadlines May 15 and December 15.

Creation Grants provide assistance up to $12,000 to assist artists in any art form by contributing toward the artist's subsistence and the project costs. Deadlines May 15 and December 15.

Presentation Grants offer assistance up to $5,000 to help cover direct costs of public presentation of the artist's work. Deadlines May 15 and December 15.

Ontario Arts Council

Literature Programs, 151 Bloor Street W., 5th Floor, Toronto, ON M5S 1T6

Phone: (416) 961-1610 or 1-800-387-0058 Fax: (416) 961-7796

E-mail: info@arts.on.ca

Web site: www.arts.on.ca

The Writers' Reserve program assists talented, emerging, and established writers in the creation of new work in fiction, poetry, writing for children, literary criticism, arts commentary, history, biography, or politics/social issues. Writers' Reserve grants are awarded through designated book and periodical publishers, who recommend authors for funding support up to a maximum of $5,000.

The Works-in-Progress program offers support ($12,000) in the completion of major book-length works of literary merit in poetry or prose by published writers.

The Chalmers Program supports arts professionals for a minimum of 1 year and consists of 2 components: arts fellowships (maximum $50,000) and professional development (maximum $15,000).

Programs are open to Ontario residents only. Write to or e-mail the Ontario Arts Council for detailed guidelines and application forms for these programs.

Prince Edward Island Council of the Arts

115 Richmond Street, Charlottetown, PE C1A 1H7

Phone: (902) 368-4410 or 1-888-734-2784 Fax: (902) 368-4418

E-mail: peiarts@peiartscouncil.com

Web site: www.peiartscouncil.com

Contact: Darrin White

Arts assistance grants are available to support Island writers. Professional development grants are offered from $500 to $1,200;

creation/production grants to a maximum of $3,000 are offered for an emerging professional artist, to $5,000 for a senior professional artist; and dissemination/presentation grants to a maximum of $1,000 are offered for an emerging professional artist, to $1,200 for a senior professional artist. Application deadlines are April 30 and October 30.

Saskatchewan Arts Board

2135 Broad Street, Regina, SK S4P 1Y6
Phone: (306) 787-4056 or 1-800-667-7526 (SK only)
  Fax: (306) 787-4199
E-mail: grants@artsboard.sk.ca
Web site: www.artsboard.sk.ca
Contact: Deron Staffen, grants co-ordinator

Creative, professional development, research, and travel grants are offered under the Independent Artists Grant Program. Creative grants assist artists to create, develop, and/or perform new work, and include professional development, research, and travel. Maximum grants are $17,000 for established artists and $6,000 for emerging artists. Professional development grants are a maximum of $7,500 for established artists and $4,000 for emerging artists. Research grants are a maximum of $5,000 for established artists and $2,000 for emerging artists. The maximum travel grants are $1,500. Deadlines for all Independent Artists Grants are March 15 and October 1.

The Indigenous Pathways Initiative is a new program that offers grants to Indigenous artists to a maximum of $6,000 for the Contemporary Arts Program, which includes the research and/or creation of literary works. The deadline is April 15.

Saskatchewan Arts Board grants are only available to Saskatchewan residents.

Yukon Department of Tourism and Culture

Arts Section, P.O. Box 2703 (L-3), Whitehorse, YT Y1A 2C6
Phone: (867) 667-8589 Fax: (867) 393-6456
E-mail: artsfund@gov.yk.ca
Web site: www.btc.gov.yk.ca/cultural/arts/index.html

Individual Yukon writers may be eligible for an Advanced Artist Award of up to $5,000 for a specific project. Training support through the Cultural Industries Training Fund is also available for writers who meet the eligibility requirements. Group projects contributing to development of the arts in the Yukon are supported through the Arts Fund.

9

PROFESSIONAL DEVELOPMENT

Writers at every level of experience can extend their skills and find fresh ideas through all manner of writing courses and workshops. Some believe creative writing is best fostered in the university or college environment by working with a good teacher who understands literary devices and structures and the power of language. Many skills peculiar to non-fiction writing, generally considered more a craft than an art, can be learned through courses or workshops led by experienced writers who have discovered not only how to refine ideas but how to research them, transform them into workable structures, and finally, market them. Some creative writers swear by the hothouse atmosphere, creative exchange of ideas, and collective reinforcement to be found in workshops led by expert facilitators.

Local branches of the Canadian Authors Association, libraries, and adult education classes offered by boards of education are some sources of writing courses and workshops. Regional writers' associations sometimes organize them, too, and are always a good source of information about what's currently available in your area.

This chapter is divided into two parts: first, a review of some of the country's most interesting writing schools, workshops, and retreats; second, a sample of the opportunities for the development of writing skills currently offered by Canadian colleges and universities. Writers' opportunities for professional development are extraordinarily diverse in Canada. Before you commit yourself, define your needs and carefully evaluate each program to see how it might meet them.

The summer courses, generally about a week long and built around small, daily workshop sessions, offer participants the chance to increase their technical skills, to submit their work to group scrutiny and critical feedback, and to enjoy, and learn from, the company of fellow writers as well as editors, agents, and other publishing professionals. Courses are sometimes streamed in order to cater to different levels of experience. Workshop facilitators are often nationally or internationally acclaimed authors, and some course participants enrol simply for the chance to work with them, but the best facilitators aren't necessarily the top literary names.

The workshop experience can be intense and demanding, and the rewards elusive. To get the most from it, bring at least one well-developed piece of writing with you, and be prepared to work hard during and outside the main sessions, but also use the opportunity to rub shoulders with other seekers, to network, and to bask in that all-too-rare sense of being part of a community of writers.

For those writers harried by family and job obligations, frustrated by the distractions of city living, and with a manuscript they simply must finish, writers' retreats and colonies offer peaceful seclusion, a beautiful rural setting, and a "room of one's own" in which to work without interruption, with meals and accommodation taken care of. Note that these are not teaching situations.

The larger section of this chapter, on creative writing and journalism courses offered at universities and colleges, surveys only some of the more significant programs, as well as a number of university-based workshops. The list is far from exhaustive. Many universities, colleges of applied arts, and community colleges offer writing courses at some level, depending on staff availability and student demand. Not all courses are taught every year, and programs can change at short notice. Continuing-education courses are open to all, but entry to credit courses is generally limited to those with specific academic prerequisites, although experienced writers can sometimes win special permission from the course convenor. Find out where you stand before developing your plans.

Creative Writing Schools, Workshops, & Retreats

The Banff Centre Writing Programs
P.O. Box 1020, Station 51, Banff, AB T1L 1H5
Phone: (403) 762-6278 Fax: (403) 763-6800
E-mail: writing_publishing@banffcentre.ca
Web site: www.banffcentre.ca

All the following programs provide opportunities for professional writers, who must choose the program that best serves their needs and objectives. Banff staff are happy to discuss this individually with applicants. Also contact the centre to discuss fee schedules and possible funding options.

The Leighton Studios for Independent Residencies
Application deadline: may apply at any time

This year-round program offers working residencies for independent professional artists engaged in the creation of new work and provides opportunities for concentrated focus in a retreat environment. Writers, screenwriters, playwrights, literary translators, composers, singer-songwriters, curators, art theorists, and professionals working in theatre, dance, and film at the conceptualization or research stage of a project are eligible. The 8 fully equipped studios are situated in a beautiful, quiet, wooded area.

Literary Journalism Program
Maclean Hunter chair: Rosemary Sullivan
April–June (off-site); July–August (on-site)
Application deadline: March

The Literary Journalism Program was established in response to an endowment from the Government of Alberta and Maclean Hunter Limited. The program offers 8 established writers of nonfiction an opportunity to develop a major essay, memoir, or feature piece. A month-long residency enables writers to work on their manuscript during individual consultations with faculty and during round-table discussions. Participants are able to advance their professional development through work with both the program chair and experienced editors, and through interaction with each other, invited guest speakers, and artists from other fields.

Applicants are usually accomplished journalists and writers who have been published in national and/or international magazines, newspapers, anthologies, or literary journals; however, writers with less experience have also been accepted to the program based on merit.

Mountain Writing Program
August–October (off-site); October–November (on-site)
Application deadline: June 1
In this unique residency program, 6 writers will delve into their own writing projects (essay, memoir, biography, poetry, feature article, or fiction) on a topic in the area of mountain culture, mountain environment, mountain life, adventure, climbing, and/or mountain history. Offers participants the time, privacy, and editorial resources to focus on their proposed piece. Writers work in a diverse and creative environment, interacting with other mountain writers and editors in group discussions and individual consultations, as well as with invited guest speakers and artists from other fields.

Self-Directed Writing Residencies
Application deadline: may apply at any time
Self-directed writing residencies provide time, space, and facilities for individual research, editing, and manuscript development. There are no formal activities organized around a self-directed writing residency; writers structure their own time and are free to maintain privacy or to engage with other artists and activities at the Banff Centre.

Wired Writing Studio
October (on-site); October–March (online)
Application deadline: June 16
The Wired Writing Studio is a unique opportunity for poets and writers of fiction and other narrative prose to pursue their artistic visions and develop their voices through one-on-one editorial assistance from experienced writers/editors, as well as through involvement in a community of working writers, both on-site at The Banff Centre and online for five months following the residency. Intended specifically for those producing work of literary merit who are at an early stage in their careers, this program offers an extended period

of writing time: 2 weeks in Banff and the remaining 20 weeks in the writer's own home or work space, working online.

Writing Studio
April–June
Application deadline: November 15

Offers a unique, supportive context for writers in the early stage of their careers to pursue a writing project. Writers spend 5 weeks at the Banff Centre working on their manuscripts in individual consultation with senior writers/editors. Enrolment is limited to 24 writers.

Writing with Style
September and April
Application deadline: May 15 and February 1

A 7-day workshop for writers at all levels, led by program director Edna Alford. Resource faculty change from year to year. The program provides writers of all levels with the opportunity to work on a novel, short fiction, memoir, poetry, travel writing, nature writing, creative non-fiction, and writing for children.

Booming Ground Writers' Community
University of B.C., 1866 Main Mall, Buch E462, Vancouver, BC V6T 1Z1
Phone: (604) 822-2469 Fax: (604) 822-3616
E-mail: bg@arts.ubc.ca
Web site: http://bg.arts.ubc.ca
Contact: Andrew Gray, director

A non-credit option that offers an innovative series of writing mentorships in poetry, fiction, non-fiction, and writing for children, as well as manuscript evaluation. Mentorships provide one-on-one feedback by e-mail directly from an instructor as students work on a writing project over 4, 6, or 8 months. Manuscript evaluations provide a constructive written report from one of our instructors, giving concrete suggestions for revisions and corrections.

Instructors include Anita Rau Badami, Gayle Friesen, Lawrence Hill, Robert Hilles, Evelyn Lau, and Pearl Luke.

Applications are accepted 3 times a year for mentorships: in January, May, and September. Manuscript evaluations may be requested at any time.

The fee for mentorship is $195/session (GST included), with a minimum of 4 sessions. Manuscript evaluations cost $270 (GST included) for up to 10 pages, double-spaced, with 12-point type (each additional page is $2.50). Fee includes a 1-year subscription to *PRISM international* magazine.

CANSCAIP's Packaging Your Imagination Workshop
40 Orchard View Boulevard, Suite 104, Lower Level, Toronto, ON
   M4R 1B9
Phone: (416) 515-1559
Web site: www.canscaip.org
Contact: Lena Coakely
   The Canadian Society of Children's Authors, Illustrators and Performers holds this day-long workshop on the first Saturday of November for anyone interested in writing, illustrating, or performing for young people. More than a dozen lectures, talks, and workshops are presented at Victoria College, the University of Toronto, by professionals respected in their fields. Those interested should contact CANSCAIP for a brochure (available in May). Workshops are $120 with lunch, $100 without. Past speakers have included Jean Little, Sheree Fitch, Paulette Bourgeois, Barbara Reid, Brian Doyle, and Kady MacDonald Denton.

Community of Writers
Tatamagouche Centre, R.R. #3, Tatamagouche, NS B0K 1V0
Phone: 1-800-218-2220
E-mail: comwrite@gmail.com
Web site:
   www.tatacentre.ca/Community%20of%20Writers/cw.htm
Contact: Gwen Davies
   A week-long writing retreat that combines intensive, small-group workshops that welcome serious beginning writers and those wanting to push deeper, and a retreat program for experienced writers. Workshops are led by a professional writer and an adult educator. The aim of the week is to discover skills, push the writing, receive support, learn from other writers, and join a community that includes writers at all levels. The schedule includes daily workshop sessions, feedback on your writing, free time to write (and

savour the grounds on Nova Scotia's North Shore), readings, and talks by writers.

Costs are modest, with largely shared accommodation and wonderful down-home cooking.

The Community of Writers is taking the year 2007 to review its program and will resume in 2008. "Visit our web site to look at where we've been and where we're going."

Emma Lake Kenderdine Campus of the Arts and Ecology Residency Program

117 Science Place, Room 133, Kirk Hall, University of Saskatchewan, Saskatoon, SK S7N 5C8
Phone: (306) 966-2463 Fax: (306) 966-5567
E-mail: emma.lake@usask.ca
Web site: www.emmalake.usask.ca
Contact: Paul Trottier, director

Writers, visual artists, performance artists, musicians, composers, critics, curators, arts administrators, ecological educators, environmentalists, and designers are invited to apply for the residency program during June and August. It provides work space, accommodation, and meals in a retreat environment where participants can work independently on their own projects for 1 to 3 weeks, depending on availability. The program also features an invited artist in residence whenever possible, although that artist is not required to provide formal instruction. Cost of the program is $400 plus taxes/week. In 2007 the residencies are from June 22 to 28, August 4 to 10, and August 11 to 17.

Gibraltar Point International Artist Residency Program

Artscape, 60 Atlantic Avenue, Suite 111, Toronto, ON M6K 1X9
E-mail: residency@torontoartscape.on.ca
Web site: www.torontoartscape.on.ca/gpiarp
Contact: Kelly Rintoul, residency program co-director

The Gibraltar Point International Artist Residency Program is an annual juried program that contributes to the development of artists and enables the creation, dissemination, and production of new work by granting participants the time and space to think, create, and experiment in a highly supportive environment. The program provides 10 professional artists with a subsidized oppor-tunity to live and work in a temporary community of artists at the Gibraltar Point Centre for the Arts on Toronto Island for 1 month. The competition is open to Canadian and international artists from a variety of disciplines who are engaged in the research or creation of new work. The residency program is managed by Artscape, a Toronto-based, non-profit enterprise that unlocks the creative potential of people and places. Guidelines for submissions are avail-able on the web site.

Another service offered by Artscape at the Gibraltar Point Centre for the Arts on Toronto Island is Artscape Lodge, an afford-able, short-term studio and bedroom rental service for artists who want to get away from life's distractions and focus on their work in a beautifully situated retreat setting. Contact bookings@toronto-artscape.on.ca for rates, availability, and additional information.

The Humber School for Writers
School of Creative and Performing Arts, Humber College,
   3199 Lake Shore Boulevard W., Toronto, ON M8V 1K8
Phone: (416) 675-6622, ext. 3449 Fax: (416) 251-7167
E-mail: antanas.sileika@humber.ca or hilary.higgins@humber.ca
Web site: www.humber.ca
Contacts: Antanas Sileika, artistic director; Hilary Higgins,
   secretary
One of Canada's best schools for writers offers a week-long writing workshop in fiction, creative non-fiction, and poetry each July. A residency option is available. The workshop fee is about $950, plus approximately $325 for full board for those who wish to stay in residence. A small number of scholarships may be available for those in need.

Each year the school also offers a unique 30-week certificate program in creative writing by correspondence, beginning in January. This extraordinary program offers promising writers the opportunity to send their work in progress (novel, short stories, or poetry) directly to their instructor, who provides editorial feedback by e-mail or post on a continuing basis for 30 weeks (January to July). Over 220 former students have been published, including Vincent Lam, the Giller Prize winner in 2006. Instructors who have taught this program include the distinguished writers Alistair

MacLeod, Guy Vanderhaeghe, Edward Albee, Roddy Doyle, Peter Carey, Timothy Findley, Elisabeth Harvor, Isabel Huggan, Paul Quarrington, and D. M. Thomas. The authors' pick for the best fiction manuscripts to emerge from the workshop are submitted to the Humber School for Writers Literary Agency.

A correspondence program in creative writing is offered at the post-graduate level. Applicants must be graduates of a college or university program, or have the equivalent in life experience (Prior Learning Assessment). Applicants must also submit a 15-page writing sample along with a proposal of the work to be completed during the course. The deadline for application is early October. Enrolment is limited. The fee is approximately $2,700. A few scholarships are available for those who demonstrate writing promise and financial need.

Pearl Luke Mentorship Program

Pearl Luke, 190 Scott Point Drive, Salt Spring Island, BC V8K 2P9
E-mail: pearl@pearlluke.com
Web site: www.pearlluke.com

Author and Commonwealth Prize-winner Pearl Luke mentors beginning and intermediate writers through any project online with personal feedback, manuscript evaluations, editing, and Q&A. Instruction is flexible and suited to the individual. Hourly and monthly programs starting from $100.

Maritime Writers' Workshop

College of Extended Learning, University of New Brunswick,
   P.O. Box 4400, Fredericton, NB E3B 5A3
Phone: (506) 453-6360
E-mail: atitus@unb.ca
Web site: http://extend.unb.ca/pers_cult/writers/index.php
Contact: Andrew Titus, program development officer

Continuing a 30-year tradition of delivering quality literary workshops in a creative, supportive, and affordable environment, the 2007 Maritime Writers Workshop and Literary Festival will run from July 8 to 14 in Fredericton. Instructors include Governor General Award–winners George Elliott Clarke (fiction) and Anne Compton (poetry), ePublishing guru Biff Mitchell (mystery and suspense), and acclaimed francophone author France Daigle. There are also public readings, adventures along the scenic St. John River Valley, and one-on-one sessions with your chosen instructor.

Dedicated to writers of all kinds and genres, from beginners to working professionals, the program offers a number of full and partial scholarships.

Sage Hill Writing Experience

P.O. Box 1731, Saskatoon, SK S7K 3S1
Phone: (306) 652-7395
E-mail: sage.hill@sasktel.net
Web site: www.sagehillwriting.ca

Sage Hill's 10-day summer writing workshops are held every August in rural Saskatchewan at St. Michael's Retreat Centre in Lumsden, in the beautiful Qu'Appelle Valley, north of Regina. The facility has private rooms with bath, meeting rooms, walking woods, and home-style cooking.

The program offers workshops at introductory, intermediate, and advanced levels in fiction, non-fiction, poetry, and playwriting (though not all these courses are available each year). The low writer-to-instructor ratio (usually 6 to 1) and high-quality faculty (all established writers) help make these workshops and colloquiums among the most highly valued in Canada.

Fees per course of $895 for the summer program include accommodation, meals, and instruction. Scholarships are available. Enrolment is limited. Applicants should send for guidelines or check them on the web site. The summer program registration deadline is April 23.

Three annual Teen Writing Experiences, primarily for Saskatchewan writers aged 14 to 18, are held in July and August. For these free, 5-day creative writing "camps," held in Saskatoon, Moose Jaw, and Regina, out-of-towners may have to arrange their own accommodation and transportation. Application deadline is May 15.

A Fall Poetry Colloquium, held in November at St. Michael's Retreat, Lumsden, is an intensive, 2-week manuscript-development seminar/retreat, also open to writers from outside Saskatchewan. This program features ample writing time, group discussions, and one-on-one critiques by the instructor, as well as online follow-up with the instructor. The fee of $1,195 includes tuition, accommodation, and meals. Application deadline is August 31.

Saskatchewan Writers/Artists Colonies & Retreats

c/o P.O. Box 3986, Regina, SK S4P 3R9

Phone: (306) 757-6310 Fax: (306) 565-8554

E-mail: skcolony@sasktel.net

Web site: www.skwriter.com/programdesc.asp?id=39

The colonies and retreats were established in 1979 to provide an environment where writers and artists (especially but not exclusively from Saskatchewan) can work free from distractions in serene and beautiful locations. They are not teaching situations but retreats, offering uninterrupted work time and opportunities for a stimulating exchange of ideas with fellow writers and artists after hours. All writers and artists may apply for a colony, while only Saskatchewan residents may apply for individual retreats. Costs are subsidized by the Saskatchewan Lotteries, SaskCulture, and the Saskatchewan Arts Board. St. Peter's Abbey is a Benedictine abbey near the town of Humboldt. Christopher Lake is in the forest country north of Prince Albert.

A 6-week summer colony (July to August) and a 3-week winter colony (February and March) are held at St. Peter's Abbey. Applicants may request as much time as they need, to a maximum of 3 weeks in winter and 4 weeks in summer, but accommodation in private rooms is limited to 10 people per week in summer and 18 in winter. There will be a third colony of 2 weeks (date and location to be announced). Individual retreats of up to 1 week per person annually are offered year round at St. Peter's, with no more than 3 individuals being accommodated at a time.

Fees for St. Peter's colonies and individual retreats, including meals, are $225 per week for Saskatchewan Writers Guild and CARFAC members, and $275 per week for non-members. Fees are subject to change. Applicants are required to submit a 10-page writing sample of recent work, a résumé, description of the work to be done at the colony, and 2 references. Consult the web site or request a brochure for complete application information.

University of Toronto School of Continuing Studies
Creative Writing Program

Writing and Literature Program, University of Toronto School of
   Continuing Studies, 158 St. George Street, Toronto, ON
   M5S 2V8

Phone: (416) 978-6714 Fax: (416) 978-6091
E-mail: scs.writing@utoronto.ca
Web site: www.learn.utoronto.ca
Contact: Lee Gowan, program director

One of Canada's largest creative writing programs that offers the broadest curriculum of any writing program in Canada. The courses are taught by outstanding writers and publishers, each of whom brings a wealth of experience and accomplishment to the classroom. Enrolment is limited to guarantee that each student receives individual attention. The school offers a certificate in creative writing and the annual Random House of Canada Student Award in Writing (3 prizes of $500), open to writers who are enrolled in the program. Winners of the prize are also published in a chapbook produced by Random House.

The wide range of courses includes an introduction to creative writing; writing short fiction; writing the novel; poetry, mystery and suspense writing; writing women's fiction; screenwriting; dramatic writing; creative non-fiction; autobiographical writing; freelance and feature writing; online mentoring; and courses on how to publish.

Instructors in the program include Michael Winter, Ken McGoogan, Helen Humphreys, Dennis Bock, Marnie Woodrow, Ray Robertson, Lee Gowan, Kim Echlin, Shyam Selvadurai, Shaughnessy Bishop-Stall, Kathy Kacer, Ken Babstock, Ken Sherman, David Donnel, Margaret Christakos, Kelli Deeth, Catherine Graham, Maureen McKeon, Alan Zweig, Hal Niedzviecki, and Kathryn Kuitenbrouwer.

Courses are 20 hours in duration and run from October to December, February to April, and April to June, and are priced at $529.

There is also a 5-day intensive workshop in early July called the U of T Summer Writing School. The program features limited enrolment, daily round-table workshops, one-on-one tutorials with the instructor, panel discussions, instructor readings, and the opportunity to meet and discuss your work with other emerging writers. The workshops in 2007 will feature Joy Fielding on writing a bestseller and a detective fiction course with Peter Robinson.

For more information, visit the web site or contact the SCS by phone, fax, or e-mail and ask for a print course calendar.

Victoria School of Writing

620 View Street, Suite 306, Victoria, BC V8W 1J6
Phone: (250) 595-3000
E-mail: info@victoriaschoolofwriting.org
Web site: www.victoriaschoolofwriting.org

This summer school offers 5 days of intensive workshops in poetry, fiction, non-fiction, and other genres. Sessions are led by experienced, established Canadian authors. The 2006 faculty included Maria Coffey, Charlotte Gill, Gary Geddes, John Lent, Susan Musgrave, Billeh Nickerson, and Kevin Patterson. The school is held during the third week of July in a residential school in Victoria, set on 22 acres of treed countryside. Registration is $595. This includes an opening reception, 5 lunches, and a final barbecue party. Accommodation and meals are available on-site.

The Writing School at Quality of Course

38 McArthur Avenue, Suite 2951, Ottawa, ON K1L 6R2
Phone: 1-800-267-1829 Fax: (613) 749-9551
E-mail: writers@qualityofcourse.com
Web site: www.qualityofcourse.com
Contact: Alex Myers

For the last 20 years, the school has offered creative writing courses by distance. These diploma courses are designed to help the student to publish. They give starting writers a thorough and practical understanding of the needs of the marketplace, and build creative and technical skills. The courses can be completed online.

The student works with his or her tutor on a variety of assignments, each structured to improve specific skills. All tutors at the school are working writers. Assignments are tailored to reflect the individual interests and abilities of each student. Course fees are $759, which cover all costs, including books, lessons, tapes, and tutorial.

The school offers prospective students a free evaluation of their work. Call the toll-free number for a free brochure detailing course contents and methodology, and for more about the evaluation service.

Creative Writing & Journalism at Colleges & Universities

Acadia University

Wolfville, NS B4P 2R6
Phone: (902) 585-1502 Fax: (902) 585-1770
E-mail: wanda.campbell@acadiau.ca
Web site: http://ace.acadiau.ca/english/cwrite.htm
Contact: Wanda Campbell, creative writing co-ordinator

The Department of English offers the following credit courses at the undergraduate level: Exploring Creative Writing: An Introduction, Advanced Creative Writing: Poetry, and Advanced Creative Writing: Fiction. There is also the option to write an honours creative writing thesis in poetry, fiction, or drama under the guidance of a published author.

University of Alberta

3 – 5 Humanities Centre, Edmonton, AB T6G 2E5
Phone: (780) 492-3258 Fax: (780) 492-8142
E-mail: english@mail.arts.ualberta.ca
Web site: www.humanities.ualberta.ca/english/
Contact: Daphne Read, Write Program director

The Department of English and Film Studies will offer the following credit courses in creative writing in 2007–08: Introductory and Intermediate Poetry, Fiction, and Non-Fiction; Projects in Genre; and Advanced Fiction and Non-Fiction.

Creative writing classes will also be available during 2007 through the extension program. Consult www.extension.ualberta.ca for details.

Algoma University College

1520 Queen Street E., Sault Ste. Marie, ON P6A 2G4
Phone: (705) 949-2301 Fax: (705) 949-6583
E-mail: gibson@auc.ca
Web site: www.auc.on.ca
Contact: Jim Gibson, associate professor, English Department

The English Department offers the following credit courses:

Creative Writing, Studies in Creative Writing, and Introduction to Creative Writing.

Algonquin College

1385 Woodroffe Avenue, Ottawa, ON K2G 1V8
Phone: (613) 727-4723 Fax: (613) 727-7707
E-mail: tarzwel@algonquincollege.com
Web site: www.algonquincollege.com
Contact: Lynn Tarzwell, co-ordinator

The Professional Writing Program offers the following credit courses: Storytelling Theory, Applied Storytelling, and Introduction to Writing for Broadcast and Film. As well, the program offers training in writing for corporate, government, and other professional environments.

The School of Media and Design offers a 2-year diploma program in print journalism.

E-publishing will be offered in fall 2007.

Publishes *The Algonquin Times*.

Brandon University

270 – 18th Street, Brandon, MB R7A 6A9
Phone: (204) 727-9790 Fax: (204) 726-0473
E-mail: lakevold@brandonu.ca
Web site: www.brandonu.ca
Contact: Dale Lakevold, assistant professor, Department of
English

Credit courses in creative writing, creative non-fiction, playwriting, short fiction, screenwriting, poetry, ecopoetics, and poetry video are offered by the English Department and the Creative Arts Program. Has the only Canada Research chair in creative writing in Canada (Di Brandt). As well, the English Department offers technical-writing courses, and the Department of Business Administration offers business communications courses.

Publishes the inter-disciplinary electronic journal *Ecclectica*. The BU Publishing Board publishes *The Quill* students' newspaper.

University of British Columbia

Creative Writing Program, Department of Theatre, Film and
  Creative Writing, Buchanan E462, 1866 Main Mall, Vancouver,
  BC V6T 1Z1
Phone: (604) 822-0699 Fax: (604) 822-3616
E-mail: patrose@interchange.ubc.ca
Web site: www.creativewriting.ubc.ca/crwr
Contact: Pat Rose, secretary

The Creative Writing Program offers courses of study leading to
BFA and MFA degrees. A wide range of creative writing courses are
available, including writing for screen and television, the novel
and novella, short fiction, stage plays, radio plays and features,
non-fiction, applied creative non-fiction, writing for children, lyric
and libretto, translation, and poetry. A joint MFA with the theatre
program is also possible. Students may choose to take a double
major in creative writing and another subject.

The literary journal *PRISM international* is edited by program
graduate students.

Brock University

500 Glenridge Avenue, St. Catharines, ON L2S 3A1
Phone: (905) 688-5550, ext. 3886 Fax: (905) 688-4461
E-mail: jsackfie@spartan.ac
Web site: www.brocku.ca/english
Contact: Robert Alexander, Writing Program director

The Department of English offers credit courses in reporting
and news writing for mass media and a creative writing course in
poetry. A BA with a major in English and professional writing is
available, as well as a minor in professional writing and a certificate
in professional writing.

University of Calgary

Department of English, Social Sciences Tower, 11th Floor,
  2500 University Drive N.W., Calgary, AB T2N 1N4
Phone: (403) 220-5470 Fax: (403) 289-1123
E-mail: engadv@ucalgary.ca
Web site: www.english.ucalgary.ca/creative
Contact: Susan Rudy, head, English Department

The Creative Writing Department offers English degrees with a concentration in creative writing. Courses include Writing the Rural, Introductory Creative Writing, Poetry Writing, Fiction, and Prose (in which a book-length manuscript is produced). The Markin-Flanagan Distinguished Writers Program ensures an annual writer-in-residence (Jaspreet Singh in 2006–7), as well as short-term visits by major writers. Some writing students also participate in the poetry magazine *dANDelion*.

Cambrian College of Applied Arts & Technology

1400 Barrydowne Road, Sudbury, ON P3A 3V8
Phone: (705) 566-8101   Fax: (705) 525-2087
E-mail: info@cambrianc.on.ca
Web site: www.cambrianc.on.ca
Contact: Brenda Bouchard, manager, liaison

The School of Business, Media, and Creative Arts offers a 2-year diploma program in Journalism – Print. Students gain practical experience by publishing *The Shield*, a publication in print and online. A 1-year Broadcast–New Media graduate certificate program is also offered. As well, credit courses are available in Business Writing Strategies, Communications, Writing a Proposal, and Writing a Feasibility Report.

Continuing Education offers the following courses through Internet delivery: creative writing, poetry writing, romance writing, beginning novel writing, and writing for publication. A creative writing course is also offered in the classroom in the evenings.

Camosun College

3100 Foul Bay Road, Victoria, BC V8P 5J2
Phone: (250) 370-3000
E-mail: english@camosun.bc.ca
Web site: www.camosun.bc.ca

The English Department offers credit courses in creative writing in fiction, poetry, and playwriting.

A variety of Continuing Education courses and programs are available in creative writing, including feature writing, travel writing, romantic writing, and selling freelance writing.

Credit courses in writing for the print and electronic media are offered as components of the 20-month, full-time Applied Communications program. Students write and produce radio and cable television programs.

Capilano College

2055 Purcell Way, North Vancouver, BC V7J 3H5
Phone: (604) 984-4957 Fax: (604) 990-7837
E-mail: humanities@capcollege.bc.ca
Web site: www.capcollege.bc.ca
Contact: Reg Johanson, co-ordinator, English
The English Department offers credit courses in creative writing.

Centennial College of Applied Arts & Technology

951 Carlaw Avenue, Toronto, ON M4K 3M2
Phone: (416) 289-5100 Fax: (416) 289-5106
E-mail: thecentre@centennialcollege.ca
Web site: www.centennialcollege.ca

The Communication Arts Department offers a 3-year diploma program in print journalism (or an 18-month "fast track") and online writing. Also a 1-year diploma program in corporate communication. Programs include courses in reporting, scriptwriting, broadcast journalism, documentary film writing, magazine writing, and newspaper feature writing. All programs emphasize practical skills. Various courses are also offered in the extension program. Courses are held online as well.

Concordia University

1455 de Maisonneuve W., Room LB 501, Montreal, QC H3G 1M8
Phone: (514) 848-2424, ext. 2342 Fax: (514) 848-4501
E-mail: sfrank@vox2.concordia.ca
Web site: http://artsandscience.concordia.ca/english/
Contact: Sharon Frank, assistant to the chair
The Creative Writing Program within the English Department offers workshops for credit in writing poetry, prose and drama, and scriptwriting, as well as editing and publishing, and other special-topic courses.

Concordia University College of Alberta

7128 Ada Boulevard, Edmonton, AB T5B 4E4
Phone: (780) 479-8481 Fax: (780) 474-1933
E-mail: marco.loverso@concordia.ab.ca
Web site: www.concordia.ab.ca
Contact: Marco LoVerso

The English Department offers 2 credit courses in creative writing: Introduction to Creative Writing – Fiction, and Introduction to Creative Writing – Non-Fiction. The fiction course is taught by published authors with graduate degrees in creative writing.

Conestoga College of Applied Arts and Technology

299 Doon Valley Drive, Kitchener, ON N2G 4M4
Phone: (519) 748-5220 Fax: (519) 748-3534
E-mail: cjonas@conestogac.on.ca
Web site: www.conestogac.on.ca

Offers a 2-year diploma in journalism print and journalism-broadcasting, which prepares the graduate for employment in various fields related to news writing and news production for Internet publishers and newspapers, magazines, and radio or TV stations. Students gain practical experience working on the college newspaper, *Spoke*; the college's FM-radio station at CJIQ; and in the television studio.

Continuing Education offers a creative writing workshop, and creative writing classes are also available online through the ontariolearn.com intercollegiate consortium.

Douglas College

P.O. Box 2503, New Westminster, BC V3L 5B2
Phone: (604) 527-5465 Fax: (604) 527-5095
Contact: Mary Burns, chair, Creative Writing Department

College credit and university transfer courses in creative writing are available. Courses include Introduction to Fiction Writing, Introduction to Playwriting, Introduction to Writing Poetry, Advanced Poetry Writing, Writing Short Fiction, Screenwriting, Personal Narrative, and Introduction to Historical Fiction Writing.

The Print Futures professional writing program is a 2-year diploma program preparing students for a professional writing career.

It includes courses in writing, research, editorial and design skills, public relations writing, and writing for magazines and trade publications. For more information, contact the program co-ordinator at (604) 527-5292 or e-mail printfutures@douglas.bc.ca.

Publishes the literary journal *Event*.

Durham College

2000 Simcoe Street N., Oshawa, ON L1H 7K4
Phone: (905) 721-2000 Fax: (905) 721-3195
E-mail: info@dca.durhamc.on.ca
Web site: http://durhamcollege.ca

The Design and Communication Arts Department offers a 3-year Journalism – Print and Broadcast program and a 2-year Journalism – Print program.

Continuous Learning offers non-credit courses in creative writing and getting published.

Publishes *The Chronicle*, a college newspaper that provides students with experience in writing, editing, design, layout, art, photography, and production.

En'owkin Centre Fine Arts Program

R.R. #2, Site 50, Comp. 8, Penticton, BC V2A 6J7
Phone: (250) 493-7181 Fax: (250) 493-5302
E-mail: pr@enowkincentre.ca
Web site: www.enowkincentre.ca

Offers the following credit courses: Introduction to Creative Writing; Writing for Children; Critical Process and World View; and Critical Process, Symbolism and Oral Tradition.

University of Guelph

Guelph, ON N1G 2W1
Phone: (519) 824-4120 Fax: (519) 766-0844
E-mail: sballant@uoguelph.ca
Web site: http://arts.uoguelph.ca/sets
Contact: Sharon Ballantyne, graduate secretary

The School of English and Theatre Studies offers Creative Writing: Fiction (in fall 2007), Creative Writing: Poetry (in winter 2008), and Seminar in Creative Writing (Fiction) (in winter 2008).

The university also offers an MFA program in creative writing.

Humber College of Applied Arts and Technology

P.O. Box 1900, 205 Humber College Boulevard, Toronto, ON
M9W 5L7
Phone: (416) 675-5000 Fax: (416) 675-2427
E-mail: enquiry@humber.ca
Web site: www.humber.ca

Offers a 3-year diploma program in print and broadcast journalism. Business writing and technical writing courses are offered by Continuing Education. Comedy scriptwriting is available in the program Comedy: Writing and Performance.

See also Humber School for Writers, p. 410–11.

University of King's College

6350 Coburg Road, Halifax, NS B3II 2A1
Phone: (902) 422-1271 Fax: (902) 423-3357
E-mail: admissions@ukings.ns.ca
Web site: www.ukings.ca

The Journalism School offers the following courses: Feature Writing, Foundations of Journalism, Reporting Techniques, Introduction to Narrative Non-Fiction, Business Reporting for Journalists, Advanced Magazine Workshop, and Investigative Workshop.

Lambton College

1457 London Road, Sarnia, ON N7S 6K4
Phone: (519) 542-7751 Fax: (519) 541-2408
Contact: Lisa Bicum, co-ordinator, English Department

Lambton offers Language and Communications, Technical Writing, Fundamentals of English, Business Correspondence, Business Reports, and Written Business Communications.

Langara College

100 West 49th Avenue, Vancouver, BC V5Y 2Z6
Phone: (604) 323-5511 Fax: (604) 323-5555
E-mail: motton@langara.bc.ca
Web site: www.langara.bc.ca
Contact: Dr. Megan Otton, chair, English Department

The Department of Journalism offers credit courses in the fundamentals of reporting, daily paper writing, magazine feature writing, advanced reporting, and specialty writing.

A variety of creative writing courses are offered by the English Department, including prose fiction, stageplay, poetry, screenwriting, and non-fiction.

A wide selection of creative writing courses are offered by Continuing Studies, including novel writing, comedy writing, writing a feature film, how to get published, travel writing, and writing for children.

Malaspina University-College

900 – 5th Street, Nanaimo, BC V9R 5S5
Phone: (250) 753-3245 Fax: (250) 740-6459
E-mail: dunstanr@mala.bc.ca
Web site: www.mala.bc.ca/www/crwrit
Contact: Richard Dunstan, chair, Department of Creative Writing and Journalism

The Department of Creative Writing and Journalism offers a variety of first- through fourth-year courses in poetry, fiction, scriptwriting, beginning journalism, news writing, feature writing, creative non-fiction, and research. Creative writing classes are also available in 2007 through online course offerings in poetry, fiction, scriptwriting, and feature writing.

Publishes *Portal*, the electronic journal *Incline*, and the student newspaper, *The Navigator*.

University of Manitoba

Department of English, 625 Fletcher Argue Building, 28 Trueman Walk, Winnipeg, MB R3T 5V5
Phone: (204) 474-9678 Fax: (204) 474-7669
E-mail: english@umanitoba.ca
Web site: www.umanitoba.ca/faculties/arts/english

The English Department offers an introduction to creative writing and advanced creative writing.

McMaster University

Centre for Continuing Education, Downtown Centre, 50 Main Street E., 2nd Floor, Hamilton, ON L8S 4L8
Phone: (905) 525-9140, ext. 23128 Fax: (905) 546-1690
E-mail: richt@mcmaster.ca

Web site: www.mcmaster.ca
Contact: Todd Rich, program manager
    The Centre for Continuing Education offers a certificate in creative writing with such courses as Forms of Writing; Introduction to Writing and Publishing; the Art of the Short Story; the On-Line Writing Workshop; the Developing Sensual (Erotic) Writing Styles Workshop, Writing Women Characters; Transforming Life into Writing; and Author Authenticity: Research and Revision.

Mohawk College
P.O. Box 2034, Hamilton, ON L8N 3T2
Phone: (905) 575-2000 Fax: (905) 575-2392
E-mail: ask@mohawkcollege.ca
Web site: www.mohawkcollege.ca
Contact: Terry Mote, director, student recruitment
    The Communications Media Department offers Writing for Media; Research and Report; Communications; and Journalism, Print and Broadcast. Continuing Education offers Novel Writing, Technical Writing, Self Publishing, and Writing Science Fiction.

Mount Royal College
4825 Mount Royal Gate S.W., Calgary, AB T3E 6K6
Phone: (403) 440-6912 Fax: (403) 440-6563
E-mail: mhaydo@mtroyal.ca
Web site: www.mtroyal.ca
Contact: Marc Chikinda, acting dean, Centre for Communication
    Studies
    The Centre for Communication Studies offers a BA in Applied Communications with specializations in journalism, technical communication, public relations, and electronic publishing.
    The centre also offers journalism and technical writing certificates, and a diploma in broadcasting.

University of New Brunswick
Department of English, P.O. Box 4400, Fredericton, NB E3B 5A3
Phone: (506) 458-7395 Fax: (506) 453-5069
E-mail: leckie@unb.ca
Web site: www.unbf.ca/english
Contact: Ross Leckie, director of creative writing

The English Department offers the following undergraduate credit courses: introduction to poetry, drama, fiction, and screenwriting, and advanced courses in poetry, fiction, drama, and screenwriting. Graduate courses include poetry, fiction, drama, and screenwriting.

Continuing Education provides a non-credit course on the fundamentals of writing.

The university has a writer-in-residence and sponsors the Maritime Writers' Workshop in mid-July each year.

Niagara College of Applied Arts and Technology

300 Woodlawn Road, Welland, ON L3C 7L3
Phone: (905) 735-2211, ext. 7753 Fax: (905) 736-6003
E-mail: pbarnatt@niagarac.on.ca
Web site: www.newsatniagara.com
Contact: Phyllis Barnatt, program co-ordinator, Journalism-Print Program

Offers a 2-year course in journalism with Special Fields of Writing I and II. Continuing Education offers a writing for publication certificate.

University of Prince Edward Island

550 University Avenue, Charlottetown, PE C1A 4P3
Phone: (902) 566-0389 Fax: (902) 566-0363
Web site: http://welcome.upei.ca
Contact: Richard Lemm, professor of English

The English Department offers 2 credit courses in creative writing and the Art and Craft of Life-Writing.

College of the Rockies

P.O. Box 8500, Cranbrook, BC V1C 5L7
Phone: 1-877-489-2687 Fax: (250) 489-1790
E-mail: ask@cotr.bc.ca
Web site: www.cotr.bc.ca
Contact: Gail Greenwood Wakulich, instructor, English and Creative Writing

The University Studies Department offers Creative Writing 101 and 102.

Ryerson Polytechnic University

350 Victoria Street, Toronto, ON M5B 2K3
Phone: (416) 979-5000 Fax: (416) 979-5277
E-mail: inquire@ryerson.ca
Web site: www.ryerson.ca
The English Department offers a creative writing course.

The School of Journalism offers a 4-year degree program with courses in reporting, freelance writing, feature writing, online journalism, and magazine writing.

Continuing Education offers a wide range of creative writing courses and workshops, including courses in short fiction and novel writing, poetry writing, playwriting, writing for children, writing romance, writing reviews, writing sitcoms, autobiographical writing, and creative non-fiction. Also has a 10-month workshop in writing the novel, short fiction, and non-fiction.

St. Jerome's University

290 Westmount Road, Waterloo, ON N2L 3G3
Phone: (519) 884-8110 Fax: (519) 884-5759
E-mail: cemcgee@uwaterloo.ca
Web site: www.sju.ca
Contact: C. E. McGee, chair, Department of English
The English Department offers a creative writing and an arts writing course, both for credit.

University of Saskatchewan

Department of English, 9 Campus Drive, Saskatoon, SK S7N 5A5
Phone: (306) 966-5486 Fax: (306) 966-5951
E-mail: nik.thomson@usask.ca
Web site: www.usask.ca/english
Contact: Nik Thomson, administrator, Department of English
The Department of English at St. Thomas More College (affiliated) offers courses in advanced creative writing for both fiction and poetry. An introduction to creative writing is occasionally offered through the Department of English.

Sheridan College

1430 Trafalgar Road, Oakville, ON L6H 2L1
Phone: (905) 845-9430, ext. 2761 Fax: (905) 815-4010

Web site: www.sheridanc.on.ca

Contacts: Joyce Wayne, professor and co-ordinator; Mary Lynn O'Shea, professor and co-ordinator

The Journalism Department offers a 2-year diploma in print journalism, as well as a 1-year postgraduate program, Journalism for New Media, which includes training in digital media for broadcast and online journalism. The Journalism Department is part of the Sheridan Centre for Animation and Emerging Technologies. Two-year-diploma students produce a weekly newspaper, *The Sheridan Sun*. Courses include newswriting for print and online publications.

A 1-year post-graduate program in Canadian journalism for internationally trained writers is also available.

Continuing Education offers various writing courses.

Simon Fraser University

Writing and Publishing Program, 515 West Hastings Street, Suite 2300, Vancouver, BC V6B 5K3

Phone: (604) 291-5093 Fax: (604) 291-5098

E-mail: wpp@sfu.ca

Web site: www.sfu.ca/wp

A large selection of creative writing classes are available through Simon Fraser's Writing and Publishing Program, the Writer's Studio (which offers a certificate in creative writing), and Continuing Studies.

University of Toronto

Toronto, ON M5S 1A1

Phone: (416) 978-6662

Web site: www.utoronto.ca

Contact: Helen Lasthiotakis, assistant vice-provost

Each year the English Department offers 2 creative writing courses, in poetry and prose, to selected students.

The School of Continuing Studies offers a certificate in creative writing and has courses in writing non-fiction, drama, short fiction, the novel, writing for children, screenwriting, and poetry.

Trent University

Peterborough, ON K9J 7B8

Phone: (705) 748-1011, ext. 1733 Fax: (705) 748-1823

E-mail: english@trentu.ca
Web site: ww.trentu.ca/english
Contact: Gordon Johnston, professor
The English Department offers an advanced seminar in creative writing.

Continuing Education offers a certificate in creative writing with courses that include Writing for Children, Writing Your Story, Novel Writing, Poetry, the Art and Craft of Travel Writing, Screenwriting, Journalism, and the Advanced Writing Workshop. After the successful completion of 4 courses, students may begin the mentorship program, working one-on-one with a seasoned writer via e-mail to polish a project of their choice.

University of Victoria
Department of Writing, P.O. Box 1700, Stn. CSC, Victoria, BC
v8w 2Y2
Phone: (250) 721-7306 Fax: (250) 721-6602
E-mail: writing@finearts.uvic.ca
Web site: www.finearts.uvic.ca/writing
Through the Department of Writing, students can major in creative writing, choosing courses (lectures and workshops) in fiction, creative non-fiction, poetry, drama, and aspects of journalism.

Writing for children, creative non-fiction, and writing the memoir are available through the Division of Continuing Studies.

University of Western Ontario
Faculty of Information and Media Studies, North Campus
Building, Room 240, London, ON N6A 5B7
Phone: (519) 661-4017 Fax: (519) 661-3506
E-mail: slong@uwo.ca
Web site: www.fims.uwo.ca/journalism
Contact: Shelley Long, graduate programs secretary
Western's 3-term (1-year) Master of Arts in Journalism is a well-rounded, professional program for candidates with an honours undergraduate degree or equivalent. The program prepares graduates for entry-level positions in newsrooms. The curriculum includes a balance of academic and practical courses, as well as a month-long internship placement, and offers a solid grounding in the basic tools and practices of print and broadcast journalism.

University of Windsor

English Language, Literature and Creative Writing,
 2 – 104 Chrysler Hall N., Windsor, ON N9B 3P4
Phone: (519) 253-3000/2289 Fax: (519) 971-3676
E-mail: englishmail@uwindsor.ca
Web site: www.uwindsor.ca
Contact: Karl Jirgens, head, Department of English
   The Department of English offers many courses in writing, ranging from introductory to advanced seminars/workshops.

University of Winnipeg

515 Portage Avenue, Winnipeg, MB R3B 2E9
Phone: (204) 786-9292 Fax: (204) 774-4134
Web site: www.uwinnipeg.ca/as/english/index.html
Contact: Catherine Hunter, associate professor, English
   Department
   The following credit courses are offered by the English Department: Introduction to Creative Writing; the Creative Process; Creative Writing; Creative Writing: Fiction; and Creative Writing: Writing for Children.

York University

210 Vanier College, 4700 Keele Street, Toronto, ON M3J 1P3
Phone: (416) 736-5910 Fax: (416) 736-5460
E-mail: suepar@yorku.ca
Web site: www.yorku.ca/human
Contact: co-ordinator of creative writing
   The Creative Writing Program offers the following credit courses: Introduction to Creative Writing, Mixed Genre, Prose Intermediate and Senior, Poetry Intermediate and Senior, and Mixed Genre Senior.
   The Professional Writing Program offers courses in print journalism.
   Publishes the literary journal *Existere*.

10

WRITERS' ORGANIZATIONS & SUPPORT AGENCIES

Access Copyright (Canadian Copyright Licensing Agency)
1 Yonge Street, Suite 800, Toronto, ON M5E 1E5
Phone: (416) 868-1620 or 1-800-893-5777 Fax: (416) 868-1621
E-mail: info@accesscopyright.ca
Web site: www.accesscopyright.ca

Alberta Foundation for the Arts
10708 – 105 Avenue, Edmonton, AB T5H 0A1
Phone: (780) 427-6315 Fax: (780) 422-1162
Web site: www.affta.ab.ca

Alberta Playwrights' Network
2633 Hochwald Avenue S.W., Calgary, AB T3E 7K2
Phone: (403) 269-8564 or 1-800-268-8564 Fax: (403) 265-6773
E-mail: admin@albertaplaywrights.com
Web site: www.albertaplaywrights.com

Alberta Romance Writers' Association
223 – 12 Avenue S.W., Suite 209, Calgary, AB T2R 0G9
Phone: (403) 269-8564 or 1-800-268-8564 Fax: (403) 265-6773
E-mail: altaromwtr@hotmail.com
Web site: www.albertaromancewriters.com

Association of Canadian Publishers
161 Eglinton Avenue E., Suite 702, Toronto, ON M4P 1J5
Phone: (416) 487-6116 Fax: (416) 487-8815
E-mail: admin@canbook.org
Web site: www.publishers.ca

Association of Canadian University Presses
10 St. Mary Street, Suite 700, Toronto, ON M4Y 2W8
Phone: (416) 978-2239, ext. 237 Fax: (416) 978-4738
E-mail: clarose@utpress.utoronto.ca

Book and Periodical Council
192 Spadina Avenue, Suite 107, Toronto, ON M5T 2C2
Phone: (416) 975-9366 Fax: (416) 975-1839
E-mail: info@thebpc.ca
Web site: www.bookandperiodicalcouncil.ca

British Columbia Arts Council
Box 9819, Stn. Prov. Govt., Victoria, BC V8W 9W3
Phone: (250) 356-1728 Fax: (250) 387-4099
E-mail: bcartscouncil@gov.bc.ca
Web site: www.bcartscouncil.ca

Burnaby Writers' Society
6584 Deer Lake Avenue, Burnaby, BC V5G 3T7
E-mail: info@bws.ca
Web site: www.bws.bc.ca

The Canadian Conference of the Arts
130 Albert Street, Suite 804, Ottawa, ON K1P 5G4
Phone: (613) 238-3561 Fax: (613) 238-4849
E-mail: info@ccarts.ca
Web site: www.ccarts.ca

The Canada Council for the Arts
350 Albert Street, P.O. Box 1047, Ottawa, ON K1P 5V8
Phone: (613) 566-4414, ext. 5537, locally or after hours, or
    1-800-263-5588 Fax: (613) 566-4410
Web site: www.canadacouncil.ca

Canadian Association of Journalists
Algonquin College, 1385 Woodroffe Avenue, Suite B224, Ottawa,
    ON K2G 1V8
Phone: (613) 526-8061   Fax: (613) 521-3904
E-mail: canadianjour@magma.ca
Web site: www.eagle.ca/caj

Canadian Authors Association (national office)
P.O. Box 419, Campbellford, ON K0L 1L0
Phone: (705) 653-0323 or 1-866-216-6222   Fax: (705) 653-0593
E-mail: admin@canauthors.org
Web site: www.canauthors.org

Canadian Children's Book Centre
40 Orchard View Boulevard, Suite 101, Toronto, ON M4R 1B9
Phone: (416) 975-0010   Fax: (416) 975-8970
E-mail: info@bookcentre.ca
Web site: www.bookcentre.ca

Canadian Intellectual Property Office
50 Victoria Street, Room C-114, Gatineau, QC K1A 0C9
Phone: (819) 977-1936 or 1-900-565-2476 ($3 flat fee)
    Fax: (819) 953-7620 (enquiries only)
E-mail: cipo.contact@ic.gc.ca
Web site: http://strategis.gc.ca/sc_mrksv/cipo

Canadian Library Association
328 Frank Street, Ottawa, ON K2P 0X8
Phone: (613) 232-9625   Fax: (613) 563-9895
E mail: info@cla.ca
Web site: www.cla.ca

Canadian Magazine Publishers Association
425 Adelaide Street W., Suite 700, Toronto, ON M5V 3C1
Phone: (416) 504-0274   Fax: (416) 504-0437
Web site: www.cmpa.ca

Canadian Science Writers' Association
P.O. Box 75, Stn. A, Toronto, ON M5W 1A2

Phone: (416) 408-4566 or 1-800-796-8595
E-mail: office@sciencewriters.ca
Web site: www.sciencewriters.ca

Canadian Society of Children's Authors, Illustrators and Performers (CANSCAIP)

40 Orchard View Boulevard, Suite 104, Lower Level, Toronto, ON M4R 1B9
Phone: (416) 515-1559
E-mail: office@canscaip.org
Web site: www.canscaip.org

The Canadian Writers' Foundation

P.O. Box 13281, Kanata Stn., ON K2K 1X4
Phone: (613) 256-6937 Fax: (613) 256-5457
E-mail: info@canadianwritersfoundation.org
Web site: www.canadianwritersfoundation.org

Conseil des arts et des lettres du Québec

79 René-Lévesque Boulevard E., 3rd Floor, Quebec, QC G1R 5N5
Phone: (418) 643-1707 or 1-800-897-1707 Fax: (418) 643-4558
500 Place d'Armes, 15th Floor, Montreal, QC H2Y 2W2
Phone: (514) 864-3350 or 1-800-608-3350 Fax: (514) 864-4160
E-mail: info@calq.gouv.qc.ca
Web site: www.calq.gouv.qc.ca/index_en.htm

Crime Writers of Canada

P.O. Box 113, 3007 Kingston Road, Scarborough, ON M1M 1P1
Phone: (416) 597-9938
E-mail: info@crimewriterscanada.com
Web site: www.crimewriterscanada.com

Editors' Association of Canada (EAC)

27 Carlton Street, Suite 502, Toronto, ON M5B 1L2
Phone: (416) 975-1379 or 1-866-226-3348 Fax: (416) 975-1637
E-mail: info@editors.ca
Web site: www.editors.ca

Federation of BC Writers
P.O. Box 3887, Stn. Terminal, Vancouver, BC V6B 2Z3
Phone: (604) 683-2057
E-mail: bcwriters@shaw.ca
Web site: www.bcwriters.com

Island Writers Association (P.E.I.)
Debbie Gamble, Pownal Road, R.R. #1, Charlottetown, PE
C1A 7J6
Phone: (902) 569-3913
E-mail: dgamble@isn.net
Web site: www.seacroftpei.com

The League of Canadian Poets
920 Yonge Street, Suite 608, Toronto, ON M4W 3C7
Phone: (416) 504-1657
E-mail: readings@poets.ca
Web site: www.poets.ca

Literary Press Group of Canada
192 Spadina Avenue, Suite 501, Toronto, ON M5T 2C2
Phone: (416) 483-1321 Fax: (416) 483-2510
E-mail: info@lpg.ca
Web site: www.lpg.ca

Literary Translators' Association of Canada
1455 Maisonneuve Boulevard W., LB 641, Concordia University,
Montreal, QC H3G 1M8
Phone: (514) 848-2424, ext. 8702
E-mail: info@attlc-ltac.org
Web site: www.attlc-ltac.org

Manitoba Arts Council
93 Lombard Avenue, Suite 525, Winnipeg, MB R3B 3B1
Phone: (204) 945-0422 or 1-866-994-2787 (toll-free in MB)
Fax: (204) 945-5925
E-mail: jthomas@artscouncil.mb.ca
Web site: www.artscouncil.mb.ca

Manitoba Writers' Guild
100 Arthur Street, Suite 206, Winnipeg, MB R3B 1H3
Phone: (204) 942-6134 or 1-888-637-5802 Fax: (204) 942-5754
E-mail: mbwriter@mbwriter.mb.ca
Web site: www.mbwriter.mb.ca

New Brunswick Arts Board
634 Queen Street, Suite 300, Fredericton, NB E3B 1C2
Phone: (506) 444-4444 Fax: (506) 444-5543
E-mail: rbryar@artsnb.ca
Web site: www.artsnb.ca

Newfoundland and Labrador Arts Council
P.O. Box 98, Stn. C, St. John's, NL A1C 5H5
Phone: (709) 726-2212 or 1-866-726-2212 Fax: (709) 726-0619
E-mail: nlacmail@nfld.net
Web site: www.nlac.nf.ca

Northwest Territories Arts Council
Department of Education, Culture and Employment,
    Government of the N.W.T., P.O. Box 1320, Yellowknife, NT
    X1A 2L9
Phone: (867) 920-6370 Fax: (867) 873-0205
E-mail: boris_atamanenko@gov.nt.ca
Web site: www.pwnhc.ca/artscouncil

Nova Scotia Department of Tourism, Culture and Heritage
1800 Argyle Street, Suite 402, P.O. Box 456, Halifax, NS B3J 2R5
Phone: (902) 424-3422 Fax: (902) 424-0710
E-mail: kirbypc@gov.ns.ca
Web site: www.gov.ns.ca/dtc

Ontario Arts Council
Literature Programs, 151 Bloor Street W., 5th Floor, Toronto, ON
    M5S 1T6
Phone: (416) 961-1660 or 1-800-387-0058 Fax: (416) 961-7796
E-mail: info@arts.on.ca
Web site: www.arts.on.ca

Ontario Ministry of Culture
900 Bay Street, 5th Floor, Toronto, ON M7A 1L2
Phone: (416) 212-0644 or 1-866-454-0049
E-mail: general_info@ontario.ca
Web site: www.culture.gov.on.ca

Outdoor Writers of Canada
P.O. Box 20008, Pioneer Park P.O., Kitchener, ON N2P 2B4
E-mail: outdoorswithbill@rogers.com
Web site: www.culture.gov.on.ca

P.E.I. Writers Guild
P.O. Box 1, 115 Richmond Street, Charlottetown, PE C1A 1H7
E-mail: r.mischler@pei.sympatico.ca
Web site: www.peiwriters.ca

PEN Canada
24 Ryerson Avenue, Suite 301, Toronto, ON M5T 2P3
Phone: (416) 703-8448 Fax: (416) 703-3870
E-mail: info@pencanada.ca
Web site: www.pencanada.ca

Playwrights Guild of Canada
54 Wolseley Street, 2nd Floor, Toronto, ON M5T 1A5
Phone: (416) 703-0201 Fax: (416) 703-0059
E-mail: info@playwrightsguild.ca
Web site: www.playwrightsguild.ca

Playwrights Theatre Centre
1398 Cartwright Street, Suite 201, Vancouver, BC V6H 3R8
Phone: (604) 685-6228 Fax: (604) 685-7451
E-mail: plays@playwrightsthreatre.com
Web site: www.playwrightsthreatre.com

Praxis Centre for Screenwriters
515 West Hastings Street, Suite 3120, Vancouver, BC V6B 5K3
Phone: (604) 268-7880 Fax: (604) 268-7882
E-mail: praxis@sfu.ca
Web site: www.praxisfilm.com

Prince Edward Island Council of the Arts
115 Richmond Street, Charlottetown, PE C1A 1H7
Phone: (902) 368-4410 Fax: (902) 368-4418
E-mail: info@peiartscouncil.com
Web site: www.peiartscouncil.com

Professional Writers Association of Canada
215 Spadina Avenue, Suite 123, Toronto, ON M5T 2C7
Phone: (416) 504-1645 Fax: (416) 913-2327
E-mail: info@pwac.ca
Web site: www.pwac.ca

Public Lending Right Commission
P.O. Box 1047, 350 Albert Street, Ottawa, ON K1P 5V8
Phone: (613) 566-4378 or 1-800-521-5721 Fax: (613) 566-4418
E-mail: plr@canadacouncil.ca
Web site: www.plr-dpp.ca

Quebec Writers' Federation
1200 Atwater Avenue, Montreal, QC H3Z 1X4
Phone: (514) 933-0878
E-mail: admin@qwf.org
Web site: www.qwf.org

Saskatchewan Arts Board
2135 Broad Street, Regina, SK S4P 3V7
Phone: (306) 787-4056 or 1-800-667-7526 (SK)
   Fax: (306) 787-4199
E-mail: sab@artsboard.sk.ca
Web site: www.artsboard.sk.ca

Saskatchewan Writers Guild
P.O. Box 3986, Regina, SK S4P 3R9
Phone: (306) 291-7742 Fax: (306) 565-8554
E-mail: ed.swg@sasktel.net
Web site: www.skwriter.com

Scarborough Arts Council
1859 Kingston Road, Scarborough, ON M1N 1T3

Phone: (416) 698-7322 Fax: (416) 698-7972
E-mail: info@scarborougharts.com
Web site: www.scarborougharts.com

SF Canada (speculative fiction)
2333 Scarth Street, Suite 303, Regina, SK S4P 2J8
E-mail: ewillett@sasktel.net
Web site: www.sfcanada.ca

Storytellers of Canada
P.O. Box 25, Corner Brook, NL A2H 6C3
E-mail: coordinator@sc-cc.com
Web site: www.sc-cc.com

Toronto Arts Council
141 Bathurst Street, Toronto, ON M5V 2R2
Phone: (416) 392-6800 Fax: (416) 392-6920
E-mail: mail@torontoartscouncil.org
Web site: www.torontoartscouncil.org

Vancouver Children's Literature Roundtable
Ron Jobe, Department of Language and Literacy, Faculty of
    Education, 2125 Main Mall, University of B.C., Vancouver, BC
    V6T 1Z4
Phone: (604) 822-5233
E-mail: ron.jobe@ubc.ca
Web site: www.library.ubc.ca/edlib/table

Vancouver Office of Cultural Affairs
453 West 12th Avenue, Vancouver, BC V5Y 1V4
Phone: (604) 873-7011
E-mail: oca@vancouver.ca
Web site: www.city.vancouver.bc.ca/commsvcs/oca

The Word Guild
P.O. Box 34, Port Perry, ON L9L 1A2
Phone: (905) 294-6482
E-mail: info@thewordguild.com
Web site: www.thewordguild.com

Writers' Alliance of Newfoundland and Labrador
P.O. Box 2681, St. John's, NL A1C 6K1
Phone: (709) 739-5215 Fax: (709) 739-5931
E-mail: wanl@nf.aibn.com
Web site: http://writersalliance.nf.ca

The Writers' Circle of Durham Region
P.O. Box 323, Ajax, ON L1S 3C5
Phone: (905) 259-6520
E-mail: info@wcdr.org
Web site: www.wcdr.org

The Writers' Federation of New Brunswick
P.O. Box 37, Stn. A, Fredericton, NB E3B 4Y2
Phone: (506) 459-7228 Fax: (506) 459-7228
E-mail: wfnb@nb.aibn.com
Web site: www.umce.ca/wfnb

Writers' Federation of Nova Scotia
1113 Marginal Road, Halifax, NS B3H 4P7
Phone: (902) 423-8116 Fax: (902) 422-0881
E-mail: talk@writers.ns.ca
Web site: www.writers.ns.ca

Writers Guild of Alberta
11759 Groat Road, Edmonton, AB T5M 3K6
Phone: (780) 422-8174 Fax: (780) 422-2663
E-mail: mail@writersguild.ab.ca
Web site: www.writersguild.ab.ca

Writers Guild of Canada
366 Adelaide Street W., Suite 401, Toronto, ON M5V 1R9
Phone: (416) 979-7907 or 1-800-567-9974 Fax: (416) 979-9273
E-mail: info@wgc.ca
Web site: www.wgc.ca

Writers in Electronic Residence
317 Adelaide Street W., Suite 300, Toronto, ON M5V 1P9
Phone: (416) 591-6300, ext. 235 Fax: (416) 591-5345

E-mail: wier@wier.ca
Web site: www.wier.ca

The Writers' Trust of Canada
90 Richmond Street E., Suite 200, Toronto, ON M5C 1P1
Phone: (416) 504-8222 Fax: (416) 504-9090
E-mail: info@writerstrust.com
Web site: www.writerstrust.com

The Writers' Union of Canada
90 Richmond Street E., Suite 200, Toronto, ON M5C 1P1
Phone: (416) 703-8982 Fax: (416) 504-9090
E-mail: info@writersunion.ca
Web site: www.writersunion.ca

Young Alberta Book Society
11759 Groat Road, Edmonton, AB T5M 3K6
Phone: (780) 422-8232 Fax: (780) 422-8239
E-mail: info@yabs.ab.ca
Web site: www.yabs.ab.ca

Yukon Department of Tourism and Culture
Arts Section, P.O. Box 2703 (L-3), Whitehorse, YT Y1A 2C6
Phone: (867) 667-8589 Fax: (867) 393-6456
E-mail: artsfund@gov.yk.ca
Web site: www.btc.gov.yk.ca/cultural/arts/index.html

11

RESOURCES

For those seeking practical advice and inspiration about their craft, there is a cornucopia of writers' resource books on the market: style guides, practical handbooks, personal meditations, marketing primers, as well as more advanced "workshops" on the narrative and descriptive arts. In addition, there are increasing numbers of writers' web sites that offer everything from dictionaries to articles on how to deal with rejection.

With a growing industry in writing about writing, it is possible to offer only a short selection of resources here. As you'll see, the following listing includes books from the United States and Britain, as well as from Canada. Most are available here in good bookstores or through the Internet; a few are out of print but may still be held in libraries.

Stylebooks, Handbooks, & Guides

Appelbaum, Judith. *How to Get Happily Published* (5th ed.), Harper Perennial, New York, 1998.

Armstrong, David. *How Not to Write a Novel*, Allison & Busby Limited, London, 2003.

Aslett, Don, and Carol Cartaino. *Get Organized, Get Published: 225 Ways to Make Time for Success*, Writer's Digest Books, Cincinnati, 2001.

Bacia, Jennifer. *Chapter One: Everything You Want to Know About Starting Your Novel*, Allen & Unwin, St. Leonards, Australia, 1999.

Baker, Edward. *A Writer's Guide to Overcoming Rejection*, Summersdale Publishers, Chichester, U.K., 1998.

Ballon, Rachel Friedman. *Breathing Life into Your Characters*, Writer's Digest Books, Cincinnati, 2003.

Bates, Jefferson D. *Writing with Precision*, Penguin Books, New York, 2000.

Bell, Julia, and Paul Magrs (eds.). *The Creative Writing Coursebook*, Macmillan, London, 2001.

Bernstein, Theodore M. *Miss Thistlebottom's Hobgoblins: The Careful Writer's Guide to the Taboos, Bugbears and Outmoded Rules of English Usage*, Centro Books, New York, 2006.

Berton, Pierre. *The Joy of Writing*, Anchor Canada, Toronto, 2003.

Blackburn, Bob. *Words Fail Us: Good English and Other Lost Causes*, McClelland & Stewart, Toronto, 1993.

Blamires, Harry. *The Penguin Guide to Plain English*, Penguin Books, London, 2000.

Bly, Carol. *Beyond the Writers' Workshop: New Ways to Write Creative Nonfiction*, Anchor Books, New York, 2001.

Bly, Robert W. *Secrets of a Freelance Writer* (2nd rev. ed.), Owl, New York, 1997.

Braine, John. *Writing a Novel*, Methuen, London, 1974.

Brandeis, Gayle. *Fruitflesh: Seeds of Inspiration for Women Who Write*, HarperCollins Canada, 2004.

Brown, Judy, and Ramona Montagnes. *Canadian Writer's Handbook* (4th ed.), Oxford University Press, Toronto, 2004.

Bulman, Colin. *Creative Writing: A Guide and Glossary to Fiction Writing*, Polity, Cambridge, U.K., 2007.

The Canadian Writer's Guide: Official Handbook of the Canadian Authors Association (13th ed.). Fitzhenry & Whiteside, Toronto, 2003.

Cheney, Theodore A. Rees. *Getting the Words Right* (2nd ed.), Writer's Digest Books, Cincinnati, 2005.

The Chicago Manual of Style (15th ed.). University of Chicago Press, Chicago, 2003.

Clark, Eliza. *Writer's Gym*, Penguin Books, Toronto, 2007.

Clayton, Joan. *Journalism for Beginners: How to Get into Print and Get Paid for It*, Piatkus, London, 2000.

Cropp, Richard, Barbara Braidwood, and Susan M. Boyce. *Writing Travel Books and Articles*, Self-Counsel Press, Vancouver, 1997.

Driscoll, Susan, and Diane Gedymin. *Get Published!* iUniverse, Inc., Lincoln, NE, 2006.

Dufresne, John. *The Lie That Tells a Truth*, W. W. Norton & Co., New York, 2004.

Editing Canadian English (2nd ed.), Editors' Association of Canada, Macfarlane Walter & Ross, Toronto, 2000.

Ellis, Sherry (ed.). *Now Write! Fiction Writing from Today's Best Writers and Teachers*, Jeremy P. Tarcher/Penguin, New York, 2006.

Embree, Mary. *The Author's Toolkit*, Allworth Press, New York, 2003.

Estleman, Loren D. *Writing the Popular Novel*, Writer's Digest Books, Cincinnati, 2004.

Evanovich, Janet. *How I Write*, St. Martin's Press, New York, 2006.

Fee, Margery, and Janice McAlpine. *Guide to Canadian English Usage*, Oxford University Press, Toronto, 2000.

Formichelli, Linda, and Diana Burrell. *The Renegade Writer* (2nd ed.), Marion Street Press, Oak Park, IL, 2005.

Frank, Steven. *The Pen Commandments*, Anchor Books, New York, 2004.

Frank, Thaisa, and Dorothy Wall. *Finding Your Writer's Voice: A Guide to Creative Fiction*, St. Martin's Press, New York, 1994.

Frey, James N. *How to Write a Damn Good Mystery*, St. Martin's Press, New York, 2004.

Gardner, John. *The Art of Fiction: Notes on Craft for Young Writers*, Vintage, New York, 1983.

Gerard, Philip. *Writing a Book That Makes a Difference*, Writer's Digest Books, Cincinnati, 2000.

Gibaldi, Joseph. *MLA Style Manual and Guide to Scholarly Publishing* (2nd ed.), The Modern Language Association of America, New York, 1998.

Goldberg, Natalie. *Thunder and Lightning: Cracking Open the Writer's Craft*, Bantam Books, New York, 2001.

Grobel, Lawrence. *Endangered Species: Writers Talk About Their Craft, Their Visions, Their Lives*, Da Capo Press, Cambridge, MA, 2001.

Harper, Timothy (ed.). *The ASJA Guide to Freelance Writing*, St. Martin's Press, New York, 2003.

Hart, Jack. *A Writer's Coach*, Pantheon Books, New York, 2006.

Heffron, Jack. *The Writer's Idea Workshop*, Writer's Digest Books, Cincinnati, 2003.

Hemley, Robin. *Turning Life into Fiction*, Gray Wolf Press, Saint Paul, MN, 2006.

Herman, Jeff, and Deborah Levine Herman. *Write the Perfect Book Proposal*, John Wiley & Sons, New York, 2001.

Hicks, Wynford. *English for Journalists* (3rd ed.), Taylor & Francis, London, 2006.

Hodgins, Jack. *A Passion for Narrative: A Guide for Writing Fiction* (revised ed.), McClelland & Stewart, Toronto, 2001.

Jenkins, Jerry B. *Writing for the Soul*, Writer's Digest Books, Cincinnati, 2006.

Kane, Thomas S., and Karen C. Ogden, *The Canadian Oxford Guide to Writing*, Oxford University Press, Toronto, 1993.

Kelton, Nancy Davidoff. *Writing From Personal Experience: How to Turn Your Life into Salable Prose*, Writer's Digest Books, Cincinnati, 2000.

Kercheval, Jesse Lee. *Building Fiction: How to Develop Plot and Structure*, University of Wisconsin Press, Madison, WI, 2003.

King, Stephen. *On Writing: A Memoir of the Craft*, Pocket Books, New York, 2000.

Kiteley, Brian. *The 3 A.M. Epiphany: Uncommon Writing Exercises That Transform Your Fiction*, Writer's Digest Books, Cincinnati, 2005.

Konner, Linda. *How to Be Successfully Published in Magazines*, St. Martin's Press, New York, 1990.

Kress, Nancy. *Characters, Emotion & Viewpoint*, Writer's Digest Books, Cincinnati, 2005.

LaRocque, Paula. *The Book on Writing*, Marion Street Press, Oak Park, IL, 2003.

Larsen, Michael. *How to Write a Book Proposal* (3rd ed.), Writer's Digest Books, Cincinnati, 2003.

Leland, Christopher T. *The Art of Compelling Fiction: How to Write a Page-Turner*, Story Press, Cincinnati, 1998.

Lerner, Betsy. *The Forest for the Trees: An Editor's Advice to Writers*, Riverhead Books, New York, 2005.

Levin, Donna. *Get That Novel Written: From Initial Idea to Final Edit*, Writer's Digest Books, Cincinnati, 1996.

Levin, Martin P. *Be Your Own Literary Agent: The Ultimate Insider's Guide to Getting Published,* Ten Speed Press, Berkeley, CA, 2002.

Levinson, Jay Conrad, Rick Frishman, and Michael Larsen. *Guerrilla Marketing for Writers: 100 Weapons for Selling Your Work,* Writer's Digest Books, Cincinnati, 2001.

Lukeman, Noah. *The First Five Pages: A Writer's Guide to Staying Out of the Rejection Pile,* Fireside, New York, 2005.

Lyon, Elizabeth. *A Writer's Guide to Fiction,* Berkley Publishing Group, New York, 2004.

Maisel, Eric. *The Art of the Book Proposal,* Jeremy P. Tarcher/ Penguin, New York, 2004.

Mandell, Judy. *Book Editors Talk to Writers,* John Wiley & Sons, New York, 1996.

Marshall, Evan. *The Marshall Plan for Getting Your Novel Published,* Writer's Digest Books, Cincinnati, 2004.

Masello, Robert. *Robert's Rules of Writing,* Writer's Digest Books, Cincinnati, 2005.

Mayer, Bob. *The Novel Writer's Toolkit,* Writer's Digest Books, Cincinnati, 2003.

McFarlane, J. A., and Warren Clements. *The Globe and Mail Style Book* (9th ed.), McClelland & Stewart, Toronto, 2003.

McKeown, Thomas W., and Carol M. Cram. *Better Business Writing,* Clear Communications Press, Vancouver, 1990.

McKercher, Catherine, and Carman Cumming. *The Canadian Reporter: News Writing and Reporting,* Harcourt Brace Canada, Toronto, 1998.

Mencher, Melvin. *News Reporting and Writing* (8th ed.), McGraw-Hill Ryerson, Toronto, 2000.

Mettee, Stephen Blake. *The Fast-Track Course on How to Write a Nonfiction Book Proposal,* Quill Driver Books, Fresno, CA, 2001.

Miller, Peter. *Get Published! Get Produced!* Lone Eagle Publishing, Los Angeles, 1998.

Neubauer, Bonnie. *The Write-Brain Workbook,* Writer's Digest Books, Cincinnati, 2006.

Oxford Style Manual, Oxford University Press, Oxford, 2003.

Perkins, Lori. *The Insider's Guide to Getting an Agent,* Writer's Digest Books, Cincinnati, 1999.

Pfeiffer, William S., and Jan Boogerd. *Technical Writing: A Practical Approach,* Prentice-Hall Canada, Toronto, 1997.

Roth, Martin. *The Writer's Partner: 1001 Breakthrough Ideas to Stimulate Your Imagination*, Michael Wiese Productions, Studio City, CA, 2001.

Rubens, Philip (ed.). *Science and Technical Writing: A Manual of Style*, Routledge, New York, 2001.

Rubie, Peter. *The Everything Get Published Book*, Adams Media Corp., Avon, MA, 2000.

Seidman, Michael. *The Complete Guide to Editing Your Fiction*, Writer's Digest Books, Cincinnati, 2000.

Staw, Jane Anne. *Unstuck: A Supportive and Practical Guide to Working through Writer's Block*, St. Martin's Press, New York, 2003.

Stevens, Mark A. *Merriam Webster's Manual for Writers and Editors*, Merriam-Webster, Springfield, MA, 1998.

Stone, Todd A. *Novelist's Boot Camp*, Writer's Digest Books, Cincinnati, 2006.

Strunk, William, Jr., and E. B. White. *The Elements of Style* (4th ed.), Allyn and Bacon, Boston, 2000.

Tasko, Patti (ed.). *The Canadian Press Stylebook* (14th ed.), The Canadian Press, Toronto, 2006.

Truss, Lynne. *Eats, Shoots & Leaves*, Gotham Books, New York, 2003.

Watson, Don. *Death Sentences*, Viking Canada, Toronto, 2003.

Williams, Malcolm (ed.). *The Canadian Style: A Guide to Writing and Editing*, Dundurn Press, Toronto, 1997.

Words into Type (3rd ed. rev.). Prentice-Hall, Englewood Cliffs, NJ, 1974.

Zinsser, William. *On Writing Well: The Classic Guide to Writing Non-fiction* (30th anniversary ed.), HarperCollins, New York, 2006.

Dictionaries & Thesauruses

The Canadian Oxford Dictionary (2nd ed.), ed. Katherine Barber, Oxford University Press, Toronto, 2006.

Canadian Thesaurus, ed. J. K. Chambers, Fitzhenry & Whiteside, Markham, ON, 2001.

Collins English Dictionary (Canadian ed.), HarperCollins, Glasgow, 2005.

Collins Gage Canadian Paperback Dictionary, HarperCollins Canada, Toronto, 2006.

The Concise English Dictionary (8th ed.), HarperCollins, Glasgow, 2006.

Gage Canadian Thesaurus, ed. T. K. Pratt, Gage Learning Corp., Toronto, 1998.

Merriam-Webster's Collegiate Dictionary (11th ed.), ed. Frederick C. Mish, Merriam-Webster, Springfield, MA, 2003.

Microsoft Encarta College Dictionary, ed. Anne H. Soukhanov, St. Martin's Press, New York, 2001.

The New Fowler's Modern English Usage (3rd ed. rev.), ed. R. W. Birchfield, Oxford University Press, Oxford, 2000.

The Oxford Compact Thesaurus (2nd ed.), ed. Maurice Waite, Oxford University Press, Oxford, 2001.

The Oxford Writers' Dictionary, ed. R. E. Allen, Oxford University Press, Oxford, 1990.

The Penguin English Dictionary, ed. Robert Allen, Penguin Books, London, 2003.

Random House Webster's Unabridged Dictionary (revised ed.), ed. Wendalyn R. Nichols, Random House, New York, 2005.

Roget's International Thesaurus (6th ed.), ed. Barbara Ann Kipfer, HarperCollins, New York, 2001.

Yearbooks, Almanacs, & Other Regularly Published Reference Sources

The Book Trade in Canada (annual), *Quill & Quire*, Toronto.

Canadian Almanac & Directory (annual), Micromedia ProQuest, Toronto.

The Canadian Global Almanac, John Wiley & Sons, Toronto, 2005.

CARD (Canadian Advertising Rates & Data) (monthly), Rogers Media, Toronto.

Canadian Publishers Directory (biannual), supplement to *Quill & Quire* magazine, Toronto.

Guide to Literary Agents (annual), Writer's Digest Books, Cincinnati.

Literary Market Place (annual), R. R. Bowker, New York.

Matthews Media Directory (biannual), Canadian Corporate News, Toronto.

Novel and Short Story Writer's Market (annual), Writer's Digest Books, Cincinnati.

Poet's Market (annual), Writer's Digest Books, Cincinnati.

Publication Profiles, published annually with the May issue of *CARD* (see above), Rogers Media, Toronto.

Writers' & Artists' Yearbook (annual), A. & C. Black, London.

Writer's Market and *Writer's Market Online* (annual), Writer's Digest Books, Cincinnati.

Some Major Canadian Magazine Publishers

Annex Publishing and Printing Inc., P.O. Box 530, 105 Donly Drive S., Simcoe, ON N3Y 4N5 Phone: (519) 429-3966 Fax: (519) 429-3112 Web site: www.annexweb.com (trade)

Baum Publications Ltd., 2323 Boundary Road, Suite 201, Vancouver, DC V5M 4V8 Phone: (604) 291-9900 Fax: (604) 291-1906 Web site: www.baumpub.com (trade)

Bowes Publishers Ltd., 1147 Gainsborough Road, London, ON N6H 5L5 Phone: (519) 471-8520 E-mail: bowes@bowesnet.com Web site: www2.bowesnet.com (business, farm, newspapers)

Business Information Group, 12 Concorde Place, Suite 800, Toronto, ON M3C 4J2 Phone: (416) 442-2212 Fax: (416) 442-2191 Web site: www.businessinformationgroup.ca (business)

Canada Wide Magazines Ltd., 4180 Lougheed Highway, 4th Floor, Burnaby, BC V5C 6A7 Phone: (604) 299-7311 Fax: (604) 299-9188 E-mail: cwm@canadawide.com Web site: www.canadawide.com (business, consumer, trade)

CLB Media Inc., 240 Edward Street, Aurora, ON L4G 3S9 Phone: (905) 727-0077 Fax: (905) 727-0017 Web site: www.clbmedia.ca (trade)

Craig Kelman & Associates Ltd., 2020 Portage Avenue, 3rd Floor, Winnipeg, MB R3J 0K4 Phone: (204) 985-9780 Fax: (204) 985-9799 E-mail: info@kelman.ca Web site: www.kelman.ca (trade)

Family Communications Inc., 65 The East Mall, Toronto, ON M8Z
5W3 Phone: (416) 537-2604 Fax: (416) 538-1794 E-mail:
admin@parentscanada.com Web site: www.parentscanada.com
(consumer)

Koocanusa Publications Inc., 1510 – 2nd Street N., Suite 200,
Cranbrook, BC V1C 3L2 Phone: (250) 426-7253 Fax: (250)
426-4125 E-mail: info@kpimedia.com Web site:
www.koocanusapublications.com (business, consumer)

Metroland Printing, Publishing & Distributing Ltd., 10 Tempo
Avenue, Willowdale, ON M2H 2N8 Phone: (416) 493-1300
Fax: (416) 493-0623 Web site: www.metroland.com (business,
consumer)

Naylor (Canada) Inc., 100 Sutherland Avenue, Winnipeg, MB
R2W 3C7 Phone: (204) 975-0415 Fax: (204) 947-2047
Web site: www.naylor.com (trade)

OP Publishing Ltd., 1080 Howe Street, Suite 900, Vancouver, BC
V6Z 2T1 Phone: (604) 606-4644 Fax: (604) 687-1925
Web site: www.oppublishing.com (consumer)

Rogers Publishing Limited, 1 Mount Pleasant Road, Toronto, ON
M4Y 2Y5 Phone: (416) 764-2000 Fax: (416) 764-3943
Web site: www.rogersmedia.com (business, consumer, trade)

St. Joseph Media, 50 MacIntosh Boulevard, Concord, ON L4K
4P3 Phone: (905) 660-3111 Fax: (905) 669-1972
E-mail: communications@stjoseph.com
Web site: www.stjosephmedia.com (consumer)

Trajan Publishing, P.O. Box 28103, Lakeport P.O., St. Catharines,
ON L2N 7P8 Phone: (905) 646-7744 Fax: (905) 646-0995
Web site: www.trajan.ca (consumer)

Transcontinental Media, 1 Place Ville Marie, Suite 3315,
Montreal, QC H3B 3N2 Phone: (514) 954-4000 Fax: (514)
954-4016 Web site: www.transcontinental.com (consumer)

Tribute Publishing Inc., 71 Barber Greene Road, Toronto, ON
M3C 2A2 Phone: (416) 445-0544 Fax: (416) 445-2894
E-mail: generalinfo@tribute.ca Web site: www.tribute.ca
(consumer)

Online Resources

The following list of online resources is by no means exhaustive. Rather, it is intended to give the writer a starting-point from which to begin his or her investigation into what sites are available on the Internet.

About: Freelance Writers
www.freelancewrite.about.com
  Includes job postings, articles, newsletters, and forums.

Authorlink
www.authorlink.com
  An American site that offers writers education, information, guidance, services for writers, a writers' registry, a critique service, publication guidelines, and the opportunity to get a literary agent and sell their work to publishers throughout the English-speaking world. Fees apply to some sections of the site.

The Bible Gateway
www.biblegateway.com
  Allows you to look up any verse or phrase in many versions of the Bible.

CanadaInfo
www.craigmarlatt.com/canada
  A source of facts about Canada and its people.

Canadian Authors Association
www.canauthors.org
  News about the organization and literary awards, and extensive links of interest to writers.

The Canadian Encyclopedia
http://thecanadianencyclopedia.com
  A convenient site on which to research Canadian topics, including a selection of articles from *Maclean's* magazine since 1995.

Canadian Studies: A Guide to the Sources
www.iccs-ciec.ca/blackwell.html
Provides links to many Canadian sites of interest to researchers.

Canadian Who's Who
http://utpress.utoronto.ca/cgi-bin/cw2w3.cgi
The 1997 edition of *Canadian Who's Who*.

Chicago Manual of Style
www.chicagomanualofstyle.org
Answers queries about the 15th edition of *The Chicago Manual of Style*, and includes a guide for citing sources and tools to help authors prepare their manuscripts for publication. Subscribers have access to an online *Chicago Manual of Style*.

CopyrightLaws.com
http://copyrightlaws.com
Canadian media and copyright lawyer Lesley Ellen Harris provides information on Canadian, U.S., and international copyright law and web-related legal issues.

Creative Freelancers
www.freelancers.com
Includes classified ads for American jobs for freelance writers.

The Eclectic Writer
http://eclectics.com/writing/writing.html
Articles on all aspects of writing with lots of links.

The Elements of Style
http://bartleby.com/141/index.html
Contains rules of usage, principles of composition, and commonly misused and misspelled words.

Encyclopedia.com
www.encyclopedia.com
Contains 57,000 updated articles from the *Columbia Encyclopedia*, and subscribers have access to the HighBeam Research database with 35 million documents.

Encyclopedia Britannica **Online**
http://eb.com

Subscribers have access to the *Encyclopedia Britannica,* plus headlines from publications from around the world, graphics, maps, and related Internet links.

Familiar Quotations
www.bartleby.com/100

Searches Bartlett's, Columbia, and Simpson's Quotations.

Fiction Factor
www.fictionfactor.com

An online magazine for fiction writers that includes articles on writing, getting published, and how to promote and market a book, writing tips, and more.

Freelance Writing.com
http://freelancewriting.com

Includes a reading room, articles, author interviews, news, a career centre, a freelance job bank, and databases for magazines, freelance recruiters, and book publishers.

Literary Market Place
http://literarymarketplace.com

Subscribers have access to databases of Canadian, U.S., and other international publishers, as well as literary agents.

MediaFinder
http://mediafinder.com

Subscribers can access detailed information on 70,000 U.S. and Canadian magazines.

Merriam-Webster OnLine
www.m-w.com

May use the dictionary, thesaurus, and Spanish-English dictionary for no charge. Subscribers have access to the *Merriam-Webster* dictionaries, a thesaurus, Spanish-English and French-English dictionaries, an atlas, style guide, word games, and more.

National Writers Union
www.nwu.org

This American site provides writer alerts for book publishers, organizations, and magazines, as well as copyright information.

Oxford English Dictionary
http://oed.com

Access to the 2nd edition of the *Oxford English Dictionary* for subscribers.

Publishers' Catalogues
www.lights.com/publisher

Provides access to information on publishers around the world.

Purple Crayon
http://underdown.org/articles.htm

Articles on writing and illustrating children's books and getting them published.

Rosedog Books
www.rosedog.com

Subscribers can post their manuscripts for viewing by agents and publishers.

Shaw Guides
http://shawguides.com

Provides information about writers' conferences and workshops worldwide.

Thesaurus.com
http://thesaurus.reference.com

Contains a thesaurus, dictionary, encyclopedias, and guides to grammar and style.

The Vocabula Review
http://vocabula.com

A monthly e-zine that seeks to promote the richness and correct use of the English language.

The Writer Market
www.writemarket.com

Lists the markets and publishers for a wide selection of writing categories.

Writer Beware
http://sfwa.org/beware

Lists agents and publishers that writers should be wary of, provides sample contracts, and has articles on all aspects of writing.

Writers Guild of Canada
www.writersguildofcanada.com

Provides lists of literary agents, lawyers, available funding, employment opportunities, workshops, and seminars, as well as links of interest to writers and screenwriters.

Writer's Market
www.writersmarket.com

Subscribers have access to listings of agents and publishers, plus advice and daily industry updates.

Writer's Resource Center
www.poewar.com

Contains job listings, book reviews, and articles and exercises about all aspects of writing.

Writer's Guidelines Database
www.writerswrite.com

Provides a long list of general topics with the publications that publish writing on those topics, both paying and non-paying. Includes *The Internet Writing Journal* with articles about writing and writers.

Writing for Dollars
http://writingfordollars.com

Provides a database of markets and a newsletter covering the business side of writing.

Writing-World.com

http://writing-world.com

Offers more than 600 articles on all aspects of writing, lists of classes and contests, and job listings.

www.dictionary.reference.com

As well as an English dictionary, this site includes *Roget's Thesaurus* and dictionaries in French, German, Greek, Latin, Spanish, and more.

Your Dictionary.com

http://yourdictionary.com

A free online dictionary, a thesaurus, dictionaries in many languages, and specialty dictionaries.

INDEX OF CONSUMER, LITERARY, & SCHOLARLY MAGAZINES